**A Dictionary of Language Acquisition
A Comprehensive Overview of Key Terms in First and Second
Language Acquisition**

A Dictionary of Language Acquisition

A Comprehensive Overview of Key Terms in First and Second Language Acquisition

Hossein Tavakoli

سرشناسه:	توکلی، حسین، ۱۳۵۵-
	Tavakoli, Hossein
عنوان و نام پدیدآور:	A Dictionary of Language Acquisition: A Comprehensive Overview of Key Terms in First and Second Language Acquistion/ Hossein Tavakoli
مشخصات نشر:	تهران: رهنما، ۱۳۹۱ = ۲۰۱۲م.
مشخصات ظاهری:	۴۱۳ ص.
وضعیت فهرست‌نویسی:	فیپا
یادداشت:	انگلیسی
آوانویسی عنوان:	دیکشنری آو لنگوایج...
موضوع:	زبان‌آموزی - - اصطلاح‌ها و تعبیرها
رده‌بندی کنگره:	۱۳۹۱ ۹د۹ت/P۱۱۸
رده‌بندی دیویی:	۴۰۱/۹
شماره کتابشناسی ملی:	۲۹۴۵۵۳۹

All rights reserved. No part of this book may be reproduced in any form or by any means without the permission, in writing, from the Publisher.
RAHNAMA PRESS
Copyright © 2012
No. 112, Shohadaye Zhandarmerie St. (Moshtagh St.), Between Farvardin & Fakhre Razi, Enghelab Ave., Oppo. Tehran University, Tehran, Iran.
P.O. Box: 13145/1845 - Tel: (021) 66416604 & 66400927
E-mail: info@rahnamapress.com
http://www.rahnamapress.com
ISBN-10: 9643675343
ISBN-13: 978-9643675349

A Dictionary of Language Acquisition ، مؤلف: حسین توکلی، لیتوگرافی: رهنما، چاپ: چاپخانهٔ نقره‌فام، چاپ اول: ۱۳۹۱، تیراژ: ۱۰۰۰ نسخه، ناشر: انتشارات رهنما، آدرس: مقابل دانشگاه تهران، خیابان فروردین، نبش خیابان شهدای ژاندارمری، پلاک ۱۱۲، تلفن: ۶۶۴۰۰۹۲۷ ، ۶۶۴۱۶۶۰۴ ۶۶۴۸۱۶۶۲ فاکس: ۶۶۴۶۷۴۲۴ ، فروشگاه رهنما، سعادت‌آباد، خیابان علامه طباطبایی جنوبی، بین ۴۰ و ۴۲ شرقی، پلاک ۲۹، تلفن: ۸۸۶۹۴۱۰۲ ، آدرس فروشگاه شماره ۴: خیابان پیروزی نبش خیابان سوم نیروی هوایی، تلفن: ۷۷۴۸۲۵۰۵ ، نمایشگاه کتاب رهنما، مقابل دانشگاه تهران پاساژ فروزنده، تلفن: ۶۶۹۵۰۹۵۷ ، شابک: ۹-۵۳۴-۳۶۷-۹۶۴-۹۷۸

حق چاپ برای ناشر محفوظ است

To my parents

To my parents

Introduction

The function of "*A dictionary of language acquisition: A comprehensive overview of key terms in first and second language acquisition*" is to collect and synthesize the knowledge base that is already well accepted and that has been well researched. Thus, it is a reference guide which offers an authoritative and encyclopedic survey of key terms and concepts in the areas of language acquisition and development. The volume is intended as a resource to elucidate various concepts, issues, approaches, models, and theories of language acquisition in an efficient and accessible style. This book makes use of approximately 1000 alphabetical entries with cross references where necessary. Cross-referencing is achieved in several ways. Within each entry, any term that is itself a key idea with its own entry is printed in SMALL CAPITAL LETTERS on first use. There are also in-text entries that are defined within the body of the paragraph and are printed in **bold letters**. Other entries that are related to the term at issue that might be of interest and further investigation are either provided in the main text or listed at the end of each entry under 'see' and 'see also' respectively. In this volume, the sign 📖 has also been used for representing the sources from which the materials have been directly or indirectly reproduced or adapted.

This volume is designed to appeal to undergraduate and graduate students, teachers, lecturers, practitioners, researchers, consultants, and consumers of information across the field of both first and second language acquisition.

I would very much welcome reactions and comments from readers, especially relating to points where I may have lapsed or strayed from accuracy of meaning, consistency of style, etc., in the interests of improving coverage and treatment for future editions.

Hossein Tavakoli 2012

absolute implicational universals
a term referring to features which are found without exception in languages, if some other feature is found. For example:

- *Phonology.* If a language has mid vowels, then it has high vowels. Thus not all languages have one of /i, u/, but if a language has a mid vowel /e, o, ɛ, ɔ/, then it has at least one of /i, u/.

- *Morphology.* If a language distinguishes the categories 'dual' (i.e., exactly 2 in number) and 'singular' in its pronouns, it distinguishes the category 'plural' as well. Many languages distinguish singular and plural pronouns, as in English *he/she* versus *they*, and *I* versus *we* (a distinction absent in the 2nd person: *you* singular and plural). But relatively few languages distinguish singular and dual, as does Arabic, which also has plurals.

- *Syntax.* If a language has relative clauses, it has relative clauses whose heads are coreferential with the subject of the clause, as in the first example of 1-4, below. In the three other examples, the head of the clause is coreferential with a direct object, indirect object, and object of a preposition, respectively.

    a) people [who lend their cars to friends for dates]
    b) cars [which people lend to friends for dates]
    c) friends [who people lend their cars (to) for dates]
    d) dates [which people lend their cars to friends for]

Even though all languages have relative clauses (an ABSOLUTE NON-IMPLICATIONAL UNIVERSAL), not all of the types of relative clauses are found in all languages. Only the first, subject type, is always found. If one of the other types is found, the types above it in the hierarchy are also found, as in the following rankings:

```
    1       2          3                 4
Subject < object < indirect object > other propositional object
```

If there are relative calluses of type 4, then there are such clauses of type 3, etc. This hierarchy of possibilities is known as *noun phrase accessibility* (see ACCESSIBILITY HIERARCHY)

see also NON-IMPLICATIONAL UNIVERSAL TENDENCIES, IMPLICATIONAL UNIVERSAL TENDENCIES

📖 Hudson 2000

absolute non-implicational universals

a term referring to features which appear to be found without exceptions in languages. Some of these concern MARKEDNESS, the relationship of relative expectedness, likelihood, and often, evident simplicity between contrastive phonological or morphological features of language. For example:

- *Phonology*. An important type of absolute non-implicational universal of phonology and morphology concerns markedness between contrastive phones or features of phones. The phone or phonetic feature which is more common and has other characteristics expected of the more common and presumably more basic category is said to be *unmarked*. The phone or feature which contrasts with the unmarked phone or feature is said to be *marked*. Some unmarked and marked phonological categories are:

Unmarked	Marked
[-aspirated] stops	[+aspirated] stops
[-voiced] obstruents	[+voiced] obstruents
[+voiced] sonorants	[-voiced] sonorants
labiodental fricatives	bilabial fricatives
[-nasal] vowels	[+nasal] vowels
[+round] back vowels	[-round] back vowels

Unmarked categories have some or all of the following characteristics, which explain their relative commonality:

a) Greater frequency (likelihood of occurrence) across languages
b) Greater frequency within a language
c) Less restricted context of occurrence
d) Presence in contexts where marked categories are absent (e.g., voiceless obstruents appear word-finally where voiced stops and fricatives are absent in many languages, including Russian, German, Turkish, etc.)
e) Greater number of variants; thus there are more coronal consonants phonemes than consonants phonemes at the other places of articulations. (English, for example, has coronal (alveolar) stops and fricatives, a nasal

/n/, and alveolar /l/; the labials, dorsals (velars), and glottals are considerably fewer)
f) Simpler or lesser form

The term 'unmarked' is most appropriate for a category with lesser form, which may be said to be lesser in form by lacking the mark of a marked category. The correlation of greater frequency and lesser form is itself a universal tendency, known as ZIPF'S LAW. Often unmarked categories are found to fulfill the additional characteristics of being earlier learned by children. English learning children, for example, often have voiceless obstruents for adult word-final voiced obstruents.

Among other absolute non-implicational phonological universals are:

a) All languages have consonants and vowels.
b) All languages have at least one voiceless stop, such as [p, t, k].
c) All languages have syllables consisting of a consonant followed by one vowel (CV syllables).

- *Morphology.* Among the contrastive morphological contrastive morphological categories are singular versus plural, masculine versus feminine, and animate versus inanimate. For each of these, the former is unmarked and the latter marked. Concerning singular versus plural, for example:

  a) Singulars are much more frequent than plurals, across languages.
  b) Singulars often occur where plurals are absent; thus in many languages when a plural number is present the plural form of nouns is avoided. In English, plurality must ordinarily be marked on plural count noun; however, when speaking of measurements we say, for example, *a seven foot door* and not *a seven feet door*.
  c) Singulars typically have more variants, as in English third-person pronouns, which distinguish masculine, feminine, and neuter singular *he, she, it* versus only *they* for the plural.
  d) Singular nouns are typically unaffixed while plurals are affixed. Exceptional languages are quite rare, such as Ethiopian Cushitic Sidamo which has a singular suffix as well as plural suffixes. In all such languages, noun number may go unexpressed, so the singular suffix is still less frequent than the plural suffix of other languages.

Among other absolute non-implicational morphological universals are: All languages have nouns and verbs. That is, all languages have two morpheme classes with characteristics ordinarily recognized as those of nouns and verbs—nouns, for example functioning as subjects and objects of verbs, forming plurals, taking determiners, etc., and verbs expressing tense, aspect and modality, often showing agreement with a subject, etc. Also, all languages have a negative morpheme, whether for verbs or nouns, or both.

- *Syntax.* All languages have relative clause, clauses within noun phrases which modify the head noun of the clause.

see also NON-IMPLICATIONAL UNIVERSAL TENDENCIES, ABSOLUTE IMPLICATIONAL UNIVERSALS, IMPLICATIONAL UNIVERSAL TENDENCIES
📖 Hudson 2000

academic competence

the knowledge needed by learners who want to use the L2 primarily to learn about other subjects, or as a tool in scholarly research, or as a medium in a specific professional or occupational field. Learners with such a goal should concentrate above all on acquiring the specific vocabulary of their field or subject area, and on developing knowledge that enables them to read relevant texts fluently in that subject area. If language learners plan to study the subject at an L2-medium university, beyond specific vocabulary knowledge and reading ability, they must also put a high priority on processing oral L2 input during lectures and class discussions, i.e., on developing the ability to engage successfully in academic listening. Further, they are likely to need proficiency in L2 academic writing in order to display their knowledge on examinations that may be required for university admission and to earn academic degrees. Many students need to develop L2 writing proficiency for the academic purposes of producing term papers or theses, and researchers may need to do so for publishing articles for international information exchange. Developing L2 academic reading, listening, and writing proficiency, however, does not necessarily require fluent speaking ability, particularly for learners studying the L2 in a foreign language context.
see also INTERPERSONAL COMPETENCE
📖 Saville-Troike 2006

Accessibility Hierarchy
also **Noun Phrase Accessibility Hierarchy, NPAH,. AH**
a continuum of relative clause types such that the presence of one type implies the presence of other types higher on the hierarchy. According to them, all languages that form relative clauses form subject relative clauses; all those that can form direct object relative clauses can also form subject relatives, and so on down the hierarchy. In addition, certain relative clauses will be more difficult to process and to acquire in certain roles; the variation will be both systematic and hierarchical. The Hierarchy predicts universal constraints on the order of acquisition of relative clauses by means of an implicational scale which expresses the relative accessibility of relativization of

NP positions in a simplex main clause. The hierarchy is an example of a TYPOLOGICAL UNIVERSAL and has been widely used as a basis for SLA research. The ordering of relative clauses in the hierarchy is:

Subject > Direct Object > Indirect Object > Oblique > Genitive > Object of comparison

Subject
That's the woman [who drove away].
The boy [who asked the time] is my brother.

Direct object
That's the woman [I met last week].
The boy [John saw] is my brother

Indirect object
That's the woman [to whom I gave the parcel].
The boy [who I sent a postcard to] is my cousin.

Oblique
That's the woman [I was complaining about].
The boy [who I was complaining about] is my cousin.

Genitive
That's the woman [whose face I recognize].
The boy [whose pet was lost] told me he was sad.

Object of Comparison
That's the woman [I am older than].
The boy [who John is older than] is my cousin.

The above sentences show that the focus of attention in the noun phrase Accessibility Hierarchy is on the grammatical role (function) of the relative pronoun no matter the role taken by the head noun in the main clause.

However, relativization is not the only problem L2 learners are facing in learning relative clauses (see MARKEDNESS THEORY, TYPOLOGICAL UNIVERSALS).

Research investigating the Accessibility Hierarchy has suggested that universal principles are at the center of acquisition processes in different languages.

see also UNIVERSAL GRAMMAR

 Ellis 2008; Gass & Selinker 2008; González 2008; Keenan & Comrie 1977; Macaro et al. 2010; VanPatten & Benati 2010

Accommodation Theory

Accommodation Theory
also **Accommodative Process, Speech Accommodation Theory**
a social-psychological model of language use proposed by Giles to account for the dynamic nature of variation within the course of a conversation. Accommodation Theory is based on the notion that speakers usually unconsciously change their pronunciation and even the grammatical complexity of sentences they use to sound more like whomever they are talking to. Accommodation occurs in a wide variety of communication behaviors, including the speaker's accent, rate, loudness, register, grammar, vocabulary, and so on. Accommodation may take place at the following levels when speakers compare their own speech with that of an interlocutor: *speed of delivery* (the speed at which one talks), *pitch range* (how high or low in frequency one's voice is), *phonological variables* (sounds used by the speaker), and *vocabulary* (the choice of words used). Accommodation differs according to the status of speaker and listener and is associated with power. For L2 learners, a primary reason for accommodation depends on the extent to which they and immigrants want to be accepted into their host communities. If an individual moves to a new country and works at a new company, he would likely have a high need for social approval; therefore, speaking style would be important.

Accommodation Theory uses a social-psychological perspective to shed light on the relationship between social/situational factors and second-language use. It examines what social factors motivate the use of psycholinguistic choices. Studies regarding L2 learning have demonstrated that learners are sensitive to their interlocutors. For instance, L2 learners tend to adapt their speech to their interlocutors by using more phonological variants. As a result, L2 learners are likely to be more hesitant and briefer when addressing a listener with the same native language background as their own, and they are likely to be less prepared to negotiate any communication problems. Such a phenomenon occurs even during the early stages of learning, and learners seem to be aware of specific linguistic features that are seen as stereotypes about native speakers of the target language. L2 learners are also more aware of their own identities as well as the conversation topic than are their native-speaker interlocutors. Native speakers are comfortable conversing in their first language, whereas L2 learners tend never to forget that they are foreigners, especially when speaking a second tongue; that is, they realize that they do not sound like native speakers and therefore remain quiet during conversations. Likewise, this is true of the conversation topic. L2 learners often feel they will sound 'stupid' if they join a conversation with a native speaker when the topic is serious (philosophy, religion, war, etc.), and hence they might listen, but will not add to the conversation. Such sensitivity shows in their attitudes toward a certain topic, judging themselves as experts or nonexperts when comparing themselves with their native-speaker interlocutors. L2 learners often report that they believe they are far too slow in speaking their L2 and that native speakers are unusually fast.

According to Accommodation Theory, there are three principal types of variation, according to the nature of the adjustments which speakers make to their speech during interaction. *Convergence* occurs when the speaker adjusts his normal speech to make it more similar to the interlocutor's speech or when the speaker converges toward a prestigious norm that he believes is favored by the interlocutor. In short, the speaker accepts the interlocutor's values and seeks to demonstrate that acceptance by his own linguistic behavior. Conversely, *divergence* occurs when speakers seek to alter their speech in order to make themselves linguistically different. *Speech maintenance* occurs when speakers do not make any changes. This is viewed as a failure to converge (the expected type of behavior). Both convergence and divergence can take place in an upward or downward fashion. *Upward convergence* occurs when speakers adjust their speech to exhibit the norms of high-status individuals in their society. This is the most common type because it is based on the universal human desire for approval. *Downward convergence* involves adjustments in the direction of the speech norms from a higher class to a lower class. In fact, downward convergence involves speakers emphasizing the non-standard features in their repertoire, while upward divergence involves emphasizing the standard features.

Accommodation Theory shares certain premises with the ACCULTURATION MODEL, but it also differs from it in a number of significant ways. Like Schumann, Giles is concerned to account for successful language acquisition. Both seek the answer in the relationships that hold between the learner's social group (termed 'in-group') and the target language community (termed the 'outgroup'). However, whereas Schumann explains these relationships in terms of variables that create *actual* SOCIAL DISTANCE, Giles does so in terms of *perceived* social distance. Giles argues that it is how the in-group defines itself in relationship to the outgroup that is important in SLA. Also, where Schumann appears to treat *social* and *psychological distance* as absolute phenomena that determine the level of interaction between the learner and native speakers, Giles sees intergroup relationships as subject to constant negotiation during the course of each interaction. Thus, whereas for Schumann social and psychological distance are static (or at least change only slowly over time), for Giles intergroup relationships are dynamic and fluctuate in accordance with the shifting views of identity held by each group vis-à-vis the other. This enables Accommodation Theory to take account of the variability inherent in language-learner language and, also, the native speaker's input.

Overall, the strength of Accommodation Theory is that it encompasses language acquisition and language use within a single framework. It also relates the acquisition of a new dialect or accent to the acquisition of an L2, as both are seen as a reflection of the learner's perception of himself with regard to his own social group and the target language/dialect group. Accommodation theory helps to explain how L2 learners vary in the way they use their L2 choice in terms of pronunciation, vocabulary, and grammatical structure. However, Accommodation Theory, like Acculturation Model, does not, explain assembly mechanisms. It does not account for the developmental sequence.

see also SOCIAL IDENTITY THEORY, INTER-GROUP MODEL, SOCIO-EDUCATIONAL MODEL, LANGUAGE SOCIALIZATION

📖 Ellis 1986, 2008; Giles & Coupland 1991; González 2008; Saville-Troike 2006

accommodative process

another term for ACCOMMODATION THEORY

acculturation

a process, voluntary or involuntary, by which an individual or group adopts one or more of another group's cultural or linguistic traits, resulting in new or blended cultural or linguistic patterns. Unlike ASSIMILATION, which results in the loss of a person's original cultural or linguistic identity, acculturation involves adaptation and change. Acculturation is frequently an additive process, which can result in two or more identities that coexist harmoniously. The ability to function in a bicultural or even multicultural context is known as **situational ethnicity**.

In the field of second language acquisition, acculturation is closely associated with John Schumann's ACCULTURATION MODEL.

📖 Macaro et al. 2010

Acculturation Model

a theory of L2 acquisition developed by Schumann that the rate and level of ultimate success of second language acquisition in naturalistic settings (without instruction) is a function of the degree to which learners acculturate to the target language community. Schumann describes acculturation as the social and psychological integration of second language learners with the target language group. Within this model, social adaptation is an integration strategy which involves second language learners' adjustment to the lifestyles and values of the target language group while maintaining their own lifestyle and values for use within their own group. According to this model, L2 acquisition is one aspect of acculturation. It contends that learners will succeed in second language acquisition only to the extent they acculturate into the group that speaks the target language natively. The closer they feel to the target speech community, the better learners will become 'acculturated' and the more successful their language learning will be. According to Schumann, PIDGINIZATION in L2 acquisition results when learners fail to acculturate to the target-language group. In this model, instruction is set apart from acculturation and is less important in the SLA process than acculturation.

The extent to which learners acculturate depends on two sets of factors which determine their levels of SOCIAL DISTANCE and *psychological distance*. Social distance concerns the extent to which individual learners become members of the target-language group and, therefore, achieve contact with them. Psychological distance concerns the extent to which individual learners are comfortable with the learning task and constitutes, therefore, a *personal* rather than a *group* dimension. Among the factors which affect psychological distance are *language sock*, CULTURE SHOCK, MOTIVATION, and *ego permeability*. The social factors are primary. The psychological factors mainly come into play where social distance is indeterminate (i.e., where social factors constitute neither a clearly positive nor a negative influence on acculturation).

Because the model focuses on relative success of learners (i.e., how far along learners get in acquisition), it does not provide any explanation or insight into the internal processes responsible for the acquisition of an L2. That is, it does not attempt to explain why there are DEVELOPMENTAL SEQUENCES or ACQUISITION ORDERS, for example, and what causes them. In addition, it fails to acknowledge that factors like *integration* and *attitude* are not fixed and static but, potentially, variable and dynamic, fluctuating in accordance with the learner's changing social experiences. It also fails to acknowledge that learners are not just subject *to* social conditions but can also become the subject *of* them; they can help to construct social context of their own learning.

Although both social and psychological factors remain important in acquisition, the Acculturation Model lost favor by the early 1980s as research increasingly turned its attention toward linguistic and psycholinguistic approaches to explaining acquisition phenomena.

see also INTER-GROUP MODEL, SOCIO-EDUCATIONAL MODEL, COMPETITION MODEL, VARIABLE COMPETENCE MODEL, MONITOR MODEL, SOCIO-PSYCHOLINGUISTIC MODEL, MULTIDIMENSIONAL MODEL, NATIVIZATION MODEL, LANGUAGE SOCIALIZATION, SOCIAL IDENTITY THEORY, FUNCTIONALIST MODEL

📖 Ellis 1997, 2008; González 2008; Macaro et al. 2010; Richards & Schmidt 2010; Schumann 1986, 1978a, 1987b, 1978c; VanPatten & Benati 2010

accuracy
see FLUENCY

achieved bilingual
another term for LATE BILINGUAL

acquisition
in the study of the growth of language in children, a term referring to the process or result of learning (acquiring) a particular aspect of a language,

and ultimately the language as a whole. FIRST-LANGUAGE ACQUISITION (or child language acquisition) is the label usually given to the field of studies involved. The subject has involved the postulation of 'stages' of acquisition, defined chronologically, or in relation to other aspects of behavior, which it is suggested apply generally to children; and there has been considerable discussion of the nature of the LEARNING STRATEGIES which are used in the process of acquiring language, and of the criteria which can decide when a structure has been acquired. Some theorists have made a distinction between 'acquisition' and 'development', the former referring to the learning of a linguistic rule (of grammar, phonology, semantics), the latter to the further use of this rule in an increasingly wide range of linguistic and social situations. Others see no clear distinction between these two facets of language learning, and use the terms interchangeably. The term 'child language development' has also come to be used for discourse-based studies of child language.

Acquisition is also used in the context of learning a foreign language: 'foreign-' or 'second-language' acquisition is thus distinguished from 'first-language' or 'mother-tongue' acquisition. In this context, acquisition is sometimes opposed to 'learning'. The former is viewed as an environmentally natural process, the primary force behind foreign-language fluency; the latter is seen as an instructional process which takes place in a teaching context, guiding the performance of the speaker.

see also ACQUISITION-LEARNING HYPOTHESIS, SECOND-LANGUAGE ACQUISITION
📖 Crystal 2008

Acquisition-Learning Hypothesis

a part of MONITOR MODEL by Krashen which claims that there are two ways of developing competency in a second language: 'acquisition' and 'learning'. Acquisition is a natural process that involves the use of language in communicative settings, while learning is a more staged process that involves what Krashen calls 'knowing about language'. Acquisition occurs as we interact with others due to our need to communicate, while learning involves a more conscious manipulation of language elements, for example, in a classroom setting. Acquisition is more subconscious, informal, and based on feeling and depends on the openness or ATTITUDE of the person; learning is explicit and conscious, formal, and based on rules and depends on aptitude (see LANGUAGE APTITUDE).

The contrast between the naturalistic environment and the classroom environment is not the crucial issue, however. What is claimed to be important is the difference between meaningful communication, on the one hand, which can very well take place in the language classroom, and which will trigger subconscious processes, and conscious attention to form, on the other, which can also take place in naturalistic settings, especially with older learners who might explicitly request grammatical information from people around them.

Krashen has been criticized for his vague definition of what constitutes conscious versus subconscious processes, as they are very difficult to test in practice: How can we tell when a learner's production is the result of a conscious process and when it is not? Nonetheless, this contrast between acquisition and learning has been very influential, especially among foreign language teachers who saw it as an explanation of the lack of correspondence between error correction and direct teaching, on the one hand, and their students' accuracy of performance, on the other. If there was some kind of internal mechanism constraining learners' development, then it could account for the fact that some structures, even simple ones like the third-person singular -s in English (e.g., He likes), can be so frustrating to teach, with learners knowing the rule consciously, but often being unable to apply it in spontaneous conversation. In Krashen's terminology, learners would have learned the rule, but not acquired it.

What is also very problematic in this distinction is Krashen's claim that learning cannot turn into acquisition. That is, that language knowledge acquired or learned by these different routes cannot eventually become integrated into a unified whole. Krashen refers to this as the NON-INTERFACE POSITION. According to empirical research studies, Krashen's 'zero option' (i.e. do not ever teach grammar) is not supported in the literature. Instruction in conscious rule learning and other types of FORM-FOCUSED INSTRUCTION can indeed aid in the attainment of successful communicative competence in a second language.

📖 Ellis 1986, 1997; González 2008; Gregg 1984; Krashen 1981, 1985; Krashen & Scarcella 1978; McLaughlin 1987; Mithcell & Myles 2004

acquisition order
also order of acquisition

a theory claiming that L2 learners acquire the morphology and syntax of the target language in a fixed and predictable order and irrespective of their L1. The theory has its origins in L1 research which provided evidence that children acquire certain morphemes before others. Evidence for this claim was provided by the MORPHEME STUDIES, which investigated the order of acquisition of grammatical features such as articles and other morphological features. Dulay and Burt found a common order of acquisition among children of several native language backgrounds—an order very similar to that found by Roger Brown using the same morphemes but for children acquiring English as their first language (see FIRST LANGUAGE ACQUISITIOn). The morpheme studies have shown that L2 learners of English tend to learn verbal morphemes in the following order:

- present progressive (ring)
- prepositions (in, on)
- plural (-s)

- past irregular
- possessive (-*'s*)
- uncontractible copula (*is, am, are*)
- articles (*a, the*)
- past regular (*-ed*)
- third-person regular (*-s*)
- third-person irregular

The theory adopts a nativist perspective (see NATIVISM) asserting that certain aspects of language are neurologically pre-programmed in human brains. Therefore, we might conclude that learners from different L1s would develop their accuracy in using these morphemes following this predictable and universal order of acquisition. These findings were important in suggesting that L2 learners use internal strategies to organize and process language, and these strategies are not influenced by external factors.

However, although L2 orders were consistently found in a clutch of morpheme studies these by no means mapped perfectly onto L1 orders and as a consequence the claim of universality of orders of acquisition was undermined, and the lack of mapping partly attributed to more advanced cognition in L2 learners. Analysis of data in the morpheme studies was criticized for not accounting for variation in some of the features observed, for its coarse ranking of elements and for restricting itself to a narrow range of elements which fell short of explaining the acquisition of the entire rule-system. Furthermore, some authors have argued that what was being measured was PERFORMANCE accuracy rather than acquired COMPETENCE. The reasons why some features should be acquired before others has remained in dispute with some authors arguing that, rather than *complexity* or *saliency*, it is the *frequency* in the INPUT that may affect the order. As a result of this lack of consensus, attention has turned more to DEVELOPMENTAL READINESS, that is, how each element is acquired. Evidence of fixed sequences has given credence to a TEACHABILITY HYPOTHESIS.

 Brown 1973, 2007; Macaro et al. 2010; VanPatten & Benati 2010

ACT

an abbreviation for ADAPTIVE CONTROL OF THOUGHT MODEL

activation

an important metaphor in models of language processing, based on the way information is transmitted within the brain by electrical impulses. It is often employed in theories of lexical access. A word in the lexicon is said to be activated to the extent that evidence supports it. Thus, reading the sequence *fro-* would activate *frog, from, front, frost,* etc. for a reader. The items would not all be activated to the same degree: some (e.g., *from*) start off with an

advantage (or perhaps a lower recognition threshold) because they are more frequent. If the next letter the reader encounters is *g*, this new information boosts the activation of *frog* to a point where it 'fires', i.e., the word on the page is regarded as successfully matched to the item *frog* in the reader's lexicon. At this point, the activation of the other words (known as *competitors*) begins to decay. Activation is said to vary in relation to the strength of the connections. Thus, the connection between *foot* and *hand* would be stronger than that between *foot* and *elbow*.
see also BOTTOM-UP PROCESSING, CONNECTIONISM, INTERACTIVE ACTIVATION, MODULARITY, PRIMING
 Field 2004

active knowledge

a term used, especially in relation to language learning, for the knowledge of language which a user actively employs in speaking or writing; it contrasts with *passive knowledge*, which is what a person understands in the speech or writing of others. Native speakers' passive knowledge of vocabulary (passive vocabulary), for example, is much greater than their active knowledge (active vocabulary), i.e., people know far more words than they use.
 Crystal 2008

Activity Theory

a development of Vygotsky's views about learning. The theory emphasizes the social nature of learning, how individual's motives affect the nature of the activity they engage in, and the mediating role of artifacts in learning. The theory proposed that people possess motives that determine how they respond to a particular task. Motives can be biologically determined (e.g., the need to satisfy hunger) or, more importantly from our perspective here, socially constructed (e.g., the need to learn an L2). The learners' motives determine how they construe a given situation. Thus, people with different motives will perform the same learning task in different ways. For example, it is found that middle-class and rural uneducated mothers in Brazil responded differently in the kind of guidance they provided their children in a puzzle-copying task. The middle-class mothers' activity reflected their desire to teach their children the skill they needed to perform the task so they could perform other, similar tasks later (i.e., their motives was pedagogic). Thus, they consistently employed strategic statements like 'now look to see what comes next' and only when these failed did they resort to referential statements like 'try the red piece here'. In contrast, the rural mothers viewed the task as a labor activity of the kind they were familiar with in their daily work. In such activity, mistakes are costly, and, therefore, the mothers strove to prevent their children making errors by directing their actions through referential statements. Thus, the different motives that the two groups of mothers brought to the task led to different activities, reflected in different patterns of language use.

The main characteristics of Activity Theory are summarized in terms of the following key points:

1) Activity Theory is not a static or purely descriptive approach; rather, the use of Activity Theory implies transformation and innovation.
2) All activity systems are heterogeneous and multi-voiced and may include conflict and resistance as readily as cooperation and collaboration.
3) Activity is central. There is no student or teacher or technology centered pedagogy from an Activity Theory perspective; rather, agents play various roles and share an orientation to the activity
4) Activity systems do not work alone. Multiple activity systems are always at work and will have varying influences on the local or focus activity at hand.

One might add that activity systems are dynamic. Individuals can realign their motives in the course of carrying out an activity, thus changing the activity. For example, a student may begin by treating a communicative task as a game but in the course of performing the task re-ordinate to it as an opportunity to learn. From the perspective of Activity Theory, then, it is crucially important for SLA researchers to recognize that elicitation devices (such as tasks) do not simply provide data but rather constitute activities that need to be examined microgenetically.

 Ellis 2003, 2008; Lantolf 2000b; Lantolf & Appel 1994b; Leontiev 1981; Thorne 2004

Adaptive Control of Thought Model
also ACT Model

a cognitive model (of MEMORY), developed by Anderson, which attempts to describe how humans store and retrieve knowledge. The Adaptive Control of Thought (ACT) model is the foundation of SKILL-LEARNING THEORY that distinguished between two types of knowledge: **declarative** and **procedural knowledge**. Procedural knowledge (knowing how to follow different procedural steps to perform an action, i.e., if X then Y) is encoded in the form of production systems, while declarative knowledge (knowing facts about different things, i.e., knowing 'that') is encoded in the form of highly interconnected propositional or semantic networks. Declarative knowledge constitutes the facts we know about the world, and the events we recall; procedural knowledge enables us to perform activities, many of which are automatic. Declarative knowledge is usually explicit and capable of being expressed verbally; it includes the kinds of grammar rule that a linguist might formulate. By contrast, procedural knowledge is implicit; it includes the ability to process language without necessarily being able to put into words the rules that are being applied. According to ACT, learning begins with declarative knowledge (information is gathered and stored) and slowly becomes procedural (people move toward the ability to perform with that knowledge). Afterward, people move to a stage in which they can function effortlessly with the procedural knowledge. For example, an experienced driver uses procedural knowledge to brake suddenly when faced with a hazard but uses declarative knowledge to explain how a car's braking system works. A production system is the set of rules which need to be followed in order to perform the action or execute a skill.

Anderson intended his theory to be sufficiently broad as to provide an overarching theory of the architecture of cognition, and different cognitive processes (memory, language comprehension, reasoning, etc.) are all considered to fall under the same underlying cognitive system. A number of researchers in SLA have used the model to help understand how knowledge of L2 develops and within this view, the development of linguistic skill is considered the development of a complex cognitive skill. Language learning then is considered a form of skill learning that must develop both in terms of developing declarative knowledge of the language, but also in developing automaticity which leads to more fluent language performance. Within SLA, the claim is that learners move from declarative to procedural knowledge through three stages. In the *declarative* stage information is stored as facts for which there are no ready-made activation procedures. For example, we may be aware that *drowned* consists of *drown* and *-ed*, and yet be unable to produce *drowned* correctly in conversation. The second stage is the *associative* stage. Because it is difficult to use declarative knowledge, the learner tries to sort the information into more efficient productions sets by means of 'composition' (collapsing several discrete productions into one), and 'proceduralization' (applying a general rule to a particular instance). For example, the learner may have learned *drowned* and *saved* as two distinct items, but may come to realize that they can be represented more economically in a production set: 'if the goal is to generate a past tense verb, then add *-ed* to the verb'. This may then serve as a general procedure for generating past tense forms, including incorrect ones (such as *goed*). Anderson notes that errors are particularly likely during the associative stage. In *autonomous* stage, in which procedures become increasingly automated, the mind continues both to generalize productions and also to discriminate more narrowly the occasions when specific productions can be used. For example, the learner may modify the past tense production set (above) so that it applies to only a subset of verbs. At this stage the ability to verbalize knowledge of the skill can disappear entirely.

Anderson discusses classroom L2 learning in the light of the ACT model. He sees the kind of knowledge taught to the classroom learner as different from adult L1 knowledge. According to Anderson, we speak the learned language (i.e., the second language) by using general rule-following procedures applied to the rules we have learned, rather than speaking directly, as we do in our native language. Not surprisingly, applying this knowledge is a much slower and more painful process than applying the procedurally encoded knowledge of our own language.

However, Anderson sees the differences between L1 and foreign language learning as merely a question of the stage reached. Whereas L1 learners almost invariably reach the autonomous stage, foreign language learners typically only reach the associative stage. Thus, although foreign language learners achieve a fair degree of proceduralization through PRACTICE, and can use L2 rules without awareness, they do not reach full autonomy.

In short, the ACT model claims that learning begins with declarative knowledge which slowly becomes proceduralized, and that the mechanism by which this takes place is *practice*.

see also INFORMATION-PROCESSING MODEL, BIALYSTOK'S THEORY OF L2 LEARNING, MONITOR THEORY, SOCIO-PSYCHOLINGUISTIC MODEL, VARIABLE COMPETENCE MODE, CAPABILITY CONTINUUM PARADIGM, EXPLICIT KNOWLEDGE, IMPLICIT KNOWLEDGE

📖 Anderson 1976, 1980, 1983, 1985, 1993; Ellis 2008; Macaro et al. 2010

additive bilingualism

the result of SLA in social contexts where members of a dominant group learn the language of a minority without threat to their L1 competence or to their ETHNIC IDENTITY. In contrast, the result of SLA in social contexts where members of a minority group learn the dominant language as L2 and are more likely to experience some loss of ethnic identity and attrition of L1 skills is referred to as **subtractive bilingualism**—especially if they are children. There are many other social variables contributing to 'additive' versus 'subtractive' outcomes, including (for immigrant groups) the degree of opportunity for continued contact with their country of origin, the composition of families (e.g., whether they include grandparents or other elderly relatives), and whether the L1 continues to fulfill an institutional function such as the practice of religion.

see also EARLY BILINGUALISM, COMPOUND BILINGUALISM, SIMULTANEOUS BILINGUALISM, ATTRITION, FOSSILIZATION

📖 Lambert 1974; Saville-Troike 2006

adjacency pair

in CONVERSATION ANALYSIS, a sequence of two functionally related turns (see TURN-TAKING) each made by a different speaker. The second utterance is always a response to the first. Pairs can take various forms, for example:

- invitation – acceptance (or rejection)
- request – acceptance (or denial)
- greeting – greeting

- assessment – agreement (or disagreement)
- blame – denial (or admission)
- question – answer

The response in the second part of the turn can be categorized as preferred or dispreferred. Generally, the preferred second is the shorter, less complicated response, while the dispreferred second tends to be longer and requires more conversational work. In example 1 below, the second part of the adjacency pair is a preferred response, while example 2 shows a typical dispreferred second which contains a delay: 'hehh'; a marker: 'well'; an appreciation of the offer: 'that's awfully sweet of you'; a declination: 'I don't think I can make it this morning'; a further delay: 'hh uhm'; and an *account* (i.e., a statement to explain unanticipated or untoward behavior): 'I'm running an ad . . . and I have to stay near the phone'.

Example 1
A: Why don't you come up and see me some time?
B: I would like to.

Example 2
A: Uh, if you'd care to come and visit a little while this morning, I'll give you a cup of coffee.
B: Hehh, well, that's awfully sweet of you. I don't think I can make it this morning, hh uhm, I'm running an ad in the paper and uh I have to stay near the phone.

📖 Atkinson & Drew 1979; Baker & Ellece 2011; Schegloff & Sacks 1973

Affective Filter Hypothesis

a term which is usually associated with Krashen, and it is one of the five hypotheses that make up the larger MONITOR MODEL. The Affective Filter is a metaphor which is often used to describe the 'blockage' caused by negative emotional attitudes towards learning a second language. It proposes that learners who are *anxious* (see ANXIETY), unmotivated (see MOTIVATION), or lacking self-confidence will experience a mental block, which will impede language from being understood and retained. Krashen explains that the LANGUAGE ACQUISITION DEVICE (LAD) is the brain's processor of language. Krashen claims that when this Affective Filter is *high*, it does not allow language to reach the LAD, and therefore acquisition does not occur. Krashen has claimed that the best acquisition will occur in environments where anxiety is low and defensiveness absent, or, in Krashen's terms, in contexts where the Affective Filter is *low*. He believes that the strength of the Affective Filter increases with puberty. The filter determines which language model the learner will select, which part of the language the learner will pay attention to, when acquisition should stop, and how fast the language will be acquired.

Believing that the Affective Filter exists, and hence trying to keep it low, implies a particular attitude on behalf of the teacher and certain modifications within the classroom setting. Basically, these changes to the classroom environment are included in the 'Natural Approach' created by Terrell and Krashen. An emphasis on speech production early in the process must be avoided or lessened. Terrell discussed stages of production ranging from the SILENT PERIOD to FLUENCY. Students should be allowed a silent period, during which they can listen to and absorb the language without having to formulate language responses themselves. This silent period mirrors the process experienced by children in their first-language acquisition process and allows students to take part more actively when they feel ready. When students begin to engage in language production, their efforts should be recognized, no matter how limited they are. Error correction needs to be avoided. Teachers who overemphasize correctness over message may contribute to the filter's 'thickness'. Modeling is the way to lead students to more correct usage. According to the model, the environment and type of activities should be taken into consideration when trying to lower anxiety and heighten self-confidence and motivation. There should be quiet, comfortable places for reading. Materials can include, for example, puppets, games, puzzles, role plays, and graphic organizers. Students should feel comfortable, interested, and intrigued with language learning. They should see the benefit of learning and feel that they are in a setting that nurtures their process. A variety of activities should be embedded in context, creative and dynamic. Teachers should be positive and supportive, ensuring that students respect each other and their classmates. They should also bring different types of resources to the classroom. COMPREHENSIBLE INPUT that is aimed slightly beyond the learner's current level of skill allows the learner to advance steadily. Students should be encouraged to seek language development opportunities outside of class. The classroom environment and what happens within it can contribute to lowering the Affective Filter and an increase in language acquisition or learning.

Although both researchers and teachers would agree that affective variables play an important role in second language acquisition, Krashen's Affective Filter remains vague and atheoretical. For example, many self-conscious adolescents suffer from low self-esteem and therefore presumably have a 'high' filter. Are they therefore all bad language learners? And are all the confident and extrovert adults (with a 'low' filter) good language learners? Clearly, they are not. Moreover, how does the Affective Filter actually work? All these issues remain vague and unexplored.

 Brown 2007; González 2008; Krashen 1985; Macaro et al. 2010; Mithcell & Myles 2004; VanPatten & Benati 2010

affective strategies
see LEARNING STRATEGIES

age of arrival
also **age of onset, AOA, AO**
the point at which a learner's exposure to or experience with the second language begins, either through IMMERSION (by immigration), by home exposure (through family members), or through foreign language classroom instruction.
 Piske & Young-Scholten 2009

age of onset
another term for AGE OF ARRIVAL

agrammatism
a term traditionally used in language pathology, as part of the study of APHASIA, referring to a type of speech production characterized by telegraphic syntactic structures, the loss of function words and inflections, and a generally reduced grammatical range; also called *agrammatic speech* and noted especially in *Broca's aphasia*. There may also be problems of comprehension. The notion has come to attract research interest in neurolinguistics and psycholinguistics as part of the study of the way the brain processes language. A distinction was traditionally drawn between agrammatism (the omission of items) and *paragrammatism* (the deviant replacement of items), but as both types of symptoms are often found in the same patient, in varying degrees, the dichotomy is now felt to obscure rather than clarify the nature of the phenomenon. The terms are much more likely to be encountered in language pathology than in psycholinguistics.
 Crystal 2008

AH
an abbreviation for ACCESSIBILITY HIERARCHY

ambiguity intolerance
see AMBIGUITY TOLERANCE

ambiguity tolerance
also **tolerance of ambiguity**
a LEARNING STYLE which concerns the degree to which you are cognitively willing to tolerate ideas and propositions that run counter to your own belief system or structure of knowledge. Some people are, for example, relatively open-minded in accepting ideologies and events and facts that contradict their own views; they are ambiguity tolerant, that is, more content than others to entertain and even internalize contradictory propositions. Others, more closed-minded and dogmatic, tend to reject items that are contradictory or slightly incongruent with their existing system; in their **ambiguity intoler-**

ance, they wish to see every proposition fit into an acceptable place in their cognitive organization, and if it does not fit, it is rejected.

Advantages and disadvantages are present in each style. The person who is tolerant of ambiguity is free to entertain a number of innovative and creative possibilities and not be cognitively or affectively disturbed by ambiguity and uncertainty. In second language learning a great amount of apparently contradictory information is encountered: words that differ from the native language, rules that not only differ but that are internally inconsistent because of certain 'exceptions', and sometimes a whole cultural system that is distant from that of the native culture. Successful language learning necessitates tolerance of such ambiguities, at least for interim periods or stages, during which time ambiguous items are given a chance to become resolved. On the other hand, too much tolerance of ambiguity can have a detrimental effect. People can become 'wishy-washy', accepting virtually every proposition before them, not efficiently subsuming necessary facts into their cognitive organizational structure. Such excess tolerance has the effect of hampering or preventing meaningful SUBSUMPTION of ideas. Linguistic rules, for example, might not be effectively integrated into a whole system; rather, they may be gulped down in meaningless chunks learned by rote.

Intolerance of ambiguity also has its advantages and disadvantages. A certain intolerance at an optimal level enables one to guard against the wishy-washiness referred to above, to close off avenues of hopeless possibilities, to reject entirely contradictory material, and to deal with the reality of the system that one has built. But intolerance can close the mind too soon, especially if ambiguity is perceived as a threat; the result is a rigid, dogmatic, brittle mind that is too narrow to be creative. This may be particularly harmful in second language learning.

 Brown 2007

ambilingualism
see BALANCED BILINGUALISM

analytical strategy
a strategy used by children to analyze the INPUT into parts. They manifest systematic development involving first a one-word and then a two-word stage, etc. L2 learners who learn in this way are referred to as 'rule-formers'. It was also found that some children use **gestalt strategy** in L1 acquisition, typically remaining silent for a longer period of time before producing full sentences when they first start talking. L2 learners who learn in this way are referred to as 'data-gatherers'.
see also SILENT PERIOD
 Ellis 2008; Hatch 1974; Peters 1977

analyzed knowledge
see BIALYSTOK'S THEORY OF L2 LEARNING

anomie
feelings of social uncertainty, dissatisfaction, or homelessness as individuals lose some of the bonds of a native culture but are not yet fully acculturated in the new culture (i.e., one feels neither bound firmly to one's native culture nor fully adapted to the second culture). As individuals begin to lose some of the ties of their native culture and to adapt to the second culture, they experience feelings of chagrin or regret, mixed with the fearful anticipation of entering a new group. Anomie has been studied as an affective variable in second/foreign language learning. In learning a new language people may begin to move away from their own language and culture, and have feelings of insecurity. At the same time they may not be sure about their feelings towards the new language group. Feelings of anomie may be highest when a high level of language ability is reached. This may lead a person to look for chances to speak their own language as a relief.
 Brown 2007; Richards & Schmidt 2010

anxiety
the subjective feeling of tension, apprehension, and nervousness connected to an arousal of the autonomic nervous system. Intricately intertwined with SELF-ESTEEM, SELF-EFFICACY, INHIBITION, and RISK TAKING, the construct of anxiety plays a major affective role in second language acquisition (SLA). Anxiety has received the most attention in SLA research, along with lack of anxiety as an important component of self-confidence. Anxiety correlates negatively with measures of L2 proficiency including grades awarded in foreign language classes, meaning that higher anxiety tends to go with lower levels of success in L2 learning. In addition to self-confidence, lower anxiety may be manifested by more risk-taking or more adventuresome behaviors.

The research on anxiety suggests that anxiety, like self-esteem, can be experienced at various levels. At the deepest, or global, level, **trait anxiety** is a more permanent predisposition to be anxious. Some people are predictably and generally anxious about many things. At a more momentary, or situational level, **state anxiety** is experienced in relation to some particular event or act. As in the case of self-esteem, then, it is important in a classroom for a teacher to try to determine whether a student's anxiety stems from a more global trait or whether it comes from a particular situation at the moment. Trait anxiety, because of its global and somewhat ambiguously defined nature, has not proved to be useful in predicting second language achievement. However, recent research on language anxiety, as it has come to be known, focuses more specifically on the situational nature of state anxiety.

Three components of foreign language anxiety have been identified in order to break down the construct into researchable issues:

1) *Communication apprehension*, arising from learners' inability to adequately express mature thoughts and ideas.
2) *Fear of negative social evaluation*, arising from a learner's need to make a positive social impression on others.
3) *Test anxiety*, or apprehension over academic evaluation

Yet another important insight to be applied to our understanding of anxiety lies in the distinction between **debilitative** and **facilitative anxiety**, or what Oxford called **harmful** and **helpful anxiety**. More recently, tension is identified as a more neutral concept to describe the possibility of both 'dysphoric' (detrimental) and 'euphoric' (beneficial) effects in learning a foreign language. We may be inclined to view anxiety as a negative factor, something to be avoided at all costs. But the notion of facilitative anxiety and euphoric tension is that some concern—some apprehension—over a task to be accomplished is a positive factor. Otherwise, a learner might be inclined to be 'wishy-washy', lacking that facilitative tension that keeps one poised, alert, and just slightly unbalanced to the point that one cannot relax entirely. The feeling of nervousness before giving a public speech is, in experienced speakers, often a sign of facilitative anxiety, a symptom of just enough tension to get the job done.

There is clear evidence to show that anxiety is an important factor in L2 acquisition. However, anxiety (its presence or absence) is best seen not as a necessary condition of successful L2 learning, but rather than as a factor that contributes in differing degrees in different learners, depending in part on other individual difference factors such as their motivational orientation and personality. Research into language anxiety has attempted to relate language anxiety to the developmental aspects of language learning and to a model of language processing.

see also LEARNING STYLES, LEARNING STRATEGIES, PERSONALITY, WILLINGNESS TO COMMUNICATE, LEARNER BELIEFS, INTELLIGENCE, LANGUAGE APTITUDE, EMPATHY, MOTIVATION, ATTRIBUTION THEORY

 Alpert & Haber 1960; Brown 2007; Ellis 2008; Horwitz 2001; Horwitz et al. 1986; Oxford 1999; MacIntyre & Gardner 1989, 1991c; Scovel 1978; Spielmann & Radnofsky 2001

AO
an abbreviation for AGE OF ONSET

AOA
an abbreviation for AGE OF ARRIVAL

aphasia
a disorder in the ability to produce or to understand spoken language. It usually results from brain damage caused by an accident, a stroke or invasive surgery; but some accounts include the effects of *dementia* (i.e., progressive

cognitive dysfunction due to deterioration of brain tissue). Evidence from aphasics provides possible insights into the location of language in the brain, and into the constituent parts of language processing, some of which may be lost by an aphasic and others retained. However, it is dangerous to rely too heavily upon evidence from these atypical subjects. We cannot assume that brain damage has wiped out a given aspect of language processing. Information may have been relocated; or a process may have switched to new (and less efficient) channels than those normally employed.

Well-established syndromes are associated with damage to the two language-sensitive areas of the brain identified by Broca and Wernicke. It is important to note that the characteristics of each type are merely possible symptoms: the exact effects vary considerably from patient to patient.

- Broca's aphasia is often characterized by *agrammatism*: an absence of syntactic structure and omission of function words and inflections. Articulation may be poor and speech is generally effortful, with many hesitations. Comprehension appears to be good, but it may be that the patient is using positional, semantic or pragmatic cues to puzzle out meaning, rather than relying upon syntax. Vocabulary is weighted towards concrete nouns, with verbs sometimes under-represented.
- Wernicke's aphasia is characterized by syntactically complex and well-structured speech, containing function words and correct affixation. Speech is apparently effortless, fluent and rapid. Indeed, many of Wernicke's patients claim not to recognize that they have speech difficulties. But there may be severe problems in retrieving vocabulary, with a reliance on general or inappropriate nouns and verbs. Comprehension may be markedly impaired.

Early accounts of Broca's aphasia associated it with impaired motor activity which led to difficulty in assembling utterances; while Wernicke's aphasia was said to reflect impaired access to stored lexical information. However, Broca's aphasics show signs not just of being unable to use functors appropriately but also of being unable to understand them.

The fact that the symptoms of aphasia vary considerably from patient to patient suggests that the language-sensitive areas of the brain may be differently located in different individuals. Alternatively, particular language functions may be so localized that a great deal depends upon the exact position of the lesion which inflicts the damage. Recent brain imaging data suggests a third possibility: the reason for the vulnerability of the Broca and Wernicke areas is that they constitute a major crossroads for the neural connections which transmit widely distributed linguistic information across the brain.

Instead of relating type of aphasia to the area of the brain in which damage has occurred, clinicians prefer to analyze symptoms. A first observation might consider the extent to which lexical-semantic processing is impaired, as against grammatical or sentence processing. However, a distinction is still often made between *non-fluent aphasia* of the Broca type and *fluent* or *expressive* aphasia of the Wernicke type.

Other less-discussed aphasias are:

- *jargon aphasia*, characterized by a large number of nonsense words in the patient's speech;
- *conduction aphasia*, characterized by an inability to repeat what has just been heard (though comprehension may remain unaffected);
- *transcortical aphasia*, where the best-preserved skill is the ability to repeat words and comprehension is often severely impaired;
- *anomia*, where the main or only symptom is the inability to retrieve words.

Features of these types of aphasia are observed to different degrees in different patients. They suggest that the processing of word form can be separated from the processing of word meaning.

 Caplan 1992; Harris & Coltheart 1986; Field 2004; Lesser & Milroy 1993; Obler & Gjerlow 1999

apology

an attempt which requires the speaker to admit responsibility for some behavior (or failure to carry out some behavior) that has proved to the hearer. Thus, it can be viewed as a *face-saving act*. Apologies differ from REQUESTS in an important respect—speaker/hearer orientation. That is, they impose on the speaker rather than on the hearer. Apologies also differ from requests in that they refer to past rather than feature events. Apologies may also differ from requests in another important way. Whereas there are substantial cross-cultural differences in the way requests are realized in different situations, this does not appear to be the case with apologies.

The study of L2 apologies bears out many of the findings of the research on L2 requests. Lower-level learners may be too direct and concise while higher-level learners may be verbose. In general, however, advanced learners are more native-like. The sociocultural norms of learners' L1 influence how they apologize in an L2. The extent to which transfer takes place can be influenced by the learners' perceptions of the universality of how to apologize, transfer being *less* likely if learners recognize the language-specificity of apologies. Transfer is also more likely in situations where learners feel the need to act in accordance with sociocultural norms of native culture. The opportunity to interact in an L2-speaking environment enables learners to become more native-like.

 Ellis 2008

applied linguistics

a branch of linguistics where the primary concern is the application of linguistic theories, methods and findings to the elucidation of language problems which have arisen in other areas of experience. The most well-developed branch of applied linguistics is the teaching and learning of foreign languages, and sometimes the term is used as if this were the only field involved. But several other fields of application have emerged, including the linguistic analysis of language disorders (clinical linguistics), the use of language in mother-tongue education (educational linguistics), and developments in lexicography, translation and stylistics. There is an uncertain boundary between applied linguistics and the various interdisciplinary branches of linguistics, such as sociolinguistics and psycholinguistics, especially as several of the latter's concerns involve practical outcomes of a plainly 'applied' kind (e.g., planning a national language policy). On the other hand, as these branches develop their own theoretical foundations, the distinction between 'pure' and 'applied' is becoming more apparent, and the characterization of research as being in 'applied psycholinguistics', etc., is now more regularly encountered.
📖 Crystal 2008

approximative system

a term used by Nemser to refer to the deviant linguistic system which the learner employs when trying to use the target language. The learner passes through a number of approximative systems on the way to acquiring full target-language proficiency. Approximative system hypothesis emphasizes the developmental nature of the learner's language since with the addition of new elements the learner's linguistic system is continually being modified and developed. According to Nemser, the acquisition of a second language involves systematic stages with an approximative system at each stage. These approximative systems are internally structured and are distinct from both the source and the target language. They are by definition transient and are gradually restructured in successive stages.

The main difference between the approximative system hypothesis and the INTERLANGUAGE hypothesis is that the latter emphasizes structurally intermediate status of the learner's language system between mother tongue and target language, while the former emphasizes the transitional and dynamic nature of the system.

see also IDIOSYNCRATIC DIALECT
📖 Ellis 1986; Keshavarz 1999; Nemser 1971

aptitude-treatment interaction

another term for LEARNER-INSTRUCTION MATCHING

ascribed bilingual
another term for EARLY BILINGUAL

Aspect Hypothesis
a claim that first and second language learners will initially be influenced by the inherent semantic aspect of verbs or predicates in the acquisition of tense and aspect markers associated with or affixed to these verbs. In other words, early verbs are predominantly affiliated with a prototypical inflection (e.g., *-ing* or *-ed*) depending on their inherent lexical aspect, rather than grammatical aspect such as the progressive. This approach is semantic in nature and focuses on the influence of lexical aspect in the second language acquisition of tense-aspect morphology.

The aspect hypothesis is a rich hypothesis drawing upon many forms of linguistics. It is important to note that very early forms of temporal expressions appear without any overt linguistic marking. Four ways are suggested by which learners can express temporality: (a) build on conversational partner's discourse, (b) infer from context, (c) contrast events, and (d) follow chronological order in narration. These are essentially pragmatic means for accomplishing what cannot be accomplished linguistically.

see also MULTIDIMENSIONAL MODEL, PROCESSABILITY THEORY, CONNECTIONISM, OPERATING PRINCIPLES

📖 Andersen & Shirai 1994; Bardovi-Harlig 1999b; Gass & Selinker 2008; Piske & Young-Scholten 2009

Aspects Model
another term for STANDARD THEORY

assimilation
a voluntary or involuntary process by which individuals or groups completely take on the traits of another culture, leaving their original cultural and linguistic identities behind. The absorption of European immigrants into U.S. society and their adoption of American cultural patterns and social structures has generally been described as a process of assimilation.

📖 González 2008

attention
a cognitive process involving the ability to select and focus on particular stimuli from the environment while ignoring others. For example, while driving, a person selects and focuses on traffic, stoplights, crosswalks, and so on, while tending to ignore the sky, birds chirping in a tree, and the license plates on most other cars. In SLA, the stimuli would be linguistic items in the INPUT. Three constructs of attention are generally discussed in the literature: 'attention as capacity', 'attention as selection', and 'attention as effort'. *Attention as capacity* refers to learners' ability to allocate attention to the

processing of the information they receive. It is well established that attention involves a limited capacity; that is, people are exposed to a large number of stimuli and the brain cannot process all of them at the same time (see WORKING MEMORY). However, capacity may be modal and context dependent. That is, people may be able to eat and watch TV at the same time because these activities require different kinds of attention (e.g., eating does not require the audio modality). However, people find it difficult to carry on a full conversation on the phone while watching TV (i.e., because both tap into the attention required for listening).

The second construct within attention is *attention as selection*. It addresses how input becomes INTAKE. It is equated with 'noticing' (see NOTICING HYPOTHESIS). Assuming that there is a limited capacity to attend to stimuli, the attentional system must select from incoming information/stimuli. Detection is the process involved in selecting and registering data in working memory.

The third construct is *attention as effort*. The degree of effortful attention needed depends on the capacity demands of the task learners have to accomplish. A task differs in the modes of processing information. Automatic processing of information would require little attentional efforts for L2 learners, whereas controlled processing of information will require lots of attention and would proceed slowly.

Attention is a construct that has attracted the interest of second language researchers, and it plays a major role in some hypotheses about L2 acquisition (e.g., noticing hypothesis). The general idea of some of these hypotheses is that (1) learners must actively attend to linguistic stimuli in order to learn; and (2) attention may affect what learners can detect in the input at any given time. That is, some scholars have looked at the possibility that learners 'selectively attend' to stimuli in the input.

see also CONSCIOUSNESS-RAISING, AWARENESS, INPUT PROCESSING THEORY
📖 Ellis 2008; Robinson 1995a, 2001a, 2001b, 2003; VanPatten & Benati 2010

Attention-Processing Model
also Information-Processing Model, Information-Processing Theory

a cognitive theory of L2 acquisition, associated with McLaughlin 1980s, which claims a separation of 'controlled' from 'automatic' processes. Controlled processes are capacity limited and temporary, and automatic processes are relatively permanent. We can think of controlled processing as typical of anyone learning a brand new skill in which only a very few elements of the skill can be retained. When you first learn to play tennis, for example, you can only manage the elements of, say, making contact between ball and racquet, getting the ball over the net, and hitting the ball into the green space on the other side of the net. Everything else about the game is far too complex for your capacity-limited ability. Automatic processes, on the other hand, refer to processing in a more accomplished skill, where the 'hard drive' (to borrow a computer metaphor) of your brain can manage hundreds and thousands of bits of information simultaneously. Automatic processing is generally characterized as fast, relatively unstoppable, independent of the amount of information being processed, effortless, and unconscious. To extend the tennis example, automatic processing in tennis involves simultaneous attention to one's location on the court, your opponent's location, your and your opponent's abilities, strategies for winning the point, decisions about using forehand or backhand, and the list goes on.

Both ends of this continuum of processing can occur with either 'focal' or 'peripheral' attention to the task at hand, that is, focusing attention either centrally or simply on the periphery. It is easy to fall into the temptation of thinking of focal attention as 'conscious' attention, but such a pitfall must be avoided. Both focal and peripheral attention to some task may be quite conscious. When you are driving a car, for example, your focal attention may center on cars directly in front of you as you move forward; but your peripheral attention to cars beside you and behind you, to potential hazards, and of course to the other thoughts running through your mind, is all very much within your conscious awareness.

While many controlled processes are focal, some, like child first language learning or the learning of skills without any instruction, can be peripheral. Similarly, many automatic processes are peripheral, but some can be focal, as in the case of an accomplished pianist performing in a concert or an experienced driver paying particular attention to the road on a foggy night. It is very important to note that in virtually every act of performing something, focal and peripheral attention actually occur simultaneously, and the question is: What, specifically, occupies a person's focal and peripheral attention? So, for example, a very young child who says to a parent *'Nobody don't like me' is undoubtedly focally attending to conveying emotion, mental anguish, or loneliness, and peripherally attending to words and morphemes that underlie the central meaning. Other factors that garner attention somewhere in between centrally focal and extremely peripheral may be reading the parent's facial features, mental recall of an uncomfortable incident of rejection, awareness of a sibling overhearing the communication, and even such peripheral nonlinguistic, noncognitive factors as the temperature in the room at the moment, a light in the background, the smell of dinner cooking, or the warmth of the parent's arms enfolding the child. All of these perceptions, from highly focal to very peripheral, are within the awareness of the child. McLaughlin noted that the literature in experimental psychology indicates that there is no long-term learning (of new material) without awareness. A cognitive perspective of SLA entirely obviates the need to distinguish conscious and subconscious processing.

When applied to SLA, this approach can be summarized as follows: Learners first resort to controlled processing in the second language. This controlled processing involves the temporary activation of a selection of information nodes in the memory, in a new configuration. Such processing requires a lot of attentional control on the part of the subject, and is constrained by the limitations of the SHORT-TERM MEMORY. For example, a beginner learner wanting to greet someone in the second language might activate the following words: *good morning how are you?* Initially, these words have to be put together in a piecemeal fashion, one at a time (assuming they have not been memorized as an unanalyzed chunk).

Through repeated activation, sequences first produced by controlled processing become automatic. Automatized sequences are stored as units in the LONG-TERM MEMORY, which means that they can be made available very rapidly whenever the situation requires it, with minimal attentional control on the part of the subject. As a result, automatic processes can work in parallel, activating clusters of complex cognitive skills simultaneously. So, in the above example, once a learner has activated the sequence *good morning how are you?* a large number of times, it becomes automatic, that is, it does not require attentional control. However, once acquired, such automatized skills are difficult to delete or modify.

'Learning' in this view is seen as the movement from controlled to automatic processing via PRACTICE (repeated activation). When this shift occurs, controlled processes are freed to deal with higher levels of processing (i.e., the integration of more complex skill clusters), thus explaining the incremental (step by step) nature of learning. It is necessary for simple sub-skills and routines to become automatic before more complex ones can be tackled. Once a learner has automatized *good morning how are you?*, he is free to deal with the learning of more complex language, as the short-term memory is not taken up by the production of this particular string.

This continuing movement from controlled to automatic processing results in a constant RESTRUCTURING of the linguistic system of the second language learner. This phenomenon may account for some of the VARIABILITY characteristic of learner language. Restructuring destabilizes some structures in the INTERLANGUAGE, which seemed to have been previously acquired, and hence leads to the temporary reappearance of second language errors. Restructuring is also the result of exemplar-based representations becoming rule-based (see DUAL-MODE SYSTEM). Second language learners often start by memorizing unanalyzed chunks of language, which will later be analyzed and give rise to productive rules. For example, a learner might first memorize a question as an unanalyzed chunk, for example *have you got a pet?*, without having a productive rule for interrogatives, involving inversion. When this learner starts generating interrogatives that are not rote-learned chunks, he might produce an alternative, uninverted form, such has *you have pet?*

This account is especially convincing in its explanation of the vexed issue of FOSSILIZATION, which is so well documented in second language acquisition studies. Fossilization in this model would arise as a result of a controlled process becoming automatic prematurely, before it is native-like. As we have seen, automatic processes are difficult to modify as they are outside the attentional control of the subject. Thus, they are likely to remain in the learner's interlanguage, giving rise to a stable but erroneous construction. However, this general idea does not explain why some structures seem much more likely to fossilize than others.

see also PROCESSABILITY THEORY, PERCEPTUAL SALIENCY APPROACH, ADAPTIVE CONTROL OF THOUGHT MODEL

📖 Brown 2007; Ellis 2008; Hulstijn 1990; McLaughlin 1987, 1990a, 1990b; McLaughlin et al. 1983; McLeod & McLaughlin 1986; Mithcell & Myles 2004; Segalowitz 2003

attitude

a set of personal feelings, opinions, or biases about races, cultures, ethnic groups, classes of people, and languages. Attitudes, like all aspects of the development of cognition and affect in human beings, develop early in childhood and are the result of parents' and peers' attitudes, of contact with people who are different in any number of ways, and of interacting affective factors in the human experience. These attitudes form a part of one's perception of self, of others, and of the culture in which one is living.

It seems clear that second language learners benefit from positive attitudes and that negative attitudes may lead to decreased motivation and, in all likelihood, because of decreased input and interaction, to unsuccessful attainment of proficiency. Yet the teacher needs to be aware that everyone has both positive and negative attitudes. The negative attitudes can be changed, often by exposure to reality—e.g., by encounters with actual persons from other cultures. Negative attitudes usually emerge from one's indirect exposure to a culture or group through television, movies, news media, books, and other sources that may be less than reliable. Teachers can aid in dispelling what are often myths about other cultures, and replace those myths with an accurate understanding of the other culture as one that is different from one's own, yet to be respected and valued. Learners can thus move through the hierarchy of affectivity through awareness and responding, to valuing, and finally to an organized and systematic understanding and appreciation of the foreign culture.

📖 Brown 2007

Attribution Theory

a theory which focuses on how people explain the causes of their own successes and failures. Attribution theory is described in terms of four explanations for success and/or failure in achieving a personal objective: *ability, effort, perceived difficulty of a task,* and *luck.* Two of those four factors are internal to the learner: ability and effort; and two are attributable to external circumstances outside of the learner: task difficulty and luck. Learners tend to explain, that is, to attribute, their success on a task on these four dimensions. Depending on the individual, a number of causal determinants might be cited. Thus, failure to get a high grade on a final exam in a language class might for some be judged to be a consequence of their poor ability or effort, and by others to difficulty of exam, and perhaps others to just plain old bad luck.

This is where **self-efficacy** (i.e., belief in one's own capabilities to successfully perform an activity) comes in. If a learner feels he is capable of carrying out a given task, in other words, a high sense of self-efficacy, an appropriate degree of effort may be devoted to achieving success. Falling short of one's personal goals may then be attributable to not enough effort expended, but rarely, in the case of students with high self-efficacy, would an excuse be made attributing the bad performance to something like bad luck. Conversely, a learner with low self-efficacy may quite easily attribute failure to external factors, a relatively unhealthy psychological attitude to bring to any task. Students with low self-efficacy might also attribute failure to an initial lack of ability. Both of the latter attributions can create a self-fulfilling sense of failure at the outset.

see also SELF-ESTEEM, INHIBITION, ANXIETY, RISK TAKING, WILLINGNESS TO COMMUNICATE, EMPATHY, MOTIVATION
 Brown 2007

attrition

the loss or forgetting of language skills. Language attrition refers to the gradual forgetting of a first or second language. It may be distinguished from the term 'language shift', where the focus is on groups of speakers, and from 'language loss', a term applied to the decline of linguistic skills in individuals or speech communities. A common typology for research in attrition lists four categories of natural language attrition (rather than pathological conditions such as APHASIA):

1) attrition of first language skills (L1) in an L1 environment (e.g., ageing, dialectal loss);
2) attrition of L1 skills in an L2 environment (e.g., fading L1 in migrant populations);
3) attrition of L2 in an L1 environment (e.g., decline in school-learned L2) or decline in L2 following return to home country (e.g., returning expatriate workers or their children); and
4) attrition of L2 skills in an L2 environment (e.g., loss of L2 skills when ageing).

Language attrition is recognized as a normal part of changes in language proficiency over time, as distinct from changes caused by accident or disease. The degree and rate of language attrition may be affected by any or all of the following factors: proficiency, age, attitude, motivation and frequency of language use.

Various hypotheses have been proposed to explain language change during periods of disuse: the *regression hypothesis* maintains that the sequence of language loss is the mirror image of the sequence of acquisition, so that forms acquired late are the most vulnerable to attrition; the *threshold hypothesis* holds that there may be a level of proficiency that, once attained, enables the language learned to remain fairly stable and resist attrition for some time; the *retrieval failure theory* and the *savings paradigm* both suggest that language which has been learned is not lost but is only difficult to retrieve (i.e., forgotten) and in the latter case, may be quickly re-learned for productive use.

 De Bot & Weltens 1995; Macaro et al. 2010

auditory learner
a learner whose preferred learning style is to learn by listening (e.g., listening to lectures and audiotapes), rather than learning in some other way, such as by reading.
see ALSO KINAESTHETIC LEARNER, VISUAL LEARNER
 Brown 2007; Ellis 2008; Richards & Schmidt 2010; Reid 1987

authenticity
a term that has come to be most closely associated with 'communicative language teaching'. Authenticity in instructed SLA contexts can be divided into two broad areas: *authenticity of materials* used, and *authenticity of the discourse* among the class participants. There has been considerable debate about the value of both of these areas. In the case of authentic materials, the definition usually applied is 'text produced by a native speaker for a native speaker reader' where there is no intention to match text difficulty to learners' L2 proficiency level. A criticism of using authentic materials has been that the kinds of tasks devised to aid comprehension of authentic text have, of necessity, tended to be of low cognitive demand. More recently the use of corpora has come to be viewed as authentic text but this too has come in for criticism: 'unfiltered' examples of words and phrases in use have not yet proved themselves as promoting SLA. Authenticity of discourse has provoked even more debate and a definition of authentic classroom discourse is hard to come by. The argument is centered around whether discourse in an L2 classroom can ever be considered as authentic and that therefore, rather than simulating the outside world (e.g., through role plays), we should be considering whether the talk encountered is 'authenticated' by its participants. Authenticity is not in the nature of a piece of text, but rather is the property of a speaker's intention and a hearer's interpretation. This view consolidates earlier positions that the only 'valid language' in the classroom

is the language needed to perform everyday classroom tasks.
 Breen 1985; Macaro et al. 2010; Van Lier 1996

Autonomous Induction Theory
a theory developed by Carroll that attributes difficulties in learning a second language to PARSING problems. Acquisition moves forward when there is a failure in the parsing of utterances. Learning is an inductive process in this view (learning takes place by being presented with examples—INPUT—and making generalizations from those examples) and learning is triggered by a failure to process incoming stimuli. Carroll accepts that our mental representations of language involve a number of distinct modules, as suggested by UNIVERSAL GRAMMAR, with limited interconnections. However, she rejects parameter (re)setting as a totally inadequate metaphor for the ways in which SLA takes place, that is, it is inadequate as a transition theory. Instead, she proposes a version of inductive learning (i-learning), which is initiated when we fail to parse incoming language stimuli adequately using our existing mental representations and analysis procedures. Inductive learning is the term applied to learning by generalization from examples.

Autonomous Induction theory has been commonly criticized as inadequate with reference to language learning, because it fails to explain why learners processing the environmental language around them are so successful at working out the complexities of natural language, and in particular, why they never produce so-called WILD GRAMMARS. Carroll argues that the i-learning of Autonomous Induction theory differs from other inductive language learning theories such as the COMPETITION MODEL because it is constrained by the preexisting mental representations of language, which are strongly resistant to change. She also presents a well-developed critique of interactionist research (see SOCIAL-INTERACTIONISM), for its theoretical limitations; for example, for its neglect of the detail of language processing which converts language stimuli into interpretable input. She challenges a commonplace among interactionist researchers, who claim that increased comprehension (of second language meaning) can lead to identification and acquisition of language form, in a sequential manner. Carroll points out that this is logically impossible. For one thing, unless enough formal analysis is done so that elements such as phonemes, syllables and words are identified in the speech stimulus as it flows by the learner, there is no way of generating any interpretation of its meaning.
 Carroll 2000, 2001, 2007; Gass & Selinker 2008; Mithcell & Myles 2004

autonomy
a construct which is often associated with and sometimes used synonymously with 'independent learning'. The main thrust of the concept is that the more a learner is able to learn a language without the direct help or direction of the teacher (1) the better he is prepared for lifelong learning of that lan-

guage and other languages and (2) the more motivated he will be to pursue learning. Taking responsibility for one's own learning, and making choices in every area of learning and assessment were key principles in early representations of language learner autonomy. However, even supporters of autonomy admit that the term continues to lack precision. Little consensus has been achieved on whether autonomy is an individual learner trait or whether it is a state that manifests itself in reaction to institutional contexts; whether autonomy is a psychological phenomenon that can be nurtured by teachers or whether it is an inevitable product of the socio-cultural situation in which the learners find themselves. Most recently, there has been a focus on learner autonomy's interdependence with teacher autonomy (i.e., freedom from institutional and national constraints to develop reflective and experimental practice). Despite more than two decades of researcher and practitioner interest in autonomy, the construct has failed to achieve a high status in the research evidence and internationally has not made much headway in terms of influencing pedagogy. It is argued that this lack of progress is possibly due to the threat autonomy poses to the educational status quo.

📖 Benson 2001; Holec 1981; Lamb & Reinders 2008; Macaro et al. 2010

autonomy of language

the view that the human LANGUAGE FACULTY is independent of general mental and cognitive abilities. A young child is obliged to spend years learning to make sense of the world it is born into, and at the same time it must learn its first language. For decades there has been a controversy, sometimes called the *nature-nurture* debate or the *content-process* debate, over whether children are born with a distinctive and largely independent faculty for learning language, or whether they simply acquire a language in the same way they acquire other kinds of understanding and skills, by using their general all-purpose cognitive abilities.

The first view—represented by such proposals as the GENETIC HYPOTHESIS OF LANGUAGE and the INNATENESS HYPOTHESIS—is probably supported by a majority of linguists; certainly by Noam Chomsky and his followers, but also by others who have limited sympathy for Chomsky's ideas. The second has been supported by a number of psychologists, notably by Jean Piaget and Jerome Bruner, and more recently by Elizabeth Bates and her colleagues.

The first view holds that children are born with specialized structures or areas in their brains which are dedicated to the learning and use of languages; Chomsky's version further holds that important information about the nature of human languages is already present at birth. The second view denies this, and sees language acquisition as not different in kind from, say, learning to judge size and distance; some versions go further and claim that learning a first language is not different from learning to ice skate or to drive a car.

This last, extreme, view can probably be disposed of: the abundant evidence for the CRITICAL PERIOD HYPOTHESIS, demonstrating that first-language acquisition is rapid in children but impossible in adults, surely demonstrates that learning a first language is very different from learning to ice skate. Otherwise, though, the debate is still very much alive.

Linguists like to support the first view by pointing to the evidence from language disability: some disabilities, such as the WILLIAMS SYNDROME, appear to leave the language faculties intact while severely damaging other mental faculties; others, such as SPECIFIC LANGUAGE IMPAIRMENT, chiefly affect only linguistic behavior while leaving other mental faculties largely unscathed.

📖 Bates 1976; Bates et al. 1979; 1988; Jackendoff 1993; Macwhinney & Bates 1989; Pinker 1994b; Trask 2005

auxiliary language

a second language that learners need to know for some official functions in their immediate sociopolitical setting, or that they will need for purposes of wider communication, although their first language serves most other needs in their lives. For learners of an auxiliary language, the target language grammar, for example, may not be that of native speakers, but of educated users of the L2 in their own country; learners may not wish to identify with or fully participate in a language community for which the L2 is politically dominant.

see also HERITAGE LANGUAGE, BILINGUAL EDUCATION

📖 González 2008; Kachru 1986; Macaro et al. 2010

avoidance

a term most often used in the context of learner strategies (see LEARNING STRATEGIES) and particularly as a COMMUNICATION STRATEGY in that it is a conscious mental act with a language use goal. Avoidance behavior occurs when L2 learners attempt to avoid using structures in their production that are difficult as a result of (perceived) differences or similarities between their L1 and the target L2. Although avoidance is a complex phenomenon to describe, scholars in SLA have attempted to address the complexity of this phenomenon by identifying three main types of avoidance:

1) when learners know or anticipate that there is a problem and have at least some, sketchy idea of what the target form is like. This is the minimum condition for avoidance;
2) when learners know what the target is but find it too difficult to use in the particular circumstances (e.g., in the context of free-flowing conversation);
3) when learners know what to say and how to say it but are unwilling to actually say it because it will result in them flouting their own norms of behavior.

In all three cases it is clear that much more is involved than the learner's L1. The extent of learners' knowledge of the L2 and the attitudes learners hold toward their own and the target-language cultures act as factors that interact with L1 knowledge to determine avoidance behavior.

Avoidance can be broken down into several subcategories. The most common type of avoidance strategy is *syntactic* or *lexical avoidance* within a semantic category. Consider the following conversation between a learner and a native speaker:

L: I lost my road.
US: You lost your *road*?
L: Uh,... I lost. I lost. I got lost.

The learner avoided the lexical item *road* entirely, not being able to come up with the word *way* at that point.

Phonological avoidance is also common, as in the case of a Japanese tennis player who avoided using the word *rally* (because of its phonological difficulty) and instead opted to say, simply, *hit the ball*.

A more direct type of avoidance is *topic avoidance*, in which a whole topic of conversation (say, talking about what happened yesterday if the past tense is unfamiliar) might be avoided entirely. Learners manage to devise ingenious methods of topic avoidance: changing the subject, pretending not to understand (a classical means for avoiding answering a question), simply not responding at all, or noticeably abandoning a message when a thought becomes too difficult to express.

📖 Brown 2007; Ellis 2008; Kellerman 1992; Macaro et al. 2010; Scovel 2000

awareness

cognizance of linguistic, mental, or emotional factors through ATTENTION and focus. Awareness refers to consciousness, i.e., the degree to which people are conscious of what they are doing or learning. Three main criteria to describe awareness have been identified. Individuals are considered aware of a given experience if they can (1) show that a change (cognitive or behavioral) has taken place as a result of that experience, (2) report that they are aware of what they are experiencing (e.g., they report noticing linguistic features in the INPUT), and (3) describe their experience (e.g., verbalize an underlying rule of the L2). Also, three levels of awareness have been identified: *perception* (we might perceive a stimulus but not be aware); *noticing* (we are able to bring a stimulus into our focal attention); and *understanding* (we are able to analyze and compare a language feature with what we have already stored in our memory).

Scholars disagree about the role of awareness in SLA. Some scholars have held that acquisition is mainly an unconscious process, and conscious learning has only a monitoring function (see MONITOR HYPOTHESIS). These scholars have argued against the key role of awareness in language acquisition as the acquisition of a second language can happen without awareness. Others have argued that awareness at the level of noticing (see NOTICING HYPOTHESIS) is a necessary condition for acquisition.

However, what we are learning from these studies is that learners can indeed benefit from raised awareness of their own processes of learning. Undoubtedly, there is an optimal level of awareness that serves learners. In other words, too much awareness, too much explicit focus on grammar, or too much devotion to rules, coupled with not enough intuitive, subconscious communication, will smother learners' yearning to simply use language, unfettered by overattention to correctness. But some levels of awareness are clearly warranted, i.e., *strategic awareness*, the conscious application of appropriate strategies.

see also CONSCIOUSNESS RAISING

📖 Brown 2007; Lightbown & Spada 1990; VanPatten & Benati 2010

B

babbling
a prelinguistic stage when young children produce sounds which resemble adult consonant-vowel (CV) syllables. Children begin to babble at about 6-10 months; and the stage lasts for up to 9 months. Two types of babbling are observed: *reduplicated* babble, with the same CV sequence repeated (e.g., *bababa* or *babababa*) and *variegated* babble, with different CV sequences combined (e.g., *bamido*). Both sometimes adopt an intonation pattern which resembles adult speech. As these babble sequences become longer and more frequent, infants may display a preference for one consonant-type over others, with some favoring mainly *m*-sounds, others *b*-sounds, and others still *g*-sounds.

They soon vary the intonation contours of babble sequences too, matching the rises and falls of intonation patterns in the language around them. They also start to vary the syllables within a babble sequence, for example, *baba-ba-mamama, mememe-dede, baba-dadada*. It is harder to tell whether infants vary vowel-like sounds systematically because there tends to be more variability in these than in consonant-like sounds. For consonants, there is distinct closure for stops (e.g., p, b, t, d, k, g) at different places in the mouth and discernible near-closure for fricatives, where the sound is produced with audible friction (e.g., s, f, v), so it is possible to identify the general place and manner of articulation for babbled syllables. By ten to twelve months of age, many babbled sequences sound compatible with the surrounding language, using similar sound sequences, rhythm, and intonation contours.

There are conflicting views as to whether babbling contributes to *phonological development*. A **discontinuity hypothesis** claims that there is no link. Exponents point out that some children undergo a SILENT PERIOD between babbling and the emergence of speech and that, regardless of target language (TL), there seems to be a set order in which phonological features are acquired. A **continuity hypothesis** maintains that babbling is a precursor to speech, enabling the child to practice a range of potentially useful sounds, which increasingly resemble those of the TL. The CV syllables produced during later babbling are said to recur in the child's first words; and there is said to be a strong correlation between the frequency of sounds in babbling and their frequency in the TL. Nevertheless, it should be noted that the omnipresent English sound /ð/ emerges late, as do fricatives in general.

see also COOING, FIRST LANGUAGE ACQUISITION, PHONOLOGICAL PRODUCTION
📖 Clark 2009; De Boysson-Bardies & Vihman 1991; Elbers 1982; Field 2004; Ingram 1989; Vihman 1996

baby talk
another term for CHILD DIRECTED SPEECH

back channels
a term identified by Duncan to describe feedback that is given by a hearer in order to indicate that they are attending to someone else's speech. They can be (1) nonverbal, for example, consisting of nods, gestures or facial expressions, or (2) verbal, for example, words like *yeah*, *right*, *okay* or vocalizations like *mm* and *uh-huh*. They can also include cases where a hearer completes part of a speaker's turn.
see also TURN TAKING
📖 Baker & Ellece 2011; Duncan 1973

backsliding
a phenomenon in which the learner seems to have grasped a rule or principle and then regresses to a previous stage. Second language learners are likely to manifest correct target language forms on some occasions but deviant forms on other occasions. When this happens they are said to backslide. Backsliding involves the use of a rule belonging to an earlier stage of development. It can occur when learners are under some pressure, as, for instance, when they have to express difficult subject matter or are feeling anxious.
see also FOSSILIZATION, OVERGENERALIZATION
📖 Ellis 2008; Selinker 1972

balanced bilingualism
also **ambilingualism, equilingualism, symmetrical bilingualism**
a type of BILINGUALISM in which a person is equally proficient in two languages. It is rare if not impossible to find perfectly balanced bilinguals, where all aspects of linguistic knowledge and performance are equally developed and fluent in both languages. Individuals are therefore, often *dominant* in either one or the other language. Some researchers consider someone with even limited amounts of L2 skill as a bilingual, whereas others only consider individuals who are highly proficient in more than one language as bilingual.
see also COMPOUND BILINGUALISM, EARLY BILINGUALISM, ADDITIVE BILINGUALISM, SIMULTANEOUS BILINGUALISM
📖 Brown & Attardo 2005; Gass & Selinker 2008; Macaro et al. 2010; VanPatten & Benati 2010

Basic Interpersonal Communication Skills
also **BICS**

a term developed by Cummins which refers to the kind of L2 proficiency that learners require in order to engage effectively in face-to-face interaction. Basic Interpersonal Communication Skills (BICS) are the skills required for oral fluency and sociolinguistic appropriateness. They are *basic* in the sense that they develop naturally as a result of exposure to a language through communication. BICS is contrasted with **Cognitive Academic Language Proficiency** (**CALP**), which refers to the kind of L2 proficiency required to engage effectively in academic study.

More specifically, Cummins has proposed that language proficiency be conceptualized along two interacting continua. One continuum relates to the extent of the contextual support available for expressing or receiving meaning. At one extreme, a task might require *context-embedded language* where communication derives from interpersonal involvement in a shared reality, while at the other the task might require *context-reduced language*, where shared reality cannot be assumed. The other continuum concerns the extent to which a task is cognitively demanding. This reflects the amount of information that must be processed simultaneously or in close succession and also the extent to which the information needed to perform the task has become automatized. Thus, CALP, unlike BICS, involves the ability to communicate messages that are precise and explicit in tasks that are context-reduced and cognitively demanding. Cummins has also argued that there is a *common underlying proficiency* (CUP) between two languages. It is possible to transfer skills, ideas and concepts which students learn in their first language into the second language.

The notion of the CALP/BICS distinction has been attacked on a number of grounds, most notably that it promotes a DEFICIT THEORY since it attributes the academic failure of bilingual/minority students to low cognitive/academic proficiency rather than to inappropriate schooling. The ongoing controversy highlights the absence of consensus regarding the relationship of language proficiency to academic achievement.

see also COMMUNICATIVE COMPETENCE

📖 Cummins 1981; Ellis 2008; Macaro et al. 2010

basic variety

an early stage of L2 acquisition identified by researchers in the *European Science Foundation Project*. It is characterized by the absence of grammatical functors. Learners rely instead on pragmatic means to convey semantic concepts such as *pastness*. Learner utterances at this stage consist of noun + verb + noun or verb + noun. Verbs are non-finite. The basic variety is preceded by the pre-basic variety (characterized by nominal organization) and followed by the post-basic variety (where finite verb forms appear).

📖 Ellis 2008

behavioral psychology
see BEHAVIORISM

behaviorism
also **behaviorist theory, behaviorist psychology, behavioral psychology, behaviorist learning theory**
a psychological theory of learning dominant in the 1950s and 1960s, most closely associated with B. F. Skinner, but originating with Ivan Pavlov's well-known CLASSICAL CONDITIONING experiments with dogs. According to behaviorism, language was viewed as a process of habit formation. This process consists of three steps:

- *stimulus* (a signal from the environment that evokes a reaction)
- *response* (the learner's reaction to the stimulus)
- *reinforcement* (a reward for an appropriate response: reinforced behavior gets internalized, a behavior that is not reinforced is extinguished)

Behaviorism attempted to explain learning without reference to thinking or mental processes. Essentially, it claimed that as an organism interacts with its environment, its behavior is conditioned. Dogs that get bitten by spiders will avoid spiders in the future (negative reinforcement). Dogs that stick their paws out to shake and get a treat for doing so will stick their paws out later when told to shake (positive reinforcement). Behaviorists feel that in studying learning, the focus should be on the relationship between the environmental INPUT and an organism's behavior, since this relationship is the only measurable observable relationship. Therefore, an important tenet of behaviorist theory is that all learned behavior is based upon specific stimulus relationships in the environment.

Skinner extended his theory of *Stimulus-Response (S-R) Learning* in his book, *Verbal Behavior*. Skinner's theory of verbal behavior was an extension of his general theory of learning by OPERANT CONDITIONING.

In the L2 context, learners were to be trained to repress L1 habits (learned from the environment in response to linguistic input, reinforcement and contingencies) and acquire good L2 habits. Behavior was modified over time when learners were rewarded for responding correctly. Errors were a sign of failure that should be corrected immediately. Lado's CONTRASTIVE ANALYSIS HYPOTHESIS was influenced by behaviorism by considering the potential difficulties encountered when replacing L1 behaviors with newly learned L2 behaviors. The pedagogical and practical implications of behaviorism resulted in the *Audiolingual Method* (ALM). The ALM was an approach to language teaching based on mechanical and pattern language practice called 'drills' (e.g., repetition and substitution/transformation drills). L2 learners had to repeat, manipulate, or transform a particular form or structure in order to complete the drill.

Behavioral approach to language acquisition was heavily criticized by Noam Chomsky who argued against such an approach, triggering the cognitive revolution (see COGNITIVE PSYCHOLOGY). It was strongly criticized as it did not take into account certain properties of language, especially CREATIVITY. Similarly, the rejection of language error was considered to be a wrong approach as empirical evidence did not prove the detrimental influence of error on language acquisition. The debate continues as to the relative role of the linguistic environment in language learning, as opposed to more innate and internally driven processes as exemplified by UNIVERSAL GRAMMAR.

see also INNATENESS HYPOTHESIS

📖 Brown 2007; Chomsky 1959; Lado 1957; Macaro et al. 2010; Skinner 1957; VanPatten & Benati 2010

behaviorist learning theory
see BEHAVIORISM

behaviorist psychology
see BEHAVIORISM

behaviorist theory
see BEHAVIORISM

Bialystok's theory of L2 learning
a theory of L2 learning which is based on the distinction between IMPLICIT and EXPLICIT KNOWLEDGE but allows for an interface (see INTERFACE MODEL) between explicit and implicit knowledge. Bialystok proposed that implicit knowledge is developed through exposure to communicative language use and is facilitated by strategy of 'functional practicing' (attempts by the learner to maximize exposure to language through communication). In contrast, explicit knowledge arises when learners focus on the language code, and is facilitated by 'formal practicing', which involves either conscious study of the L2 or attempts to automatize already learned explicit knowledge. Formal practicing enables explicit knowledge to become implicit, while inferencing allows explicit knowledge to be derived from implicit. The model also distinguishes two types of output. *Type I output* is spontaneous and immediate, while *Type II output* is deliberate and occurs after a delay. As might be expected, Type I relies entirely on implicit knowledge, whereas Type II involves both implicit and explicit. A feedback loop from both types allows for continual modification of a response. Thus, Bialystok's theory is premised on an interface between the two types of knowledge.

Bialystok's position has undergone considerable revision. The development is her reconceptualization of L2 knowledge. In the early model, this was represented as a dichotomy—knowledge was either implicit or explicit—but in subsequent formulations it is represented in terms of two intersecting continua reflecting the extent to which rules and items are 'controlled' or 'analyzed'. Again, Bialystok's definition of control has shifted somewhat. Whereas initially, it concerned the ease and rapidity with which knowledge can be accessed in different types of language use, in later formulations it refers to three different functions: the selection of items of knowledge, their coordination, and the extent to which selection and coordination can be carried out automatically.

By 'analysis' of knowledge, Bialystok refers to the process by which mental representations of this knowledge are built, structured, and made explicit for the learner. One way in which this can take place is by analyzing formulas (i.e., discovering the parts that make them up). It is tempting to see this 'analysis' dimension as equivalent to the explicit/implicit distinction, with **analyzed knowledge** corresponding to explicit knowledge and **unanalyzed knowledge** to implicit knowledge. Unanalyzed knowledge is the general form in which we know most things without being aware of the structure of that knowledge; on the other hand, learners are overtly aware of the structure of analyzed knowledge. For example, at the unanalyzed extreme of this knowledge dimension, learners have little awareness of language rules, but at the analyzed end, learners can verbalize complex rules governing language. Bialystok, in fact, did equate analysis with the development of an explicit representation of knowledge, but she emphasized that analyzed knowledge need not involve consciousness.

There are a number of problems with Bialystok's views of language acquisition. In particular, the claim that language must begin with unanalyzed knowledge seems unwarranted in the case of L2 acquisition. Many instructed L2 learners begin with explicit knowledge.

see also SKILL-LEARNING THEORY, VARIABLE COMPETENCE MODEL

📖 Bialystok 1978, 1981a, 1982, 1990, 1991; Bialystok & Ryan 1985; Brown 2007; Ellis 2008; Hulstijn 1990

BICS
an abbreviation for BASIC INTERPERSONAL COMMUNICATION SKILLS

bidialectalism
also **bidialectism**

a term which refers to proficiency by a person or a community in the use of two dialects of a language, whether regional or social. Several kinds of bidialectal situation have been studied, one of the best known being the switching from a casual to a formal variety of speech (see DIGLOSSIA). More specifically, it is a principle propounded in sociolinguistics and educational linguistics wherein different dialects are attributed equal linguistic validity and recommended for use in their appropriate social settings. The principle

is of particular importance in relation to educational policy in schools, where the differences between the non-standard and the standard forms of a language can lead to considerable conflict. Bidialectalism recommends that both nonstandard and standard dialects should be encouraged in the educational process, along with the fostering of children's abilities to use CODE SWITCHING, thus developing a greater degree of understanding and control over the varieties of their language than would otherwise be the case.
 Crystal 2008

bidialectism
another term for BIDIALECTALISM

bilingual education
also **bilingual education program**
a term which refers to an educational policy whereby primary (and sometimes secondary) school children are educated through more than one language. The National Association for Bilingual Education (NABE) proposes that, in the USA, the term Bilingual Education refers specifically to educating MINORITY LANGUAGE children for whom English, the MAJORITY LANGUAGE, is not the native language, and where the most significant first exposure to the majority language is through schooling. However, bilingual education programs can be found throughout the world and therefore do not always imply *English Language Learners* (ELLs) or *English as an Additional Language* (EAL) learners. Typical developmental bilingual education programs (e.g., in the USA) are developed for minority language students where both English and the native language are used for instruction during several primary grades. *Two-way Immersion Programs* are those where both minority and majority language children are taught in the same class in both the minority L1 and the majority L2 in literacy and more general academic subjects. *Transitional bilingual programs* are aimed at language minority children where support in both the L1 and majority L2 is offered in the early years of primary education, with the child being transitioned into the majority-language only programs later on.
IMMERSION is also a form of bilingual education, but focused towards majority language students where the focus is on academic content delivered in a second language, usually an L2 that has some relevance to the wider community (such as French in Canada). Bilingual education programs throughout the world differ with respect to how much they support education in both the child's L1 and L2. For example, *developmental bilingual programs* typically aim to support full bilingual proficiency and grade-appropriate standards in academic subjects whereas *transitional programs* attempt to promote proficiency within the majority L2. Much of the research that has been carried out investigating the relative impact on different bilingual education programs illustrates that supporting the L1 in bilingual education is im-

portant as it is positively related to L2 literacy development and grade-appropriate academic standards among other positive effects.
see also BILINGUALISM
📖 Macaro et al. 2010

bilingual education program
another term for BILINGUAL EDUCATION

bilingual first language acquisition
another term for SIMULTANEOUS BILINGUALISM

bilingualism
a term which is used to describe the speaking and understanding of more than one language but can also include knowing many languages (i.e., MULTILINGUALISM). Therefore, a person who is bilingual is someone who speaks at least two languages. Bilingualism is an over-arching construct that has given rise to research in diverse areas including: child language development, educational policy and cognitive neuroscience. From a developmental perspective, researchers are interested in how children, growing up in bilingual communities, learn more than one language at the same time (see SIMULTANEOUS BILINGUALISM). From this perspective bilingualism is often differentiated from L2 learning in that the bilingual child is one growing up with two (or more languages) whereas the L2 learner is one who learns and develops knowledge of the L2 after an L1 has become more established. A sociolinguistic view of bilingualism is concerned with understanding issues such as language and identity and language choice. Researchers adopting a psycholinguistic perspective consider how bilinguals store, represent and process information within multiple languages. Bilingualism can also refer to communities or societies in which multiple languages are spoken (e.g., in Canada, Belgium) and the promotion of bilingualism can therefore be a source of controversy among educational policy makers (see BILINGUAL EDUCATION).
As can be seen from Table B.1, the terminology used in bilingualism is far-reaching and overlaps to some extent with second language acquisition. For example, *successive bilingual* describes the scope of second language acquisition research. Importantly, however, it is difficult to pigeonhole all types of bilingualism because there are numerous situations in which individuals use two languages, from growing up with two languages, to achieving bilingual status as adults, to having the second language as virtually their only language (e.g., displaced refugees). Further, there are different combinations of ability. For example, there are those who function well in some contexts (talking with one's family), but who are not literate in that language, versus those who function well academically in both languages.

bilingualism

Type	Definition
• achieved bilingual	same as *late bilingual*
• additive bilingual	someone whose two languages combine in a complementary and enriching fashion
• ambilingual	same as *balanced bilingual*
• ascendant bilingual	someone whose ability to function in a second language is developing due to increased use
• ascribed bilingual	same as *early bilingual*
• asymmetrical bilingual	see *receptive bilingual*
• balanced bilingual	someone whose mastery of two languages is roughly equivalent
• compound bilingual	someone whose two languages are learned at the same time, often in the same context
• consecutive bilingual	same as *successive bilingual*
• coordinate bilingual	someone whose two languages are learned in distinctively separate contexts
• covert bilingual	someone who conceals his knowledge of a given language due to an attitudinal disposition
• diagonal bilingual	someone who is bilingual in a nonstandard language or a dialect and an unrelated standard language
• dominant bilingual	someone with greater proficiency in one of his languages and uses it significantly more than the other language(s)
• dormant bilingual	someone who has emigrated to a foreign country for a considerable period of time and has little opportunity to keep the first language actively in use
• early bilingual	someone who has acquired two languages early in childhood
• equilingual	same as *balanced bilingual*
• functional bilingual	someone who can operate in two languages with or without full fluency for the task in hand
• horizontal bilingual	someone who is bilingual in two distinct languages which have a similar or equal status
• incipient bilingual	someone at the early stages of bilingualism where one language is not fully developed
• late bilingual	someone who has become a bilingual later than childhood
• maximal bilingual	someone with near-native control of two or more languages
• minimal bilingual	someone with only a few words and phrases in a second language
• natural bilingual	someone who has not undergone any specific training and who is often not in a position to translate or interpret with facility between two languages
• passive bilingual	same as *receptive bilingual*
• primary bilingual	same as *natural bilingual*

•	productive bilingual	someone who not only understands but also speaks and possibly writes in two or more languages
•	receptive bilingual	someone who understands a second language, in either its spoken or written form, or both, but does not necessarily speak or write it
•	recessive bilingual	someone who begins to feel some difficulty in either understanding or expressing him or herself with ease, due to lack of use
•	secondary bilingual	someone whose second language has been added to a first language via instruction
•	semibilingual	same as *receptive bilingual*
•	semilingual	someone with insufficient knowledge of either language
•	simultaneous bilingual	someone whose two languages are present from the onset of speech
•	subordinate bilingual	someone who exhibits interference in his language usage by reducing the patterns of the second language to those of the first
•	subtractive bilingual	someone whose second language is acquired at the expense of the aptitudes already acquired in the first language
•	successive bilingual	someone whose second language is added at some stage after the first has begun to develop
•	symmetrical bilingual	same as *balanced bilingual*
•	vertical bilingual	someone who is bilingual in a standard language and a distinct but related language or dialect

Table B.1. Definitions of bilingualism

Valdés illustrates what she calls a bilingual continuum in Figure B.1. The two letters represent two languages; the size and the case of the font reflect different proficiencies.

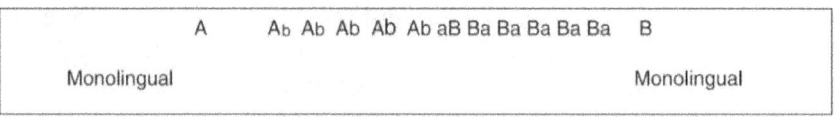

Figure B.1. Bilingual continuum

see also EARLY BILINGUAL, COMPOUND BILINGUAL, ADDITIVE BILINGUALISM
📖 Gass & Selinker 2008; Macaro et al. 2010; Valdés 2001a; VanPatten & Benati 2010

Bilingual Syntax Measure
also BSM
a term developed to elicit sentences containing specific grammatical structures, using pictures. This instrument was used in a number of MORPHEME STUDIES.
📖 Ellis 2008; Burt et al. 1973

biolinguistics
also biological linguistics
a developing branch of linguistics which studies the biological preconditions for language development and use in human beings, from the viewpoints of both the history of language in the race, and the development of language in the individual. Topics of common interest to the two subject-areas involved include the genetic transmission of language, neurophysiological models of language production, the anatomical parallels between human and other species, and the development of pathological forms of language behavior. In recent years, Chomsky has called his entire GENERATIVE GRAMMAR an exercise in biolinguistics, claiming that it is possible to ask a question beyond EXPLANATORY ADEQUACY: How did the language faculty evolve in the human species?
📖 Crystal 2008

biological linguistics
another term for BIOLINGUISTICS

bioprogram hypothesis
the hypothesis that children are born with inborn abilities to make basic semantic distinctions that lead to particular types of grammar. Human languages differ rather substantially in their grammatical structures (e.g., in their *basic word order*). However, CREOLEs all over the world appear to be strikingly similar in their grammar: all creoles look pretty much alike, regardless of where they came into existence or of which languages provided most of the input into them. The British-born American linguist Derek Bickerton has proposed an explanation for this observation. Since creoles are newly created languages, built out of the grammarless PIDGINs which preceded them, and since the children who create a creole are obliged to build its grammar for themselves, Bickerton argues that there must be some kind of innate machinery which determines the nature of that grammar. He calls this machinery the bioprogram, and he sees the bioprogram as an innate default structure for language which is always implemented by children unless they find themselves learning an adult language with a different structure, in which case they learn that instead. The bioprogram hypothesis therefore represents a rather specific and distinctive version of the INNATENESS HYPOTHE-

SIS. It has attracted a great deal of attention, but it remains deeply controversial.
 Bickerton 1984; Richards & Schmidt 2010; Trask 2005

bootstrapping
in the study of CHILD LANGUAGE ACQUISITION, a suggested discovery procedure whereby children make deductions about the semantics or syntax of a language from their observations of language use. A prelinguistic infant has no lexicon against which to match the sound sequences encountered in the speech signal. Furthermore, connected speech provides few cues to where word boundaries lie. It is therefore difficult to explain how the language-acquiring infant comes to identify word forms and to map them on to meanings relating to the real world. It has been suggested that the infant can only achieve this task by relying on some kind of technique which gives it a head start—just as straps can help one to pull on a pair of boots (the metaphor comes via computer science). This technique might be specific to the process of language acquisition or it might be the product of general cognition, reflecting, for example, a predisposition to impose patterns upon diverse information.

Three main types of bootstrapping have been proposed as follows:

- In *prosodic bootstrapping*, the infant exploits rhythmic regularities in the language it is acquiring. At the phoneme level, it can distinguish a difference between *steady-state* sequences representing full vowels and *transitional* sequences representing consonants. It is thus sensitive to syllable structure. From this and from its innate sense of rhythm, the infant acquiring English is able to recognize the difference between longer stressed syllables featuring full vowels and shorter unstressed syllables featuring weak quality vowels. It may be that the infant develops a *metrical template* which reflects the tendency of English towards an strong-weak (SW) rhythmic unit. The template encourages the child to seek words which follow an SW pattern, and provides it with the working hypothesis that a stressed syllable in the signal is likely to mark a word onset. This accounts for the following versions of adult words:

giRAFFE → raffe
MONkey → monkey
baNAna → nana

It also accounts for evidence of children joining words to form an SW pattern as in: *I like-it the elephant.*
The concept of prosodic bootstrapping has been applied to larger constituents than the word. It is suggested that infants learn to recognize intonation patterns (especially the placing of the tonic accent) and the regular

occurrence of pauses. These features, which are often heightened in CHILD DIRECTED SPEECH, provide infants with cues to phrase boundaries and to the structure of typical phrases.

- *Syntactic bootstrapping* assumes that an infant uses surface form to establish syntactic categories. The early mapping process draws upon an assumption (innate or learned) that there is a word-class which relates to objects in the real world, one which relates to actions and one which relates to attributes. Once this is established, the infant can add less prototypical items to each class (abstract nouns, state verbs) by noticing that they share grammatical properties with words that have already been acquired: in particular, their morphology and their distribution.

  It learns to associate count nouns with the frame *It's a . . .* and mass nouns with the frame *It's . . . .* Experiments with non-words (*It's a sib*, *It's sib*) have demonstrated that infants are capable of making this association as early as 17 months. Infants are also capable of using formal evidence to recognize that non-words like *nissing* refer to a potential action and non-words like *a niss* refer to a potential object.

  Later on, infants may use syntactic structure to establish distinctions of meaning. Thus, they can distinguish the senses of the words *eat* and *feed* by their distribution: eat occurring in the structure Verb + Noun (edible) while *feed* occurs in the structure Verb + Noun (animate). Among evidence cited in support of syntactic bootstrapping is the fact that blind infants manage to acquire the words *see* and *look* without difficulty. The suggestion is that they are able to do so by relating the words to the contexts in which they occur, even though they lack a concept to which to attach them.

- *Semantic bootstrapping* hypothesizes the reverse process: that infants use their world knowledge in order to recognize syntactic relationships within sentences. Assume an infant has acquired, in isolation, the nouns *rabbit* and *duck*. Presented with a sentence such as *The rabbit is chasing the duck* and evidence from a cartoon film, the infant comes to recognize that the position of the word *rabbit* in the sentence is reserved for the 'agent' or syntactic subject and the position of the word *duck* is reserved for the 'patient' or syntactic direct object. The assumptions would be confirmed if the cartoon film later showed the reverse situation and the associated sentence was *The duck is chasing the rabbit*.

  As formulated by Pinker, semantic bootstrapping also incorporates the assumption that certain linguistic concepts are innate in the infant: these include the notions of noun and verb as word classes and the notions of agent and patient as roles.

Other bootstrapping theories are:

- *Perceptual bootstrapping*, where the infant focuses its attention on the most salient parts of the input; this might explain why early utterances do not usually contain weakly stressed function words.
- *Logical bootstrapping,* a process whereby an infant systematically directs its attention first to physical objects (nouns), then to events and relationships between the objects (verbs and adjectives) and then to word order and syntax. This step-by-step building of meaning reflects the general pattern of vocabulary acquisition.

 Bates & Goodman 1999; Cutler & Mehler 1993; Crystal 2008; Field 2004; Gerken 1994; Gleitman 1990; Nusbaum & Goodman 1994; Peters 1983; Pinker 1994a

bottom-up processing

an approach to the processing of spoken or written language which depends upon actual evidence in the speech signal or on the page. Smaller units of analysis are built into progressively larger ones. There is a contrast with **top-down processing**, the use of conceptual knowledge to inform or to reshape what is observed perceptually. The terms 'bottom-up' and 'top-down' are derived from computer science, where they refer respectively to processes that are data-driven and processes that are knowledge-driven.

Bottom-up processes include: decoding from phoneme to grapheme (in listening) and from grapheme to phoneme (in reading); whole word recognition; noticing morphemes and/or segmenting words into morphemes; identifying or assembling short phrases in order to analyze them, syntactically and as units of meaning (PARSING); translating individual words, collocations and phrases into L1 (perhaps using glossaries or dictionaries); linking pronouns with their referents; linking subordinate clauses with the main clause; noticing textual clues (prosody, punctuation etc.). Thus, bottom-up processes include all text-based resources which the listener/reader appropriates in order to carry out further processing.

Top-down processing involves schema (see SCHEMA THEORY) and script (conventionally recognized sequences of events). A reader or listener will almost inevitably trigger schema and script when the first content word of a text is understood (e.g., 'snow'). As the reading/listening progresses the different schematic subsets should be activated, informed by the text-based resources being appropriated (sledge, children, fun [rather than] blizzard, frostbite, despair).

In L2 text access, the two processes act in compensatory fashion (resorting to schema in order to compensate for not recognizing words; resorting to careful text analysis in order to compensate for unfamiliarity with the text topic), and confirmatory fashion (using later text information to confirm earlier established predictions of what the text is about). Therefore, an interactive-compensatory model of text access is now generally accepted.

see also ACTIVATION, INTERACTIVE ACTIVATION, MODULARITY
📖 Field 2004; Macaro et al. 2010; Stanovich 1980

BSM
an abbreviation for BILINGUAL SYNTAX MEASURE

C

CA
> an abbreviation for CONVERSATION ANALYSIS

CAH
> an abbreviation for CONTRASTIVE ANALYSIS HYPOTHESIS

CALL
> an abbreviation for COMPUTER-ASSISTED LANGUAGE LEARNING

CALP
> an abbreviation for COGNITIVE ACADEMIC LANGUAGE PROFICIENCY

capability continuum paradigm
> a variability theory of L2 acquisition developed by Tarone to refer to the idea that L2 learners acquire a continuum of grammars for the L2 (which she calls 'styles') ranging from the most *informal* or **vernacular style**, to the most **careful style**, used when an L2 speaker is focusing on form, and trying to be as correct as possible. Tarone refers to this as the capability continuum, as illustrated in Figure C.1.

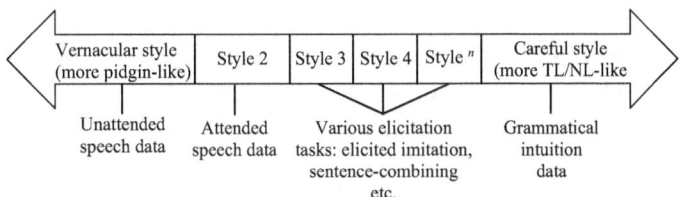

Figure C.1. Interlanguage capability continuum

The vernacular style is usually the least target-like, but the most internally consistent, while at the other pole the careful style is more target-like, perhaps incorporating grammatical knowledge which has been consciously learned by the L2 speaker. It will also be less internally consistent, involving acquired knowledge, consciously learned knowledge, and perhaps also careful style norms transferred from the L1.

According to Tarone, new forms can enter the continuum in two ways: (1) forms may be spontaneously produced first in the vernacular style; it is possible that such forms could gradually spread over time into more and more formal styles. Or (2) new forms may appear first in the most formal style where the learner can pay attention to speech production, and gradually spread over time into less and less formal styles. In the case of (1), there may be a tendency for the new forms to appear in a universal order.

see also COMPETITION MODEL, VARIABLE COMPETENCE MODEL, MONITOR MODEL, SOCIO-PSYCHOLINGUISTIC MODEL, MULTIDIMENSIONAL MODEL, ACCULTURATION MODEL, NATIVIZATION MODEL, FUNCTIONALIST MODEL

📖 Ellis 2008; Tarone 1983, 1985, 1988; Towell & Hawkins 1994

careful style
see CAPABILITY CONTINUUM PARADIGM

caregiver speech
another term for CHILD DIRECTED SPEECH

caretaker speech
another term for CHILD DIRECTED SPEECH

caretaker talk
another term for CHILD DIRECTED SPEECH

CC
an abbreviation for COMMUNICATIVE COMPETENCE

CCH
an abbreviation for CREATIVE CONSTRUCTION HYPOTHESIS

CDS
an abbreviation for CHILD DIRECTED SPEECH

cerebral dominance
another term for LATERALIZATION

channel capacity
a term which refers to the language learner's ability to process utterances. Processing language in both comprehension and production involves more than just knowing the rules of the language. It also involves being able to recover the rules from memory and to use them easily and spontaneously. Learners in the early stages of development are likely to experience difficul-

ty in accessing and using their knowledge, with the result that they have limited channel capacity.
 Ellis 1986

chaos theory
a theory developed in the physical sciences and is based on the idea that complex systems are random, non-linear, unpredictable, self-organizing, and subject to strange attractors (i.e., they tend to focus on a particular pattern that determines the boundaries of the phenomenon). Larsen-Freeman proposed that language and L2 acquisition are best viewed as complex systems. Outlining similarities between chaos theory and SLA, she argues that SLA constitutes a dynamic process characterized by VARIABILITY, this process is self-evidently complex (i.e., it involves a number of interacting factors), it is non-linear (i.e., learners do not master one item and then move on to another), the learner's INTERLANGUAGE system is self-organizing (i.e., it manifest RESTRUCTURING), and the learner's L1 functions as a strange attractor. The pathway that one learner takes in order to achieve success is different, and sometimes markedly so, from another's. Like predicting the patterns of flocking birds or the course of droplets of water in a waterfall, certain laws are axiomatic, but the sheer number and complexity of the variables involved make SLA exceedingly difficult to predict a priori.
Larsen-Freeman's application of chaos theory is fundamentally emergentist (see EMERGENTISM) in that it conflates how L2 knowledge is represented with how it is used and develops over time.
 Brown 2007; Ellis 1986, 2008; Larsen-Freeman 1997

checking
see MONITORING

child directed speech
also **CDS, caretaker speech, caretaker talk, caregiver speech, motherese, mother talk, baby talk**
a speech register used by adults when addressing young children (infants) who are learning to talk. Parents simplify their speech in consistent ways when speaking to children. For English speakers, the linguistic modifications include:

- *Phonological features*: simplification, higher pitch, emphatic stress, greater pausing, longer pauses, a slower speech rate.
- *Lexical features*: restricted vocabulary, local topics, special forms.
- *Syntactic features*: shorter utterances, less complex utterances.

In addition, child directed speech (CDS) is characterized by less dysfluency than adult speech and much repetition and rephrasing. It may employ its own lexical variants. Many of these modifications potentially assist the child in the BOOTSTRAPPING process of identifying words and recognizing phrase boundaries, or in making matches between words and objects in the real world.

An interest in CDS originated when researchers began trying to understand language development from an interactionist point of view (see INTERACTIONIST THEORY). Within this perspective of language learning, researchers have investigated the extent to which CDS is important in guiding the child towards ULTIMATE ATTAINMENT of their native language, potentially making specific features of language more salient to the child (e.g., by segmenting the speech stream). However, in the light of Chomsky's POVERTY OF THE STIMULUS argument, the major issue is whether CDS is accurate, explicit and comprehensive enough to provide the child with the data it needs in order to acquire a language. In fact, CDS is not as 'degenerate' as Chomsky argued. It is generally well formed syntactically, though it contains more imperatives and questions than normal conversation. While nativists (see NATIVISM) are correct in asserting that adults rarely correct infants' language, a great deal of indirect teaching takes place when parents echo, revise or expand their child's utterances. Parents also support acquisition with SCAFFOLDING, where the adult's initiating utterance provides a syntactic and lexical framework for the infant's responses (e.g., *You want milk? You want juice? You want milk or juice?*). Furthermore, it appears that adults fine-tune their CDS as the child's understanding of language progresses.

CDS thus provides a richer source of linguistic data than was once assumed. However, it has proved difficult to establish precisely how the modifications to adult speech assist the infant. No correlation has been found between the degree of simplification in the carer's CDS and the rate at which the infant acquires language. Furthermore, CDS does not appear to be universal. In non-western societies, it may have different characteristics. There are even cultures in which the child is exposed to adult discourse but no language is specifically directed towards it.

Within a given culture, CDS is strikingly consistent across carers—suggesting either that it is transmitted as folk knowledge or that the speaker somehow taps into their own experience of language acquisition. Similarities have been traced between CDS, FOREIGNER TALK and some PIDGINS and CREOLES. One nativist view holds that, in constructing any of these forms, speakers draw upon an innate sense of what constitutes the basic properties of language. This may be a relic of the UNIVERSAL GRAMMAR which enabled children to acquire their first language.

see also INTERLANGUAGE TALK

 Ellis 2008; Field 2004; Gallaway & Richards 1994; Macaro et al. 2010; Snow 1986, 1995; Valian 1996

child language acquisition
another term for FIRST LANGUAGE ACQUISITION

Chomskyan theory
Noam Chomsky formulated what is currently the leading model of language, GENERATIVE GRAMMAR. His goal was to create a set of rules to account for the 'creativity' of language: the way in which a potentially infinite number of sentences can be generated from a finite set of words. A Chomskyan grammar offers a symbolic representation of the system which native speaker-hearers internalize in acquiring the language, a system which enables them to formulate or to understand sentences that they may never have said or heard before. The grammar is generative in that its rules serve to specify all possible sentences which are grammatically correct and to exclude from consideration all those which are not. These 'rules' are not the prescriptive rules of traditional grammar. They are more like the laws of physics, which account for disparate natural phenomena in terms of general underlying principles.

Chomskyan theory highlights the fact that language is *structure dependent*, and provides models of standard phrase types. These are taken to represent the underlying form of an utterance, its *deep structure*. In the first version of the theory, a set of *transformational rules* showed how the user might reorganize the constituents of a deep structure string to produce a *surface structure* one. For example, they showed, in stages, how a speaker derived a passive sentence from an underlying active form.

Current theory has replaced the cumbersome transformational rules with *movement rules*. These show diagrammatically how the deep structure (now *D-structure*) constituents are moved to new slots to provide a derived *S-structure* pattern. An important feature of this revised theory, sometimes referred to as GOVERNMENT AND BINDING THEORY, is that when a constituent is moved it leaves behind a *trace* (*t*). This enables the listener to retrieve the original deep structure from the sentence that is heard. Studies in psycholinguistics have attempted to verify the existence and effect of such traces.

Chomskyan theory has recently taken a new direction, known as MINIMALISM, which emphasizes the importance of simplicity in formulating syntactic rules. One development is that much of what is traditionally represented as syntax can be explained by reference to the constraints which are imposed by lexis. Thus, if one decides to construct a sentence around the verb *give*, the choice of verb determines the possible structure VP + NP + NP (Elizabeth gave Philip a book). This information is stored as part of the lexical entry for *give* in the user's lexicon.

Chomskyan theory provided a boost for COGNITIVE PSYCHOLOGY. It moved the discussion on from the simplified accounts provided by BEHAVIORISM; and redirected attention to the mental processes involved in the production and understanding of language, processes which behaviorism regarded as inaccessible or non-existent. Chomsky made an important distinction between COMPETENCE, the set of principles which enable a native speaker to generate an infinite set of grammatically acceptable sentences and PERFORMANCE, the spoken/written language to which the system gives rise. This differs somewhat from de Saussure's distinction between *langue* and *parole*. Where de Saussure defines 'langue' in relation to the speech community which shares the language in question, Chomsky relates competence to the individual user of the language.

Chomsky argues that linguistic theory needs to be based upon competence, not performance. The goal of the linguist should be to specify the means by which the native speaker-hearer constructs grammatically correct sentences rather than to analyze what he/she actually says. Generative grammar thus assumes an *ideal* speaker-hearer, one from whose speech idiolectal, dialectal and hesitational features have been removed. It is here that linguistic approaches and psychological ones diverge, since the data upon which a psychologist traditionally works is provided by examples of human behavior in performance.

In psycholinguistics, those who work within the Chomskyan tradition follow a theory-driven approach which seeks evidence of the psychological reality of Chomsky's constructs. However, they face a problem in attempting to tap into competence rather than relying on performance data. A solution adopted by many researchers is to ask subjects to make *grammaticality judgments*. They might, for example, be asked to decide if a sentence such as *Who did you introduce the man you got the present from to?* is grammatically acceptable.

A second complication is that Chomsky's grammar is specifically a model of language. Chomsky has much to say on the human mind; but he does not claim that phrase structure and movement rules represent the actual process taking place within the mind of the user as he constructs a sentence. Hence there is discussion as to whether these generative rules are *psychologically real*. Early research in *syntactic* PARSING attempted to demonstrate that the complexity of a transformational rule did, indeed, influence the listener's ability to process a sentence. The hypothesis was not supported.

Chomskyan thought has had a strong impact on language acquisition. Chomsky argues strongly for a nativist view (see NATIVISM). His main point relates to the POVERTY OF THE STIMULUS afforded by CHILD DIRECTED SPEECH. The language to which the infant is exposed in its early years could not possibly, he suggests, cover the whole range of possible sentences. Furthermore, it is 'degenerate' in that it constitutes performance data (complete with ungrammatical forms, hesitations, false starts, etc.). How then can the infant succeed in deriving competence from it in a comparatively short time?

Chomsky concludes that we can only account for FIRST LANGUAGE ACQUISITION by assuming that a child is born with an innate knowledge of the principles of language and a predisposition to employ them in analyzing the speech which it encounters. Current theory attempts to bridge the gap between the universal principles with which we are born and the specific form of the language which we finally acquire. We are said to be endowed with a UNIVERSAL GRAMMAR (UG) in the form of an innate awareness of the nature of language and the various forms that language adopts. UG is represented in terms of a set of principles common to all languages and a set of parameters which are adjusted to reflect the characteristics of the specific language to which the infant is exposed.

📖 Cook & Newson 1996; Field 2004; Lyons 1970; Smith 1999

classical conditioning
also **respondent conditioning, Pavlovian reinforcement**

a learning theory within the context of BEHAVIORIST PSYCHOLOGY. Classical conditioning is a form of conditioning and learning which highlights the formation of associations between stimuli and responses that are strengthened through rewards. It was first demonstrated by the Russian psychologist Pavlov, who at the turn of the twentieth century conducted a series of experiments in which he trained a dog to salivate to the tone of a bell through a procedure that has come to be labeled classical conditioning. For Pavlov the learning process consisted of the formation of associations between stimuli and reflexive responses. All of us are aware that certain stimuli automatically produce or elicit rather specific responses or reflexes, and we have also observed that sometimes that reflex occurs in response to stimuli that appear to be indirectly related to the reflex. Pavlov used the salivation response to the sight or smell of food (an *unconditioned response*) in many of his pioneering experiments. In the classical experiment he trained a dog, by repeated occurrences, to associate the sound of a bell with food until the dog acquired a *conditioned response*: salivation at the sound of the bell. A previously neutral stimulus (the sound of the bell) had acquired the power to elicit a *response* (salivation) that was originally elicited by another stimulus (the smell of meat).

With reference to language learning, , the first stage of learning is based on unconditioned stimulus and unconditioned response, e.g., a child responds with anticipation to chocolate. The second stage of learning is based on the conditioned stimulus and conditioned response: when showing chocolate, the mother repeats the word chocolate. Afterwards, the child associates the word with the object and responds to the word itself, anticipating the experience from the first stage of learning.

Drawing on Pavlov's findings, Watson coined the term BEHAVIORISM. Watson contended that human behavior should be studied objectively, rejecting mentalistic notions of innateness (see INNATENESS HYPOTHESIS) and instinct.

He adopted the classical conditioning theory as the explanation for all learning: by the process of conditioning, we build an array of stimulus-response connections, and more complex behaviors are learned by building up series or chains of responses. Later, Thorndike expanded on classical conditioning models by showing that stimuli that occurred after a behavior had an influence on future behaviors. Thorndike's *law of effect* paved the way for another psychologist, B. F. Skinner, to modify our understanding of human learning.

see also OPERANT CONDITIONING

📖 Brown 2007; Watson 1913

classroom discourse

the observed interaction between teacher and learners and between learners and learners. It is often claimed to constitute a distinct discourse domain. That is, it contains content features, structural relationships, and rituals which make it distinct from, for example, day-to-day informal conversation or the discourse of interviews. Classroom discourse is of interest to SLA researchers because:

1) the L2 (in broadly *communicative* classrooms) represents both the content of the lesson and the medium through which the content is understood (thus it differs from other subjects on the curriculum);
2) in many contexts teacher INPUT is the main exposure to the L2 that learners receive, thus the interaction represents a unique opportunity for learning;
3) TEACHER TALK often contains the pedagogical intentions of the teacher which may not be obvious to observers or understood by learners;
4) classroom discourse is highly complex in that it often operates on several 'planes' and utterances can be directed at any number and combinations of participants in the interaction.

Analysis of classroom discourse has been proposed as a tool for language teacher development. Research has centered on: how teachers modify their speech to make it comprehensible (see COMPREHENSIBLE INPUT); the use of controlling mechanisms which teachers deploy (e.g., through topic selection and TURN-TAKING patterns); the cognitive demands of teacher questions; how communication breakdown is repaired; how teachers provide FEEDBACK to learner errors; how learners become socialized via the interaction. These diverse research themes reflect different research traditions adopted and there is disagreement as to which analytical methods best explain the phenomenon—socio-cultural (how interaction shapes society), psycholinguistic (how the interaction leads to learning) or 'neutral-descriptive' (the quantification and classification of talk).

📖 Chaudron 1988; Macaro et al. 2010

CM
an abbreviation for COMPETITION MODEL

cocktail party effect
another term for COCKTAIL PARTY PHENOMENON

cocktail party phenomenon
also **cocktail party effect**
the ability that humans have in social gatherings to listen selectively to speech coming from one source (e.g., a conversation some distance away) while ignoring other sources (e.g., the speech of other guests, even those who are closer). Redundancy in conversation helps make this possible, but the phenomenon is a specific example of the more general human ability to pay attention selectively to some stimuli while ignoring others.
see also ATTENTION
📖 Richards & Schmidt 2010

code switching
the practice of alternating between two languages (or dialects) during communication. In bilinguals (see BILINGUALISM), code switching is the act of inserting words, phrases, or even longer stretches of one language into the other. It can take place in a conversation when one speaker uses one language and the other speaker answers in a different language. A person may start speaking one language and then change to another one in the middle of their speech, or sometimes even in the middle of a sentence.
There are a number of principles underlying this switching although exceptions or violations of these principles have been recorded:

1) it is normally accepted that one language is the dominant language and the other the *embedded language*;
2) that switching can take place intrasententially or intersententially (the latter sometimes known as *code-mixing*);
3) that the grammar of either language is not violated.

In uninstructed settings, code switching is considered to be a bilingual competence, not a symptom of language deficiency, and one of a series of COMMUNICATION STRATEGIES through which meaning can be expressed. Functions of code switching include its use for sociocultural effect, for establishing social relationships, for signaling utterances on different textual planes, for communicating more precisely a concept not existing in the dominant language, and for using appropriate metalanguage among professionals. Use of code switching in formal bilingual classrooms is somewhat contentious and even more so in monolingual foreign language classrooms where it is sometimes considered pejoratively as resorting to L1 use due to its effect of

reducing exposure to L2, undermining the communicative orientation of the classroom, and depriving learners of the opportunity to infer meaning. Supporters of code switching in instructed settings argue that, on limited occasions, communicative tasks can be advanced via judicious teacher code switching, and learning can be enhanced by making reference to the learner's L1. They posit, moreover, that SLA instruction should be concerned with creating bilinguals not emulating native speakers, and that to prohibit learners from using their own L1 can be a form of linguistic imperialism. Researchers are trying to establish a series of principles for judicious use of code switching which might inform practice.
📖 Macaro et al. 2010; Myers-Scotton 1989; Richards & Schmidt 2010

cognition
the use or handling of knowledge; hence, (a) the faculty which permits us to think and reason and (b) the process involved in thought and reasoning. It is sometimes contrasted with **metacognition**, which can be defined as 'thinking about thinking' and involves preplanning a cognitive process, exercising control over the process or taking steps to ensure that its results are stored long term. Metacognition involves some degree of awareness, whereas cognitive processes may not be available to report.

An important issue is whether language is part of general cognition or is a separate faculty. One argument supporting the latter (modular) view is the fact that all normally developing infants achieve a first language whatever their cognitive capacities in other areas.
see MODULARITY
📖 Field 2004

Cognitive Academic Language Proficiency
see BASIC INTERPERSONAL COMMUNICATION SKILLS

cognitive constructivism
see CONSTRUCTIVISM

cognitive development
also **stage theory of development, Piagetian stages of development**
developmental changes in cognitive abilities, processes, and structures. The best known theory of childhood cognitive development is that of Jean Piaget. For Piaget language was both a social and a cognitive phenomenon. It was not an independent *modular* faculty but part of general cognitive and perceptual processing. Language acquisition was thus dependent upon cognitive development. The child's level of language was determined by whether it had acquired certain fundamental concepts and by the complexity of the processing operations of which it was capable. Piaget suggested that cognitive development fell into four phases. They constitute a gradual progression in

which previous stages are revisited cyclically. The age at which a particular child goes through each stage varies considerably. Each stage has implications for linguistic development.

1) *Sensorimotor* (*birth to 2 years*). The child achieves recognition of *object permanence* (the fact that an object still exists even when it is not in view). This is a prerequisite to the formation of concepts (including lexical concepts). It may be a dawning awareness of object permanence which first leads the child to name things and gives rise to the '*vocabulary spurt*' at around 18 months. The first relational words ('*no*' '*up*' '*more*' '*gone*') also reflect object permanence, with those indicating presence emerging before those ('*all gone*') relating to absence.
   The child's language has its origins in simple signals (a bottle signifies eating) and then in *indexical relationships* (a career with a coat on signifies going out). Early words are employed for *symbolic reference* (*doggie* referring to one specific dog that is present) but later acquire *symbolic sense* (*doggie* referring to the class of dogs). The child's productions may show an awareness of *means-ends* (the word *milk* gets the child a drink) and limited spatial awareness.
2) *Preoperational* (*2 to 6 or 7 years*). The child's behavior reflects *egocentric thought*: it is unable to identify with the views of others. The child's language progresses through *echolalia* (repeating others' utterances) to *monologues* (speaking aloud what would normally be private thoughts). It may engage in *collective monologues* with other children, in which participants appear to be taking turns, but express their own ideas without responding to those of others.
3) *Concrete operational* (*6/7 to 11/12*). The child's vocabulary shows signs of organization into hierarchical categories. It develops the concept of *conservation* (the recognition that size or quantity is not dependent upon the container) and shows signs of *decentration*, the ability to consider multiple aspects of a physical problem. It learns to receive and respond to outside ideas.
4) *Formal operational* (*11/12 to adult*). The adolescent becomes capable of abstract reasoning. It learns to construct its own argument structures, can represent hypothetical situations and engages mentally and verbally in problem-solving.

see also VYGOTSKYAN
📖 Boden 1979; Field 2004; McShane 1991; Piattelli-Palmarini 1980

cognitive organizer
a term used by Dulay and Burt to refer to that part of the learner's internal processing system that is responsible for organizing the INPUT into a system.

Thus, the internal organizer is responsible for the transitional stages through which the learner passes. The cognitive organizer operates subconsciously.
 Dulay and Burt 1977; Ellis 1986

cognitive pruning
see SUBSUMPTION

cognitive psychology
the study of human behavior and processes which includes investigating how people perceive, learn, remember and think, as opposed to BEHAVIORAL PSYCHOLOGY, which focuses on overt, observable, empirically measurable behavior. Issues of attention and consciousness, how knowledge is represented in the human mind, how humans process information, how MEMORY is organized, how people reason and make decisions and solve problems are all areas that fall within the broader discipline of cognitive psychology. It is therefore a highly interdisciplinary domain which draws from research and literature in psychology, neuroscience, linguistics, computer science and biology (among others). An important sub-domain within cognitive psychology is language, and questions on how language is learned, how knowledge of language is represented and retrieved from memory, how language is produced and understood are prominent issues in cognitive psychology. Therefore, theories within the study of both first and second language learning and processing draw heavily from key issues within cognitive psychology.
In the context of SLA, two somewhat different cognitive paradigms can be identified. One of these draws on a COMPUTATIONAL MODEL of L2 acquisition, which characterizes acquisition in terms of INPUT, the internal computation of data from the input, and output. This is the mainstream model informing SLA. The second account is perhaps better characterized as sociocognitive (see SOCIOCULTURAL THEORY) rather than cognitive. It affords a sociocultural explanation of L2 use and acquisition by viewing acquisition as originating in use and involving subsequent processes of internalization. Both the computational and the sociocultural paradigms share a point in common: they treat L2 acquisition as essentially similar in nature to other kinds of learning in drawing on a common set of processes. In this respect, both paradigms contrast with the linguistic paradigm, which treats linguistic knowledge as unique and separate from other knowledge systems, and sees acquisition as guided by mechanisms that are (in part at last) specifically linguistic in nature.
see also INFORMATION PROCESSING THEORY, ADAPTIVE CONTROL OF THOUGHT MODEL, ATTENTION, AWARENESS, INDIVIDUAL LEARNER DIFFERENCES, MULTIDIMENSIONAL MODEL, NATIVIZATION MODEL, PARALLEL DISTRIBUTED PROCESSING MODEL, COGNITIVE DEVELOPMENT
 Ellis 2008; Lantolf & Tarone 1996, 2006; Macaro et al. 2010; VanPatten & Benati 2010

cognitive strategies
see LEARNING STRATEGIES

cognitive style
see LEARNING STYLES

cognitive theory
a theory that describes phenomena in terms of mental constructs in the mind of individuals. Cognitive theory attempts to understand how humans create and use knowledge. As such, it is not domain specific. That is, for cognitivists, there are no special places in the mind for language, math, or any other knowledge system (which stands in stark contrast to those who work in contemporary linguistic theory (e.g., UNIVERSAL GRAMMAR). Cognitive researchers are thus interested in learning processes, and a good deal of cognitive research centers on LEARNING STYLES, understanding (i.e., how people make sense of something), APTITUDE, INFORMATION PROCESSING, and other areas. Within cognitive theory, all learning (no matter the object of that learning) utilizes the same general principles for human understanding and learning. Thus, language learning would utilize the same mechanisms for learning as would, say, history learning and chess learning.

Applied to SLA, cognitive theory views language acquisition as the formation of a knowledge system that L2 learners must eventually tap for speaking and understanding. However, unlike linguists and psycholinguists, scholars within a cognitive psychology approach would be more interested in the learning factors that affect acquisition such as how learners come to understand the nature of a particular feature and what strategies (see LEARNING STRATEGIES) learners go about to master a concept. Under the umbrella of cognitive theory, then, would fall INDIVIDUAL LEARNER DIFFERENCES such as language aptitude, MOTIVATION, MEMORY, and others. A related area of interest would be RESTRUCTURING, that is, how the learning of new information causes changes in already existing knowledge. SKILL THEORY is a particular branch within cognitive theory. In fact, some psychologists would prefer to speak of cognitive theories or even cognitive approaches.
 VanPatten & Benati 2010

cognitivism
approaches to language acquisition which view the process as closely linked to general cognition and to COGNITIVE DEVELOPMENT. Some accounts leave open the extent to which certain aspects of language are innate; but all take the view that acquisition is primarily driven by the way in which the infant's cognitive abilities are brought to bear upon the INPUT to which it is exposed. These cognitive abilities may reflect developing awareness of objects, spatial relations, defining characteristics, etc., or they may take the form of percep-

tual biases which incline the child to recognize patterns in linguistic material. Among views on acquisition which can be characterized as cognitive are:

- *An infant cannot express concepts in language unless it has previously developed them.* Example: A child cannot use language to refer to objects that are not visible unless it has grasped the idea of object permanence. For Piaget, language was the product of cognitive and perceptual processes. His research with children led him to conclude that there were four stages of COGNITIVE DEVELOPMENT. They represent a gradual progression and not a sudden shift in behavior; and the age at which a particular child goes through each varies considerably. However, they are closely linked to linguistic development.
- *Both language and cognition are part of a staged maturation program, in which they operate in parallel, supporting each other.* For Vygotsky, thought exists pre-verbally. There is initially a separation between thought and language: the infant's first words are devoid of thought. During three phases, the separate roles of thought and language become established (see VYGOTSKYAN).
- *Innate cognitive tendencies may predispose us*:
  a) *To find patterns in language data* (as in data in general). A theory of syntactic BOOTSTRAPPING postulates that infants reach conclusions about words on the basis of their inflections and other grammatical properties: thus the child learns that the difference between *It's sib* and *It's a sib* serves to distinguish real-world entities that are mass from those that are count.
  b) *To adopt certain strategies in response to language data.* Slobin concludes that infants apply a set of universal strategies or OPERATING PRINCIPLES in order to deconstruct the input to which they are exposed. (Pay attention to the ends of words. Pay attention to the order of words and morphemes.) More cognitively complex features are acquired later.
  c) *To apply individual learning styles to language data.* Some infants appear to break the input into words, while others acquire chunks of language in a holistic manner

- *The infant's limited cognitive capacity renders it more sensitive to the features of language than it might be before or later.* The 'less is more' argument holds that it may be the very limitations of the infant's early cognitive state which enable it to identify structure in language and to recognize that language constitutes a set of inter-related symbols.

📖 Bates et al. 1995; Deacon 1997; Field 2004; Piattelli-Palmarini 1980; Slobin 1973

communication strategies

strategic options which relate to output, how one productively expresses meaning, and how one effectively delivers messages to others. While LEARNING STRATEGIES deal with the receptive domain of intake, memory, storage, and recall, communication strategies pertain to the employment of verbal or nonverbal mechanisms for the productive communication of information.

While the research of the last decade does indeed focus largely on the compensatory nature of communication strategies, more recent approaches seem to take a more positive view of communication strategies as elements of an overall STRATEGIC COMPETENCE in which learners bring to bear all the possible facets of their growing competence in order to send clear messages in the second language. Moreover, such strategies may or may not be 'potentially conscious'; support for such a conclusion comes from observations of first language acquisition strategies that are similar to those used by adults in second language learning contexts.

Perhaps the best way to understand what is meant by communication strategy is to look at a typical list of such strategies. Table C.1 offers a taxonomy that reflects accepted categories over several decades of research.

Table C.1. Communication strategies

Avoidance Strategies
1. *Message abandonment*: Leaving a message unfinished because of language difficulties
2. *Topic avoidance*: Avoiding topic areas or concepts that pose language difficulties

Compensatory Strategies
3. *Circumlocution*: Describing or exemplifying the target object of action (e.g., *the thing you open bottles with* for *corkscrew*)
4. *Approximation*: Using an alternative term which expresses the meaning of the target lexical item as closely as possible (e.g., *ship* for *sailboat*)
5. *Use of all-purpose words*: Extending a general, empty lexical item to contexts where specific words are lacking (e.g., the overuse of *thing, stuff, what-do-you-call-it, thingie*)
6. *Word coinage*: Creating a nonexisting L2 word based on a supposed rule (e.g., *vegetarianist* for *vegetarian*)
7. *Prefabricated patterns*: Using memorized stock phrases, usually for 'survival' purposes (e.g., *Where is the_____* or *Comment allez-vous?* where the morphological components are not known to the learner)
8. *Nonlinguistic signals*: Mime, gesture, facial expression, or sound imitation
9. *Literal translation*: Translating literally a lexical item, idiom, compound word, or structure from LI to L2
10. *Foreignizing*: Using a LI word by adjusting it to L2 phonology (i.e., with a L2 pronunciation) and/or morphology (e.g., adding to it a L2 suffix)
11. *Code-switching*: Using a LI word with LI pronunciation or a L3 word with L3 pronunciation while speaking in L2

12. *Appeal for help*: Asking for aid from the interlocutor either directly (e.g., *What do you call . . .?*) or indirectly (e.g., rising intonation, pause, eye contact, puzzled expression)
13. *Stalling or time-gaining strategies*: Using fillers or hesitation devices to fill pauses and to gain time to think (e.g., *well, now let's see, uh, as a matter of fact*)

📖 Brown 2007; Bongaerts & Poulisse 1989; Dörnyei 1995

communicative competence
also CC

a term which was coined by Dell Hymes, a sociolinguist who was convinced that Chomsky's notion of COMPETENCE was too limited. Chomsky's 'rule-governed creativity' that so aptly described a child's mushrooming grammar at the age of 3 or 4 did not, according to Hymes, account sufficiently for the social and functional rules of language. So Hymes referred to communicative competence (CC) as that aspect of our competence that enables us to convey and interpret messages and to negotiate meanings interpersonally within specific contexts.

Seminal work on defining CC was carried out by Michael Canale and Merrill Swain, still the reference point for virtually all discussions of CC in relation to second language teaching. In Canale and Swain's and later in Canale's definition, four different components, or subcategories, made up the construct of CC. The first two subcategories reflected the use of the linguistic system itself; the last two defined the functional aspects of communication:

1) **Grammatical competence** is that aspect of CC that encompasses knowledge of lexical items and of rules of morphology, syntax, sentence-grammar semantics, and phonology. It is the competence that we associate with mastering the linguistic code of a language, the **linguistic competence** of Hymes and Paulston.
2) The second subcategory is **discourse competence**, the complement of grammatical competence in many ways. It is the ability we have to connect sentences in stretches of discourse and to form a meaningful whole out of a series of utterances. Discourse means everything from simple spoken conversation to lengthy written texts (articles, books, and the like). While grammatical competence focuses on sentence-level grammar, discourse competence is concerned with intersentential relationships.
3) **Sociolinguistic competence** is the knowledge of the sociocultural rules of language and of discourse. This type of competence requires an understanding of the social context in which language is used: the roles of the participants, the information they share, and the function of the interac-

tion. Only in a full context of this kind can judgments be made on the appropriateness of a particular utterance.
4) The fourth subcategory is **strategic competence**, a construct that is exceedingly complex. Canale and Swain described strategic competence as the verbal and nonverbal COMMUNICATION STRATEGIES that may be called into action to compensate for breakdowns in communication due to performance variables or due to insufficient competence. Savignon paraphrased this as the strategies that one uses to compensate for imperfect knowledge of rules—or limiting factors in their application such as fatigue, distraction, and inattention. In short, it is the competence underlying our ability to make repairs, to cope with imperfect knowledge, and to sustain communication through paraphrase, circumlocution, repetition, hesitation, avoidance, and guessing, as well as shifts in register and style (see COMMUNICATION STRATEGIES).

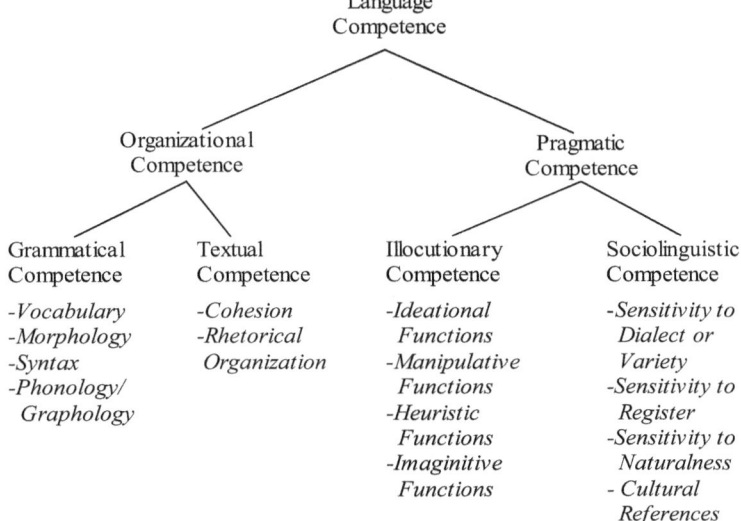

Figure C.2. Components of language components

Canale and Swain's model of CC has undergone some other modifications over the years. These newer views are perhaps best captured in Lyle Bachman's schematization of what he simply calls 'language competence', as shown in Figure C.2. Bachman places grammatical and discourse (renamed 'textual') competence under one node, which he appropriately calls *organizational competence*: all those rules and systems that dictate what we can do with the forms of language, whether they be sentence-level rules (grammar) or rules that govern how we 'string' sentences together (discourse). Canale and Swain's sociolinguistic competence is now broken down into two separate pragmatic categories: functional aspects of language (*illocutionary competence*, pertaining to sending and receiving intended meanings) and sociolinguistic aspects (which deal with such considerations as politeness, formality, metaphor, register, and culturally related aspects of language). And, in keeping with current waves of thought, Bachman adds strategic competence as an entirely separate element of communicative language ability (see Figure C.3). Here, strategic competence almost serves an 'executive' function of making the final 'decision', among many possible options, on wording, phrasing, and other productive and receptive means for negotiating meaning.

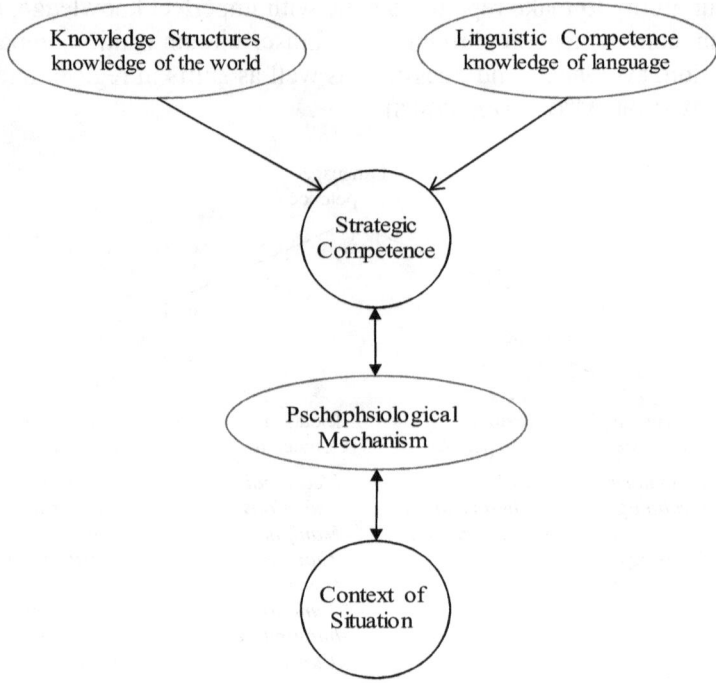

Figure C.3. Components of communicative language ability in communicative language use

As SLA research progressed in the 1970s, how L2 learners communicated with limited L2 ability became a matter of interest. And because tests of speaking ability in a second language needed to include more than just information about formal accuracy (e.g., whether a learner could successfully accomplish a given communicative task in a given context), researchers interested in L2 assessment increasingly turned their attention to models of communicative competence to talk about testing. At the same time, language teaching and curriculum development became increasingly concerned with the development of communicative ability, moving away from the more nar-

row focus of the structural syllabus that had dominated language teaching until then.
📖 Bachman 1990; Brown 2007; Canale 1983; Canale & Swain 1980; Chomsky 1965; Hymes 1972, 1967; Macaro et al. 2010; Savignon 1983

community language
    another term for HERITAGE LANGUAGE

compensation strategies
    see LEARNING STRATEGIES

competence
a term which refers to one's underlying knowledge of a system, event, or fact. Competence is the nonobservable *ability* to do something, to perform something. In reference to language, competence is one's underlying knowledge of the system of a language—its rules of grammar, its vocabulary, all the pieces of a language and how those pieces fit together. More specifically, within Chomskyan linguistics (see CHOMSKYAN THEORY), competence is the implicit and abstract knowledge of a language possessed by native speakers, which allows them to produce, and distinguish the difference between, grammatical and ungrammatical forms. It is *implicit* because speakers generally are unaware of this knowledge and, even if aware, cannot articulate its contents. It is also *abstract* because it does not consist of rules such as 'verbs must agree with their subjects', but instead, of other syntactic operations that yield sentences that can be described as having verbs that agree with their subjects. What is more, competence contains information that not only generates grammatical sentences, but also informs speakers of what is impossible in their languages. For example, the native speaker of English has competence that allows the sentences *John thinks Mary brought what?* and *What does John think Mary brought?* At the same time, that competence allows the sentence *John wonders who brought Mary what* but disallows the sentence **What does John wonder who brought Mary?*
As another example, the simple definition of 'subject of a sentence' eludes the average person. A subject is not the 'doer of the action', as verbs such as *seem* do not have 'doers' but entities that experience something (e.g., *What did John do? He ate*. But not *What did John do? He seemed sad.*). A subject is not the thing that comes before the verb in English as demonstrated by *John comes to class* and *Here comes John*. In short, the notion of 'subject of a sentence' is an abstract and implicit notion, and yet, every English speaker intuitively knows what a subject is, or would not be able to make well-formed sentences in English.
Again, competence is not a list or set of rules and grammatical forms, but instead a complex interaction of abstract constraints and principles of language that interact to make sentences look the way they look to us. Compe-

tence is often contrasted with **performance**, which is the overtly observable and concrete manifestation or realization of competence. It is the *actual doing* of something: walking, singing, dancing, speaking. In reference to language, performance refers to the individual's actual language use. It is actual production (speaking, writing) or the comprehension (listening, reading) of linguistic events. For example, a mature speaker of a language (e.g., English) might make an error and produce an utterance such as '*I will be home yesterday*'. The adult speaker of English who makes this error knows that this constitutes an ill-formed utterance, and can easily recognize it as such. However, *performance* errors like these are fairly common in adult speech and can result from such performance variables as memory limitations, distractions, shifts of attention and interest, errors, and hesitation phenomena, such as repeats, false starts, pauses, omissions, and additions, for example. Chomsky likened competence to an 'idealized' speaker-hearer who does not display such performance variables. Chomsky's point was that a theory of language had to be a theory of competence lest the linguist try in vain to categorize an infinite number of performance variables that are not reflective of the underlying linguistic ability of the speaker-hearer.

While many researchers both within L1 and L2 research (see INTERLANGUAGE) are interested in understanding the nature of a learner's underlying competence, all language behavior is ultimately performance, and therefore a tension exists between measures of linguistic knowledge (i.e., competence) which necessarily have to rely on human behavior (i.e., performance). Researchers interested in understanding linguistic competence need to be diligent therefore to use measures which minimize performance errors.

📖 Brown 2007; Macaro et al. 2010; VanPatten & Benati 2010

Competition Model
also **CM**

a functional model of language use and language acquisition proposed initially by Bates and MacWhinney, for understanding both L1 and L2 learning. It views the task of language learning as that of discovering the particular form-function mappings that characterize the target language. It is argued that the forms of natural languages are created, governed, constrained, acquired and used in the service of communicative functions. Any one form may realize through a number of functions and, conversely, any one function can be realized through a number of forms. The learner's task is to discover the particular form-function mappings that characterize the target language. Form-function mappings are characterized as being of varying strengths in different languages. This is usually illustrated with reference to the function of 'agency', which has a number of possible formal exponents:

1) *Word order*: in the case of transitive constructions, the first noun mentioned in a clause is likely to function as the agent. For example, in the

English sentence *Mary kissed John*, 'Mary' is the agent.
2) *Agreement*: the noun phrase which functions as agent may agree in number with the verb. Thus, in English, a singular noun phrase functioning as agent takes a singular verb form (e.g., *She likes ice-cream*), while a plural noun phrase takes a plural verb form (e.g., *They like ice-cream*). The object of the sentence has no effect on the verb form.
3) *Case*: the noun phrase functioning as agent may be morphologically marked in some way. For example, the agent is signaled in German by nominative case marking on the article, while the object is signaled by means of accusative case marking (e.g., *Der Mann isst den Apfel* = *The man is eating the apple*).
4) *Animacy*: agents are normally animate, patients are normally inanimate.

Any one language is likely to utilize several devices for signaling the 'agent' of a sentence. English, for example, uses all four, as illustrated in these sentences:

Mary kissed John. (word order)
Money they like. (agreement)
She kissed him. (case)
This book Mary likes a lot. (animacy)

However, a language is likely to assign different weights to these devices in terms of the probability of their use in signaling a given function. English, as the above examples show, relies primarily on word order to encode agency, while Russian uses case marking, and Japanese, animacy. Like VARIABILITY models, the Competition Model (CM) is probabilistic in nature.

The model takes its name from the 'competition' that arises from the different devices or cues that signal a particular function. For example, in a sentence like *that lecturer we like a lot* there is competition between 'lecturer', 'we', and 'lot' for the role agent of the verb. 'Lot' rapidly loses out because, unlike 'lecturer' and 'we', it is inanimate, and because it follows rather than precedes the verb. The candidacy of 'lecturer' is promoted by its position in the sentence—it is the first noun—but, ultimately, this cue is not strong enough to overcome two other cues. 'We' is the strongest candidate for agent because it is nominative in case and because it agrees in number with the verb.

The task facing the L2 learner is to discover (1) which forms are used to realize which functions in the L2, and (2) what weights to attach to the use of individual forms in the performance of specific functions. This is what is meant by 'form-function mapping'. The INPUT supplies the learner with cues of four broad types: word order, vocabulary, morphology, and intonation.

The usefulness of a cue is determined by several factors: *cue availability*, *cue reliability*, and *conflict validity*. Availability refers to how present or frequent the cue is in the input. In English, word order is a readily available cue for what a subject is; however, subject-verb agreement is not (i.e., only in the present tense and with third-person singular do we see person-number marking on verbs). Reliability refers to how often the cue leads to the correct sentence interpretation. In English, word order almost always leads to correct interpretation of what the subject is as English is rigidly subject-verb-object. Conflict validity refers to how valid a cue is for correct sentence interpretation when it is in conflict with another. That is, whether a cue 'wins' or 'loses' when it appears in competitive environments. In a language like Hebrew, case marking has high conflict validity because Hebrew sentences can be either subject-verb-object or object-verb-subject (or possibly other combinations). If people normally expect subjects to appear before verbs, then object-verb order is in conflict with case marking, but case marking would win out because it is more reliable (i.e., subjects are always marked one way and objects are always marked another). This is not the case in German. Although German consistently marks articles for case, the markings themselves are not always unique. Masculine definite articles are either *der* for subject or *den* for object. But for feminine, the article is always *die*. Thus, when case marking is in conflict with word order in German (German allows object-verb-subject and requires certain orders in embedded clauses and other constructions), case marking has high conflict validity only for masculine nouns indicating subject and object. In language acquisition, cues that are available, highly reliable, and have high conflict validity will be acquired before those that do not possess the same characteristics. The CM also claims that L2 learners will transfer the cue strengths of their L1 to the L2 in the initial stages of acquisition. Language learning within the view of the CM is, therefore, driven by the input and not by a set of prespecified internal linguistic constraints as in UNIVERSAL GRAMMAR. Learners have to detect linguistic cues which are distributed within the linguistic input and by detecting these cues will be able to learn language. Thus, the model provides a minimalist, empiricist prediction for the ways cues are acquired.

The CM has informed a number of studies of L2 acquisition. These studies take the form of sentence-interpretation experiments using bilingual subjects in a within-subject, cross-language design. That is, speakers of different languages are asked to identify the function of different cues in L1 and L2 sentences that have been designed to reflect both the coordination and competition of cues. For example, they may be asked to say which noun is the agent of an action in acceptable sentences like *The boy is chopping the log* and in semantically unlikely sentences such as *The logs are shopping the boy*, where the animacy cue is in competition with the word order cue, but the agreement cue is in coordination. The studies then compare the responses of learners with different language backgrounds.

MacWhinney, later, outlined a development of the CM, which he called the **Unified Model** because it sought to provide an account of both L1 and L2 learning. According to this model, forms are stored in associative maps for syllables, lexical items, constructions, and mental models. For example, in lexical maps, words are viewed as associations between forms and functions. Construction maps consist of patterns that show how a predicate (verb, adjective, preposition) can combine with its arguments. The idea of self-organizing associative maps is derived from computer modeling of language learning. These show learning involving three phases. In the first phase, all units in the model are activated by the input with each unit computing its current activation. In the second phase, units compete with the best matching unit emerging as the winner. In the third phase, the weights of the responding unit are adjusted to increase the precision of future activation. Within these associative maps, learning is self-organized, modulated by a number of processes—'buffering', 'chunking', and 'resonance'. *Buffering* serves as a mechanism for the final form/interpretation. *Chunking* (the process of storing formulaic sequences) provides a data base from which grammar can emerge through analogic processing. *Resonance* is the process by which robust connections within neural structure of the brain are formed. It is achieved through careful timing of practice to stimulate resonant activation of the relevant neurons.

The strength of the CM is that it provides a convincing account of a number of aspects of L2 acquisition which any theory must consider: the role of the L1, the effect of input, and the gradual way in which native-like ability is acquired. There are, of course, other aspects which it does not address, at least not at the moment. It is not clear, for instance, what kind of knowledge (implicit or explicit) learners use in sentence interpretation. The early version of the model did not have much to say about the cognitive mechanisms responsible for the obtaining INTAKE from input or for using L2 knowledge in production. However, the later Unified Model with its account of buffering, chunking, and resonance has largely filled this gap.

Probably the main weakness of the model is over-reliance on rather artificial interpretation tasks, a problem that is aggravated by the unnatural sentences that figure in such tasks. The justification for such a methodology is the **Ecological Validity Hypothesis**, according to which the processing of both grammatical and ungrammatical sentences proceed by reference to the same set of cues and processing patterns. It might be further argued that L2 acquisition take place as a result of 'utterance processing' rather than 'sentence processing', the distinguishing feature being that utterances are contextualized whereas sentences are not. Utterance processing involves pragmatic procedures, which are ignored in the kind of sentence-processing tasks on which the CM has relied. Nevertheless, the CM is a powerful theory, like PROCESSABILITY THEORY, it affords very precise prediction about L2 acquisition, which have received uniform support in the studies that have investigated the model.

The CM has been subsumed under CONNECTIONISM in recent years, but research on the CM made important contributions to SLA research in the 1990s.

see also MULTIDIMENSIONAL MODEL, VARIABLE COMPETENCE MODEL, CAPABILITY CONTINUUM PARADIGM, MONITOR MODEL, SOCIO-PSYCHOLINGUISTIC MODEL, NATIVIZATION MODEL, ACCULTURATION MODEL, FUNCTIONALIST MODEL, EMERGENTISM

 Bates & MacWhinney 1982; Ellis 2008; Gass & Selinker 1994; Macaro et al. 2010; MacWhinney 2001, 2007b; MacWhinney et al. 1984; MacWhinney et al. 1985; VanPatten & Benati 2010

complete access view

a view which states that the whole of UNIVERSAL GRAMMAR (UG) is available to second language learners, in the same way as it is to first language learners. Within this view, there are different hypotheses about the initial grammars of second language learners:

- *Full access/no transfer*: Flynn adopts this position (see PARAMETER-SETTING MODEL). That is, she argues that UG continues to underpin SLA, for adults as well as children, and that there is no such thing as a 'critical period' (see CRITICAL PERIOD HYPOTHESIS) after which UG ceases to operate. If it can be shown that learners can acquire principles and/or parameter settings of the second language, which differ from those of their first language, the best interpretation is the continuing operation of UG. According to this view, it appears that L2 learners do construct grammars of the new target languages under the constraints imposed by UG; those principles of UG carefully investigated indicate that those not instantiated or applying vacuously in the LI but operative in the L2, are in fact acquirable by the L2 learner. We are thus forced to the conclusion that UG constrains L2 acquisition; the essential language faculty involved in LI acquisition is also involved in adult L2 acquisition.
- *Full transfer/full access*: this model also believes that second language learners have full access to UG principles and parameters, whether or not they are present in the learners' first language. But in this view, second language learners are thought to transfer all the parameter-settings from their first language in an initial stage, and subsequently to revise their hypotheses when the second language fails to conform to these first language settings. Learners then develop new hypotheses that are constrained by UG. In this view, UG is accessed via the first language in a first stage, and directly thereafter when the second language INPUT cannot be accommodated within the first language settings.

- *Full access/impaired early representations*: several researchers also believe that learners can 'reset' parameters to the second language values, but that initially, learners are lacking functional categories altogether. The 'Minimal Trees approach' has been highly influential and forms the starting point for a number of recent accounts of the development of syntax: only lexical categories are projected initially, which transfer from the first language. Functional categories develop later, but are not transferred from the first language. A similar approach is that of Eubank and is called the 'Valueless Features hypothesis'. In this view, both lexical and functional categories are transferred early on (with a short stage in which only lexical projections are present), but functional categories lack values such as tense, agreement, etc., and are present as syntactic markers only (i.e., inflections may be lacking, but the syntactic operations linked to these categories will be in place).

see also NO ACCESS VIEW, PARTIAL ACCESS VIEW, DUAL ACCESS VIEW
Eubank 1996; Flynn 1996, 1984, 1987; Mithcell & Myles 2004; Schwartz & Sprouse 1994, 1996; Vainikka & Young-Scholten 1996b, 1998

compound bilingualism

the theory that a bilingual person relates words to their meanings in one of two ways. Compound bilinguals were thought to be those who learn their languages in a single environment and develop a single mental representation for both. They attribute identical meanings to corresponding lexical units in the two languages (e.g., *dog* in English and *chien* in French are simply two words for the same concept). In contrast, **coordinate bilingual**s are those who learn their languages in distinctively separate contexts, associate them with different cultures, and develop different mental representations. They thus attribute partly or wholly different meanings to corresponding lexical units in the two languages (e.g. *dog* in English would mean something different from *chien* in French). Practically speaking, foreign language learners are often coordinate bilinguals. There are problems with this distinction as a model of BILINGUALISM, but the labels are often used in studies of vocabulary learning.

see also EARLY BILINGUALISM, SIMULTANEOUS BILINGUALISM, ADDITIVE BILINGUALISM
Brown & Attardo 2005; Crystal 2008

comprehensible input

see INPUT HYPOTHESIS

comprehensible output hypothesis

another term for OUTPUT HYPOTHESIS

computational model

a model of L2 acquisition which adopts the INFORMATION PROCESSING approach common in COGNITIVE PSYCHOLOGY. It views acquisition as the result of processing mechanisms that operate on INPUT to construct INTERLANGUAGE systems that evolve gradually over time.

see also SOCIOCULTURAL THEORY, INFORMATION PROCESSING THEORY, ADAPTIVE CONTROL OF THOUGHT MODEL, ATTENTION, AWARENESS, INDIVIDUAL LEARNER DIFFERENCES, MULTIDIMENSIONAL MODEL, NATIVIZATION MODEL, PARALLEL DISTRIBUTED PROCESSING MODEL, COGNITIVE DEVELOPMENT, CONNECTIONISM

 Ellis 2008

computer-assisted language learning
also **CALL**

the use of a computer in the teaching or learning of a second or foreign language. Computer Assisted Language Learning (CALL) is often perceived, somewhat narrowly, as an approach to language teaching and learning in which the computer is used as an aid to the presentation, reinforcement, and assessment of material to be learned, usually including a substantial interactive element. CALL may take place in classrooms, homes, libraries, computer cafés, etc. It also happens at different times and in different economic, cultural, political, social, and linguistic realms that embody different understandings, goals, and standards.

CALL has been divided into seven general types of activity. One of the most important is *writing*. This includes word processing, text analysis, and desktop publishing, often combined with communication over a local area network (LAN). Though student use of spell checkers and grammar checkers is common in these types of activities, much more sophisticated and interactive approaches are also possible. Many second language (L2) teachers, for example, now request their students to use computers to write essays then to e-mail each other what they have written or to post their essays on a LAN. The students then discuss and correct each other's writing, engaging in meaningful discourse and creating knowledge through interaction.

A second type of CALL is *communicating*. This includes e-mail exchanges, student discussions with each other or with their teacher on LANs, MOOs (sites on the Internet where student do role-playing games and talk with each other), and real-time chat. These activities are particularly useful for foreign language teaching where students share the same first language because they create the need to use the foreign language for authentic communication.

Another CALL activity is use of *multimedia*. This includes courseware presented on CD-ROM or online for study of specific skills such as pronunciation or grammar, and integrated skills-based or communicative practice where hyperlinks allow students to access a range of supplementary material for learning support. Often teacher-created programs are course-specific and are designed to quiz students over material covered in class.

Other CALL activities involve the *Internet*, such as Web searches for information and student construction of home pages. Related to this is the field of *information literacy*, a concept similar to *computer literacy* and referring to the ability to obtain information from the Internet and process it selectively and critically. The tremendous amount of online resources means that teacher evaluation of Web sites and L2 learning materials has now become an important aspect of Internet-based activities.

An additional use of CALL is *concordancing* and referencing, or using a corpus to examine the range of usages for grammar and vocabulary items, and using online dictionaries for definitions and usage information.

Yet another significant use of CALL is *distance learning*. Some college professors teach some or all of their courses online. Research on distance learning and courses with online components suggests that online students make the same gains as those achieved by students receiving a regular 'brick-and-mortar' lecture. An additional aspect of distance learning is the teacher creation of Web pages to disseminate their lesson plans, course material, research papers, and other material. Many teachers routinely take attendance online and post course outlines, specific activities, tests, drills, and so on, on their home pages. Veteran teachers may recall when there was often a filing cabinet of time-tested activities, lessons, and tests in the teachers' office for instructors to browse through and copy. Now this 'filing cabinet' has moved online to hundreds of sites, including listening laboratories, Test of English as a Second Language (TOEFL) practice, reading and writing activities and exercises, tests, holiday-related and other types of cultural activities, Web page design, and so forth.

Another important use of CALL is *test taking*. There is extensive research on computer-assisted language testing (CALT), suggesting that computer-based tests, particularly those that respond to learners' choices by presenting subsequent items at varying levels of difficulty, are effective in building language skills because they provide immediate feedback and multimedia support by access to dictionaries, grammatical explanations, and audio and video material for study of test items.

With new learning programs arriving regularly, today, CALL is one of the more dynamic areas in applied linguistics.

📖 Egbert & Petrie 2005; Fotos & Browne 2004; Levy 1997; Tavakoli 2012a

concept-oriented approach

an approach that maps language functions that a learner wants to express to the form that he needs to express it. The concept-oriented approach begins with the assumption that learners begin with the need to express a given concept—for example, an event in the past. With adult learners, the function (i.e., concept) is already known as the relevant concepts are available

through their first language. Andersen discusses the possibility of multifunctionality, recognizing that there are times when a learner needs to 'search' the INPUT to understand additional meanings expressed in the input. An example might be the present progressive, which can mean an act in the present (*I am writing these words now*) or an act in the future (*I am flying to Shanghai tomorrow*).
📖 Andersen 1990; Gass & Selinker 2008

conceptual transfer
a term referring to how L1-specific world view affects the acquisition of another language. That is, transfer effects are seen as not just linguistic but as reflecting the underlying ways in which learners perceive and conceptualize the world. Conceptual transfer is closely linked to the notion of LINGUISTIC RELATIVITY.
📖 Ellis 2008

connectionism
a nonlinguistic approach to studying language acquisition that has important ties with psychology and general learning. Connectionism is a theory (led by McClelland and Rumelhart) which likens the brain to a computer that would consist of neural networks: complex clusters of links between information nodes. These links or connections become strengthened or weakened through activation or non-activation, respectively. Learning in this view occurs on the basis of associative processes, rather than the construction of abstract rules. In other words, the human mind is predisposed to look for associations between elements and create links between them. These links become stronger as these associations keep recurring, and they also become part of larger networks as connections between elements become more numerous. When applied to the learning of language, connectionism claims that learners are sensitive to regularities in the language INPUT (i.e. the regular co-occurrence of particular language forms) and extract probabilistic patterns on the basis of these regularities. Learning occurs as these patterns become strengthened by repeated activation.
Connectionism is thus the computer modeling of the *constructivist* (see CONSTRUCTIVISM) or *emergentist* (see EMERGENTISM) views of language learning. Connectionism attempts to develop computationally explicit PARALLEL DISTRIBUTED PROCESSING models of IMPLICIT LEARNING in well-understood, constrained, and controllable experimental learning environments. The models allow the assessment of just how much of language acquisition can be done by extraction of probabilistic patterns of grammatical and morphological regularities. Because the only relation in connectionist models is strength of association between nodes, they are excellent modeling media in which to investigate the formation of associations as a result of exposure to language. An example of a connectionist network is shown in Figure C.4.

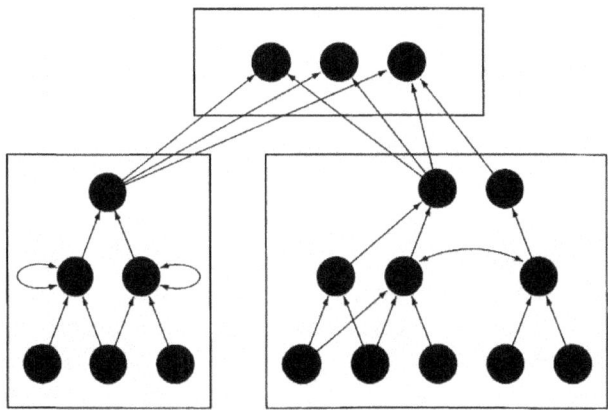

Figure C.4. A complex network consisting of several modules (arrows indicate the direction of flow of excitation or inhibition, for example)

The connectionist approach does not believe that the learning of rules underlies the construction of linguistic knowledge, but rather that this happens through the associative processes. This goes against the view that language is a set of modules (syntax, morphology, phonology) with an accompanying lexicon, and that the task facing language learners is to extract rules from the language around them in order to build up their own mental set of those rules as well as learning the lexicon which will then fit into the slots made available by the grammar. Saying, as connectionists do, that learning is not rule-governed, but is based on the construction of associative patterns, is a fundamental departure from most currently held views. Connectionism is seen as an alternative to symbolic accounts of language acquisition: rule-like behavior does not imply rule-governed behavior.

It is a transition theory that aims to explain how these associative patterns emerge in learners. Whereas property theories characterize the language that learners develop, connectionism attempts to model the dynamic acquisition of that language. If language learning is all about the building of billions of associations and the extraction of patterns resulting in rule-like behavior, how do these come about? Connectionism provides the computational tools for exploring the conditions under which emergent properties arise.

Connectionist models of language learning constitute an enormous challenge to *nativist* theories (see NATIVISM) of language and acquisition. Not surprisingly, therefore, they have been criticized by researchers working in Chomskyan paradigm (see CHOMSKYAN THEORY). According to them, the fact that a computer model behaves intelligently without rules does not show that humans lack rules. Thus, connectionist theories have been criticized for being 'revisionist' (i.e., behaviorist) in a way that is not scientifically defensible.

Connectionist models are also referred to as *artificial neural network* models.

see also COMPETITION MODEL

📖 N. Ellis 1996b, 2003; N. Ellis & Schmidt 1997; Macaro et al. 2010; McClelland et al. 1986; Mithcell & Myles 2004; Piske & Young-Scholten 2009; Rumelhart & McClelland 1986; VanPatten & Benati 2010

consciousness raising
also intake enhancement

techniques that encourage learners to pay attention to language form in the belief that an AWARENESS of form will contribute indirectly to language acquisition. Consciousness raising (CR) involves an attempt to equip the learner with an understanding of a specific grammatical feature—to develop DECLARATIVE rather than PROCEDURAL KNOWLEDGE of it. The main characteristics of CR activities are the following:

1) There is an attempt to *isolate* a specific linguistic feature for focused attention.
2) The learners are provided with *data* which illustrate the targeted feature and they may also be supplied with an *explicit rule* describing or explaining the feature.
3) The learners are expected to utilize *intellectual effort* to understand the targeted feature.
4) Misunderstanding or incomplete understanding of the grammatical structure by the learners leads to *clarification* in the form of further data and description or explanation.
5) Learners may be required (although this is not obligatory) to articulate the rule describing the grammatical structure.

CR is contrasted with **practice**, whose aim is to cause the learners to absorb the structure thoroughly; or to put it another way, to transfer what they know from short-term to LONG-TERM MEMORY. Practice is essentially a pedagogical construct. It assumes that the acquisition of grammatical structures involves a gradual automatization of production, from controlled to automatic, and it ignores the very real constraints that exist on the ability of the teacher to influence what goes on inside the learner's head. Practice may have limited psycholinguistic validity. In fact, practice is directed at the acquisition of IMPLICIT KNOWLEDGE of a grammatical structure—the kind of tacit knowledge needed to use the structure effortlessly for communication. CR is directed at the formation of EXPLICIT KNOWLEDGE—the kind of intellectual knowledge which we are able to gather about any subject, if we so choose. CR, unlike practice, does not involve the learner in *repeated production*. This is because the aim of CR is not to enable the learner to perform a structure correctly by simply to help her to *know about it*. CR is considered as a potential facilitator for the acquisition of linguistic competence and has nothing directly to do with the use of that competence for achievement of specific communicative objectives, or with the achievement of fluency. Whereas practice is primarily behavioral, CR is essentially concept forming in orientation. While practice work cannot take place without some degree of CR (even if this is incidental), the obverse is not the case. CR can occur without practice.

Thus, it is perfectly possible to teach grammar in the sense of helping learners to understand and explain grammatical phenomena without having them engage in activities that require repeated production of the structures concerned.

Although CR does not contribute directly to the acquisition of implicit knowledge, it does so indirectly. In other words, CR facilitates the acquisition of grammatical knowledge needed for communication. CR, then, is unlikely to result in immediate acquisition. More likely, it will have a delayed effect.

There are, of course, limitations to CR. It may not be appropriate for young learners. Some learners (e.g., those who like to learn by *doing* rather than studying) may dislike it. It can only be used with beginners if the learners' first language is used as the medium for solving the tasks. However, the alternative in such situations is not practice. Rather, it is to provide opportunities for meaning-focused language use, for communicating in the L2, initially perhaps in the form of listening tasks. All learners, even those who are suited to a CR approach, will need plenty of such opportunities. CR is not an alternative to communication activities, but a supplement.

see also INPUT ENHANCEMENT
📖 Ellis 2002a; Richards & Schmidt 2010

consecutive bilingualism
another term for SEQUENTIAL BILINGUALISM

Construction Grammar
see DUAL-MODE SYSTEM

constructions
recurrent patterns of linguistic elements that serve some well-defined linguistic function. They can be at sentence level or below. Many constructions are based on particular lexical items which can be single words or whole sentences (i.e., they are formulaic in nature, see FORMULAIC LANGUAGE). Constructions can also be abstract such as the ditransitive pattern with verbs like 'fax' (e.g., *Pat faxed Bill the letter*) or the caused motion pattern with verb like 'push' (e.g., *Pat caused the napkin off the table*). These abstract patterns cater to the creativity of language, allowing speakers to construct unique utterances such as *Pat sneezed the napkin off the table*. It is argued

that the acquisition of constructions involves a developmental sequence from formula, through low-scope pattern (involving the partial analysis of formulaic chunks that enables learners to discover how particular lexical items work syntactically) to construction.

Emergentist (see EMERGENTISM) accounts of L2 acquisition view acquisition as a process of internalizing and subsequently analyzing constructions.

📖 N. Ellis 2003; Ellis 2008

constructivism

a theory of knowledge (epistemology) concerned with how humans come to understand the world and differentiate between justified belief and opinion. It is often regarded as the opposite of *positivism* (a philosophical movement that began in the early twentieth century, characterized by an emphasis on the scientific method as the only source of knowledge and a desire to rebuild society on the basis of 'positive' knowledge), and proposes that reality only exists as seen through the filter or lens of the human mind operating both individually and collectively. There are two branches of constructivism: 'cognitive' and 'social'. In the **cognitive constructivism**, emphasis is placed on the importance of learners constructing their own representation of reality. Learners must individually discover and transform complex information if they are to make it their own, suggesting a more active role for students in their own learning than is typical in many classrooms. Such claims are rooted in Piaget's. For Piaget, learning is a developmental process that involves change, self-generation, and construction, each building on prior learning experiences.

Social constructivism emphasizes the importance of social interaction and cooperative learning in constructing both cognitive and emotional images of reality. It is argued that constructivist research tends to focus on individuals engaged in social practices, on a collaborative group, or on a global community. The champion of social constructivism is Vygotsky (see VYGOTSKYAN), who advocated the view that children's thinking and meaning-making is socially constructed and emerges out of their social interactions with their environment. One of the most popular concepts advanced by Vygotsky was the notion of a ZONE OF PROXIMAL DEVELOPMENT in every learner.

Researchers studying first and second language acquisition have demonstrated constructivist perspectives through studies of conversational discourse, sociocultural factors in learning, and interactionist theories. In many ways, constructivist perspectives are a natural successor to cognitively based studies of UNIVERSAL GRAMMAR, INFORMATION PROCESSING, MEMORY, ARTIFICIAL INTELLIGENCE, and INTERLANGUAGE *systematicity* (see VARIABILITY).

see also COGNITIVE DEVELOPMENT, CONNECTIONISM, EMERGENTISM, SOCIOCULTURAL THEORY

📖 Brown 2007; Kaufman 2004; Piaget 1954, 1955, 1970; Piaget & Inhelder 1969; Slavin 2003; Spivey 1997; Tavakoli 2012

context

knowledge based on what has already been read or heard in a specific text or situation, as well as an understanding of what the writer's or speaker's intentions are, and the overall structure of the discourse pattern being used.
A term sometimes used loosely to cover any of:

- Immediate situation: knowledge of speaker/writer; analogy with a similar linguistic exchange.
- Meaning representation built up from the text so far.
- Topic: world knowledge in the form of pre-established schemas.
- Co-text: a group of words which provides syntactic or semantic evidence for the words which occur next.

Contextual information appears to be used by readers in two different ways. Weaker readers use it to compensate for inadequate decoding skills, while stronger ones use it to enrich their interpretation of the text.
📖 Field 2004; Saville-Troike 2006

continuity hypothesis
see BABBLING

Contrastive Analysis Hypothesis
also **CAH**

a hypothesis as formulated by Lado claims that that the principal barrier to second language acquisition is first language INTERFERENCE (i.e., negative transfer from L1 to L2), and that a scientific analysis of the two languages in question enables the prediction of difficulties a learner will encounter. Contrastive Analysis Hypothesis (CAH) had both a psychological aspect and a linguistic aspect. The psychological aspect was based on BEHAVIORIST LEARNING THEORY, and the linguistic aspect was based, in the first place at least, on STRUCTURALIST LINGUISTICS. The psychological rational takes a 'strong' and a 'weak' form. The *strong version* of the CAH contended that all L2 errors could be predicted by identifying the differences between learners' native language and the target language. It stipulates that the prime cause, or even the sole cause, of difficulty and error in language learning is interference coming from the learner's native language. Where languages are more distinct and different from each other, the more interference would arise and thus make learning the L2 form more difficult. But where the two languages were similar, *positive transfer* would result and thus the L2 form was predicted to be easier to learn.

However, the empirical evidence suggested that many errors were not the result of transfer. Therefore, the second position—the *weak position*—was formulated. The weak form of the hypothesis claims only to be diagnostic.

According to view, only some errors were traceable to transfer, and contrastive analysis could be used only *a posteriori* to explain rather than predict. In other words, errors are studied *after* they have been committed by second language learners and explanations based on a contrastive analysis of those areas in question are offered as why the errors have occurred. The so-called weak version of the CAH is what remains today under the label CROSSLINGUISTIC INFLUENCE, suggesting that we all recognize the significant role that prior experience plays in any learning act, and that the influence of the native language as prior experience must not be overlooked. In fact, it claims a less powerful role for the L1 than the strong version of the hypothesis.

A comparison of two languages can be carried out using any of several different models of grammar. Initially the model used was that of structuralist linguists. This emphasized the importance of detailed scientific description of languages based on a description of the different categories that make up the patterns of a language. These categories were defined in formal terms and they were established inductively. Most of the contrastive studies carried out have been based on surface structure characteristics, such as those described by the structuralists. The procedure followed was (1) *description* (i.e., a formal description of the two languages was made), (2) *selection* (i.e., certain areas or items of the two language were made), (3) *comparison* (i.e., the identification of areas of difference and similarity), and (4) *prediction* (i.e., determining which areas were likely to cause errors).

In (3), *comparison*, the simplest procedure was to identify which aspects of the two languages were similar and which were different. However, contrastive analysts soon realized that there were *degrees* of similarity and difference. The best known attempt was made by Stockwell, Bowen, and Martin, who proposed what they called a *hierarchy of difficulty* by which a teacher or linguist can make a prediction of the relative difficulty of a given aspect of the second language. They constructed a hierarchy of difficulty for phonological and grammatical structures of two languages in contrast. Later, Clifford Prator captured the essence of this grammatical hierarchy in six categories of difficulty. Prator's hierarchy was applicable to both grammatical and phonological features of language. The six categories, in ascending order of difficulty, are listed below:

- Level 0—*Transfer*. No difference or contrast is present between the two languages. The learner can simply transfer (positively) a sound, structure, or lexical item from the native language to the target language. Examples: English and Spanish cardinal vowels, word order, and certain words (*mortal, inteligente, arte, americanos*).
- Level 1—*Coalescence*. Two items in the native language become coalesced into essentially one item in the target language. This requires that learners overlook a distinction they have grown accustomed to. Exam-

ples: English third-person possessives require gender distinction (*his/her*), and in Spanish they do not (*su*); an English speaker learning French must overlook the distinction between *teach* and *learn* and use just the one word *apprendre* in French.
- Level 2—*Underdifferentiation*. An item in the native language is absent in the target language. The learner must avoid that item. Examples: English learners of Spanish must forget such items as English *do* as a tense carrier, possessive forms of *wh*-words (*whose*), or the use of *some* with mass nouns.
- Level 3—*Reinterpretation*. An item that exists in the native language is given a new shape or distribution. Example: An English speaker learning French must learn a new distribution for nasalized vowels. Similarly, the Persian learner of English, for example, must learn a new allophone for the phoneme /l/. That is, Persian /l/ is a clear /l/; whereas this phoneme may be clear or dark in English depending on the phonological environment.
- Level 4—*Overdifferentiation*. A new item entirely, bearing little if any similarity to the native language item, must be learned. Example: An English speaker learning Spanish must learn to include determiners in generalized nominals (Man is mortal/*El hombre es mortal*), or, most commonly, to learn Spanish grammatical gender inherent in nouns. Similarly, the native speaker of Persian must learn some new English phonemes such as /θ/, /ð/, and /ʌ/.
- Level 5—*Split*. One item in the native language becomes two or more in the target language, requiring the learner to make a new distinction. Example: An English speaker learning Spanish must learn the distinction between *ser* and *estar* (to be), or the distinction between Spanish indicative and subjunctive moods. Similarly, the Persian learners of English have to make a distinction between 'he' and 'she' as the equivalent of these two pronouns in Persian is one single form, namely /uː/.

The first, or 'zero', degree of difficulty represented complete one-to-one correspondence and transfer, while the fifth degree of difficulty was the height of interference.

The CAH had its heyday in the 1960s, but gradually fell out of favor in the 1970s. There were several reasons for this. The strong form became untenable when it was shown that many errors were apparently not caused by interference. These errors either looked like those that children learning the L1 would make, or their source was ambiguous. In addition, many errors predicted by the CAH did not actually occur. However, the weak form is also problematic. First, *a posteriori* contrastive analysis is something of a 'pseudo procedure' in the sense that it makes little sense to undertake a lengthy comparison of two languages simply to confirm that errors suspected of being caused by transfer are indeed so. It was argued that a contrastive analysis was only worthwhile if it was predictive. It was also argued that an *a priori* contrastive analysis was needed in order to identify those areas of the L2 system which learners might try to avoid. Neither version of the CAH was convincing, therefore; the strong version was theoretically untenable and the weak version was impractical and inadequate. It was not surprising to see contrastive analysis lose ground to ERROR ANALYSIS in the 1970s.

Theoretical attacks on the validity of behaviorist accounts of language learning also helped to create a crisis in CAH. Gradually, however, the role of the L1 was reappraised rather than rejected out of hand. The appraisal took two forms. The nature of language transfer was reexamined to take into account of AVOIDANCE, the need for there to be a degree of similarity between the first and second language items for interference to take place, and the multifactor nature of learner error. Also the contribution made by the L1 was recast in a more cognitive framework to make it more acceptable to the mentalist views (see MENTALISM) which dominated discussion of language acquisition following Chomsky's attack on Skinner's neo-behaviorist theory (see OPERANT CONDITIONING). The key concept in this new framework was that of 'strategy' for communicating when there were insufficient L2 resources (see COMMUNICATION STRATEGIES). More recently, interest in contrastive analysis has shifted to reflect current developments in linguistic which emphasize the communicative uses of language. This development is known as CONTRASTIVE PRAGMATICS.

📖 Brown 2007; Dulay & Burt 1974a; Ellis 1986, 2008; James 1998; Kellerman 1995; Kellerman & Sharwood-Smith 1986; Keshavarz 1999; Lado 1957; Macaro et al. 2010; Odlin 2003; Prator 1967; Schachter 1974; Sharwood-Smith 1996; Stockwell, Bowen, & Martin 1965; VanPatten & Benati 2010; Wardhaugh 1970; Whitman 1970, 1987; Whitman & Jackson 1972

contrastive interlanguage analysis

a term used by Granger to refer to the contrastive study of the INTERLANGUAGEs of learners with different L1s. It has been made possible by the advent of concordancing tools for analyzing learner corpora (see CALL).

📖 Ellis 2008; Granger 1998a

contrastive pragmatics

the study of cultural differences in the way speech acts and other aspects of speaking are realized, such as by comparing differences between the ways people from two different cultures realize the speech act of 'apologizing'. It was argued that that the basic idea of contrasting languages is a correct one. The problem lies not in the idea, but in the way in which the contrast has been carried out. According to this view, contrastive analysis needs to be undertaken with reference to communicative networks, rather than purely linguistic parameters. One way is to take a particular function (e.g., apolo-

gizing) and then contrast its linguistic realizations in two or more languages. Another approach is to examine the different functions served by the same linguistic structure in two languages. Yet another, more ambitious, possibly is to compare the discourse structure of representative interactions in the two languages.
see also CONTRASTIVE ANALYSIS HYPOTHESIS, CONTRASTIVE RHETORIC
📖 Ellis 1986; Richards & Schmidt 2010; Riley 1981; Sajavaara 1981b

contrastive rhetoric
the study of similarities and differences between writing in a first and second language or between two languages, in order to understand how writing conventions in one language influence how a person writes in another. Writing in a second language is thought to be influenced to some extent by the linguistic and cultural conventions of the writer's first language, and this may influence how the writer organizes written discourse (discourse structure), the kind of script or scheme the writer uses, as well as such factors as topic, audience, paragraph organization, and choice of vocabulary or register.
Kaplan presented a schematic diagram of how two different languages and three language families conventionally organize an essay. English and Russian (languages) and Semitic, Oriental, and Romance (language families) were described through what have now been dubbed 'doodles' to characterize the structure of an essay So, for example, English was depicted through a straight line from one point to another, Semitic languages with a jagged set of lines and Oriental languages through a spiral. Kaplan's descriptions were clearly inspired by the *Whorfian Hypothesis*. The point of Kaplan's conclusions about how we write was, of course, that learners of English bring with them certain predispositions, which come from their native languages, about how to organize their writing. If English writers get straight to the point, and Chinese writers spiral around the point, then a Chinese speaker who is learning English will encounter some difficulty in learning to write English discourse.
Kaplan's claims raised various criticisms. Some researchers claimed that what Kaplan was characterizing as contrastive rhetorical patterns in L2 student writing were in fact due to developmental issues (i.e., the students were not writing effectively in the L2 because they were not yet competent enough to do so, not because their L1 rhetorics were interfering). Others worried about the implied ethnocentrism of the claims and/or about the deterministic pedagogy that it suggested or at least appeared to privilege. Earlier work on contrastive rhetoric was also criticized for ignoring issues of genre and audience.
Although there were some serious problems with Kaplan's study, there was and still is a ring of truth to his claims. No one can deny the effect of one's native culture, or one's predispositions that are the product of perhaps years of schooling, reading, writing, thinking, asserting, arguing, and defending.

But rather than holding a dogmatic or predictive view (that certain writers will experience difficulty because of their native language), teachers must adopt a weak position in which they must consider a learner's cultural/literary schemata as only one possible source of difficulty. A theory of contrastive rhetoric is influenced by more than first language patterns; factors such as LINGUISTIC RELATIVITY, theory of rhetoric, text linguistics, discourse types and genres, and translation all contribute toward a comprehensive theory of contrastive rhetoric. One important conclusion from this renewed wave of research is the significance of valuing learners' native-language-related rhetorical traditions, and of guiding them through a process of understanding those schemata while not attempting to eradicate them. That self-understanding on the part of learners may then lend itself to a more effective appreciation and use of English rhetorical conventions.

see also CONTRASTIVE ANALYSIS HYPOTHESIS, CONTRASTIVE PRAGMATICS

 Brown 2001, 2007; Connor 1996; Connor et al. 2008; Kaplan 1966; Leki 1991; Matsuda 1997; Mohan & Lo 1985; Richards & Schmidt 2010

conversational analysis
another term for CONVERSATION ANALYSIS

conversation analysis
also **conversational analysis, CA**
a method for analyzing social interaction in order to uncover their orderliness, structure, and sequential patterns. Conversational analysis (CA) provides a tool for conducting microanalysis of classroom discourse and, in particular, for examining the sequential development of classroom talk. CA is concerned with the structure of conversation, dealing with such matters as TURN-TAKING, topic change and conversational structure—rules governing the opening and closing of the conversation (e.g., on the phone). CA has been used as a tool in SLA research to study the different types of interaction relevant to language acquisition, including issues related to discourse management, like topic nomination and communication breakdown.

CA derives from a branch of sociology—ethnomethodology. Five key principles of this method of inquiry have been identified as follows: Indexicality (i.e., the use that interactants make of shared background knowledge and context), 2) the documentary method of interpretation (i.e., each real-world action is treated as an exemplar of a previously known pattern), 3) the reciprocity of perspectives (i.e., the interactants' willingness to follow the same norms in order to achieve intersubjectivity), 4) normative accountability (i.e., there are norms that are constitutive of action and enable speakers to produce and interpret actions), and 5) reflexivity (i.e., the same methods and procedures apply to the production and interpretation of actions). In accordance with these principles, CA seeks to explain how talk in interaction takes place. It aims to characterize the organization of interaction by abstracting from exemplars of specimens of interaction and to uncover the *emic* logic underlying the organization. This emic perspective, which contrasts with the *etic* perspective of mainstream SLA accounts of interaction is achieved by recording naturally occurring interaction, transcribing them narrowly and deriving bottom-up interpretations of the underlying order.

CA has been used to contrast the interactions that occur in naturalistic settings with those that occur in classrooms, the organization of turn-taking, the structure of repair sequences, the basic structure of classroom discourse, and how context is jointly constructed by the participants.

'CA for SLA', the term coined by Markee and Kasper, affords rich and illuminative accounts of classroom interaction. It serves as a tool for researchers to be able to assess what environment may be more or less conducive to learning because such settings would recommend themselves as scenes on which to focus research efforts. However, there are limits to its adequacy. One concerns the principle of 'reciprocity of perspectives' as it cannot be assumed that students (as L2 learners) do act in accordance with the same norms as the teacher (native or non-native speaker). It is noted that it is not so easy to interpret the participants' orientation to such phenomena as silence, stretched syllables, and non-verbal behavior in the L2 classroom as in interaction involving co-members. It is argued that CA alone is not capable for 'learning' as opposed to language use. Other disadvantages include the difficulty of generalizing results and the danger of ignoring superordinate variables relating to the learners' social context.

see also ETHNOGRAPHY OF COMMUNICATION
 Ellis 2008; Johnson & Johnson1999; Markee and Kasper 2004

cooing
the earliest use of speech-like sounds by an infant in the first few months. During the first few months of life, the child gradually becomes capable of producing sequences of vowel-like sounds, particularly high vowels similar to [i] and [u]. By four months of age, the developing ability to bring the back of the tongue into regular contact with the back of the palate allows the infant to create sounds similar to the velar consonants [k] and [g], hence the common description as 'cooing' or 'gooing' for this type of production. Speech perception studies have shown that by the time they are five months old, babies can already hear the difference between the vowels [i] and [a] and discriminate between syllables like [ba] and [ga].

see also BABBLING, FIRST LANGUAGE ACQUISITION
 Yule 2006

coordinate bilingual
see COMPOUND BILINGUALISM

corrective feedback
another term for FEEDBACK

correspondence hypothesis
also **derivational theory of complexity, DTC**
a view which attracted considerable psycholinguistic interest in the 1960s, especially with reference to language acquisition studies. Correspondence hypothesis states that the number or sequence of rules used in the grammatical derivation of a sentence corresponds to the amount of psychological processing that takes place in speech production and speech perception. Evidence in its favor came from several experiments which showed that the time it took for speakers to process sentences with more complex derivations was longer than their less complex counterparts (e.g., passives as opposed to actives, negatives as opposed to affirmatives). Further experimental evidence, in the late 1960s, was less convincing, however, and methodological problems were raised (e.g., how one separates out effects due to length and meaning, as well as transformational history); there have also been radical theoretical changes in the notions of transformation involved. As a result, the correspondence hypothesis is no longer influential as a research paradigm.
 Crystal 2008

covert prestige
the status of a speech style or feature as having positive value, but which is 'hidden' or not valued similarly among the larger community. For example, many lower-working-class speakers do not change their speech style from casual to careful as radically as lower-middle-class speakers. They value the features that mark them as members of their social group and consequently avoid changing them in the direction of features associated with another social group. They may value group solidarity (i.e., sounding like those around them) more than upward mobility (i.e., sounding like those above them). Among younger speakers in the middle class, there is often covert prestige attached to many features of pronunciation and grammar (*I ain't doin' nuttin'* rather than *I'm not doing anything*) that are more often associated with the speech of lower-status groups. This kind of prestige is covert, because it is usually manifested subconsciously between members of a group,
Covert prestige contrasts with **overt prestige**, which is generally recognized as 'better' or more positively valued in the larger community. It is associated with the undeniable social power of upper-class speakers, may be required for higher-status jobs and upward mobility, and are promulgated by the agents of standardization in society, such as the mass media and school teachers. Unlike the case of overt prestige, the forms to be valued are publicly recommended by powerful social institutions.
see also HYPERCORRECTION, HYPOCORRECTION
 Crystal 2008; Labov 1972

CPH
an abbreviation for CRITICAL PERIOD HYPOTHESIS

Creative Construction Hypothesis
also **CCH**
a hypothesis which was emerged from the open criticism toward BEHAVIORISM and particularly the CONTRASTIVE ANALYSIS HYPOTHESIS, along with the early research on SLA in the 1970s. Under creative construction, SLA is considered to be very much like L1 acquisition in that SLA is a process in which learners make unconscious hypotheses on the basis of the INPUT they get from the environment. Creative construction viewed acquisition as a learner-internal driven process, guided by innate mechanisms that are impermeable to outside influences such as instruction and CORRECTIVE FEEDBACK. Very often, creative construction is viewed as the 'L1 = L2 hypothesis'; namely, that L1 acquisition and SLA are basically the same in terms of how acquisition happens.

The major evidence for creative construction consisted of the MORPHEME STUDIES, in which learners of different L1 backgrounds seemed to acquire features of language in the same order (discounting the strong TRANSFER hypothesis). Additional important research centered on *developmental sequences* (see FIRST LANGUAGE ACQUISITION), which revealed that learners with different L1 backgrounds tended to traverse the same stages of acquisition of a given structure (e.g., negation, question formation) over time. Thus, major features of the Creative Construction Hypothesis were: (1) L1 transfer is negligible; and (2) there is universality in acquisition sequences.

As an account of acquisition, creative construction was subsumed under MONITOR MODEL, and by the late 1980s had all but disappeared from the active discourse on SLA as other theories and accounts began to surface.
 VanPatten & Benati 2010

creativity
a term which refers to the capacity of language learners to produce and understand an indefinitely large number of sentences, most of which they will not have heard or used before. CHILD LANGUAGE LEARNING shows creativity because it always results in utterances by children which they have not heard. They cannot be imitating these utterances, and so must be guessing, or creating, what would be said in their language. English-speaking children, for example, say things like *goed*, *mans*, and *mommy sock*, which they have not heard from others. That is, they create these words and phrases.

As a property of language, it refers to the 'open-endedness' or productivity of patterns, whereby a finite set of sounds, structures, etc., can be used to produce a potentially infinite number of sentences. In contrast with studies of animal communication, linguistic creativity is considered to be a 'species-specific' property: the creation of new sentences is not a feature of animal communication systems.

The notion of creativity has a long history in the discussion of language, but it has become a central feature of contemporary studies since the emphasis placed upon it by Noam Chomsky (see CHOMSKYAN THEORY). One of the main aims of linguistic enquiry, it is felt, is to explain this creative ability, for which such constructs as generative rules have been suggested. Care must, however, be taken to avoid confusing this sense of 'creative' with that found in artistic or literary contexts, where notions such as imagination and originality are central.

 Crystal 2008; Hudson 2000

creole

a PIDGIN language that has become the native language of a group of speakers. A pidgin is not a natural language, but only a crude system of communication stitched together by people who have no language in common. If a pidgin establishes itself in a multilingual society, then there may well come a time when a generation of children is produced who have only the pidgin to use among themselves. In this case, the children will almost inevitably take the pidgin and turn it into a real language, complete with a large vocabulary and a rich grammatical system. This new natural language is a creole, and the children who create it are the first native speakers of the creole. The process of turning a pidgin into a creole is **creolization**.

Countless creoles have come into existence during the last few centuries, often because of the activities of European colonists. Speakers of English, French Spanish, Portuguese and Dutch have established colonies in Africa, Asia and the Americas, in areas where the local languages were very different, and in many cases the Europeans imported African slaves speaking any of dozens of African languages. The Caribbean has been a particularly fertile area for creoles, as Europeans and Africans (and to a lesser extent native Americans) were forced to construct innumerable local pidgins, very many of which went on to be converted to creoles.

At one time, there was a widespread belief that all creoles were descended from a single ancestral creole by massive vocabulary replacement (*relexification*), but this idea is no longer taken seriously.

When a creole remains in contact with the prestige language from which it was largely constructed, it may undergo significant **decreolization**—adjustment toward that prestige standard—and the result may be a **creole continuum**, a range of varieties from a highly conservative version of the creole (the *basilect*) through increasingly decreolized versions (the *mesolects*) to something more or less identical to the prestige standard (the *acrolect*).

Linguists studying contemporary *language change* have found creolization to be a rich source of information, particularly from the point of view of the

construction of new grammatical systems. The remarkable similarities in grammar among creoles all over the world have led to the proposing of the BIOPROGRAM HYPOTHESIS.
📖 Trask 2005

creole continuum
see CREOLE

creolization
see CREOLE

Critical Period Hypothesis
also **CPH**
the claim that there is a biological timetable before which and after which language acquisition, both first and second, is more successfully accomplished. It is a construct often discussed in the L1 and L2 literature as a potential explanation for why older learners have more apparent difficulty learning a (second) language than younger learners. The term 'critical period' is used in biology to refer to a phase in the development of an organism during which a particular capacity or behavior must be acquired if it is to be acquired at all. An example typically cited is that of imprinting in certain species. Thus, for instance, immediately after hatching, ducklings follow and become irreversibly attached to the first moving object they perceive—usually their mother. This following behavior occurs only within a certain time period, after which the hatchlings develop a fear of strange objects and retreat instead of following. Within these time limits is what is seen as the critical period for the following behavior. Another example is provided by the acquisition of birdsong: for instance, if a young chaffinch does not hear an adult bird singing within a certain period, the bird in question will apparently never sing a full song. If language acquisition in human beings is constrained by the limits of a critical period on this kind of definition, the implication is that unless language acquisition gets under way before the period ends it simply will not happen. There may also be an implication that, even if language acquisition begins within the critical period, it does not continue beyond the end of that period and that additional languages acquired beyond the critical period will not ever be completely or 'perfectly' acquired.

Critical Period Hypothesis (CPH) was first related to language development by Penfield and Roberts and later by Lenneberg who argued that the human brain loses its capacity for language learning as maturation proceeds. Penfield and Roberts argued that after the age of nine the human brain becomes 'progressively stiff ' while Lenneberg argued that the critical period for language learning was between the ages of 2 years and puberty, a period of time which corresponds to when brain function becomes associated with specific brain regions (see LATERALIZATION). Singleton has demonstrated that there are many different versions of the CPH and many disagreements in both the L1 and L2 literature concerning whether it is applicable either to L1 or L2 development, and when the onset and the offset of the critical period might be for different aspects of linguistic knowledge. The term **sensitive period** has often been used in lieu of critical period to accommodate the idea that unlike other animal learning paradigms, human language development (either L1 or L2) does not seem to be subject to such a tightly defined time frame but rather suggests a time frame where the effects of a particular stimulus (i.e., linguistic environment) on behavior (i.e., learning) are particularly strong. In the sensitive period formulation, the sensitivity does not disappear at a fixed point; instead it is thought to fade away over a longer period of time, perhaps covering later childhood, puberty and adolescence. In other words, the critical period represents a well-defined window of opportunity, whereas the sensitive period represents a progressive inefficiency of the organism. Such a suggestion acknowledges that certain language skills are acquired more easily at particular times in development than at other times, and some language skills can be learned even after the critical period, although less easily. It seems reasonable to deduce from research that age does have an influence on L2 development, but the nature of influence will depend on which INTAKE factors, when, and in what combination, are brought to bear on the learning experience of an individual learner.

📖 Clark & Clark 1977; De Villiers & De Villiers 1978; Hinkel 2011; Hyltenstam & Abrahamsson 2003; Kumaravadivelu 2006; Lenneberg 1967; Lorenz 1961; Macaro et al. 2010; Penfield & Roberts 1959; Singleton 2007; Singleton & Muñoz 2011; Thorpe 1954

crosslinguistic influence

a cover term proposed by Sharwood Smith and Kellerman to refer to such phenomena as TRANSFER, INTERFERENCE, AVOIDANCE, borrowing, and L2-related aspects of language loss and thus permitting discussion of the similarities and differences between these phenomena. Whereas the term transfer is closely associated with BEHAVIORIST LEARNING THEORY, crosslinguistic influence is theory-neutral.

see also CONTRASTIVE ANALYSIS HYPOTHESIS

📖 Brown 2007; Ellis 2008; Odlin 2003

crosssectional study

an application of the general use of this term in the field of child language acquisition, referring to one of the two main procedures used in order to study the process of language development. In a cross-sectional study, the language of a group of children of the same or different ages is compared at a given point in time. This method contrasts with a **longitudinal study**, which follows the course of language acquisition in a single child or group over a period of time.

📖 Crystal 2008; Tavakoli 2012a

cultural transmission
a suggested defining property of human language, whereby the ability to speak a language is transmitted from generation to generation by a process of learning, and not genetically. This is not to deny that children may be born with certain innate predispositions towards language (see INNATENESS HYPOTHESIS), but it is to emphasize the difference between human language, where environmental learning has such a large role to play, and animal systems of communication, where instinct is more important.
📖 Crystal 2008

culture shock
feelings of estrangement, anger, hostility, indecision, frustration, unhappiness, sadness, loneliness, homesickness, and even physical illness which a person may have when they enter another culture. For example, when a person moves to live in a foreign country, they may have a period of culture shock until they become familiar with the new culture. Persons undergoing culture shock view their new world out of resentment and alternate between self-pity and anger at others for not understanding them. It is common to describe culture shock as the second of four successive stages of culture acquisition:

- Stage 1 is a period of excitement and euphoria over the newness of the surroundings.
- Stage 2—culture shock—emerges as individuals feel the intrusion of more and more cultural differences into their own images of self and security. In this stage individuals rely on and seek out the support of their fellow countrymen in the second culture, taking solace in complaining about local customs and conditions, seeking escape from their predicament.
- Stage 3 is one of gradual, and at first tentative and vacillating, recovery. This stage is referred to as 'culture stress': some problems of ACCULTURATION are solved while other problems continue for some time. But general progress is made, slowly but surely, as individuals begin to accept the differences in thinking and feeling that surround them, slowly becoming more empathic with other persons in the second culture.
- Stage 4 represents near or full recovery, either assimilation or adaptation, acceptance of the new culture and self-confidence in the 'new' person that has developed in this culture.

The culture shock stage of acculturation need not be depicted as a point when learners are unwitting and helpless victims of circumstance. It is argued that culture shock, while surely possessing manifestations of crisis, can also be viewed more positively as a profound cross-cultural learning experi-

ence, a set of situations or circumstances involving intercultural communication in which the individual, as a result of the experiences, becomes aware of his own growth, learning and change. As a result of the culture shock process, the individual has gained a new perspective on himself, and has come to understand his own identity in terms significant to himself. The cross-cultural learning experience, additionally, takes place when the individual encounters a different culture and as a result (1) examines the degree to which he is influenced by his own culture, and (2) understands the culturally derived values, attitudes and outlooks of other people.
📖 Adler 1972; Brown 2007; Larson & Smalley 1972

D

debilitative anxiety
see ANXIETY

declarative knowledge
see ADAPTIVE CONTROL OF THOUGHT MODEL

decreolization
see CREOLE

deductive instruction
see INDUCTIVE INSTRUCTION

deficit hypothesis
also **deficit theory, verbal deficit hypothesis**
the hypothesis that working-class children have an inadequate command of grammar and vocabulary to express complex ideas. In the 1960s, the British educational theorist Basil Bernstein proposed that a given language can be regarded as possessing two fundamentally different styles, or codes. A *restricted code*, in this view, has a limited vocabulary and a limited range of grammatical constructions; it is adequate for talking to people with very similar backgrounds about everyday experiences, but it is highly inexplicit and depends for success upon a large degree of shared experience. It is too inexplicit and too limited to express complex and unfamiliar ideas in a coherent manner. An *elaborated code*, in contrast, possesses a large vocabulary and a wide range of grammatical constructions, and it is entirely suitable for communicating complex ideas, in a fully explicit manner, to people who do not share the speaker's background.

Bernstein's deficit hypothesis holds that, while middle-class children have full control over both codes, working-class children have access only to the restricted code. Hence working-class children cannot communicate effectively in the manner expected in educational institutions, and so they cannot hope to succeed in school.

This hypothesis has generated a storm of discussion and debate. Linguists, led by William Labov, have mostly been critical and dismissive of it. They defend instead the **difference hypothesis**—by which working-class speech is

merely different from middle-class speech, and not inferior to it in expressiveness—and, hence, that working-class children in school are penalized only for being different, and not for being incompetent. The difference hypothesis views all dialects as intrinsically equal and able to express ideas of any complexity, though children who speak non-standard dialects may not have had the same kind of opportunity or motivation to use their language in demanding educational contexts.
see also MOTHER TONGUE MAINTENANCE
📖 Crystal 2008; Trask 2005

deficit theory
another term for DEFICIT HYPOTHESIS

depidignization
see NATIVIZATION MODEL

depth of knowledge
a term used in vocabulary acquisition research to refer to the extent to which learners have acquired various properties of words such as their syntactical functions and their collocations.
📖 Ellis 2008

derivational theory of complexity
another term for CORRESPONDENCE HYPOTHESIS

descriptive adequacy
see GENERATIVE THEORY

developmental linguistics
a term occasionally used for the branch of linguistics concerned with the study of the acquisition of language in children. The subject involves the application of linguistic theories and techniques of analysis to child language data, in order to provide a precise description of patterns of development and an explanation of the norms and variations encountered, both within individual languages and universally. In relation to the task of explanation, particular attention is paid to the role of non-linguistic factors, such as COGNITION, social background, the nature of the experimental task, and so on, and as a consequence there has been an increasingly multidisciplinary approach to the problem. Because of the particular relevance of psychological factors, the subject is more commonly referred to as **developmental psycholinguistics**.
📖 Crystal 2008

developmental psycholinguistics
see DEVELOPMENTAL LINGUISTICS

developmental readiness

a concept which forms part of the larger theory of processability (see PRO-CESSABILITY THEORY) which attempts to predict which grammatical structures are able to be processed by a learner at a certain stage in his development. It has its origins also in ACQUISITION ORDERS. Its main thesis is that a learner's L1 may inhibit the acquisition of certain L2 structures. As a consequence the brain will not be 'ready' to acquire a structure until sufficient exposure to INPUT (both positive and negative) has occurred. However, certain complex structures (such as question forms in English or negatives in German) may be acquired in stages with each stage requiring the learner to be 'ready' for the next stage. For example, in the case of English questions the following stages were identified and the notion of readiness to move up a stage was noted:

1) Single words or fragments (without verb): *spot on the dog?*
2) SVO with rising intonation: *a boy throw ball?*
3) Fronting: *do the boy is beside the bus?*
4) Wh-with copula; yes/no questions with auxiliary inversion: *where is the space ship?; Is there a dog on the bus?*
5) Wh-with auxiliary second: *what is the boy throwing?*

However, it is argued that counter-evidence to the need for readiness may be found in a learner's ability to subsume earlier stages of a sequence if he is exposed to sufficient later (more difficult) stages of that sequence. What 'readiness' may mean in psychological or biological terms remains open to question and the practical applications of developmental readiness may only be evident with very small classes where individual differentiation may be achievable.

Macaro et al. 2010; Mackey & Philp 1998; Spada & Lightbown 1999

dichotic listening

an experimental technique used in auditory phonetics to determine which hemisphere of the brain is more, or less, involved in the processing of speech or other sounds. This technique uses the generally established fact that anything experienced on the right-hand side of the body is processed in the left hemisphere, and anything on the left side is processed in the right hemisphere. So, a basic assumption would be that a signal coming in the right ear will go to the left hemisphere and a signal coming in the left ear will go to the right hemisphere. Listeners are presented simultaneously with competing stimuli to each ear (e.g., the syllable *ga* or the word *dog* to one and *da* or *cat* to the other) and must then report what they hear—in the left ear, in the right ear, or without specifying which. When asked to say what was heard, the listeners more often correctly identify the sound that came via the right ear.

This is known as the *right ear advantage* for linguistic sounds. The process involved is best understood with the help of the accompanying illustration.

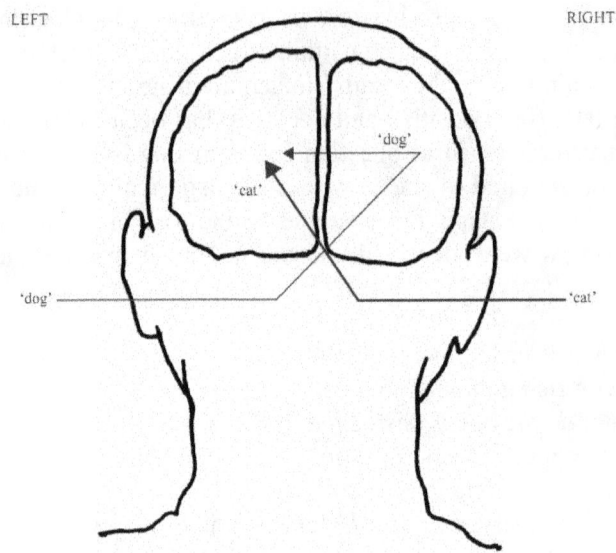

In this process, the language signal received through the left ear is first sent to the right hemisphere and then has to be sent to the left hemisphere (language center) for processing. This non-direct route takes longer than a linguistic signal received through the right ear and going directly to the left hemisphere. First signal to get processed wins.

The right hemisphere appears to have primary responsibility for processing a lot of other incoming signals that are non-linguistic. In the dichotic listening test, it can be shown that non-verbal sounds (e.g. music, coughs, traffic noises, birds singing) are recognized more often via the left ear, meaning they are processed faster via the right hemisphere. So, among the specializations of the human brain, the right hemisphere is first choice for non-language sounds (among other things) and the left hemisphere specializes in language sounds (among other things too).

These specializations may actually have more to do with the type of processing, rather than the type of material, that is handled best by each of the two hemispheres. The essential distinction seems to be between analytic processing, such as recognizing the smaller details of sounds, words and phrase structures in rapid sequence, done with the 'left brain', and holistic processing, such as identifying more general structures in language and experience, done with the 'right brain'.

📖 Crystal 2008; Yule 2006

difference hypothesis
see DEFICIT HYPOTHESIS

differential localization
a term which refers to the existence of neurobiological differences within the same hemisphere of the brain in bilinguals. It contrasts with **hemispheric differential**. Early studies of BILINGUALISM suggested that a second language is stored differently from the first language. Whereas the latter is (usually) housed in the left hemisphere of the brain, the former was believed to involve both hemispheres. However, later research has shown that there is no clear hemispheric differentiation of the two languages.
 Ellis 2008

Diffusion Model
another term for GRADUAL DIFFUSION MODEL

diglossia
a term which refers to a situation where two very different varieties of a language co-occur throughout a speech community, each with a distinct range of social function. Both varieties are standardized to some degree, are felt to be alternatives by native-speakers and usually have special names. Sociolinguists usually talk in terms of a high (H) variety and a low (L) variety, corresponding broadly to a difference in formality: the high variety is learned in school and tends to be used in church, on radio programs, in serious literature, etc., and as a consequence has greater social prestige; the low variety tends to be used in family conversations, and other relatively informal settings. Diglossic situations may be found, for example, in Greek (High: Katharevousa; Low: Dhimotiki), Arabic (High: Classical; Low: Colloquial), and some varieties of German (H: Hochdeutsch; L: Schweizerdeutsch, in Switzerland). A situation where three varieties or languages are used with distinct functions within a community is called **triglossia**. An example of a triglossic situation is the use of French, Classical Arabic and Colloquial Tunisian Arabic in Tunisia, the first two being rated H and the last L.

In terms of language acquisition, children in diglossic situations may encounter reading difficulties. For example, in some Arabic-speaking countries, the local dialect and literary Arabic, and the language of school books and instruction, differ greatly.
 Crystal 2008; Macaro et al. 2010

Direct Contrast Hypothesis
a hypothesis proposed by Saxton which is defined within the context of child language acquisition. According to Direct Contrast Hypothesis, when the child produces an utterance containing an erroneous form, which is responded to immediately with an utterance containing the correct adult alternative

to the erroneous form (i.e., when NEGATIVE EVIDENCE is supplied), the child may perceive the adult form as being in contrast with the equivalent child form. Cognizance of a relevant contrast can then form the basis for perceiving the adult form as a correct alternative to the child form. An example will make this clear.

Child: I thought they were all womans
Adult: They're not all women

It is suggested that this exchange can provide two bits of information which are important as a child learns correct forms: the appropriate grammatical form and the potential ungrammaticality of his own form.

The fact that a correct and an incorrect form are adjacent is important in creating a conflict for the learner. The mere fact of a contrast or a conflict draws a learner's attention to a deviant form, thereby highlighting the contrast through RECASTs or negotiation work. Saxton specifically tested two competing hypotheses, one based on NATIVISM and one relying on *contrast theory*. The nativist hypothesis suggests that negative evidence, even when occurring adjacent to a child error, is no more effective than POSITIVE EVIDENCE in bringing about language change, whereas the contrast theory-based hypothesis suggests that the former is more effective than the latter. Saxton's research with children suggested that contrast theory was a more reliable predictor; that is, children reproduced correct forms more frequently when the correct form was embedded in negative evidence than in positive evidence.

The important point for SLA literature reported on earlier is to ensure that correct forms as a result or contrast not be limited to immediate responses. Long-term effectiveness must be ensured in order to claim that there is validity to this approach.

This is not unlike what has been dealt with in the SLA literature under the rubric of 'noticing the gap'—that is, noticing where learner production differs from target language forms. Conversation provides the means for the contrasts to become apparent. The immediate juxtaposition of correct and erroneous forms may lead learners to recognize that their form is in fact erroneous. However, many questions remain. What is the function of WORKING MEMORY? What happens when learners take the next step, which (at least in the case of syntax or morphosyntax) will undoubtedly involve some sort of analysis? Contrasts occurring within the context of conversation often do not have an immediate outcome. Research has not yet been successful at predicting when a single exposure—for example, through a negotiation sequence or a recast—will or will not suffice to effect immediate learning.

📖 Doughty 2003; Gass & Selinker 2008; Saxton 1997, 2000

direct negative evidence
see NEGATIVE EVIDENCE

direct strategies
see LEARNING STRATEGIES

discontinuity hypothesis
see BABBLING

discourse competence
see COMMUNICATIVE COMPETENCE

Down's Syndrome
also **DS**
Studies of Down's Syndrome suggest a connection between cognitive impairment and failure to acquire full linguistic competence. Down's sufferers show limitations of attention, short-term memory and perceptual discrimination; they also have difficulty with symbolic representation of any kind. All of this appears to affect language performance, though there is great variation between individuals. Phonological development is slow. Only a limited vocabulary is acquired, and utterances usually remain short and 'telegraphic' (see TELEGRAPHIC SPEECH). There has been much discussion as to whether language development in Down's sufferers is different in kind from that of unaffected children or simply delayed. The issue is hard to resolve because of the wide differences in individual performance, and because a delay in one area of language (say, a limited vocabulary) might well affect the course of another (say, length of utterance).
see WILLIAMS SYNDROME, SAVANT, SPECIFIC LANGUAGE IMPAIRMENT
Crystal & Varley 1999; Field 2004

DS
an abbreviation for DOWN'S SYNDROME

DTC
an abbreviation for DERIVATIONAL THEORY OF COMPLEXITY

dual access view
a view advanced by Felix according to which adults have continued access to UNIVERSAL GRAMMAR (UG) but also make use of a general problem solving module, which competes with the language specific system. Felix claims that the problem-solving system is a fundamentally inadequate tool to process structures beyond a certain elementary level and that this account for why adults fail to attain native-speaker levels of competence. Thus, when learners reach the *Piagetian stage of formal operations* (see COGNITIVE DEVELOPMENT) at the onset of puberty, they develop the ability to form hypotheses about abstract phenomena. They are now able to call on two distinct and autonomous cognitive systems to deal with abstract linguistic information.

Adult learners are unable to suppress the operation of the problem-solving module. This interferes with UG, which alone is capable of ensuring complete GRAMMATICAL COMPETENCE. This position assumes that adult learners can only be fully successful providing they rely on UG.
see also PARTIAL ACCESS VIEW, COMPLETE ACCESS VIEW, NO ACCESS VIEW
 Ellis 1997, 2008; Felix 1985

dual language education
a term which refers to a bilingual *minority* IMMERSION PROGRAM. It is common in the United States. There has been considerable opposition to bilingual programs for linguistic minorities, as reflected in the Official English Movement—the attempt to have English designated as the official language of the United States and to ensure that educational resources are directed towards teaching English rather than some other language. It is argued that the debate has centered on two arguments, both of which are mistaken. Supporters of minority bilingual programs have advanced the 'linguistic mismatch' argument, according to which minority children will be retarded academically if they are required to learn exclusively through the L2. This is mistaken because the French Canadian immersion programs have shown conclusively that early instruction through the medium of the L2 has no negative effects. Critics of bilingual immersion programs have also advanced the 'maximum exposure' argument, according to which bilingual education is detrimental because it deprives learners of the exposure to the L2 necessary for successful acquisition. This is refuted by programs which show that minority children who spend less time on English while they are developing L1 literacy skills ultimately do just as well in L2 academic skills as those who are educated exclusively thorough the L2. It is argued that minority programs that are designed in such a way that they reflect the INTERDEPENDENCY PRINCIPLE and the comprehensible input hypothesis (see INPUT HYPOTHESIS) have been shown to be successful. However, it is argued that the success of minority immersion programs also depends on changing the sociocultural fabric of the school.
see also SUBMERSION, MOTHER TONGUE MAINTENANCE, SEGREGATION
 Cummins 1988; Ellis 1997, 2008; Genesee 1987

Dual-Mechanism Model
a model according to which computation of regular morphological features such as past tense *-ed* in English involves rule-based or symbolic processing, whereas irregular features such as irregular past tense forms like *swam* are stored as items.
see also DUAL-MODE SYSTEM
 Ellis 2008; Pinker 1999

dual-mode system
a model of L2 knowledge proposed by Skehan that a person's knowledge of language (first or second) is comprised of two distinct system—a *rule-based system* and a *memory-based system*, where exemplars are stored. This view corresponds to that of DUAL-MECHANISM MODEL. It is argued that much of language is *exemplar* rather than *rule-based*, reflecting the claims of **Construction Grammar** (a claim that grammar is represented in the mind as a set of items and, possibly also, ready-made patterns that are required from the INPUT on the basis of their frequency). An implication of this position is that linguistic memory is not compact and efficiently organized but rather large and highly redundant, with multiple representations of the same item in what Skehan called 'item bundles'. Memory is organized in this way for convenience of use. That is, speaking (and, one might add, probably also rapid writing) is possible because of the way language is represented. Learners are able to draw on their exemplar-based system to obtain quick and easy access to the linguistic means needed to construct a phonetic plan. It is for this reason that speakers need to acquire a solid repertoire of formulaic chunks. Skehan's position echoes instance-based theories of fluency, which claim that fluent speech is not based on the rapid computation of rules but on the retrieval of ready-made exemplars that require minimal processing capacity because they are accessed as wholes. According to this view, then, language must be represented as an exemplar-based system because, if it was not, normal fluent speech would be impossible.

However, a memory-based system is limited and not all language use involves real-time processing. There are times when language users need to formulate precise and novel propositions. This requires a rule-based system and, when users are not under pressure to perform rapidly online, they have the time to access such a system. A rule-based system makes creativity and flexibility in what is said possible. Another advantage of such a system is its parsimony. It consists of a finite set of representations that can fit into a small memory space.

Thus, according to Skehan, two system co-exist, the rule-based analytic, on the one hand, and the formulaic, exemplar-based on the other hand. The rule-based system consists of powerful 'generative rules' and is required to compute well-formed sentences. The exemplar-based system is capacious, with the contents organized in accordance with the 'idiom principle', and is required for fast, fluent language use. It is argued that language users can move between these systems, and do so quite naturally.

see also BIALYSTOK'S THEORY OF L2 LEARNING, MONITOR THEORY, EXPLICIT LEARNING, IMPLICIT LEARNING, EXPLICIT KNOWLEDGE, IMPLICIT KNOWLEDGE, INTENTIONAL LEARNING, INTENTIONAL LEARNING, SOCIO-PSYCHOLINGUISTIC MODEL, VARIABLE COMPETENCE MODEL, CAPABILITY CONTINUUM PARADIGM
 Ellis 2008; Skehan 1998b

dual-route model
the hypothesis that the reader of an alphabetic language has two ways of matching the form of a word on the page to a mental representation. The first (the *lexical route*) seeks a match for the word as a whole; the second (the *sub-lexical route*) interprets the letters phonologically, by means of *grapheme-phoneme correspondence* (GPC) rules. In normal reading, the lexical route is faster and more efficient; but it is argued that readers need the sub-lexical route when encountering a word which they have not seen before in written form, an unusual proper noun, a neologism, a non-word, etc.

The dual-route model faces problems in situations where a sequence of letters permits of more than one interpretation. The model assumes that the sub-lexical route offers access to standard GPC rules, while the lexical route handles 'exception' words. On this analysis, a reader would take the same time to identify *gope* as a non-word as to identify *heaf*. However, *neighborhood* effects are found to apply. Words like *gope* with only 'friends' (*hope, rope*) are identified faster than those like *heaf* with 'enemies' (*leaf* vs. *deaf*). One solution to this is found in analogy theory which suggests that words are interpreted phonologically by analogy with others, perhaps mainly on the basis of their rime. Another is to assume that the sub-lexical route contains information on all possible interpretations of a particular letter or digraph (*-ea-* being recognized as potentially both /i:/ and /e/); hence the slower reaction time.

The strongest evidence supporting a dual route model comes from studies of acquired DYSLEXIA. One type, *surface dyslexia*, seems to involve impairment of the lexical route but permits use of the sub-lexical. Subjects thus regularize irregular words. A second type, *phonological dyslexia*, seems to involve an intact lexical route but an impaired sub-lexical one. The subjects can pronounce familiar words, both regular and irregular, but are incapable of suggesting pronunciations for non-words.

The extent to which the sub-lexical route is employed may vary from language to language. A relatively *opaque* orthography like the English one may involve greater dependence upon the lexical route than the *transparent* orthography of Spanish. However, there is some evidence from Spanish dyslexics of semantic exchanges (when a word like *ape* is read as *monkey*); this suggests that both whole-word and phonological routes are employed.
 📖 Balota 1994; Field 2004; Harris & Coltheart 1986

dysfluency
in speech-language pathology, widely used as a synonym for 'stuttering.' As such, it denotes a situation-specific speech production disorder in which fluency of speech is disrupted by a lack of motor co-ordination in the muscles involved in articulation, phonation, or respiration. Two symptoms are generally distinguished: (a) tonic dysfluency (stuttering), characterized by interruptions in articulatory movements due to a spasm in the articulatory mus-

cles; and (b) clonic dysfluency (stammering) due to a quick sequence of contractions of the speech muscles that causes repetitions of sounds, syllables, or words. Both symptoms can occur isolated or combined. Stuttering is more common in male than in female speakers. In North America, stuttering and stammering are not sharply distinguished. The term 'dysfluency' can also be used more generally to refer to any sort of breakdown in speech fluency, such as cluttering.
 Bussmann 1996

dyslexia
 a certain disability affecting reading and writing. Strictly, dyslexia (often informally called *word blindness*) is a disability with reading, while the related disability with writing is *dysgraphia*, but the two very commonly occur together. (The terms *alexia* and *agraphia* are often preferred in North America.) A sufferer has difficulty in perceiving a printed page: the words on the page often appear distorted, as though viewed through a misshapen lens; both the order and the shapes of the letters may be perceived wrongly. Similar problems affect writing: letters may be put down in the wrong order or turned upside-down or backwards. Both in reading and in writing, mirror-image letters like *b, d, g* and *q* may be confused. In more severe cases, called *deep dyslexia*, words may be confused with totally unrelated words, even those of very different appearance, which are somehow similar in sound, meaning or grammatical class: for example, *saw* with *was*, *dinner* with *food*, *rib* with *ride*, *bun* with *cake*, *saucer* with *sausage*, *for* with *and*.
As is usual with disabilities, individual sufferers vary significantly in the particular symptoms they exhibit, but specialists have nonetheless identified certain recurring patterns of disability and given them names. Also, as with other disabilities, dyslexia and dysgraphia may be present from early childhood in children showing no sign of brain damage, or they may be acquired in adulthood as a result of brain damage; the two cases are called *developmental dyslexia* and *acquired dyslexia*, respectively. The former belief that dyslexia could be traced to a single uniform cause is now known to be false: dyslexia can in fact result from any of a number of different causes, and many specialists suspect that any given case of dyslexia probably results from the interaction of several distinct factors.
Dyslexia is very commonly accompanied by some detectable degree of other types of language disability. In addition, there is evidence that it tends to be accompanied by certain non-linguistic features, such as poor or mixed handedness, poor short-term memory, clumsiness, and a poor sense of direction, including left—right confusion, though no single sufferer ever exhibits all of these traits.
Individuals with the milder kinds of dyslexia, especially the developmental kind, can often overcome their handicap and make successful careers in

business, politics, entertainment, academia, or any other kind of work.
📖 Trask 2005

E

EA
an abbreviation for ERROR ANALYSIS

EAL
an abbreviation for ENGLISH AS AN ADDITIONAL LANGUAGE

early bilingual
also ascribed bilingual
one who learns more than one language prior to the age of 4, that is, prior to the (relatively) complete acquisition of another language. (Children are said to have native-like competence in most formal areas of language by the age of 5.) Early BILINGUALISM may be complete or not; that is, early bilinguals may possess strong knowledge and skills in two languages or may possess strong knowledge and skill in only one language. Early bilinguals may or may not belong to a larger speech community in which two languages are spoken. A child born in Barcelona may grow up speaking Spanish and Catalan where both languages are spoken in the community. A child born in Lubbock, Texas, with Spanish speaking parents may learn Spanish at home, but English would be the language spoken in the larger community. 'Heritage speakers' (see HERITAGE LANGUAGE) is another term for these latter early bilinguals.

In contrast, **late bilingual** (also called **achieved bilingual**) are those who acquire a second language after a first language is already in place; although in practice late bilingualism refers to people who acquire a second language after childhood. Thus, SLA is a type of bilingualism. It does not matter whether a late bilingual receives instruction or not, and like early bilinguals, late bilinguals may possess strong knowledge/skills in two languages or not. In both early and late bilingualism, however, most people are dominant in one language. Even if a person seems relatively fluent in two languages, most likely that person will exhibit dominance in one language in either overt or subtle ways. For example, the person may have a larger vocabulary in one language as opposed to another, or greater facility with rhetoric and discourse. A person may be better with language A in one kind of context (e.g., science) but better with language B in another context (e.g., interpersonal communication).

see also COMPOUND BILINGUALISM, ADDITIVE BILINGUALISM SIMULTANEOUS BILINGUALISM, BALANCED BILINGUALISM
📖 VanPatten & Benati 2010

echoic memory
see SENSORY MEMORY

Ecological Validity Hypothesis
see COMPETITION MODEL

EFL
an abbreviation for ENGLISH AS A FOREIGN LANGUAGE

egocentric speech
in child language acquisition, speech which does not take into account the needs of the listener, but is used for such purposes as self-expression and language play. The notion was introduced by Swiss psychologist Jean Piaget and elaborated by Russian psychologist Lev Vygotsky as part of a basic classification of types of speech observed in young children; it contrasts with the *socialized speech* which is used for communication with others.
📖 Crystal 2008

elaborative simplification
see RESTRICTIVE SIMPLIFICATION

E-language
an abbreviation for EXTERNALIZED LANGUAGE

emergentism
an approach in psycholinguistics which posits an interaction between biological (see NATIVISM) and environmental (see EMPIRICISM) processes in language acquisition, and provides an alternative to earlier theories which focused exclusively on one set of factors (e.g., innateness, cognition, INPUT). Acquisition is seen to be the result of both innate constraints and environmental input, which dynamically interact to yield language. For example, the child's early guesses about word meaning are viewed as the result of an interaction between parental input, the child's cognitive awareness, and the way information is stored and retrieved in the child's brain. There is particular interest in the ways higher-order structures emerge from lower-order interactions ('upward causation') and the ways higher-order interactions can affect lower levels ('downward causation').
In emergentist accounts of language acquisition, knowledge is not seen as rules, nor is there any distinction drawn between DECLARATIVE and PROCEDURAL KNOWLEDGE. Probably the most influential emergentist model in SLA

is CONNECTIONISM, which affords a unified model of cognition, straddling the traditional competence/performance distinction. The COMPETITION MODEL is another emergentist theory of L2 acquisition and is entirely compatible with connectionist theory.
see also SOCIO-EDUCATIONAL MODEL, SOCIOCULTURAL THEORY
📖 Crystal 2008; Ellis 2008

empathy
the process of putting yourself into someone else's shoes, of reaching beyond the self to understand what another person is feeling. It is probably the major factor in the harmonious coexistence of individuals in society. Language is one of the primary means of empathizing, but nonverbal communication facilitates the process of empathizing and must not be overlooked. In more sophisticated terms, empathy is usually described as the projection of one's own personality into the personality of others in order to understand them better. Empathy is not synonymous with **sympathy**. Empathy implies more possibility of detachment; sympathy connotes an agreement or harmony between individuals. Guiora et al. defined empathy as a process of comprehending in which a temporary fusion of self-object boundaries permits an immediate emotional apprehension of the affective experience of another. Psychologists generally agree with Guiora's definition and add that there are two necessary aspects to the development and exercising of empathy: first, an awareness and knowledge of one's own feelings, and second, identification with another person. In other words, you cannot fully empathize—or know someone else—until you adequately know yourself.
Communication requires a sophisticated degree of empathy. In order to communicate effectively, a learner needs to be able to understand the other person's affective and cognitive states; communication breaks down when false presuppositions or assumptions are made about the other person's state. From the very mechanical, syntactic level of language to the most abstract, meaningful level, learners assume certain structures of knowledge and certain emotional states in any communicative act. In order to make those assumptions correctly, they need to transcend their own ego boundaries, or to 'permeate' their ego boundaries so that they can send and receive messages clearly.
Oral communication is a case in which, cognitively at least, it is easy to achieve empathetic communication because there is immediate feedback from the hearer. A misunderstood word, phrase, or idea can be questioned by the hearer and then rephrased by the speaker until a clear message is interpreted. Written communication requires a special kind of empathy—a 'cognitive' empathy in which the writer, without the benefit of immediate feedback from the reader, must communicate ideas by means of a very clear empathetic intuition and judgment of the reader's state of mind and structure of knowledge.

Thus, in a second language learning situation, the problem of empathy becomes acute. Not only must learner-speakers correctly identify cognitive and affective sets in the hearer, but they must do so in a language in which they are insecure. Then, learner-hearers, attempting to comprehend a second language, often discover that their own states of thought are misinterpreted by a native speaker, and the result is that linguistic, cognitive, and affective information easily passes in one ear and out the other.

see also SELF-ESTEEM, INHIBITION, ANXIETY, RISK TAKING, WILLINGNESS TO COMMUNICATE, MOTIVATION, ATTRIBUTION THEORY

📖 Brown 2007; Guiora et al. 1972b; Hogan 1969

empiricism

an application in linguistics of the general sense of this term in philosophy to refer to a view of language, and especially of language acquisition, in which sense experience is seen as the ultimate source of learning. It is opposed to **rationalism**, which asserts that knowledge about language can derive from sources other than sense experience (see INNATENESS HYPOTHESIS). In empiricism, language acquisition is seen as a process of generalization from experience; in rationalism, it results from maturation of a language faculty (organ) governed by various innate principles.

see also BEHAVIORISM, EMERGENTISM, MENTALISM

📖 Crystal 2008

English as a foreign language

see ENGLISH AS A SECOND LANGUAGE

English as an additional language

also **EAL**

a term typically used to identify school-aged students who come from a home linguistic background that is not English but who are being educated in English schools (i.e., in communities where English is the language spoken and used by the majority of the population). The term English as an additional language (EAL) is analogous to the term 'English Language Learners' (ELLs) which is the term used in North America. EAL learners typically tend to be a heterogeneous group, coming from a range of different language backgrounds, cultures and socio-economic status bands. While some EAL learners go on to excel academically and become highly proficient in their two languages (home language and English), on the whole, EAL children tend to lag behind their native English-speaking peers on a range of academic and linguistic achievements. A range of factors have been identified as contributing to the success EAL (ELL) students have at both learning English and achieving expected-level performance on academic outcomes. These variables include the level of literacy development in the home language, and the level of education and socio-economic status of the caregivers (par-

ents) of the EAL (ELL) child. Additionally, the quality of the educational experience and the kind of educational program the EAL (ELL) child receives has also been shown to play a significant role in how successfully the EAL (ELL) child is able to learn English and perform at the expected level academically.
📖 August & Shanahan 2008; Genesee et al. 2006; Macaro et al. 2010

English as a Second Language
also **ESL**

a basic term with several somewhat different definitions. In a loose sense, English is the second language of anyone who learns it after learning their first language in infancy in the home. Using the term this way, no distinction is made between second language, third language, etc. However, English as a second language is often contrasted with **English as a foreign language** (also called **EFL**). Someone who learns English in a formal classroom setting, with limited or no opportunities for use outside the classroom, in a country in which English does not play an important role in internal communication (China, Japan, and Korea, for example), is said to be learning English as a foreign language. Someone who learns English in a setting in which the language is necessary for everyday life (for example, an immigrant learning English in the US) or in a country in which English plays an important role in education, business, and government (for example in Singapore, the Philippines, India, and Nigeria) is learning English as a second language.

Two global developments, however, mitigate the clarity of identifying a simple EFL context: (1) The current trend toward immigrant communities establishing themselves within various countries (e.g., Spanish or Chinese or Russian communities in a large city in the United States) provides ready access to users of so-called foreign languages. (2) In the case of English, the penetration of English-based media (especially television, the Internet, and the motion picture industry) provides further ready access to English even in somewhat isolated settings.

The problem with the ESI/EFL terminology is that it seems to have created a worldview that being a native speaker of English will somehow bestow on people not only unquestionable competence in the use and teaching of the language but also expertise in telling others how English ought to be taught. Native-speaker models do not necessarily exemplify the idealized competence that was once claimed for them. The multiplicity of contexts for the use of English worldwide demands a careful look at the variables of each situation before making the blanket generalization that one of two possible models, ESL or EFL, applies.

see also FOREIGN LANGUAGE LEARNING
📖 Brown 2007; Nayar 1997; Richards & Schmidt 2010

enriched input

a type of FORM-FOCUSED INSTRUCTION which can take the form of oral or written texts that learners simply listen to or read (i.e., input-flooding) or texts where the target structure has been highlighted in some way (e.g., through the use of underlining or bold print). Three groups of enriched input studies can be identified: (1) studies designed to investigate whether the forms targeted in the enriched input are noticed by learners (see NOTICING HYPOTHESIS), (2) studies designed to investigate whether enriched input promotes acquisition, and (3) studies comparing the effects of enriched input with some other instructional option (see INPUT PROCESSING THEORY).

There is some evidence that enriched input involving either highlighting or orienting learners to attend to form induces noticing of target features. However, little is yet known about which approach to enrichment works best. There is fairly convincing evidence that enriched input can help L2 learners acquire some new grammatical features and use partially learned features more consistently, although it may not enable learners to eradicate erroneous rules from their INTERLANGUAGE. Also, clear positive effects may only be evident when the treatment provides learners with extensive exposure to the target features and is relatively prolonged.

see also CONSCIOUSNESS RAISING, INPUT ENHANCEMENT
  Ellis 2008

entrenchment

linguistic forms, including INTERLANGUAGE forms, that are in constant use become entrenched in the learners' interlanguage system. One source of entrenchment is the learner's L1. Entrenchment is a feature of FOSSILIZATION.
  Ellis 2008

equilibration

progressive interior organization of knowledge in a stepwise fashion, and is related to the concept of *equilibrium*. That is, COGNITION develops as a process of moving from states of doubt and uncertainty (disequilibrium) to stages of resolution and certainty (equilibrium) and then back to further doubt that is, in time, also resolved. And so the cycle continues. Piaget claimed that conceptual development is a process of progressively moving from states of disequilibrium to equilibrium and that periods of disequilibrium mark virtually all cognitive development up through age 14 or 15, when *formal operations* (see COGNITIVE DEVELOPMENT) finally are firmly organized and equilibrium is reached.

It is conceivable that disequilibrium may provide significant MOTIVATION for language acquisition: language interacts with cognition to achieve equilibrium. Perhaps until that state of final equilibrium is reached, the child is cognitively ready and eager to acquire the language necessary for achieving the cognitive equilibrium of adulthood. That same child was, until that time, de-

creasingly tolerant of cognitive ambiguities. Children are amazingly indifferent to contradictions, but intellectual growth produces an awareness of ambiguities about them and heightens the need for resolution. Perhaps a general intolerance of contradictions produces an acute awareness of the enormous complexities of acquiring an additional language, and so perhaps around the age of 14 or 15, the prospect of learning a second language becomes overwhelming, thus discouraging the learner from proceeding a step at a time as a younger child would do.
📖 Brown 2007; Piaget 1970; Sullivan 1967

equilingualism
see BALANCED BILINGUALISM

equivalence classification
In L2 acquisition some sounds of the new language may sound different from any sound in the L1 or any other language a given speaker may have learned already. In some cases these unfamiliar sounds are substituted in a highly systematic way by sounds from a language acquired before (see TRANSFER), because the former are perceived as equivalent to the latter. For example, speakers of German tend to perceive English /θ/ as [s] or /æ/ as [ɛ]. Equivalence classification denotes the method of classifying sounds as to their equivalencies.
📖 Piske & Young-Scholten 2009

error
the use of a linguistic item (e.g., a word, a grammatical item, a speech act, etc.) in a way which a fluent or native speaker of the language regards as showing faulty or incomplete learning. Errors can be taken as red flags; they provide windows onto a system—that is, evidence of the state of a learner's knowledge of the L2. They are not to be viewed solely as a product of imperfect learning; hence, they are not something for teachers to throw their hands up in the air about. As with research on CHILD LANGUAGE ACQUISITION, it has been found that second language errors are not a reflection of faulty imitation. Rather, they are to be viewed as indications of a learner's attempt to figure out some system, that is, to impose regularity on the language the learner is exposed to. Learners of English who ask *Does John can sing?* are in all likelihood reflecting a competence level in which all verbs require a pre-posed *do* auxiliary for question formation. As such, they are evidence of an underlying rule-governed system.

Error is distinguished from **mistake**, which refers to a performance error that is either a random guess or a slip, in that it is a failure to utilize a known system correctly. All people make mistakes, in both native and second language situations. Native speakers are normally capable of recognizing and correcting such lapses or mistakes, which are not the result of a deficiency in competence but the result of some sort of temporary breakdown or imperfection in the process of producing speech. These hesitations, slips of the tongue, random ungrammaticalities, and other performance lapses in native-speaker production also occur in second language speech. Mistakes, when attention is called to them, can be self-corrected.

The fact that learners do make errors, and that these errors can be observed, analyzed, and classified to reveal something of the system operating within the learner, led to a surge of study of learners' errors, called ERROR ANALYSIS.

📖 Corder 1967; Gass & Selinker 2008; Brown 2007

error analysis
also EA

the study and analysis of the errors made by second language learners. Error analysis (EA) involves a set of procedures for identifying, describing, and explaining language errors made by learners in terms of linguistic level (pronunciation, grammar, lexis, style, etc.) and with attempting to ascribe the causes of errors to particular sources, such as the application of conventions and rules in a learner's mother tongue (i.e., INTERFERENCE) or faulty application of target language rules. According to Corder, errors were seen as evidence of a built-in syllabus significant in three respects: informing the teacher what needed to be taught; providing the researcher with insights into how learning proceeded; and providing the learners with a means of testing their hypotheses about the target language.

There are different typologies of language errors as follows:

- *Surface strategy taxonomy* This taxonomy classifies errors according to the way surface structures are altered:
  - *omission*: skipping an item that is required in a correct utterance (*I went to movie,* definite article *the* omitted).
  - *addition*: adding an item that must not appear in a correct utterance (e.g., *Does can he sing?*).
  - *misinformation*: using the wrong form of a morpheme or structure (*I lost my road,* instead of *way*).
  - *misordering*: the incorrect position of a morpheme in an utterance (e.g., *I to the store went*).
- *Language competency taxonomy* Errors resulting from gaps in language competence can be divided into two types:
  - *overt errors*: an error that is unquestionably ungrammatical at the sentence level; a sentence level error.
  - *covert errors*: an error that is grammatically well formed at the sentence level but not interpretable within the context of communication; a discourse level error.

- Corder distinguished three types of errors according to their relation to the stage of the learner's linguistic development:
  - *presystematic stage*: random errors occur when the learner does not know a particular rule (e.g., *John cans sing*).
  - *systematic stage*: it signals that the learner has discovered a rule which is incorrect. The most salient feature of this stage is that the learners are able to correct their errors when they are pointed out.
  - *postsystematic* (or *stabilization*) *stage*: it signals that the learner knows the correct rule but does not always follow it. This stage is characterized by the learner's ability to self-correct.
- *Error gravity taxonomy* This taxonomy is based on the relative gravity of an error which concerns the seriousness of an error. Error gravity is assessed with reference to such criteria as *intelligibility*, *acceptability*, and *irritation*.
  - **local error** does not prevent a message from being understood, usually due to a minor violation of one segment of a sentence, allowing the hearer/reader to make an accurate guess about the intended meaning. *A scissors*, for example, is a local error.
  - **global error** hinders communication; it prevents the hearer from comprehending some aspect of the message. For example, *Well, it's a great hurry around* in whatever context, may be difficult to interpret.

EA became distinguished from CONTRASTIVE ANALYSIS by its examination of errors attributable to *all* possible sources, not just those resulting from negative transfer (i.e., interference) of the native language. In fact, errors arise from several possible general sources: **interlingual errors**—errors which results from interference from the native language, **intralingual errors**—errors which results from faulty or partial learning of the target language, rather than from language transfer; these errors may be caused by the influence of one target language item upon another. For example, a learner may produce *He is comes*, based on a blend of the English structures *He is coming*, *He comes*), the context of learning (see INDUCED ERROR), the sociolinguistic context of communication, psycholinguistic or cognitive strategies, and no doubt countless affective variables.

EA has made a substantial contribution to SLA research. It served as a tool for providing empirical evidence for the *behaviorist/mentalist* (see BEHAVIORISM, MENTALISM) debates of the 1970s, showing that many of the errors that learners make cannot be put down to interference. It helped to make errors respectable—to force recognition that errors were not something to be avoided but were an inevitable feature of the learning process.

EA lost popularity as a result of its perceived weaknesses. These weaknesses include methodological problems involving all stages of analysis and, also, limitations in the scope of EA. Focusing solely on the errors which learners produce at a single point in time can only provide a partial picture. It takes no account of what learners do correctly, of development over time, and of AVOIDANCE phenomena. However, some work in EA continued and, recently, it has had something of a rebirth with the advent of computer-based analysis of learner language. Also, EA continues to have a role to play in remedial approaches to the teaching of writing.

📖 Brown 2007; Corder 1967, 1973, 1974; Ellis 1994, 2008; Larsen-Freeman 1991; Macaro et al. 2010

error treatment
another term for FEEDBACK

ESL
an abbreviation for ENGLISH AS A SECOND LANGUAGE

ethnic identity
a term that can be viewed from two perspectives. From a structural perspective, ethnic identity is seen as determined by the social contexts in which learners find themselves. From an interactional perspective, ethnic identity is seen as something that is constantly negotiated by learners and as a result is ambivalent, contested, and dynamic.

A number of points about the relationship between ethnic identity and L2 acquisition are highlighted as follows:

- Ethnic identity is both a social and an individual construct and for that reason alone it is of special importance for SLA.
- Acquiring an L2 is likely to involve some change or addition to the learner's sense of identity.
- A change or addition to the learner's identity may involve the learner overcoming a number of social obstacles and the extent to which this is achieved will affect how successfully the L2 acquired.

Research into L2 learners' ethnicity has been informed by normative, social-psychological, socio-structural, and post-structural views of the relationship between ethnicity and L2 acquisition. A *normative view* emphasizes the effect of cultural distance on L2 learning; learners who are close to the target-language culture are likely to outperform those who are more distant.

A *social-psychological model* emphasizes the role of ATTITUDES. In general, learners with positive attitudes towards their own ethnic identity and towards the target culture can be expected to develop a strong MOTIVATION and high levels of L2 proficiency, while also maintaining their own L1. Successful L2 learning is also possible, however, in learners with non-integrative attitudes towards the target culture.

In a *socio-structural model*, attitudes based on learners' sense of ethnic identity influence learning through the interactions in which learners participate. Learners who are status- and person-centered are more likely to converge on L2 norms and therefore more likely to be successful learners than those whose solidarity with their own in-group encourages divergence. This view has been explored within the general theoretical framework of interpersonal accommodation (see ACCOMMODATION THEORY).

A *post-structural model* does not clearly distinguish between ethnic identity and other forms of identity. It views identity as multiple and dynamic; identity and language learning are interrelated, each influencing the other.
see also SOCIAL IDENTITY THEORY
📖 Ellis 2008; Gardner 1985; Gardner & Lambert 1972; Gatbonton et al. 2005; Giles & Johnson 1981; Giles & Ryan 1982; Lambert 1974; Pavlenko 2002; Svanes 1988

ethnography
Literally the word ethnography means the description (*graphy*) of cultures (*ethno*). Ethnography is the in-depth study of naturally occurring behavior within a culture or entire social group. It seeks to understand the relationship between culture and behavior, with culture referring to the shared beliefs, values, concepts, practices, and attitudes of a specific group of people. It examines what people do and interprets why they do it. Ethnographers typically describe, analyze, and interpret culture over time using observations, interviews, questionnaires, and field work as the data collecting strategies. The final product is a *cultural portrait* that incorporates the views of participants as well as views of researcher. Ethnographic studies consider where people are situated and how they go about daily activities as well as cultural beliefs. Because of the increasingly situated nature of much recent SLA research, ethnography has been utilized for the contextualized analysis of classroom discourse and school learning. In studies of language learning and use, the term ethnographic research is sometimes used to refer to the observation and description of naturally occurring language (e.g., between mother and child or between teacher and students), particularly when there is a strong cultural element to the research or the analysis. However, much of this research is quasi-ethnographic at best, since the requirements of prolonged observation and thick description are frequently not met.
📖 Ellis 2008; Tavakoli 2012a

ethnography of communication
also ethnography of speaking
the study of the norms of communication in a speech community, including verbal, non-verbal and social factors. Ethnography of communication has its origin in anthropology and, in particular, in the work of Dell Hymes. It relates language use to broader social and cultural contexts, and applies ethno-

graphic methods of data collection and interpretation to study of language acquisition and use.

Every society has its own norms for communicative behavior. If you are sitting at the dinner table and you want the salt, which is out of reach, you might say *Would you mind very much passing me the salt?* or *Could you pass the salt, please?* or *Gimme that salt*; you might even say nothing, but just reach over the person next to you to grab the salt. Some of these behaviors are more acceptable than others, depending on the circumstances, and some would perhaps never be acceptable at all.

The key point is that the norms are not everywhere the same; instead, they vary substantially from culture to culture. In a traditional Basque household, the master of the house may indicate that he wants his wine glass refilled simply by banging it, without saying a word; this would probably never be acceptable in an English-speaking society (nor is it normal among younger Basques).

Anthropological linguists have long stressed the importance of examining communicative behavior in the context of a culture. Investigators have looked at a broad range of variables in a number of speech communities: loudness of voice, pitch of voice, distance between speakers, expressions and postures, eye contact, terms of address, rules for initiating conversations, and many others.

Mexicans in conversation prefer to stand much closer together than do Americans, which can lead to comical results when a Mexican is talking to an American. English-speakers who meet each other but have nothing in particular to say will begin talking about the weather, since silence is considered unacceptable; but Chinese-speakers in the same position may choose to remain silent without giving offence. In Japanese and in Javanese, even the simplest utterance may assume any of a number of very different forms, depending on the relative status of the speaker, the addressee and the person being talked about, and also on the circumstances in which the conversation takes place. Italians punctuate their speech with animated gesticulations; Swedes do not. In the British House of Commons, it is considered technically improper for one MP to address another directly, and hence all speeches and remarks are formally directed at the Speaker.

The ethnography of communication differs from CONVERSATIONAL ANALYSIS in that it looks for strategies and conventions governing larger units of communication and involves more holistic interpretation.

The ethnographic tradition has been particularly evident in research into bilingual classrooms or mainstream classrooms containing L2 learners. Such research has three advantages: (1) it can account for learners who do not participate actively in class, (2) it can provide insights into the conscious thought processes of participants, and (3) it helps to identify variables which have not previously been acknowledged. Many of the disadvantages noted

for conversational analysis also apply to ethnography of communication. In particular, studies in this tradition have not typically shown how the interactional opportunities afforded a learner in a classroom contribute to learning.
 Ellis 2008; Gaies 1983; Hymes 1966, 1974; Saville-Troike 1996, 2006; Trask 2005

ethnography of speaking
another term for ETHNOGRAPHY OF COMMUNICATION

ethnolinguistic identity theory
a theory which addresses how people from different ethnic groups communicate with each other. It is proposed that the members of an in-group may or may not adopt positive linguistic distinctiveness strategies when communicating with members of an out-group.
see also ACCOMMODATION THEORY, ETHNIC IDENTITY, SOCIAL IDENTITY THEORY
 Ellis 2008; Giles and Jonson 1981

event probabilities
the likelihood that a situation occurs under one condition as opposed to another. In terms of verbs and events expressed by verbs, the likelihood that one noun as opposed to another represents the agent of the action. For the verb *correct* and the nouns *teacher* and *student*, either teacher or student can correct the other, but it is more likely that teachers correct students than the other way around. Thus, teachers correcting students has a higher event probability than students correcting teachers.
 Piske & Young-Scholten 2009

explanatory adequacy
see GENERATIVE THEORY

explicit feedback
see FEEDBACK

explicit instruction
see FORM-FOCUSED INSTRUCTION

explicit knowledge
the knowledge of rules and items that exists in an analyzed form so that learners are able to report what they know. Explicit knowledge is conscious, declarative, anomalous, and inconsistent (i.e., it takes the form of 'fuzzy' rules inconsistently applied) and generally only accessible through controlled processing in planned language use. It is verbalizable, in which case it entails semi-technical or technical metalanguage. Like any type of factual knowledge, it is potentially learnable at any age.

Explicit knowledge is closely linked to *multilingual knowledge*. Explicit knowledge has given rise to considerable theorizing as to the nature of its construct, its measurement and its role in language learning. It is generally accepted that the explicit knowledge of an L2 that a learner has is accessible in WORKING MEMORY and is knowledge of which the learner is consciously aware and can articulate. This does not mean that explicit knowledge is necessarily correct. It is argued that explicit knowledge takes place on two planes: the breadth of facts a learner has about language and the depth of refinement about each of those facts. Thus, an L2 learner may be able to articulate a number of rules of English but at a superficial or unsophisticated level. It is also hypothesized that explicit knowledge is stored in *declarative* LONG-TERM MEMORY but the nature of that storage is as yet unclear. Moreover, its relationship with IMPLICIT KNOWLEDGE (that which can be articulated 'by feel' as in 'that feels right to me') remains an area for investigation. It is likely that a learner will resort to explicit knowledge when 'feel' proves insufficient to accomplish a language task and that a learner will draw more on implicit knowledge when examining a grammatical sentence and on explicit knowledge when examining an ungrammatical one. A variety of *grammaticality judgment* tests have been used to measure and distinguish explicit knowledge, and it is believed that the less time a participant has to judge the correctness of a sentence the less likely he is to be using explicit knowledge. A number of studies have shown that correctness is not necessarily dependent on explicit knowledge. However, the evidence suggests that explicit knowledge gives, as it were, added value in a variety of language tasks where some reflection is possible.

see also MONITOR THEORY, ADAPTIVE CONTROL OF THOUGHT MODEL, INFORMATION-PROCESSING MODEL, DUAL-MODE SYSTEM, EXPLICIT LEARNING, IMPLICIT LEARNING, INTENTIONAL LEARNING, INCIDENTAL LEARNING, INTERFACE MODEL, NON-INTERFACE MODEL, WEAK INTERFACE MODEL

📖 Ellis 2004, 2008; Bialystok 1979; Macaro et al. 2010

explicit learning

a conscious process and is also likely to be intentional. Often proposed in contrast to IMPLICIT LEARNING, explicit learning of second language morphosyntactic patterns and the semantic properties of a lexical item entails conscious reflection on that information in its declarative form, for example: in French, some adjectives are placed before a noun but most come after; in some cultures 'pig' has a different meaning to ours; in the present tense 'she' is a subject pronoun which has an effect on the verb's ending. Thus, explicit learning may include the involvement of metalinguistic information. In explicit language learning, a learner arrives at an understanding of a rule through a global explanation involving logical reasoning (deductively), followed by examples which give credence to that explanation.

The term is sometimes wrongly associated with INTENTIONAL LEARNING but there are clear differences in that one may learn something intentionally without it being explicit. An additional complication with this term is that it is sometimes used synonymously with EXPLICIT KNOWLEDGE (that a learner has or demonstrates) but if one adopts the INTERFACE MODEL, then that which has been learned through explicit processes may well become implicit knowledge which may no longer be easily articulated (and vice versa).
see also, IMPLICIT KNOWLEDGE, MONITOR THEORY, ADAPTIVE CONTROL OF THOUGHT MODEL, INFORMATION-PROCESSING MODEL, DUAL-MODE SYSTEM, NON-INTERFACE MODEL, WEAK INTERFACE MODEL
 Macaro et al. 2010

explicit memory
memory that is based on conscious recollections of events and phenomena. Explicit memory houses EXPLICIT KNOWLEDGE. Explicit memory contrasts with **implicit memory**, which is the memory that does not depend on conscious recollections of events and phenomena. It houses IMPLICIT KNOWLEDGE. It is suggested that implicit memory consists of multiple systems rather than a single system. It is possible, therefore, that implicit linguistic knowledge is better conceptualized in terms of separate stores for a perceptual and a conceptual system.
 Ellis 2008; Eysenck 2001

extended core program
a Canadian term for a kind of program that combines traditional Language As Subject (LAS) and a low dose of IMMERSION in a foreign language. Students are introduced to the new language via the core program which is a traditional LAS program. At some point in time the latter is extended by the addition of an immersion component in that some subjects are taught in the new language. Programs comparable to the Canadian extended core model exist in many parts of the world.
 Piske & Young-Scholten 2009

externalized language
see INTERNALIZED LANGUAGE

external variation
see VARIABILITY

extrinsic motivation
see MOTIVATION

extroversion
the extent to which a person has a deep-seated need to receive ego enhance-

ment, self-esteem, and a sense of wholeness from other people, as opposed to receiving that affirmation within oneself, as opposed to **introversion**, which is the extent to which a person derives a sense of wholeness and fulfillment from 'within', apart from a reflection of this self from other people. Extroverts actually need other people in order to feel 'good'. But extroverts are not necessarily loudmouthed and talkative. They may be relatively shy but still need the affirmation of others. Introversion, on the other hand, is the extent to which a person derives a sense of wholeness and fulfillment apart from a reflection of this self from other people. Contrary to our stereotypes, introverts can have an inner strength of character that extroverts do not have. Extroversion is commonly thought to be related to EMPATHY, but such may not be the case. The extroverted person may actually behave in an extroverted manner in order to protect his own ego, with extroverted behavior being symptomatic of defensive barriers and high ego boundaries. At the same time the introverted, quieter, more reserved person may show high empathy—an intuitive understanding and apprehension of others—and simply be more reserved in the outward and overt expression of empathy.

The extent to which individuals verge towards one of these types is usually measured by analyzing responses to self-report questions such as those in the *Eysenck Personality Inventory* or the *Myers-Briggs Type Indicator*.

There are two major hypotheses regarding the relationship between extroversion/introversion and L2 learning. The first—which has been the most widely researched—is that extroverted learners will do better in acquiring BASIC INTERPERSONAL COMMUNICATION SKILLS. The rationale for this hypothesis is that sociability (an essential feature of extroversion) will result in more opportunities to practice, more INPUT, and more success in communicating in the L2. The second hypothesis is that introverted learners will do better at developing COGNITIVE ACADEMIC LANGUAGE PROFICIENCY. The rationale for this hypothesis comes from studies which show that introverted learners typically enjoy more academic success, perhaps because they spend more time reading and writing. There is some support for the first hypothesis. However, not all studies have shown that extraversion is positively related to learners' oral language. The second hypothesis has received less support.

see also SELF-ESTEEM, INHIBITION, ANXIETY, RISK TAKING, WILLINGNESS TO COMMUNICATE, EMPATHY, MOTIVATION, ATTRIBUTION THEORY

📖 Brown 2007; Ellis 2008; Eysenck & Eysenck 1964; Myers & Briggs 1976

F

facilitative anxiety
see ANXIETY

Failed Functional Features Hypothesis
a hypothesis developed by Hawkins and Chan which claims that parameterized functional features (e.g., gender agreement) cannot be acquired after childhood unless they are instantiated in the L1. A key assumption of this hypothesis is that functional categories determine the parametric differences between languages with regard to grammatical features such as inflections on nouns, adjectives, and verbs. A second assumption is that parameterized functional features are subject to a *critical period* (see CRITICAL PERIOD HYPOTHESIS). When this is past, learners no longer have access to the virtual, unspecified features that constitute UNIVERSAL GRAMMAR but only to how these features are encoded in the lexical entries of their L1. These assumptions serve as the basis for claiming that (1) the main difference between L1 and L2 learners lies in the properties of the INPUT that they can assimilate into their mental grammars, and (2) that when the critical period is past learners are unable to assimilate features from the input unless they are also instantiated in some form in their L1. In the case of a grammatical area such as gender agreement, therefore, it follows that adult learners whose L1 lacks gender agreement will experience difficulty in acquiring L2 gender agreement whereas those adult learners whose L1 contains gender agreement will have no such (or less) difficulty.
 Ellis 2008; Hawkins & Chan 1997

FDH
an abbreviation for FUNDAMENTAL DIFFERENCE HYPOTHESIS

FD style
an abbreviation for FIELD DEPENDENCE STYLE

feedback
also **corrective feedback, error treatment**
a general term used in both SLA research and L2 pedagogy for the information that a teacher provides in response to a learner production (spoken or

written) and is most commonly associated with inaccuracy rather than with praising interesting or accurate productions. Feedback can take one of two forms: 'implicit' or 'explicit'. In the case of **implicit feedback** there is no overt indicator that an error has been committed, whereas in **explicit feedback** there is. Clarification requests, confirmation checks, repetitions, and RECASTs occurring during communicative interactions may serve as forms of implicit feedback. Explicit feedback can take several forms: it may draw attention to the *source of problem indicated* (e.g., *Not goed*), where only NEGATIVE EVIDENCE is provided; it may provide *explicit correction* (e.g., *No, we don't say 'goed' in English; we say 'went'*), where the feedback clearly indicates that what the learner has said as incorrect and supplies the correct form, thus providing both negative and POSITIVE EVIDENCE; *elicitation* which refers to at least three techniques that teachers use to directly elicit the correct form from the student. First, teachers elicit completion of their own utterance by strategically pausing to allow students to 'fill in the blank'. Such 'elicit completion' moves may be preceded by some metalinguistic comment such as *No, not that. It's a...* or by a repetition of the error. Second, teachers use questions to elicit correct forms (e.g., *How do we say X in French?*). Such questions exclude the use of yes/no questions: A question such as *Do we say that in French?* is metalinguistic feedback, not elicitation. Third, teachers occasionally ask students to reformulate their utterance; or it may offer **metalinguistic feedback** (e.g., *You need past tense*), defined as comments, information or questions related to the well-formedness of the learner's utterance, which again only provides negative evidence, i.e., there is an error somewhere. Metalinguistic information generally provides either some grammatical metalanguage that refers to the nature of the error (e.g., *It's masculine*) or a word definition in the case of lexical errors. Metalinguistic questions also point to the nature of the error but attempt to elicit the information from the student (e.g., *Is it feminine?*).

It has been proposed that feedback may lead to L2 development through helping to make problematic aspects of learners' INTERLANGUAGE salient and giving them additional opportunities to focus on their production or comprehension, possibly promoting awareness of L1 strategies that do not work in processing the L2. Feedback may also be facilitative of SLA in allowing learners to subdivide complex production tasks into more manageable ones, to the effect that they are able to perform them better than they might have done otherwise.

📖 Ellis 2008; Lyster & Ranta 1997; Macaro et al. 2010; Mackey 2007; VanPatten & Benati 2010

FFI

an abbreviation for FORM-FOCUSED INSTRUCTION

field dependence style
also **FD style**
the tendency to be 'dependent' on the total field so that the parts embedded in the field are not easily perceived, although that total field is perceived more clearly as a unified whole. Field dependence often contrasts with **field independence style** (**FI style**), which refers to ability to perceive a particular, relevant item or factor in a 'field' of distracting items. In general psychological terms, that field may be perceptual, or it may be more abstract and refer to a set of thoughts, ideas, or feelings from which your task is to perceive specific relevant subsets. Field dependence is synonymous with *field sensitivity*, a term that may carry a more positive connotation.

A field independent (FI) style enables you to distinguish parts from a whole, to concentrate on something (like reading a book in a noisy train station), or to analyze separate variables without the contamination of neighboring variables. On the other hand, too much FI may result in cognitive 'tunnel vision': you see only the parts and not their relationship to the whole. 'You cannot see the forest for the trees', as the saying goes. Seen in this light, development of a field dependent (FD) style has positive effects: you perceive the whole picture, the larger view, the general configuration of a problem or idea or event. It is clear, then, that both FI and FD are necessary for most of the cognitive and affective problems we face.

Affectively, persons who are more predominantly FI tend to be generally more independent, competitive, and self-confident. FD persons tend to be more socialized, to derive their self-identity from persons around them, and are usually more empathic and perceptive of the feelings and thoughts of others.

With reference to second language learning, two conflicting hypotheses have emerged. First, we could conclude that FI is closely related to classroom learning that involves analysis, attention to details, and mastering of exercises, drills, and other focused activities. Indeed, research supports such a hypothesis. It was found that FI correlated positively and significantly with language success in the classroom. Some studies found relatively strong evidence in groups of adult second language learners of a relationship between FI and formal measures of language performance, which in some respects require analytical abilities.

The second of the conflicting hypotheses proposes that a FD style will, by virtue of its association with EMPATHY, social outreach, and perception of other people, yield successful learning of the communicative aspects of a second language. While no one denies the plausibility of this second hypothesis, little empirical evidence has been gathered to support it. The principal reason for the dearth of such evidence is the absence of a true test of FD.

The two hypotheses deal with two different kinds of language learning. One kind of learning implies natural, face-to-face communication, the kind of

communication that occurs too rarely in the average language classroom. The second kind of learning involves the familiar classroom activities: drills, exercises, tests, and so forth. It is most likely that 'natural' language learning in the 'field', beyond the constraints of the classroom, is aided by a FD style, and the classroom type of learning is enhanced, conversely, by a FI style.
see also LEFT-BRAIN DOMINANCE, REFLECTIVE STYLE
📖 Brown 2007; Johnson et al. 2000; Hansen 1984; Hansen & Stansfield 1981; Jamieson 1992; Naiman et al.1978; Stansfield & Hansen 1983

field independence style
see FIELD DEPENDENCE STYLE

final state
also **ultimate attainment**
the outcome of L1 or L2 learning. The final state of L1 development is native linguistic competence. While vocabulary learning and cultivation of specialized registers (such as formal academic written style) may continue into adulthood, the basic phonological and grammatical systems of whatever language(s) children hear around them are essentially established by the age of about five or six years, along with vocabulary knowledge and interaction skills that are adequate for fulfilling communicative functions. This is a universal human achievement, requiring no extraordinary aptitude or effort.
On the other hand, the final state of L2 development can never be totally native linguistic competence, and the level of proficiency which learners reach is highly variable. Some learners reach 'near-native' or 'native-like' competence in L2 along with native competence in L1, but many cease at some point to make further progress toward the learning target in response to L2 INPUT, resulting in a final state which still includes instances of L1 interference or creative structures different from any that would be produced by a native speaker of the L2 (a 'frozen' state of progress known as FOSSILIZATION in SLA). The complex of factors which contribute to differential levels of ultimate multilingual development is of major interest for both SLA theory and second language teaching methods.
see also INITIAL STATE, LOGICAL PROBLEM OF LANGUAGE ACQUISITION
📖 Saville-Troike 2006

first language
also **L1**
chronologically the first language acquired by a learner or a person's mother tongue. In multilingual communities, however, where a child may gradually shift from the main use of one language to the main use of another (e.g., because of the influence of a school language), first language may refer to the language the child feels most comfortable using. Often this term is used syn-

onymously with **native language** (**NL**). First language is also known as L1.
📖 Piske & Young-Scholten 2009; Richards & Schmidt 2010

first language acquisition
also **child language acquisition**
the process of learning a native language. It seems that normal children all over the world go through similar stages, use similar constructions in order to express similar meanings, and make the same kinds of errors. The stages of development can be summarized as follows:

Language stage	Beginning age
Crying	Birth
Cooing	6 weeks
Babbling	6 months
Intonation patterns	8 months
One-word utterances	1 year
Two-word utterances	18 months
Word inflections	2 years
Questions, negatives	2 years 3 months
Rare or complex constructions	5 years
Mature speech	10 years

These stages are not language-specific, although their actual realization obviously is.

Similarly, when studying the emergence of a number of structures in English, a consistent order of acquisition was found. Brown's so-called 'morpheme study' is probably the best-known first language study of that time, and was to be very influential for second language acquisition research (see MORPHEME STUDIES, ACQUISITION ORDER). In an in-depth study of three children of different backgrounds, he compared the development of 14 grammatical morphemes in English. Brown found that although the rate at which children learnt these morphemes varied, the order in which they acquired them remained the same for all children, as listed below in a simplified form:

- Present progressive — *boy sing**ing***
- Prepositions — *dolly **in** car*
- Plural — *sweet**ies***
- Past Irregular — ***broke***
- Possessive — *Baby**'s** biscuit*
- Articles — ***a** car*
- Past regular — *want**ed***
- Third person singular — *eat**s***
- Auxiliary *be* — *he **is** running*

What is striking is that, not only do children acquire a number of grammatical morphemes in a fixed order, but they also follow fairly rigid stages during the acquisition of a given area of grammar. For example, children all over the world not only acquire negatives around the same age, but they also mark the negative in similar ways in all languages, by initially attaching some negative marker to the outside of the sentence: *no go to bed, pas faut boire* (= not need drinking), etc., and gradually moving the negative marker inside the sentence, following the stages exemplified below for English:

- Stage 1: Negative utterances consist of a 'nucleus' (i.e., the positive proposition) either preceded or followed by a negator.

  wear mitten no
  no mitten
  no sit there
  not a teddy bear

- Stage 2: Negators are now incorporated into affirmative clauses. Negators at this stage include *don't* and *can't*, used as unitary items, and with *no* and *not*, are increasingly used in front of the verb rather than at the beginning of the sentence. Negative commands also appear.

  there no squirrels
  you can't dance
  don't bite me yet
  He no bite you

- Stage 3: Negators are now always incorporated into affirmative clauses. Other auxiliary forms such as *didn't* and *won't* appear while the typical stage 1 forms disappear. The 'Auxiliary + not' rule has been acquired, as *don't, can't*, etc., are now analyzed. But some mistakes still occur (e.g., copula *be* is omitted from negative utterances and double negatives occur). A very late acquisition is the negative form *isn't*, with the result that some stage 2 forms (with *not* instead of *isn't*) continue to be used for quite a long time.

  I don't have a book
  I didn't caught it
  She won't let go
  Paul can't have one
  I not crying
  no one didn't come
  This not ice cream

These developmental sequences are not unlike the stages followed by second language learners. The study of the developing use of negative forms has produced some delightful examples of children operating their own rules for negative sentences. One famous example also shows the futility of overt adult 'correction' of children's speech.

CHILD: *Nobody don't like me.*
MOTHER: *No, say 'nobody likes me'.*
CHILD: *Nobody don't like me.*
(Eight repetitions of this dialog)
MOTHER: *No, now listen carefully; say 'nobody likes me'.*
CHILD: *Oh! Nobody don't likes me.*

Similar phenomena can be observed for the acquisition of interrogatives and other structures. For example, in forming questions, the child's first stage has two procedures. Simply add a Wh-form (e.g., Where, Who) to the beginning of the expression or utter the expression with a rise in intonation towards the end, as in these examples:

Where kitty?
Doggie?
Where horse go?
Sit chair?

In the second stage, more complex expressions can be formed, but the rising intonation strategy continues to be used. It is noticeable that more Wh-forms come into use, as in these examples:

What book name?
You want eat?
Why you smiling?
See my doggie?

In the third stage, the required inversion of subject and verb in English questions appears (*I can go* → *Can I go?*), but the Wh-questions do not always undergo the required inversion. In fact, children beginning school in their fifth year may still prefer to form Wh-questions (especially with negatives) without the type of inversion found in adult speech. Apart from the occasional lack of inversion and continuing trouble with the morphology of verbs, stage 3 questions are generally quite close to the adult model, as in these examples:

Can I have a piece?
Did I caught it?
Will you help me?
How that opened?
What did you do?
Why kitty can't stand up?

Another important characteristic of child language is that it is rule-governed, even if initially the rules children create do not correspond to adult ones. As early as the two-word stage, children express relationships between elements in a sentence, such as possession, negation or location, in a consistent way. Also, it has been demonstrated convincingly that when children produce an adult-like form which is the result of the application of a rule, such as for example adding *-s* to dog in order to produce the plural form dogs, they are not merely imitating and repeating parrot-fashion the adult language around them.
From the account of first language acquisition research, the following characteristics emerge:

- children go through stages
- these stages are very similar across children for a given language, although the rate at which individual children progress through them is highly variable
- these stages are similar across languages
- child language is rule-governed and systematic, and the rules created by the child do not necessarily correspond to adult ones
- children are resistant to correction
- children's processing capacity limits the number of rules they can apply at any one time, and they will revert to earlier hypotheses when two or more rules compete.

see also COOING, BABBLING, ONE-WORD STAGE, TWO-WORD STAGE, TELEGRAPHIC SPEECH
 Aitchison 1989; Berko 1958; Cazden 1972; Ellis 1994; Klima & Bellugi 1966; McNeill 1966; Mithcell & Myles 2004; Yule 2006

FI style
an abbreviation for FIELD INDEPENDENCE STYLE

Flow Theory
a school of thought that highlights the importance of an experiential state characterized by intense focus and involvement that leads to improved performance on a task. Flow Theory claims that as a result of the intrinsically

rewarding experience associated with flow, people push themselves to higher levels of performance. Others have characterized flow as optimal experience, being 'in the groove', when 'everything gelled'. Flow research has found that such optimal performance is a result of such factors as a perceived balance of skills and challenge, ability to focus intently on clear task goals, positive feedback that one is succeeding at a task, a lack of self-consciousness, and the perception of time passing quickly. All of this research supports the ultimate importance of intrinsic involvement of learners in attaining one's proficiency goals in a foreign language. Overall, Flow Theory offers a way of conceptualizing and evaluating tasks and environments that may help us to better understand the processes of teaching and learning.
see also MOTIVATION
📖 Brown 2007; Egbert 2003; Egbert & Petrie 2005; Ellis 2008

fluency

the features which give speech the qualities of being natural and normal, including native-like use of pausing, rhythm, intonation, stress, rate of speaking, and use of interjections and interruptions. A working definition of fluency might be the rapid, smooth, effortless, accurate, lucid, and efficient translation of thought or communicative intention into language under the temporal constraints of on-line processing. The notion is chiefly applied to oral fluency (speech), but is also used with reference to ability in writing, reading, and signing. Curiously, the skill of listening is not usually considered in terms of fluency. If speech disorders cause a breakdown in normal speech (e.g., as with APHASIA or stuttering), the resulting speech may be referred to as dysfluent, or as an example of DYSFLUENCY.

In spoken production, fluency can be investigated either in a holistic and subjective sense (not very fluent to near native) or in a narrow, usually quantitative and highly objective sense. It is the latter that has most interested researchers who have experimented with various components of fluency including:

1) speech rate (usually the number of syllables uttered per minute)
2) repetitions
3) false-starts
4) self-corrections
5) pauses ('number of' and 'length of'; 'filled' and 'unfilled')
6) average length of uninterrupted 'runs' between pauses.

It is particularly the last of these that appears to correlate with increased general proficiency, amount of exposure to the L2 and with holistic judgments of fluency. Various theories have been considered as affecting these measures. For example, different components of LEVELT'S MODEL OF SPEECH PRODUCTION may adversely affect fluency because of problems: in the conceptualizer (lack of ideas slowing down expression), in the formulator (lack of vocabulary or grammar slowing down expression), in the articulator (difficulties related to the speech organs), and through use of the monitor (thinking about the accuracy of the previous utterance or rehearsing the next utterance before articulating it). An alternative theoretical approach is to examine the relative use of FORMULAIC LANGUAGE or chunks of language that have become automatized, this being a characteristic which is believed to distinguish native and non-native speakers. Researchers are currently investigating the effectiveness of technology for measuring fluency as the implications for language testing (in which fluency plays an important part) could be considerable.

In foreign language teaching, the notion of fluency is sometimes distinguished from **accuracy**, which refers to the ability to produce grammatically correct sentences. It refers to the extent to which the language produced conforms to target language norms. A typical measure of accuracy is percentage of error-free clauses.

📖 Crystal 1992; Ellis 2003, 2008; Lennon 1990, 2000; Macaro et al. 2010; Richards & Schmidt 2010; Skehan 1996; Towell et al. 1996

focus on form
also **FonF**

within a communicative approach, a term which refers to learners and teachers addressing formal features of language that play a role in the meanings that are being negotiated. Usually attributed to Long, focus on form (FonF) adheres to the principle that L2 teaching should essentially both involve and promote communication of meaning but that, at certain moments in the lesson when learners reveal a gap in their knowledge, the focus should switch from communicating messages to drawing the learners' attention to formal aspects of the language, particularly its grammar. By adhering to the communicative principle, it distances itself from what Long labeled **focus on forms** (**Fonfs**) which is a teaching method that begins with and is governed by an analysis of the formal properties of the L2. Focus on Forms is characterized by a structuralist, synthetic approach to language, where the primary focus of classroom activity is on language forms rather than the meanings they convey. In other words, it involves the pre-selection of specific features based on a linguistic syllabus and the intensive and systematic treatment of those features. A good example of a focus-on-forms lesson is one conducted by means of 'PPP' (i.e., a three stage lesson involving the *presentation* of a grammatical structure, its *practice* in controlled exercises and the provision of opportunities to *produce* it freely).

In contrast, in focus-on-form instruction the primary focus of attention is on meaning. The attention to form arises out of meaning-centered activity derived from the performance of a communicative task. For example, students might be asked to perform an information-gap task and in the course of doing so have their attention drawn to one or more linguistic forms which are needed to perform the activity or that are causing the students problems. Proponents of FonF, therefore, argue that positive INPUT alone is not sufficient to promote acquisition of the whole of the L2 morpho-syntactic system and that even *negotiation of meaning* may in some instances not allow sufficient attentional resources to be directed at the new language element, simply because of the demands of understanding the message. FonF may be proceduralized in many ways by the teacher, ranging from a simple RECAST to a full (but brief) explanation of how a rule works in the L2 or is different from the L1.

Two types of focus-on-form instruction can be distinguished; **planned focus-on-form** and **incidental focus-on-form**. The former involves the use of focused tasks, i.e., communicative tasks that have been designed to elicit the use of a specific linguistic form in the context of meaning-centered language use. In this case, then, the focus-on-form is pre-determined. For example, a same-or-different task could be used to present pairs of pictures which would necessitate learners using 'at' and 'in' (the target forms) in order to determine whether the pictures are the same or different. This type of focus-on-form instruction is similar to focus-on-forms instruction in that a specific form is pre-selected for treatment but it differs from it in two key respects. First, the attention to form occurs in interaction where the primary focus is on meaning. Second, the learners are not made aware that a specific form is being targeted and thus are expected to function primarily as 'language users' rather than as 'learners' when they perform the task.

Incidental focus-on-form involves the use of unfocused tasks, i.e., communicative tasks designed to elicit general samples of the language rather than specific forms. Such tasks can be performed without any attention to form whatsoever. However, it is also possible that the students and teacher will elect to incidentally attend to various forms while performing the task. In this case, of course, attention to form will be extensive rather than intensive—that is, many different forms are likely to be treated briefly rather than a single form addressed many times. For example, while performing an opinion-gap task, students might make a number of different errors which the teacher corrects or students might feel the need to ask the teacher about a particular form, such as the meaning of a key word they do not know.

It should be noted that whether focus on form is planned or incidental is not so much a matter of the task that is used as the teacher's orientation to the task. Both types of focus on form require the use of a communicative task. In the case of planned focus-on-form, the teacher elects to use a task to target a specific linguistic feature and this then influences how the task is performed in the classroom. In the case of incidental focus on form, the forms attended to are not pre-determined but arise naturally out of the performance of the task. Even when the focus on form is planned, incidental attention to a range of forms in addition to the targeted form can occur.

There are, however, many questions for which clear answers are not yet available. These include:

1) To what extent should teachers engage in focus-on-form? A communicative language lesson has a dual purpose—to improve the students' FLUENCY and confidence in using the target language and to help them build their linguistic competence. By restricting the amount of attention to form the teacher can ensure the first of these purposes is achieved but at the expense of the second. By regularly focusing on form the teacher can create the conditions that promote the acquisition of language but runs the risk of inhibiting student fluency. It is sometimes recommended that teachers make a note of forms that cause students problems during a communicative activity and address them when it is over. However, this ignores one of the key reasons for employing focus-on-form, namely to make learners aware of specific forms at the time they need to use them.

2) Should focus-on-form be conversational or didactic? This is related to the preceding question. Conversational focus-on-form belongs naturally to communicative activity as it provides the means for solving communication difficulties whenever these arise. However, didactic form is the product of the classroom context; it reflects the fact that even when performing communicative activities the classroom participants are motivated to teach/learn the language. Given that many communicative activities do not result in much negotiation-of-meaning, didactic focus-on-form may be needed to provide sufficient opportunities for students to attend to form. But such activity can endanger the 'communicativeness' of an activity.

3) Should focus-on-form be implicit or explicit? Again, this concerns whether the orientation to an activity is to be entirely communicative, in which case implicit focus-on-form is appropriate, or more pedagogic, when explicit focus-on-form becomes acceptable. Students are more likely to notice the form that is being addressed if the focus is made explicit.

4) Should teachers pre-empt attention to form during a communicative activity? Teacher pre-emption of form is probably the option most likely to disrupt the communicative flow. It tells the students that the teacher is really concerned about form rather than meaning. Also, the forms teachers pre-empt may not constitute actual gaps in the students' L2 knowledge. Nevertheless, there may be occasions when the teacher pre-

empting form is useful (e.g., when students are planning a communicative activity).
5) What role is there for student-initiated attention to form? Students, especially motivated adult students, are likely to ask questions about form during the course of a communicative activity. How should the teacher deal with them? There are three possibilities—answer them immediately, ignore them, or deflect them (i.e., until later). Clearly, the strategy a teacher adopts needs to be informed by social as well as psycholinguistic considerations. Teachers cannot afford to antagonize their students by refusing to address their questions but equally whatever they do must be motivated by a concern for what will aid learning.

📖 Carter & Nunan 2001; Ellis et al. 2002; Long 1991; Macaro et al. 2010

focus on forms
see FOCUS ON FORM

FonF
an abbreviation for FOCUS ON FORM

Fonfs
an abbreviation for FOCUS ON FORMS

foreigner talk
also **FT**
the type of speech often used by native speakers of a language when communicating with non-native speakers who are not proficient in the language. Foreigner talk (FT) promotes communication, signals, implicitly or explicitly, speakers' attitudes towards their interlocutors, and teaches the target language implicitly. FT resembles CARETAKER TALK in some respects, but also differs from it in others (e.g., there are fewer yes/no questions). Both ungrammatical and grammatical FT occur, although it is not possible to identify the precise social conditions that favor one over the other. In the case of grammatical FT, three processes are evident: *simplification, regularization*, and *elaboration*. The modifications are continuous, influenced by the learner's stage of development, and age. It should be noted that whereas simplification involves an attempt on the part of native speakers to simplify the language forms they use, regularization and elaboration are directed at simplifying the learners' task of processing the INPUT and can, in fact, result in the use of language that is not always simple in itself. This is important because it means that FT provides not only simple input, correspondingly perhaps to what learners already know, but also input containing linguistic features that they have not yet learned.

One way of simplifying is by adjusting temporal variables such as speech rate (measured usually in syllables per second), articulation rate (measured by calculating the ratio of the total number of syllables to the total articulation time) and silent pause phenomena (pause duration, pause distribution, and pause frequency). Regularization entails the selection of forms that are in some way basic or explicit. Examples include: fewer false starts; a preference for full forms over contracted forms; a preference for canonical word order. Elaboration is the opposite of simplification, but to claim that FT evidences both is not contradictory, as both processes can occur at different times. Elaboration often involves lengthening sentences in an attempt to make the meaning clear. Native speakers often use analytic paraphrases of lexical items they consider difficult.

Many of the formal characteristics of FT are very similar to those found in other simplified registers such as learner language, caretaker talk, and PIDGIN. This suggests that it reflects universal processes of simplification, knowledge of which constitutes part of a speaker's linguistic competence.

Table F.1 presents the list of adjustment made in foreigner talk.

see also INTERLANGUAGE TALK, MODIFIED INPUT

Ellis 2008; Larsen-Freeman 1991

Linguistic adjustments
Phonology
Slower rate of delivery
More use of stress and pauses
More careful articulation
Wider pitch range/exaggerated intonation
More use of full forms/avoidance of contractions
Morphology and syntax
More well-formed utterances/fewer disfluencies
Shorter utterances (fewer words per utterance)
Less complex utterances
More regularity/use of canonical word order
More retention of optional constituents
More overt marking of grammatical relations
More verbs marked for present/fewer for non-present temporal reference
More questions
More yes-no and intonation questions/fewer WH-questions
Semantics
More overt marking of semantic relations
Lower type-token ration
Fewer idiomatic expressions
Higher average lexical frequency of nouns and verbs
Higher proportion of copulas to total verbs

Marked use of lexical items

Fewer opaque forms (greater preference for full NPs over pronouns, concrete verbs over dummy verbs, like *do*)

Conversational adjustments

Content

More predictable/narrower range of topics more here-and now orientation

Briefer treatment of topics

interactional structure

More abrupt topic-shifts

More willing relinquishment of topic-choice to interlocutor

More acceptable of unintentional topic-switches

More use of questions for topic-initiating moves

More repetition (self- and other-, exact and semantic, complete and partial)

More comprehension checks

More confirmation checks

More clarification requests

More expansions-and-answer strings

More decomposition

Table F.1. Language adjustments in foreigner talk

foreign language
also non-native language

a language which is not the native language of large numbers of people in a particular country or region, is not used as a medium of instruction in schools, and is not widely used as a medium of communication in government, media, etc. Foreign languages are typically taught as school subjects for the purpose of communicating with foreigners or for reading printed materials in the language.

📖 Richards & Schmidt 2010

foreign language learning

a term which refers to the learning of a non-native language in the environment of one's native language (e.g., French speakers learning English in France or Spanish speakers learning French in Spain, Argentina, or Mexico). This is most commonly done within the context of the classroom. On the other hand, **second language learning**, generally refers to the learning of a non-native language in the environment in which that language is spoken (e.g., German speakers learning Japanese in Japan or Persian speakers learning English in the United Kingdom). This may or may not take place in a classroom setting. The important point is that learning in a second language environment takes place with considerable access to speakers of the language being learned, whereas learning in a foreign language environment usually does not.

see also ENGLISH AS A SECOND LANGUAGE
📖 Gass & Selinker 2008

formal learning
see L2 = L1 HYPOTHESIS

form-focused instruction
also **FFI**

teaching which focuses on control of formal aspects of language such as the grammatical features of a specific type of discourse or text, e.g., narrative. Different types of form-focus instruction can be distinguished including **explicit instruction** and **implicit instruction**. Explicit form-focused instruction (FFI) involves some sort of rule being thought about during the learning process. In other words, learners are encouraged to develop metalinguistic awareness of the rule. This can be achieved deductively *or* inductively. Implicit FFI is directed at enabling learners to infer rules without awareness. Thus, it contrasts with explicit FFI in that there is an absence of externally-prompted awareness of what is being learned. Implicit FFI and explicit FFI are differentiated in terms of a number of characteristics, as shown in Table F.2.

Implicit FFI	Explicit FFI
• *attracts* attention to target form	• directs attention to target form
• is delivered *spontaneously* (e.g., in an otherwise communication-oriented activity)	• is *predetermined* and planned (e.g., as the main focus and goal of a teaching activity)
• is unobtrusive (minimal interruption of communication of meaning)	• is obtrusive (interruption of communicative meaning)
• presents target forms in context	• present target forms in isolation
• makes no use of metalanguage	• uses metalinguistic terminology (e.g., rule explanation)
• encourages free use of the target form	• involves controlled practice of target form

Table F.2. Implicit and explicit FFI

It should be noted that the terms explicit and implicit instruction can only be defined from a perspective *external* to the learner—i.e., the teacher's, material writer's, or course designer's perspective. In contrast, the terms IMPLICIT and EXPLICIT LEARNING and INTENTIONAL and INCIDENTAL LEARNING refer to the learner's perspective. These distinctions should not be treated as isomorphic. That is, it does not follow that implicit instruction result in implic-

it/incidental learning nor that explicit instruction necessarily leads to explicit/intentional learning.
📖 Dekeyser 1995, 2003; Ellis 2008; Housen & Pierrard 2006a

formulaic language
also **formulaic speech**
a sequence, continuous or discontinuous, of words or other elements, which is, or appears to be, prefabricated: that is, stored and retrieved whole from memory at the time of use, rather than being subject to generation or analysis by the language grammar. Formulaic speech differs from *creative speech*, which is speech that has been constructed by stinging together individual lexical items, often by drawing on underlying abstract patterns or rules. Everyday native-speaker speech is composed of a mixture of formulaic sequences and creative elements. Examples of formulaic language include idioms, set expressions, rhymes, songs, prayers, and proverbs; they may also be taken to include recurrent turns of phrase within more ordinary sentence structures.
In SLA research, formulaic expressions are difficult to identify because we may not know how a certain phrase was produced. However, a number of criteria help us with identification: they are produced fluently and without hesitation; they are morpho-syntactically above the level one would expect of the learner; they are used frequently/repeatedly and in particular situations; they may be used erroneously with respect to the meaning intended. Formulaic phrases permit even beginner learners to express themselves despite a poor command of grammar. For example, a learner can say '*I'd like* a return ticket' without needing to have been taught the conditional tense, modal verbs or rules governing contractions. Formulas learned in early stages can be analyzed later and/or 'slots' in them changed to convey different meaning. Alternatively, constructed phrases, when frequently used over a period of time, can become formulaic language in that they are stored and produced automatically as chunks thus freeing up working memory capacity.
📖 Ellis 2008; Macaro et al. 2010; Schmitt 2004; Weinert 1995; Wray 2002

formulaic speech
another term for FORMULAIC LANGUAGE

fossilization
a term introduced by Selinker referring to a permanent cessation in learning before the learner has attained target language norms at all levels of linguistic structure and in all discourse domains in spite of the learner's positive ability, abundant linguistic INPUT, opportunity, and MOTIVATION to learn and acculturate into target society. Irrespective of their age (but especially if they start in adolescence or later), many learners do not achieve full native-speaker competence—they stop short, continuing to manifest grammatical

and lexical errors in their L2 production and, even if overcoming these, failing to achieve a native-like pronunciation or to behave in accordance with the pragmatic norms of the target language (TL).

Fossilization is not an all-or-nothing phenomenon. First, there is considerable variation in the extent to which individual learners fossilize. That is, learners vary at what point in their development of an L2 they fossilize, with some ceasing development at a very elementary level, manifesting continued pidginized forms (see PIDGIN) in their production, and others at a much more advanced level. Second, there is 'intra-learner differential success/failure'. That is, a learner may reach target-language norms in some aspects of the L2 but not in others. Differential success/failure can also arise within the grammatical system of the L2 itself. Syntactical features (e.g., basic subject-verb-object word order) are relatively easy to acquire while morphological features (e.g., subject-verb agreement in English) are much more difficult. Thus, it is perfectly possible for a learner to be fossilized in some aspects of the L2 but to continue to develop in others.

Fossilization should not be viewed as some sort of terminal illness, in spite of the forbidding metaphor that suggests an unchangeable situation etched in stone. In fact, the more relevant object of study for researchers becomes **stabilization**, not fossilization, which leaves open the possibility for further development at some point in time. Stabilization refers to a state of L2 development where fluctuation has temporarily ceased. Many L2 learners are familiar with a situation where they appear to plateau, failing to develop despite their continuing efforts to do so, but then make a breakthrough some time later. Stabilization is easier to demonstrate empirically as it does not constitute a permanent condition—that is, a stabilized L2 system can subsequently become destabilized. All that is required to demonstrate that a learner has stabilized is evidence to show that over a given period of time some specific non-target feature of the learner's L2 system has persisted. In contrast, to demonstrate fossilization it is necessary to provide evidence that the learner's L2 system is permanently stabilized. This requires showing that even after many years of exposure to the language the learner continues to manifest the same non-target features.

There is another reason for preferring stabilization to fossilization. Talk of fossilization positions L2 learners as failures but, in fact, many achieve very considerable success in acquiring an L2. A key factor in determining success is undoubtedly instruction; learners who have received some instruction generally outperform those who rely entirely on naturalistic learning. Instructed learners, then, may be successful in acquiring the morphological features the absence of which has taken as a defining characteristic of a fossilized learner. It would follow that a learner who displays stabilization might be able to continue learning with the help of instruction.

Han 2004; Long 2003; Macaro et al. 2010; Mithcell & Myles 2004; Selinker 1972; Selinker & Lakshmanan 1992; Selinker & Lamendella 1978

fragile features
see RESILIENT FEATURES

free variation
see VARIABILITY

frequency analysis
also **interlanguage analysis**
the method of analyzing learner language that involves identifying the variations of a given structure and examining the frequency of occurrence of each variant. For example, a learner may make negative utterances using (1) 'no' + verb, (2) 'don't' + verb and (3) auxiliary + verb. A frequency analysis of the negative utterances produced by this learner would involve counting each occurrence of the three variants.
  Doughty & Varela 1998; 2008; Ellis & Barkhuizen 2005

Frequency Hypothesis
a hypothesis, initially formulated by Hatch & Wagner-Gough, which states that the order of development in L2 acquisition is determined by the frequency with which different linguistic items occur in the INPUT. The hypothesis deals with the relationship between input and accuracy rather than that between input and acquisition. The justification rests on the claim that the accuracy order mirrors the acquisition order.
There is now sufficient theory and empirical evidence to make the case that input frequently plays a major role in L2 acquisition. However, it is also clear that input frequency alone cannot explain L2 acquisition. This is, in fact, obvious. For example, the English definite and indefinite articles are both among the most frequent forms in both oral and written input but they pose considerable learning problems for all learners and are acquired later than other forms that occur much less frequently. Other factors that interact with input frequency in determining acquisition include syntactic category (in particular, whether the feature is regular or irregular), phonological salience, the learner's L1, communicative value (e.g., third person -*s* is acquired late because it is redundant) and innate constraints on learning.
see also INPUT HYPOTHESIS, NOTICING HYPOTHESIS, INTERACTION HYPOTHESIS, MORPHEME STUDIES, ACQUISITION ORDER
  N. Ellis 1996, 2002a; R. Ellis 2008; Hatch & Wagner-Gough 1976

FT
an abbreviation for FOREIGNER TALK

functionalist model
a model of L2 acquisition which views the task of learning a language as involving the construction of form-function networks. That is, learners have

to discover which forms perform which meanings in the L2. Thus, from this perspective, L2 knowledge is comprised of a network of form-function mappings. Initially, the network is a relatively simple one but it gradually complexifies as the learner acquires new L2 forms, matches these to existing functions and uses them to realize new functions. Functionalist models recognize that learners are likely to construct idiosyncratic form-function networks (i.e., use forms to perform functions not performed by these forms in the target language). They emphasize the role that communication plays in the acquisition process.

A good example of a functional approach to SLA research can be found in much of the literature on the acquisition of 'tense' and 'aspect'. What a researcher might ask is, 'How do people express tense (past, present, future) in their speech?', with the expression of temporality being the function and the linguistic devices people use as the form. In SLA, learners might begin to express the function of temporality through adverbs and not verb inflections with *Last night John study very much*. In this case, the adverb is the only form the learner uses to express temporality. In terms of acquisition, what the functionalist would want to know is how the learner's expression of temporality changes over time and what the interplay is between all the linguistic resources available to him at any given point in time during acquisition.

see also SOCIAL-INTERACTIONISM, SYSTEMIC LINGUISTICS

 Ellis 2008; Klein 1991; Perude 1991; VanPatten & Benati 2010

Fundamental Difference Hypothesis
also **FDH, no access view**

a hypothesis which claims that first language acquisition and adult second language acquisition are fundamentally different. Fundamental Difference Hypothesis (FDH) rests on two related claims. The first is that adult L2 acquisition is very different from L1 acquisition. The second is that this difference arises because whereas L1 features make use of their language faculty, adult L2 learners resort to general LEARNING STRATEGIES. According to this position, UNIVERSAL GRAMMAR (UG) is not available to adult L2 learners. L1 and L2 acquisition are fundamentally different. Adult L2 learners will normally not be able to achieve full COMPETENCE and their INTERLANGUAGE may manifest impossible rules (i.e., rules that would be prohibited by UG).

The FDH is predicated upon a number of observations about SLA, among which we highlight the following.

- Children always achieve complete grammatical knowledge of their native language, whereas adult L2 learners seem to rarely achieve full target language competence (see FOSSILIZATION).
- Unlike first language acquisition, which is uniformly successful across children (i.e., all native speakers converge on the same mental representation regarding the formal properties of language), adult L2 learners show

considerable VARIATION in their language learning success. In other words, L2 learners vary as to how far they get with an L2 and to what degree they approximate what native speakers know about language and can do with it.
- First language acquisition is constrained and guided by innate mechanisms (e.g., UG) and is not really influenced by external factors. SLA, especially with adults, seems to be influenced by (1) L1 TRANSFER, (2) INDIVIDUAL DIFFERENCES, and (3) social-communicative contexts of learning, among factors.

Proponents of the FDH take the above observations (and others) to mean that at their core, L1 and L2 acquisition cannot be the same and thus are different. In particular, the FDH claims that, whereas child L1 acquisition is guided by innate mechanisms, adult SLA is guided by general cognitive learning or problem solving principles and not by any innate linguistic knowledge. Thus, implicit in the FDH is that there is probably a 'critical period' (see CRITICAL PERIOD HYPOTHESIS) for language acquisition, after which such things as UG and other language-specific mechanisms are no longer available for learning language.
see also PARTIAL ACCESS VIEW, DUAL ACCESS VIEW, COMPLETE ACCESS VIEW
📖 Clahsen & Muysken 1986; Ellis 1997, 2008; Meisel 1991; VanPatten & Benati 2010

G

garden path sentences
a term used in psycholinguistics for sentences which, viewed from left to right one word at a time, mislead the listener/reader into an interpretation which later information in the sentence shows to be incorrect. We have been 'led up the garden path'. Put differently, garden path sentences are sentences which temporarily mislead the reader or listener when they are being processed *on-line* (word by word). The initial part of the sentence is ambiguous and permits of at least two possible endings. One of them is strongly indicated by semantic probability: *The lawyer questioned . . . (the witness* is more likely than by the police confessed); or by syntactic frequency: *The old man . . . (retired* is more likely than *the boats*).
Interest lies in establishing:

- Whether readers are strongly biased towards the more predictable outcome (raising the question of whether, during processing, they carry multiple possible interpretations of a sentence or prefer a single one).
- The impact upon the reader of encountering an unpredictable resolution.
- Whether listeners use phonetic and prosodic cues to anticipate the correct syntactic structure before the disambiguation point.

see also PARSING
 Aitchison 1998; Crystal 2008; Field 2004

Gass' model of second language acquisition
a model of second language acquisition, developed by Gass, which identifies five stages to account for the conversion of INPUT to OUTPUT. It also incorporates a role for output in the acquisitioned process:

1) *Apperceived input*: this occurs when the learner realizes that there is a gap in his L2 knowledge. Apperception is an internal cognitive act in which a linguistic form is related to some bit of existing knowledge (or gap in knowledge). Thus, the stage of the model draws on NOTICING HYPOTHESIS. Gass also acknowledged the role played by INPUT FREQUENCY.
2) *Comprehended input*: Gass stressed the difference between comprehensible and comprehended input. Whereas COMPREHENSIBLE INPUT

positions the speaker as controlling comprehensibility, comprehended input focuses on the learner. She also noted that comprehension is not an all-or-nothing affair; there are different levels, reflecting the difference between processing input for meaning and for learning. This stage draws on criticisms of Krashen's INPUT HYPOTHESIS.
3) *Intake*: this referred to the process of assimilating linguistic material; it refers to the mental activity that mediates input and grammars. It is where noticing-the-gap or cognitive comparisons occur. Gass viewed interaction, in conjunction with the learner's innate knowledge of linguistic universals and his L1 knowledge as instrumental in causing intake.
4) *Integration*: Gass identified four possibilities. The first involves the acceptance or rejection of an existing INTERLANGUAGE (IL) hypothesis. The second involves the use of the intaken feature to strengthen an existing IL hypothesis. The third involves storage. That is, the intaken feature is not immediately incorporated into the L1 system but is rather treated as an item and placed in the learner's lexicon. Later, however, when the learner has gathered more evidence, the learner may be also able to utilize this item to confirm or disconfirm an IL hypothesis. The final possibility is that learner makes no use of the intaken feature.
5) *Output*: Gass viewed output both as an overt manifestation that acquisition has taken place and also as a source of acquisition when it serves as a means for testing hypotheses. She drew explicitly on COMPREHENSIBLE OUTPUT HYPOTHESIS, envisaging a loop back to input.

Gass' model constitutes the fullest and clearest statement of the roles played by input and interaction in L2 acquisition currently available. It is a standard COMPUTATIONAL MODEL, reflecting the information-processing approach common in COGNITIVE PSYCHOLOGY.
see also INFORMATION PROCESSING, INFORMATION-PROCESSING MODEL
Ellis 2008; Gass 1988, 1997

GB
an abbreviation for GOVERNMENT-BINDING THEORY

general nativism
see NATIVISM

general self-esteem
see SELF-ESTEEM

generative grammar
a type of grammar that attempts to define and describe by a set of rules or principles all the grammatical sentences of a language and no ungrammatical ones. This type of grammar is said to generate, or produce, grammatical sen-

tences. The notion of generative grammar originated with Chomsky and this approach has been the focus of a considerable amount of work within theoretical linguistics resulting in different versions of grammatical theory. Underlying this idea is the notion that, in acquiring language, children cannot be simply memorizing the sentences to which they are exposed in the INPUT (as implied by Skinner) but must rather be more actively generating novel sentences out of a knowledge of the grammatical principles of their (native) language. The assertion is that all languages have an infinite number of possible sentences, and therefore, these sentences would be impossible to memorize. Rather, a finite set of phrase structure rules are acquired which allows the language user to generate an infinite number of sentences from a finite set of grammatical rules. Associated with this idea of generative grammar is the notion of UNIVERSAL GRAMMAR which claims that the ability to acquire this necessary grammatical knowledge is innately specified for the human species. A significant branch of research within second language acquisition is situated within a generative grammar framework, and attempts to understand the grammatical knowledge available to the L2 learner and the extent to which universal grammar is available and/or accessible to L2 learners.

📖 Chomsky 1957; Macaro et al. 2010; Richards & Schmidt 2010

generative theory
a cover term for a variety of linguistic theories that have the common goals of (a) providing an account of the formal properties of language, positing rules that specify how to form all the grammatical sentences of a language and no ungrammatical ones (the principle of **descriptive adequacy**), while (b) explaining why grammars have the properties they do and how children come to acquire them in such a short period of time (the principle of **explanatory adequacy**). The major versions of generative theory (all associated with the pioneering work of the linguist Noam Chomsky) that have influenced the fields of first and second language acquisition have been: **transformational grammar** (also **transformational-generative grammar**, **generative-transformational grammar**, **TG**), an early version of the theory that emphasized the relationships among sentences that can be seen as transforms or transformations of each other, for example the relationships among simple active declarative sentences (e.g., *He went to the store*), negative sentences (*He didn't go to the store*), and questions (*Did he go to the store?*). Such relationships can be accounted for by transformational rules. The **Standard Theory** (also **Aspects Model**) proposed in the mid-1960s, which specified a base component that produces or generates basic syntactic structures called *deep structures*; a transformational component that changes or transforms those basic structures into sentences called *surface structures*; a phonological component, which gives sentences a phonetic representation so that they can be pronounced; and a semantic component, which deals with the meaning of sentences. GOVERNMENT-BINDING THEORY, which dominated

formally orientated work in first and second language acquisition during the 1980s and 1990s. MINIMALISM, a version of generative theory developed in the late 1990s.
📖 Richards & Schmidt 2010

generative-transformational grammar
another term for TRANSFORMATIONAL GRAMMAR

genetic hypothesis of language
the hypothesis that the human language faculty is rooted in our genes. This hypothesis holds that our distinctive language faculty is a trait which we have evolved over time, just like our upright posture and our opposable thumb. According to this view, language just grows in children, much as their teeth grow, except that language learning requires exposure to speech; that is, the hypothesis sees our language faculty as a distinct and specific part of our genetic endowment. It is seemingly supported by the nature of certain genetically based disabilities, which disrupt language while affecting little else, or which leave language largely unaffected while disrupting most other cognitive abilities. It is perhaps further supported by the existence of the astonishing LANGUAGE INSTINCT in children. While controversial, this hypothesis is now widely accepted by linguists. The INNATENESS HYPOTHESIS is a more specific version of it. Nevertheless, the genetic hypothesis has been vigorously criticized.
see also AUTONOMY OF LANGUAGE
📖 Bates 1976; Bates et al. 1979; Bates et al. 1988; Macwhinney & Bates 1989; Pinker 1994; Sampson 1997; Trask 2005

gestalt strategy
see ANALYTICAL STRATEGY

global error
see ERROR ANALYSIS

global self-esteem
another term for GENERAL SELF-ESTEEM

Government and Binding Theory
another term for GOVERNMENT-BINDING THEORY

Government-Binding Theory
also **GB, Government and Binding Theory**
a version of Noam Chomsky's UNIVERSAL GRAMMAR according to which linguistic expressions, though infinite in number, can be generated with the help of a restricted number of rules. Government-Binding (GB) Theory pro-

poses a system of innate principles and constrains which govern all languages and a set of parameters that define the syntax of particular languages. Its machinery is divided up into about eight distinct modules, or components. Each of these modules is responsible for treating different aspects of sentence structure, and each is subject to its own particular principles and constraints. A sentence structure is well-formed only if it simultaneously meets the independent requirements of every one of the modules. Two of those modules—those treating *government* and *binding*—give GB its name. Government addresses the nature of abstract syntactic relations whereas binding deals with the referents of features such as pronouns. GB is a modular framework. Just like TRANSFORMATIONAL GRAMMAR, GB sees every sentence as having both an abstract underlying structure (the former *deep structure*, now renamed *D-structure*) and a superficial structure (the former *surface structure*, now renamed *S-structure*). There is also a third level of representation, called *logical form* (LF). Certain requirements apply to each one of these three levels, while further requirements apply to the way in which the three of them are related.

The motivation for all this, of course, is the hope of reducing the grammars of all languages to nothing more than minor variations upon a single theme, the unvarying principles of universal grammar. But the task is far from easy, and Chomsky, confronted by recalcitrant data, has been forced into the position of claiming that the grammar of every language consists of two quite different parts: a *core*—which alone is subject to the principles of universal grammar—and a *periphery*—consisting of miscellaneous language-specific statements not subject to universal principles. This ploy has been seen by critics as a potentially catastrophic retreat from the whole basis of the Chomskyan research program.

GB was an abstract framework to begin with, but it has become steadily more abstract, as its proponents, confronted by troublesome data, have tended to posit ever greater layers of abstraction, in the hope of getting their universal principles to apply successfully at some level of representation. Critics have not been slow to see this retreat into abstraction as a retreat from the data altogether, that is as an attempt to shoehorn the data into *a priori* principles which themselves are sacrosanct. The more outspoken critics have declared the GB framework to be more a religious movement than an empirical science. Nevertheless, GB has for years been by far the most influential and widely-practiced theory of grammar in existence.

Recently, however, Chomsky has, to general surprise, initiated the MINIMALIST PROGRAM, in which almost all of the elaborate machinery of GB is rejected in favor of a very different approach.

📖 Chomsky 1981, 1892; Ellis 2008; Trask 2005

Gradual Diffusion Model
also **Diffusion Model**
a model developed by Gatbonton to account for the way that learners develop and change their internal rules, gradually sorting out how to use forms correctly. Gatbonton's Gradual Diffusion Model identifies two broad phases in L2 acquisition: an 'acquisition phase' and a 'replacement (development) phase'. In the former, the learner first uses one form in his INTERLANGUAGE in a variety of situations and contexts, and then introduces another form which is used in FREE VARIATION with the first in all contexts. In the replacement phase, each form is restricted to its own contexts through gradual elimination of the other in first one context and then another (see SYSTEMATIC VARIATION).
 Ellis 1986, 2008; Gatbonton 1978

grammatical competence
see COMMUNICATIVE COMPETENCE

graphic organizers
a specific type of *advance organizer* (i.e., making a general but comprehensive preview of the organizing concept or principle in an anticipated learning activity) and are usually applied to listening and reading comprehension pre-task activities. The idea is that access to the text will be facilitated if the listener or reader prepares their mind (more specifically their schema) before being faced with the text. This can be achieved by the teacher presenting a 'concept map' (words connected in meaning radiating out from a central word) or by the teacher conducting an initial elicitation activity, producing a graph on the board in the middle of which is the central core word (e.g., 'famine') and from which a mind-map is formed linking all possible connecting words to it (e.g., 'hunger, starvation, poverty, drought'). This activation of schema is said to allow the student to predict what words are likely to occur in the text and therefore reduce the cognitive load by, as it were, having done some of the comprehension beforehand, or by regrouping the INPUT into more manageable chunks. Other types of advance organizers are 'structural overview' (predicting 'who/what/when/how'), text related questions or feasible 'statements' about the text. Although there is some evidence that these organizers facilitate comprehension in the immediate task, there is as yet little evidence that they transfer to other tasks or result in long-term improvement of comprehension.
 Herron et al. 1998; Macaro et al. 2010; Teichert 1996

H

harmful anxiety
 another term for DEBILITATIVE ANXIETY

helpful anxiety
 another term for FACILITATIVE ANXIETY

hemispheric differentiation
 see DIFFERENTIAL LOCALIZATION

heritage language
 also **community language**
 a term which is used to refer to a language spoken in a child's home or home community which is different from the language spoken in the majority of the community (MAJORITY LANGUAGE). Heritage language and MINORITY LANGUAGE are therefore largely synonymous. However, the term heritage language does not have associated with it any potentially offensive or pejorative aspects associated with the societal standing of the child's home language and heritage language is often associated with a language that may have originated in the country in which it is no longer the majority language (e.g., Mohawk in Canada).
 Issues concerning children's heritage language development are most commonly considered within the domain of BILINGUAL EDUCATION, as there have been a number of different educational programs around the world which promote heritage language education. Heritage language education is a 'strong form' of bilingual education where children use their heritage, or native/home language in the school as a medium of instruction—in addition to learning the L2 or majority language. Examples of heritage language education programs include education through Navajo and Spanish in the USA, Basque in Spain, Welsh in Wales (Great Britain) and Maori in New Zealand. The primary aim of these programs is to promote ADDITIVE BILINGUALISM, and protect and promote the child's development and use of their heritage or home language.
 Heritage language learners have knowledge of two languages (the home language and the language of the environment/school), and they are usually dominant in the second language. There is a wide range of linguistic

knowledge that heritage speakers have, including those who were born in the second language environment and those who came to the second language environment during their school years. Another consideration is the amount of INPUT in the home, ranging from only the heritage language spoken in the home (with perhaps parents only speaking the heritage language) to those situations in which the heritage language is spoken only sporadically.

Nonetheless, it is generally accepted that the nature of language learning for heritage language learners differs from language learning involving non-heritage language learners. Heritage speakers often possess a subtly different knowledge base of the heritage language than L2 learners of that language with no prior background. In addition, they often differ from monolingual speakers of their heritage language. Sometimes these differences may be subtle and sometimes they may be quite fundamental. Some recent studies have investigated the linguistic differences between heritage language and non-heritage language learners.

see also IMMIGRANT LANGUAGE

📖 Macaro et al. 2010; Gass & Selinker 2008

heuristic function
see SYSTEMIC LINGUISTICS

holism
see MODULARITY

holophrastic stage
another term for ONE-WORD STAGE

homogeneous competence paradigm
a theory of INTERLANGUAGE developed by Adjemian to refer to the view that learners have grammatical intuitions which the linguist may use as data in modeling that competence. Variation is a phenomenon which occurs in speech performance and not in the grammatical intuitions on the basis of which the grammar itself is written. This paradigm is inadequate because it does not satisfactorily account for the results of VARIABILITY research, which show that the 'careful style' (see CAPABILITY CONTINUUM PARADIGM) is more permeable to invasion from the target language than the 'vernacular style'. The homogeneous competence paradigm predicts the opposite.

📖 Adjemian 1976; Ellis 2008; Tarone 1983

horizontal variation
see VARIABILITY

hypercorrection
also **hypercorrectness, hyperurbanism, overcorrection**
a term used in linguistics to refer to the movement of a linguistic form beyond the point set by the variety of language that a speaker has as a target. The phenomenon usually takes place when speakers of a non-standard dialect attempt to use the standard dialect and 'go too far', producing a version which does not appear in the standard, e.g., putting a long /ɑː/ in place of a short /æ/ in such words as *cap*, *mat*, etc. Analogous behavior is encountered in second language learning. It has been suggested that this process is analogous to OVERGENERALIZATION in L2 acquisition.
see also COVERT PRESTIGE, HYPOCORRECTION
📖 Crystal 2008; Ellis 2008; Preston 1989

hypercorrectness
another term for HYPERCORRECTION

hyperurbanism
another term for HYPERCORRECTION

hypocorrection
a term which refers to the retention of an old norm in the speech of the working class because it has COVERT PRESTIGE. It has been suggested that this is analogues to NEGATIVE TRANSFER in L2 acquisition.
see also COVERT PRESTIGE, HYPERCORRECTION
📖 Ellis 2008; Preston 1989

hypothesis testing
It has been suggested that during SLA, the learners form hypotheses about the nature of the target-language rules and then tests them out. A hypothesis in this sense is an internalized rule which is used in the speech community. Once a learner has formed a hypothesis about a language rule, he can consciously or subconsciously test it out in a variety of ways in order to confirm or reject it:

1) *receptively* (i.e., the learner attends to L2 INPUT and compares his hypotheses with the data provided—by means of INTAKE analysis;
2) *productively* (i.e., the learner produces L2 utterances containing rules representing the hypotheses he has formed and assesses their correctness in terms of the FEEDBACK received);
3) *metalingally* (i.e., the learner consults a native speaker, teacher, grammar, or dictionary to establish the validity of a hypothesis;
4) *interactionally* (i.e., the learner elicits a repair from his interlocutor.

As a result of hypothesis testing carried out in one or more of these ways, the learner is in a position either to confirm or reject an initial hypothesis. The constant revision of INTERLANGUAGE rules is the result of the learner responding to evidence that requires modification of hypotheses. SLA ceases either when the learner no longer receives contrary evidence (see NEGATIVE EVIDENCE), or when he stops testing out hypotheses (i.e., because he is satisfied with his existing competence).

There have been several criticisms of the hypothesis testing view of SLA. Most of these have to do with the role of feedback. It has been observed that the provision of negative feedback (i.e., corrections) does not appear to lead to more accurate performance, at least not immediately. Even when the negative feedback is provided in the course of ordinary conversation (e.g., in the form of expansions and paraphrases serving as confirmation checks and requests for clarification), there is still no evidence to suggest that the learner amends his hypothesis immediately. Moreover, it makes little sense to talk about learners actively seeking out negative feedback. The falsification of idea is not feasible.

Nevertheless, the hypothesis testing model is still viable. These criticisms relate to how hypotheses are rejected. The important process, however, may be hypothesis confirmation. The learner often builds two or more hypotheses relating to the form of a single rule. The role of feedback may be to enable him to decide which hypothesis to accept finally. He is unlikely to come to a conclusion until he has received substantial feedback to test each of these hypotheses fully. As a result, the alternative hypotheses are maintained for some time, with perhaps a gradual tendency to favor one rather than the other(s). Eventually one of the competing hypotheses wins through and becomes a permanent L2 rule. This view of hypothesis testing meets the objections described above and also gives due recognition to interlanguage as a variable phenomenon. The entire process is a subconscious one; that is, the learner does not carry out hypothesis testing in order to learn L2, but as part of the process of communication. Thus, different types of communication can hinder or facilitate the process.

📖 Ellis 1986; Long 1977

I

ICLE
an abbreviation for INTERNATIONAL CORPUS OF LEARNER ENGLISH

iconic memory
see SENSORY MEMORY

identity hypothesis
another term for L2 = L1 HYPOTHESIS

idiosyncratic dialect
a term used by Corder to refer to the learner's language as idiosyncratic dialect to emphasize the idea that the learner's language is unique to a particular individual and the grammar of this language is peculiar to that individual alone. Corder maintains that idiosyncratic dialects are regular, systematic, meaningful, and unstable. Corder further explains that the language of the second language learner is not the only kind of idiosyncratic dialects. One class of idiosyncratic dialects is the language of poems, where parts can be deliberately deviant; another is the speech of an aphasic (see APHASIA), which categorizes as pathologically deviant. A third class of idiosyncratic dialects is that of an infant learning his mother tongue. However, the idiosyncratic dialect of the second language learner differs from the native language and the target language while maintaining some of its own, i.e., some of the rules and characteristics are idiosyncratic.
Corder further claims that every sentence of the second language learner is to be regarded as idiosyncratic until shown otherwise. A learner's sentence, therefore, may be superficially 'well-formed' and yet be idiosyncratic as opposed to those overtly idiosyncratic, i.e., sentences which are superficially 'ill-formed' in terms of the rules of the target language. Corder suggests that the interpretation of the learner's utterances is to be done by reconstructing the correct utterance of the target language and then matching the erroneous utterance with its equivalent in the learner's native language.
see also APPROXIMATIVE SYSTEM, INTERLANGUAGE
📖 Corder 1971a; Keshavarz 1999

I-language
an abbreviation for INTERNALIZED LANGUAGE

illocutionary act
see SPEECH ACT

imaginative function
see SYSTEMIC LINGUISTICS

immersion
also **immersion program, immersion education program, IM**

a term used to denote a type of BILINGUAL EDUCATION PROGRAM that was developed in Canada in the 1970s by Lambert and Tucker where children were educated within the medium of a second language and therefore 'immersed' in this L2 with a view to becoming a competent user of that language with no cost to their academic achievement. The focus of the immersion classroom was not on the L2 per se, but rather on the content of the academic curriculum. The L2 in the immersion setting is therefore not the subject matter, but rather the medium of instruction. As it was originally formulated in Canada, immersion was developed for English-speaking children to learn French. The aims of the original programs in Canada were to encourage the students involved in immersion programs to become competent in French in both speaking, reading and writing, to develop an appreciation of different cultural aspects of the L2 community and to reach expected-level academic achievement. The original French immersion classes proved to be highly successful and have led to successful immersion education programs throughout the world (e.g., Australia, Finland, Hong Kong, South Africa). There are different types of immersion education programs which vary with respect to two different variables: *age* and amount of *time* spent in immersion, i.e., whether the program begins *early* (e.g., in kindergarten) or *late* (e.g., in Grade 4 or 7), and whether it is *full* (more or less all instruction is conducted in the L2) or *partial* (only part of the curriculum is taught through the L2).

The term immersion has also come to be used to refer to a variety of programs for minority students: 'L2 monolingual immersion programs for minority students' which provide English-only instruction directed at classes consisting entirely of L2 learners; 'L1 bilingual immersion programs for minority students', which begin with L1-medium instruction, introducing L2-medium instruction some time later; 'L2 bilingual immersion programs for minority students', which emphasize instruction in and on the L2 but which also promote L1 skills.

A number of core features of immersion programs are identified as follows:

1) The L2 is the medium of instruction.
2) The immersion curriculum parallels the local L2 curriculum.
3) Overt support for the L1 exists.
4) The program aims for ADDITIVE BILINGUALISM.
5) Exposure to the L2 is largely confined to the classroom.
6) Students enter with similar (and limited) levels of proficiency.
7) The teachers are bilingual.
8) The classroom culture is that of the local L1 community.

There is general agreement that immersion programs are very effective in promoting L2 development in an educational setting. There are many reasons for the success of immersion programs. One undoubtedly, has to do with the fact that the immersion settings ensure a plentiful supply of INPUT that has been tailored to the learners' L1 and their ETHNIC IDENTITY is not threatened, so it is easy for the learners to adjust to the immersion setting. Furthermore, the immersion programs are optional and, therefore, are supported by those parents who elect to send their children to them.
see also DUAL LANGUAGE EDUCATION, SUBMERSION, MOTHER TONGUE MAINTENANCE, SEGREGATION, EXTENDED CORE PROGRAM
📖 Ellis 2008; Cummins 1988; Johnson & Swain 1997; Lambert & Tucker 1972; Macaro et al. 2010

immigrant language

a language spoken in a country by a sizeable number of people who have only recently immigrated there. For centuries large numbers of people have been leaving their homelands and migrating to other countries in the hope of finding a better life. In some cases, the chief languages of the immigrants have already displaced the indigenous languages of the receiving countries as the national languages: Portuguese in Brazil, English in Australia, New Zealand, the USA and much of Canada, Spanish in most of the rest of Latin America. These languages can no longer be regarded as immigrant languages.
see also HERITAGE LANGUAGE, MINORITY LANGUAGE
📖 Trask 2005

implicational scaling

a technique which is used by sociolinguists and some SLA researchers to represent VARIATION in L2 performance. It rests on the notion that the presence of one linguistic form in learner language occurs only if one or more forms are also present. Thus, one form 'implicates' other forms.
📖 Ellis 2008

implicational universal tendencies
a term referring to features which strongly tend to be found in languages, if some other feature is found. Implicational universals take the form of 'if/then' statements. For example:

- *Phonology*. If a language has a nasal consonant, this is probably /n/. That is, the major allophone of the one nasal consonant phoneme is /n/.
- *Morphology*. If a language distinguishes the singular and plural of nouns by an affix, this is probably the plural rather than singular morpheme, an implication which follows from the unmarkedness of singulars. English is a typical case, with a plural suffix. Sidamo is one of the exceptional languages with a singular affix.
- *Syntax*. If a language has VO order (the direct object or other verb complement follows the verb), then modifiers tend to follow their heads generally in the language. We may understand a direct object to be modifier of its verb, which is the head of VP. OV order, then, is a case—perhaps the leading case—of the generalization that modifiers tend to precede their heads. Thus, VO and OV languages tend to have the opposite word order for heads and modifies.

see also ABSOLUTE NON-IMPLICATIONAL UNIVERSALS, NON-IMPLICATIONAL UNIVERSAL TENDENCIES, ABSOLUTE IMPLICATIONAL UNIVERSALS
 Hudson 2000

implicit feedback
see FEEDBACK

implicit instruction
see FORM-FOCUSED INSTRUCTION

implicit knowledge
knowledge that is automatically and spontaneously used in language tasks and thus cannot be directly reported. Implicit knowledge is intuitive, tacit, procedural, systematically variable, automatic, and thus available for use in fluent, unplanned language use. According to some theories, it is only learnable before learners reach a critical age (e.g., puberty). The knowledge that most speakers have of their L1 is implicit. The study of LINGUISTIC COMPETENCE is the study of a speaker-hearer implicit L2 knowledge. Children implicitly learn phonological, syntactic, semantic, and pragmatic rules for language, but do not have access to an explanation, explicitly, of those rules. Implicit processes enable a learner to perform language but not necessarily to cite rules governing the performance.
The acquisition of implicit knowledge involves three processes:

162 implicit learning

1) *noticing* (the learner becomes conscious of the presence of a linguistic feature in the INPUT, whereas previously he had ignored it).
2) *comparing* (the learner compares the linguistic feature noticed in the input with his own mental grammar, registering to what extent there is a *gap* between the input and his grammar).
3) *integrating* (the learner integrates a representation of new linguistic feature into his mental grammar.

The first two processes involve conscious attention to language; the third process takes place at a very deep level, of which the learner is generally not aware. Noticing and comparing can take place at any time; they are not developmentally regulated. But integration of new linguistic material into the store of implicit knowledge is subject to the kinds of psycholinguistic constraints.
see also EXPLICIT KNOWLEDGE, MONITOR THEORY, ADAPTIVE CONTROL OF THOUGHT MODEL, INFORMATION-PROCESSING MODEL, DUAL-MODE SYSTEM, EXPLICIT LEARNING, IMPLICIT LEARNING, INTENTIONAL LEARNING, INCIDENTAL LEARNING, INTERFACE MODEL, NON-INTERFACE MODEL, WEAK INTERFACE MODEL, NOTICING HYPOTHESIS
 Brown 2007; Ellis 2002, 2008

implicit learning
the acquisition of knowledge about the underlying structure of a complex stimulus environment by a process which takes place naturally, simply and without conscious operations. Implicit learning contrasts with EXPLICIT LEARNING, which is a more conscious operation where the individual makes and tests hypotheses in a search for structure. Not to be confused with INCIDENTAL LEARNING, where information or skills are acquired which were not part of the original learning intention or task.
It has been argued that implicit learning may play a part in second language acquisition. Experiments have been conducted with *artificial grammars* consisting of strings of letters whose order and co-occurrence is determined by specific rules. After extended exposure to these letter strings, subjects have proved capable, at a level higher than chance, of distinguishing strings which are 'grammatical' (permissible) from those which are not. However, this result may be attributable to an 'analogy' effect, where subjects learn to recognize certain recurrent patterns rather than necessarily accessing the rules which underlie them. Questions have also been raised as to whether the acquisition of a 'grammar' of this kind can be said to model the acquisition of normal grammatical rules. The grammar can be said to possess 'phrase structure' but it is not meaningful or contextualized in the way that natural language data is; nor is there any speaker-listener interaction to support acquisition.

see also EXPLICIT KNOWLEDGE, IMPLICIT KNOWLEDGE, MONITOR THEORY, ADAPTIVE CONTROL OF THOUGHT MODEL, INFORMATION-PROCESSING MODEL, DUAL-MODE SYSTEM, INTENTIONAL LEARNING, INTERFACE MODEL, NON-INTERFACE MODEL, WEAK INTERFACE MODEL
📖 Ellis 1994; N. Ellis 1994a, 1994b; Field 2004; Gass & Selinker 2008

implicit memory
see EXPLICIT MEMORY

impression management
a term which concerns the way speakers make use of their linguistic resources in interaction to create social meanings favorable to themselves. For example, L2 learners may make deliberate use of primitive INTERLANGUAGE forms to mitigate the force of threatening SPEECH ACTs.
📖 Ellis 2008

impulsive style
see REFLECTIVE STYLE

incidental focus-on-form
see FOCUS ON FORM

incidental learning
a type of learning which is characterized by an absence of intentionality to learn, but may involve *ad hoc* conscious attention to some features of L2. Often proposed in contrast to INTENTIONAL LEARNING, incidental learning may occur when learners' attention is focused predominantly (but not exclusively) on the message contained in an utterance or a text rather than the form through which that message is being conveyed. That attention cannot be focused exclusively on the message is argued on the basis that some AWARENESS of the form of a new word, or unfamiliar grammatical element, must occur in order for 'noticing' (and subsequent processing of that word or element) to take place and leading to possible acquisition. For example, when reading a text containing an unknown word an L2 learner may be able to understand (or think they understand) the meaning of the sentence in which that word is contained without stopping, reflecting on and inferring the word's possible meaning from its context. However, in order for the new word to be acquired, some processing in WORKING MEMORY must occur which links the word's shape or components to its meaning. Hence, although generally accepted that incidental learning may arise spontaneously (i.e., without any prior planning), the idea that incidental learning is totally unmotivated and unintentional, has been challenged. This notion has formed the basis of some pedagogical practice in which focus on form episodes arise incidentally during interaction the pedagogical intention of which is predom-

inantly communicative. Studies suggest that incidental learning is less effective for both vocabulary and grammar than intentional learning but the lack of a precise definition of 'incidental' makes synthesis of these studies untrustworthy. Research into incidental learning has been carried out almost exclusively within a psycholinguistic framework although a few authors have adopted a socio-cultural perspective by situating it within ACTIVITY THEORY.

see also EXPLICIT LEARNING, IMPLICIT LEARNING, NOTICING HYPOTHESIS, FORM-FOCUSED INSTRUCTION, FOCUS ON FORM

📖 Ellis 2008; Loewen 2005; Macaro et al. 2010; McCafferty et al. 2001

indirect negative evidence
see NEGATIVE EVIDENCE

indirect strategies
see LEARNING STRATEGIES

individual learner differences
also **individual differences, IDs**
a term which refers to the differences in how learners learn an L2, how fast they learn, and how successful they are. These differences include LANGUAGE APTITUDE, LEARNING STYLES, LEARNING STRATEGIES, PERSONALITY, MOTIVATION, ANXIETY, WILLINGNESS TO COMMUNICATE, and LEARNER BELIEFS. These differences can be cognitive, effective, or social in nature.
📖 Ellis 2008

induced error
an error which has been caused by the way in which a language item has been presented or practiced. Students often make errors because of a misleading explanation from the teacher, faulty presentation of a structure or word in a textbook, or even because of a pattern that was rotely memorized in a drill but improperly contextualized. Two vocabulary items presented contiguously—for example, *point at* and *point out*—might in later recall be confused simply because of the contiguity of presentation.
📖 Ellis 2008; Richards & Schmidt 2010

inductive instruction
in FORM-FOCUSED INSTRUCTION, a form of explicit instruction that involves requiring learners to induce rules from examples given to them or simply from the opportunity to practice the rules. It contrasts with **deductive instruction** which involves providing learners with an explicit rule which they then practice in one way or another. This distinction underlies the language teaching controversy of the 1960s and early 1970s, in which the claims of an empiricist (see EMPIRICISM) approach (such as the Audiolingual Method)

were pitted against those of a rationalist approach (such as the Cognitive Code Method).
Several studies have compared deductive and inductive explicit instruction when these are combined with practice activities. A tentative general conclusion might be that deductive instruction is more effective then inductive instruction (when both involve practice activities) but it is possible that this may in part depend on the learner's preferred LEARNING STYLES.
📖 Diller 1978; Eisenstein 1980; Ellis 2008

infant bilingualism
another term for SIMULTANEOUS BILINGUALISM

inferencing
an INTAKE process which involves making a series of intelligent guesses to derive tentative hypotheses about various aspects of the target language (TL) system. Inferences are normally made by using all available, at times inconclusive, linguistic and nonlinguistic evidence based on the learner's IMPLICIT and EXPLICIT KNOWLEDGE base. Similarly, inferencing can be made using inductive as well as deductive reasoning. That is, learners can infer how a particular subsystem of language works by moving inductively from the particular to the general (i.e., from examples to rules), or moving deductively from the general to the particular.
Furthermore, L2 learners may benefit from the processes of OVERGENERALIZATION and LANGUAGE TRANSFER to make inferences about the TL system. Using *intralingual* cues, they may overgeneralize certain features of the TL system on the basis of any partial learning that may have already taken place. Some of the COMMUNICATION STRATEGIES such as paraphrase or word coinage that learners employ in order to get across their message while using their still-developing INTERLANGUAGE system are an indication of this process of overgeneralization. Similarly, using *interlingual* cues, learners may transfer certain phonological, morphological, syntactic, or even pragmatic features of their first language. Language transfer, as a cognitive process, has been considered to be essential to the formation of interlanguage.
Inferencing is particularly useful when the learners are able to pay attention to the new features presented in the INPUT data in order to find the gap between what is already known and what needs to be learned anew. The process of inferencing can be expected to vary from learner to learner because it reflects individual cognitive capabilities involving the connections made by learners themselves and not the connections inherently found in the input data. It can lead to working hypotheses that in turn may lead to interim conclusions that are tested against new evidence and are subsequently rejected or refined. Inferencing thus may entail framing new insights or reframing

what is already vaguely or partially known.
see also STRUCTURING, RESTRUCTURING
📖 Kumaravadivelu 2006; Selinker 1992

informal learning
see L2 = L1 HYPOTHESIS

information processing
a general term for the processes by which meanings are identified and understood in communication, the processes by which information and meaning are stored, organized, and retrieved from MEMORY and the different kinds of decoding which take place during reading or listening. The study of information processing includes the study of memory, decoding, and hypothesis testing, and the study of the processes and strategies (see LEARNING STRATEGIES) which learners use in working out meanings in the target language.
see also INPUT, COGNITIVE PSYCHOLOGY, INFORMATION-PROCESSING MODEL, PROCESSABILITY THEORY, PERCEPTUAL SALIENCY APPROACH, ADAPTIVE CONTROL OF THOUGHT MODEL
📖 Richards & Schmidt 2010

Information-Processing Model
another term for ATTENTION-PROCESSING MODEL

Information-Processing Theory
another term for ATTENTION-PROCESSING MODEL

inhibition
apprehension over one's self-identity or fear of showing self-doubt, leading to building mechanisms of protective self-defense. A variable that is closely related to, and in some cases subsumed under, the notion of SELF-ESTEEM and SELF-EFFICACY is the concept of inhibition. All human beings, in their understanding of themselves, build sets of defenses to protect the ego. The newborn baby has no concept of its own self; gradually it learns to identify a self that is distinct from others. In childhood, the growing degrees of awareness, responding, and valuing begin to create a system of affective traits that individuals identify with themselves. In adolescence, the physical, emotional, and cognitive changes of the preteenager and teenager bring on mounting defensive inhibitions to protect a fragile ego, to ward off ideas, experiences, and feelings that threaten to dismantle the organization of values and beliefs on which appraisals of self-esteem have been founded. The process of building defenses continues into adulthood. Some persons—those with higher self-esteem and ego strength—are more able to withstand threats to their existence, and thus their defenses are lower. Those with weaker self-esteem

maintain walls of inhibition to protect what is self-perceived to be a weak or fragile ego, or a lack of self-confidence in a situation or task.

The human ego encompasses **language ego** or the very personal, egoistic nature of second language acquisition. Meaningful language acquisition involves some degree of identity conflict as language learners take on a new identity with their newly acquired competence. An adaptive language ego enables learners to lower the inhibitions that may impede success.

Anyone who has learned a foreign language is acutely aware that second language learning actually necessitates the making of mistakes. Children learning their first language and adults learning a second can really make progress only by learning from their mistakes. If we never ventured to speak a sentence until we were absolutely certain of its total correctness, we would likely never communicate productively at all. But mistakes can be viewed as threats to one's ego. They pose both internal and external threats, to hearken back to ATTRIBUTION THEORY. Internally, one's critical self and one's performing self can be in conflict: the learner performs something 'wrong' and becomes critical of his own mistake. Externally, learners perceive others to be critical, even judging their very person when they blunder in a second language.

It is argued that language learning involves a number of forms of 'alienation': alienation between the critical me and the performing me, between my native culture and my target culture, between me and my teacher, and between me and my fellow students. This alienation arises from the defenses that we build around ourselves. These defenses inhibit learning, and their removal can therefore promote language learning, which involves self-exposure to a degree manifested in few other endeavors.

see also SELF-ESTEEM, ANXIETY, RISK TAKING, WILLINGNESS TO COMMUNICATE, EMPATHY, MOTIVATION, ATTRIBUTION THEORY, SOCIAL IDENTITY THEORY, ETHNIC IDENTITY

📖 Brown 2007; Ehrman 1996; Guiora et al. 1972a; Stevick 1976b

initial state

the starting point for language acquisition. Initial state is thought to include the underlying knowledge about language structures and principles that are in learners' heads at the very start of L1 or L2 acquisition. While the initial state in children's minds for L1 almost surely is an innate capacity (see INNATENESS HYPOTHESIS) to learn language, it is not at all certain whether or not such natural ability is part of the initial state in older learners for L2 acquisition. Some linguists and psychologists believe that the genetic predisposition which children have from birth to learn language remains with them throughout life, and that differences in the final outcomes of L1 and L2 learning are attributable to other factors. Others believe that some aspects of the innate capacity which children have for L1 remain in force for acquisition of subsequent languages, but that some aspects of this natural ability are lost with advancing age. Still others believe that no innate capacity for language acquisition remains beyond childhood, and that subsequent languages are learned by means which are more akin to how older learners acquire other domains of knowledge, such as mathematics or history.

Because it is impossible for us to observe mental capacity for language learning directly, the different beliefs are based largely on theoretical assumptions and are tested by indirect methods which individuals who come from different disciplinary perspectives may not agree on. For example, many linguists rely on learners' ability to judge which L2 utterances are not possible, an aspect of children's L1 competence which is attributed to innate capacity. Many who take a social perspective tend to reject such judgments of (un)grammaticality as convincing evidence because they result from artificial tasks which do not include actual circumstances of L2 interpretation and use. Many who take a psychological perspective in turn reject socially constituted evidence (such as natural language production) because the many variables which go along with actual social usage cannot be controlled for experimental investigation. So, although the question of the extent to which innate capacity for language acquisition remains available in SLA is a very interesting and important one, it is likely to remain unresolved for some years to come.

There is complete agreement, however, that since L2 acquisition follows L1 acquisition, a major component of the initial state for L2 learning must be prior knowledge of L1. This entails knowledge of how language (in general) works, as well as a myriad of language-specific features which are only partially relevant for production of the new L2. This prior knowledge of L1 is responsible for the TRANSFER from L1 to L2 during second language development.

L2 learners also already possess real-world knowledge in their initial state for language acquisition which young children lack at the point they begin learning their L1. This has come with COGNITIVE DEVELOPMENT and with experience by virtue of being older. The initial state for L2 learning also includes knowledge of means for accomplishing such interactional functions as requesting, commanding, promising, and apologizing, which have developed in conjunction with L1 acquisition but are not present in the L1 initial state.

The initial state of L1 learning thus is composed solely of an innate capacity for language acquisition which may or may not continue to be available for L2, or may be available only in some limited ways. The initial state for L2 learning, on the other hand, has resources of L1 competence, world knowledge, and established skills for interaction, which can be both an asset and an impediment.

see also FINAL STATE, LOGICAL PROBLEM OF LANGUAGE ACQUISITION, FUNDA-
MENTAL DIFFERENCE HYPOTHESIS, PARTIAL ACCESS VIEW, DUAL ACCESS VIEW,
COMPLETE ACCESS VIEW
 Mithcell & Myles 2004; Saville-Troike 2006

innateness hypothesis
also **nativist hypothesis, innatist hypothesis,, rationalist hypothesis**
the view that children bring a biologically endowed abstract knowledge to the task of learning a first language, and this abstract knowledge constrains the shape of the target linguistic system they learn. This innate knowledge allows them to discover the underlying rules of a language system and minimizes guessing and hypothesis formation. According to the innateness hypothesis which was developed by Noam Chomsky, a number of important characteristics of language are built into our brains at birth, as part of our genetic endowment, and hence we are born already 'knowing' what a human language can be like. In this view, then, learning a particular language is merely a matter of learning the details which distinguish that language from other languages, while the universal properties of languages are already present and need not be learned.

The innateness hypothesis was controversial from the start, and a number of critics, among them philosophers and psychologists, took vigorous issue with Chomsky's position, arguing that there is no evidence for innate linguistic knowledge, and that the acquisition of a first language could be satisfactorily explained in terms of the all-purpose cognitive faculties which the child uses to acquire other types of knowledge about the world. This controversy reached a head in 1975, when Chomsky debated the issue with one of his most distinguished critics, the Swiss psychologist Jean Piaget.

Chomsky and his supporters have responded in several ways. First, they attempt to point to identifiable universal properties of language, what they call UNIVERSAL GRAMMAR (itself a deeply controversial notion); these properties they claim to be arbitrary, unexpected and in no way deducible from general cognitive principles. Second, they point out that children never make certain types of ERRORs which we might have expected. For example, having learned *The dog is hungry*, they can produce *They dog looks hungry*, yet, having learned *Susie is sleeping*, they never produce **Susie looks sleeping*. Third, they invoke the POVERTY OF THE STIMULUS. By this term they mean that the data available to the child are quite inadequate to account for the knowledge which the child eventually acquires. For example, the usual rules of question-formation in English seem to predict that a statement like *The girls who were throwing snowballs have been punished* should have a corresponding question **What have the girls who were throwing been punished?* In fact, every English-speaker knows that this is impossible, and no child or adult ever tries to construct such questions.

However, there seems to be no way that this constraint could possibly be inferred from what the child hears, and Chomsky therefore invokes a universal principle, supported by comparable data from other languages, which he takes as part of our innate linguistic endowment.
 Trask 2005

inner-directed learners
see SILENT PERIOD

inner speech
also **silent self-directed speech**
Vygotsky's term for the unvocalized self-talk that many adults use to control their own thought and behavior. Inner speech is linked, but also different from, *sub-vocalization* in that the latter is language which is articulated through the speech organs albeit at a very low volume. Inner speech is also distinguished from PRIVATE SPEECH which technically is not private in that the speaker may say *right, so what I need to do now is X* in front of other people but will be doing so in order to regulate his thinking in carrying out that task. In SLA inner speech has often been interpreted from a sociocultural perspective, drawing on the work of Vygotsky, and is concerned with, for example, whether the L1 is used in preference to the L2 in L2 problem-solving tasks; whether inner speech is used in order to maintain, in WORKING MEMORY, recently seen or heard language; planning processes in writing; rehearsing prior to speaking; the relationship between inner speech and (outward) gestures or facial expressions. One of the obvious problems in researching inner speech is that it can only be mediated through spoken or written language and therefore the validity of using stimulated recall or think-aloud procedures is called into question. There is some evidence that bilingual children develop different characteristics of inner speech than do adults learning an L2 in more formal environments.
see also PRIVATE SPEECH
 Cohen & Macaro 2007; De Guerrero 2005; Macaro et al. 2010

input
the language to which a listener or reader is exposed; a term used especially in relation to first and second language acquisition. Different kinds of input have been discussed over the years, including COMPREHENSIBLE INPUT (i.e., language that learners can readily understand for its meaning) and MODIFIED INPUT (i.e., language that is adjusted so that learners can better comprehend the speaker's meaning). Some have referred to input as *primary linguistic data*. The reason for this is that all current theories of acquisition believe that input is the data source for acquisition as opposed to, say, practice, grammar explanations, FEEDBACK, and NEGATIVE EVIDENCE. Thus, learners' develop-

ing linguistic systems are a result of input interacting with learners' internal mechanisms used for processing and storing language.

Although all theories of L2 acquisition acknowledge a role for input, they differ greatly in the importance that is attached to it. Behaviorist theories (see BEHAVIORISM) of L2 acquisition propose a direct relationship between input and output. They emphasize the possibility of shaping L2 acquisition by manipulating the input to provide appropriate stimuli and by ensuring that adequate feedback is always available. Acquisition is thus controlled by external factors, and the learner is viewed as a passive medium.

Mentalist theories (see MENTALISM) view input as only a 'trigger' that sets off internal language processing. Learners are equipped with innate knowledge of the possible forms that any single language can take, and use the information supplied by the input to arrive at the forms that apply to the L2 they are trying to learn. A common assertion of mentalist theories is that the input is indeterminate, i.e., the information that it supplies is, by itself, insufficient to enable learners to arrive at the rules of the target language (see POVERTY OF THE STIMULUS).

*Interactionist theories (*see SOCIAL-INTERACTIONISM) on input view verbal interaction as being of crucial importance for language learning in a number of ways. Interaction provides learners with input containing the data they need for acquisition. It also affords opportunities to experiment through production and to receive feedback on these attempts, thereby making the 'facts' of the L2 salient. However, it is argued that an interactionist model is agnostic as to whether input determines acquisition or feeds the learner's innate LANGUAGE ACQUISITION DEVICE.

The final theory offers a very different view of the relationship between input and learning. SOCIOCULTURAL THEORY does not distinguish between input and output but rather views language acquisition as an inherently social practice that takes place within interaction as learners are assisted to produce linguistic forms and functions that they are unable to perform by themselves. Subsequently, internalization takes place as learners subsequently move from assisted to independent control over a feature.

📖 Ellis 2008; VanPatten & Benati 2010

input enhancement

a term used by Sharwood-Smith to refer to directing learners' attention to formal features of language while at the same time maintaining a focus on meaning. As such, input enhancement is a pedagogical tool meant to assist learners' development regarding formal properties of language. Input enhancement is an externally conducted activity; that is, it is teachers and/or materials that enhance INPUT. It is not an activity that originates from within the learner (as opposed to CONSCIOUSNESS RAISING which refers to an internal state of the learner).

Input enhancement entails any effort to make formal features of the language more salient to learners and comes in two varieties: 'positive' and 'negative'. *Positive input enhancement* involves manipulating input in certain ways to make formal features more obvious to learners. Such manipulations include louder voice or increased acoustic stress on something while the teacher is talking; bolding or highlighting particular features (among other manipulations) would be used in written input. *Negative input enhancement* is basically FEEDBACK: The teacher draws a learner's attention to an incorrect production in order to signal that the learner has violated target norms. There is a relationship between input enhancement and FOCUS ON FORM, as both involve simultaneous attention to form and meaning in the input.

A major assumption of input enhancement is that learners must attend to formal features in the input. In particular, they must pick up and process linguistic examples that their internal mechanisms can subsequently use as data for the developing system.

see also ENRICHED INPUT

 Sharwood-Smith 1993; VanPatten & Benati 2010

Input Hypothesis

a term which is usually associated with Stephen Krashen, and it is one of the five hypotheses that make up the larger MONITOR MODEL. Input hypothesis claims that the way humans acquire language is by understanding messages or by receiving **comprehensible input**. In the late 1970s, Krashen referred to comprehensible input as INTAKE. About a decade earlier, Corder had distinguished *intake*—language that a learner understands, takes in, and uses—from INPUT—any stretch of language available to the learner. Krashen originally claimed that intake alone was both necessary and sufficient for second-language acquisition. His preliminary writings focused on the acquisition of grammatical structures, mainly morphemes. By the mid-1980s, he extended his claims about comprehensible input to include the acquisition of lexical items embedded in messages and the acquisition of literacy.

The input hypothesis asserts that learners become more proficient in a second language when they understand language input that includes grammatical structures slightly beyond their current proficiency levels. Messages directed to the learner that contain language structures too far beyond the learner's current proficiency do not help the learner develop greater or expanded proficiency, because they leave gaps in understanding and therefore in production. Krashen uses the expression $i + 1$ to capture the idea of language input that is 'slightly beyond' the learner's current level of competence. In the expression, the term i equals the learner's current competency level, so that $i + 1$ is the next level or stage the learner is ready to acquire. Messages to the learner that contain structures that extend well beyond the learner's current proficiency level, say, $i + 5$ or $i + 9$, are by definition incomprehensible, and thus, because the learner cannot process the structures in the message, the structures will not be acquired.

Krashen points out, however, that this is a theoretical and conceptual portrayal. Comprehensible input does not need to be finely tuned to each learner's *i + 1* level to be useful for acquisition. In a classroom where language learners are at different levels of proficiency, a teacher cannot possibly adjust for all the variations in level present in the classroom. The teacher's role is to make sure that learners understand what is being communicated to them orally or in writing. If learners understand the input and there is an ample amount of it, learners are likely to receive *i + 1* geared to their acquisition needs. This is what Krashen refers to as 'casting a net' of language wide enough to ensure that there are multiple instances of the individual student's *i + 1*. According to Krashen, speaking is a result of acquisition and not its cause. Speech cannot be taught directly but 'emerges' on its own as a result of building competence via comprehensible input.

Krashen's Input hypothesis has been frequently criticized for being vague and imprecise. Despite the substantial contribution the input hypothesis and comprehensible input have had on second-language acquisition studies, it has received strong rebukes from several researchers, who criticize the term as being atheoretical, unmeasurable, and extremely vague.

Kevin Gregg argues that the input hypothesis does not stand up to conditions that any theory of second-language acquisition needs to meet. In particular, Krashen does not adequately define the terms he uses in his writings on comprehensible input. For example, Krashen interchanges the term language with grammatical structures, when he apparently really means a particular set of grammatical morphemes. There is no way to measure comprehensible input.

Lydia White rejects the input hypothesis because it places too much emphasis on comprehensible input, when, for her, it is *incomprehensible input* that is crucial for second-language acquisition. If the input is comprehensible, then there is no need for learners to negotiate for meaning. White contends that comprehension difficulties provide important negative FEEDBACK to learners, enabling them to adjust their developing language based on feedback provided in the conversational repair work.

Susan Gass questions whether it is *comprehensible* or comprehended input that is responsible for second-language acquisition. For her, comprehensible input implies that the speaker controls the comprehensibility through MODIFIED INPUT, use of extralinguistic support, and focus on the here-and-now. In comprehended input, the onus for comprehension is on the learner and the focus is on the extent to which the learner understands language addressed to him. So which is it, comprehensible or comprehended input that matters to second-language acquisition? Krashen argues that in order for learners to move to the next level of competency, they must process the *i + 1* they receive. It is not enough for speakers to modify their input to, or in interaction with, learners; ultimately, the learner has to comprehend the language for it to be useful for acquisition.

Merrill Swain also makes the argument that in addition to comprehensible input, learners need to produce *comprehensible output* in order to develop proficiency in a second language. Swain argues that comprehensible input may be necessary for the beginning stages of language development, but in order to develop complex syntax required for long stretches of language used in descriptions, explanations, justifications, and summaries, learners need to practice with comprehensible output. As Krashen pointed out, one of the corollaries of the input hypothesis is that speaking is the result of acquisition, not its cause. Swain argues that nudging learners to speak moves them from semantic processing to syntactic processing. When learners are forced to produce language, they may recognize the gap between what they want to produce and what they are able to, and because of this, they may pay closer attention to how native speakers use language for extended discourse. *Pushed output* involves providing learners with useful and consistent feedback, which encourages self-repair; this may lead to more accurate and precise language use.

Finally, there is the problem of how comprehensible input becomes intake and how intake leads to acquisition. As indicated by Park, most studies involving comprehensible input assume that some combination of speech modifications, extralinguistic support, a here-and-now emphasis, and negotiations for meaning involving judicious push output stimulate acquisition. However, in fact, as claimed by Long, most studies involving comprehensible input have focused on showing that language and conversational modifications promote the comprehension of input. Park argues that few studies have been able to show that comprehensible input promotes acquisition, mainly because the construct of acquisition has not been sufficiently explained or operationalized. Moreover, all of the research used to support the input hypothesis comes from Western settings involving mainstream middle-class, well-educated people. There are many examples of CAREGIVER SPEECH interaction in non-Western societies in which caregivers do not adjust their speech to young children, making no attempt to provide comprehensible input, and yet children in all of these settings acquire the language of their communities. Thus, even the supposed link between language/conversational adjustment and comprehensible input is questionable.

Despite the long-term debates over the role of comprehensible input in second language acquisition, there is considerable support for the idea that when learners can negotiate comprehensible input and are also encouraged to repair their output in order for it to be more comprehensible, such 'interactional contexts' are more conducive to language development than just providing comprehensible input. Moreover, though there is little value in pursuing the role of comprehensible input as the single reason for second language acquisition, the idea of providing language learners with lots of comprehensible input is highly regarded among classroom teachers working with language learners and native speakers together.

see also FREQUENCY HYPOTHESIS, NOTICING HYPOTHESIS, INTERACTION HYPOTHESIS

📖 González 2008; Faltis 1984; Gregg 1994; Krashen 1985; Krashen & Terrell 1983; Long 1981, 1982; McLaughlin 1987; Mithcell & Myles 2004; Park 2002; White 1987

Input Processing Theory
a theory of SLA in instructed contexts which refers to how learners connect meaning and function with formal features of language in the INPUT, and the strategies or mechanisms that guide and direct how learners do this. Input Processing (IP) Theory is associated originally with the work of VanPatten. The theory attempts to explain why grammar acquisition does not automatically result from COMPREHENSIBLE INPUT by proposing that the natural tendency is to listen for meaning rather than to attend to form and that it is difficult for both to happen simultaneously because of processing limitations. Moreover, listeners tend to focus on content words rather than function words or morphemes (because many of these are redundant for meaning) and in particular on the first noun of an utterance. Therefore in instructed contexts the teacher will have to manipulate the input in such a way that the listener cannot arrive at meaning without attending to grammatical clues in the input. In the most widely cited model of IP, learners are claimed to take certain strategies for processing input in particular ways. These strategies are couched in the form of principles such as the *First Noun Principle*: Learners tend to process the first noun or pronoun they encounter in the sentence as the subject. This kind of strategy works fine for languages that are rigidly subject-verb-object or subject-object verb, but many languages are not so rigid. Thus, learners make errors in comprehending object-verb-subject sentences and deliver incorrect linguistic information about sentence structure to their developing system. Other principles within this model of IP include the *Lexical Preference Principle* (i.e., learners will process lexical forms for meaning before grammatical forms when both encode the same semantic information) and the *Sentence Location Principle* (i.e., learners tend to process items in sentence initial position before those in final position and those in medial position).

A problem with IP instruction is that VanPatten proposes that IP sequences should begin with some EXPLICIT INSTRUCTION making it difficult to completely distinguish IP classes from traditional grammar teaching classes. A further criticism is that there is evidence that attentional capacity is not as limited as is suggested and therefore learners can attend to both form and meaning.

see also NOTICING HYPOTHESIS, ATTENTION, AWARENESS
📖 Allen 2000; DeKeyser et al. 2002; Ellis 2008; VanPatten 1996; VanPatten & Benati 2010

instructed language acquisition
see NATURALISTIC LANGUAGE ACQUISITION

instructional conversation
a term which refers to pedagogic interaction that is teacher-led and directed towards a curricular goal (e.g., enabling students to perform a structure that they have not yet internalized), but is conversational in nature (e.g., it manifests equal TURN-TAKING rights and is unpredictable).
📖 Ellis 2008; Tharp & Gallimore 1988

instrumental conditioning
another term for OPERANT CONDITIONING

instrumental function
see SYSTEMIC LINGUISTICS

instrumental learning
another term for OPERANT CONDITIONING

instrumental motivation
see MOTIVATION

intake
a term which normally used to describe those parts of the comprehended input which are, at least in part, attended to and processed by the learner. The term intake has been used in different ways by different scholars and theories. It was originally coined in by Corder to be distinct from the term INPUT, which is the language that learners are exposed to. It was Corder's intention to distinguish what learners are exposed to from what they actually 'take in'. The reason the term has been used differently by different scholars is that the notion of 'take in' itself is not clear. For example, for Corder, the term meant what the learner actually processes and acquires, that is, becomes part of his competence. In other models, intake refers only to linguistic data that is processed from the input and held in WORKING MEMORY, but not yet acquired. That is, the data are taken into working memory, but may or may not be processed further and/or can be rejected by other mechanisms responsible for the storage of linguistic data and its relationship to the learner's competence. In still other models, intake can refer to a process and not a product. In such cases, intake is defined as the process of assimilating linguistic data or the mental activity that mediates between the input 'out there' and the competence 'inside the learner's head'. The product view identifies intake as a sub-

set of input *before* the input is processed by learners. In other words, intake *is* input, even though it is only a part of it. The process view, however, identifies intake as what comes *after* psycholinguistic processing. That is, intake is already part of the learner's INTERLANGUAGE (IL) system. According to the product view, intake then is *unprocessed* language input; according to the process view, it is *processed* language input. The two views can be diagrammatically represented, as shown in Figure I.1 and Figure I.2.

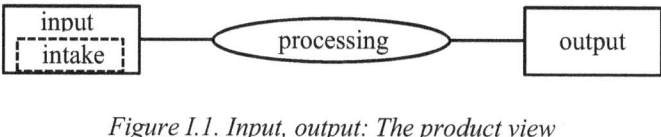

Figure I.1. Input, output: The product view

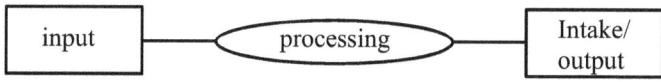

Figure I.2. Input, intake, output: The process view

The product view of intake appears to be severely flawed. It implies that there is no need to differentiate input from intake because intake, after all, is no more than a part of input and is independent of language-learning processes. In such a scenario, the distinction between input and intake, crucial to the nature of L2 development, becomes insignificant if not irrelevant. Furthermore, without such a distinction, we will not be able to account for the fact that input is not perceived and processed by different learners in an identical manner.

Intake, then, is an abstract entity of learner language that has been fully or partially processed by learners, and fully or partially assimilated into their developing IL system. It is the result of as yet undetermined interaction between input and intake factors (see next page) mediated by intake processes. It is not directly observable, quantifiable, or analyzable; it is a complex cluster of mental representations. What is available for empirical verification is the product of these mental representations, generally called OUTPUT. Intake is treated as a subset of input only to the extent that it originates from a larger body of input data. Features of learners' output can be traced, not only to the input they are exposed to, but to the dynamics of intake processes as well. The relationship between input, intake, and output can be diagrammatically represented, as shown in Figure I.3.

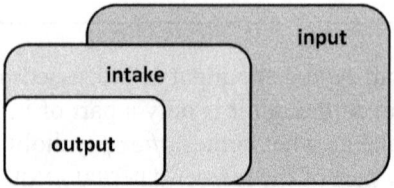

Figure I.3. Input, intake: A quantitative view

This figure shows that, output is a subset of what has been internalized, which in turn is a subset of input. However, there is no simple part-whole relationship between intake and input, and between intake and output. Furthermore, parts of learner intake and learner output can go beyond the boundaries of language input because the learners' developing system provides instances of grammatically deviant utterances that are not part of input. This happens when a learner imposes regularities on the data or uses native language markedness values. It may also happen when learners use various COMMUNICATION STRATEGIES that result in linguistically deviant forms of expression. What part of input gets converted into intake is determined by certain **intake factors**, and **intake processes**. Intake factors refer to learner internal and learner external factors that are brought to bear on the psycholinguistic processes of language learning, such as individual factors, negotiation factors, tactical factors, affective factors, knowledge factors, environmental factors. Intake processes are cognitive mechanisms that at once mediate between, and interact with, input data and intake factors. They consist of mental operations that are specific to language learning as well as those that are required for general problem-solving activities. As procedures and operations that are internal to the learner, intake processes remain the most vital and the least understood link in the input-intake-output chain. The intake processes that appear to shape L2 development may be grouped under three broad and overlapping categories: INFERENCING, STRUCTURING, and RESTRUCTURING. These processes appear to govern what goes on in the learners' mind when they attempt to internalize the TL system, that is, infer the linguistic system of the TL from the available and accessible input data, structure appropriate mental representations of the TL system, and restructure the developing system in light of further exposure and experience.

📖 Corder 1967; Gass 1988; Kumaravadivelu 2006; Stern 1983; VanPatten & Benati 2010

intake enhancement
another term for CONSCIOUSNESS RAISING

integrative motivation
see MOTIVATION

intelligence
the general set of cognitive abilities involved in performing a wide range of learning tasks. Intelligence constitutes a general sort of aptitude that is not limited to a specific performance area but is transferrable to many sorts of performance. Intelligence, WORKING MEMORY, and LANGUAGE APTITUDE are clearly all closely linked. They all refer to cognitive capacities and the difference between their conceptualizations lies largely in how broad and how language-specific the terms are.

Intelligence has traditionally been defined and measured in terms of linguistic and logical-mathematical abilities. The notion of IQ (Intelligence Quotient) is based on several generations of testing of these two domains. Success in educational institutions and in life in general seems to be a correlate of high IQ. In terms of MEANINGFUL LEARNING MODEL, high intelligence would no doubt imply a very efficient process of storing items that are particularly useful in building conceptual hierarchies and systematically pruning those that are not useful. Other cognitive psychologists have dealt in a much more sophisticated way with memory processing and recall systems.

Gardner described seven different intelligences which, in his view, provided a much more comprehensive picture of intelligence. Since then, he has added one more intelligence (naturalist), and has even toyed with further possible forms of intelligence (spiritual, existential, moral). Beyond the traditional two forms of intelligence (listed as 1 and 2 below), the following eight *multiple intelligences* are typically listed in Gardner's work:

1) *Linguistic intelligence*: the ability to acquire easily and effectively the use of sounds, words, and grammar orally and in the written form. It includes a sensitivity to codes and linguistic nuance at both the sentence and text level. These abilities are employed to achieve one's goals in fields such as law, writing, and public speaking/oratory. Lawyers, writers, editors, and interpreters are often strong in linguistic intelligence.
2) *Logical-mathematical intelligence*: the ability to learn and employ mathematical calculation and computation in solving problems, the ability to work logically through tasks, and a capacity to use traditional scientific procedure in defining, analyzing, and working through problems. This type of intelligence is often found in doctors, engineers, programmers, and scientists.
3) *Musical intelligence*: the ability to perceive and create pitch and rhythmic patterns, as is strong in singers, and composers.
4) *Spatial intelligence*: the ability to find one's way around an environment, to form mental images of reality, and to transform them readily, something architects, decorators, sculptors, and painters are good at.
5) *Bodily-kinesthetic intelligence*: having a well-coordinated body, something found in athletes and craftspersons.

6) *Interpersonal intelligence*: the ability to understand others, how they feel, what motivates them, how they interact with one another, which is strong in salespeople, politicians, and teachers.
7) *Intrapersonal intelligence*: the ability to understand one's own intentions, dispositions, motivations, strengths, and weaknesses and to use this information to effectively regulate one's intellectual, emotional, and social behavior.
8) *Naturalist intelligence*: the ability to recognize and classify things of the natural world (e.g., plants, animals) as well as other aspects of the environment (e.g., sounds, objects, measurements).

Gardner maintained that by looking only at the first two categories we rule out a great number of the human being's mental abilities; we see only a portion of the total capacity of the human mind. Moreover, he showed that our traditional definitions of intelligence are culture-bound. His more recent work has focused on applications of his multiple intelligences theory to daily human interactions as we manipulate those around us in order to accomplish a variety of purposes.

In a likewise revolutionary style, Robert Sternberg has also shaken up the world of traditional intelligence measurement. In his triarchic view of intelligence, Sternberg proposed three types of 'smartness':

1) *Componential ability* for analytical thinking.
2) *Experiential ability* to engage in creative thinking, combining disparate experiences in insightful ways.
3) *Contextual ability*: 'Street smartness' that enables people to play the game of manipulating their environment (others, situations, institutions, contexts).

Sternberg contended that too much of psychometric theory is obsessed with mental speed, and therefore dedicated his research to tests that measure insight, real-life problem solving, 'common sense', getting a wider picture of things, and other practical tasks that are closely related to success in the real world.

Finally, Daniel Goleman's work on *emotional intelligence* is persuasive in placing emotion, or what might be called EQ (Emotional Quotient), at the seat of intellectual functioning. The management of even a handful of core emotions—anger, fear, enjoyment, love, disgust, shame, and others—drives and controls efficient mental or cognitive processing. Even more to the point, Goleman argued that the emotional mind is far quicker than the rational mind, springing into action without even pausing to consider what it is doing. Its quickness precludes the deliberate, analytic reflection that is the hallmark of the thinking mind. Gardner's sixth and seventh types of intelligence (interpersonal and intrapersonal) are of course laden with emotional processing, but Goleman would place emotion at the highest level of a hierarchy of human abilities.

By expanding constructs of intelligence as Gardner, Sternberg, and Goleman have done, we can more easily discern a relationship between intelligence and second language learning. In its traditional definition, intelligence may have little to do with one's success as a second language learner: people within a wide range of IQs have proven to be successful in acquiring a second language. But Gardner attaches other important attributes to the notion of intelligence, attributes that could be crucial to second language success. Musical intelligence could explain the relative ease that some learners have in perceiving and producing the intonation patterns of a language. Music also appears to provide a natural facilitator of learning. Bodily-kinesthetic modes have been discussed in connection with the learning of the phonology of a language. Interpersonal intelligence is of obvious importance in the communicative process.

One might even be able to speculate on the extent to which spatial intelligence, especially a 'sense of direction', may assist the second culture learner in growing comfortable in a new environment. Sternberg's experiential and contextual abilities cast further light on the components of the 'knack' that some people have for quick, efficient, unabashed language acquisition. Finally, the EQ (emotional quotient) suggested by Goleman may be far more important than any other factor in accounting for second language success both in classrooms and in untutored contexts.

see also LEARNING STYLES, LEARNING STRATEGIES, PERSONALITY, MOTIVATION, ANXIETY, WILLINGNESS TO COMMUNICATE, LEARNER BELIEFS, LANGUAGE APTITUDE

📖 Brown 2007; Dörnyei 2005; Ellis 2008; Gardner 1999, 1983, 2004; Goleman 1995, 1998; McGinn et al. 2005; Schumann et al. 2004; Sternberg 1985, 1988, 1997, 2003

intentional learning

a type of learning in which a person consciously sets out to learn something. Often proposed in contrast to INCIDENTAL LEARNING, intentional learning involves a deliberate attempt to learn. For example, a learner may set out to read a book with the express purpose of increasing his vocabulary and is therefore likely to consciously attend to new words in the text. Intentional learning is investigated by making learners aware of what they are supposed to learn and then testing whether they have learned it.

see also EXPLICIT LEARNING, IMPLICIT LEARNING, NOTICING HYPOTHESIS, FORM-FOCUSED INSTRUCTION, FOCUS ON FORM

📖 Ellis 2008; VanPatten & Benati 2010

interactional act

an utterance which is considered in terms of its structural function in discourse, for example, whether it opens, closes, or continues a conversation.
📖 Ellis 2008

interactional function

see SYSTEMIC LINGUISTICS

interactional modification

L2 learners do not always obtain access to the kinds of input modifications (see MODIFIED INPUT) found in FOREIGNER TALK. More ubiquitous are interactional modifications. A useful distinction can be made between those interactional modifications that involve *discourse management* and those that involve *discourse repair*. The former are motivated by the attempt to simplify the discourse so as to avoid communication problems, while the latter occur when some form of communication breakdown has taken place or in response to a learner utterance that contains an error of some kind (factual, linguistic, or discourse).

The need for discourse repair arises when some kind of problem occurs. Two different kinds of problems can be identified: (1) communication problems and (2) linguistic problems. Frequently, the two coincide, especially when the source of the problem lies in something the non-native speaker (NNS) has said, as in the example below. Here the non-native speaker's incorrect pronunciation of 'closed' leads to a communication breakdown. In solving the communication problem, however, the linguistic problem is addressed—by the native speaker (NS).

NNS: The windows are crozed.
NS: The windows have what?
NNS: Closed?
NS: Crossed? I'm not sure what you are saying here.
NNS: Windows are closed.
NS: Oh, the windows are closed, OK, sorry.

Native speakers have been noted to try to manage discourse by frequently checking whether the learner has understood. Comprehension checks (e.g., *You understand?*, *Okay?*) have been found to occur more frequently in NS-NNS discourse than in NS-NS discourse. TEACHER TALK, in particular, seems to be rich in comprehension checks. It was found that ESL teacher were more likely than native speakers in informal conversations to check comprehension.

see also NEGOTIATION OF MEANING
📖 Ellis 2008; Long 1981; Pica 1994b

interactional sociolinguistics
see SOCIOLINGUISTICS

interaction analysis
a research procedure which is used to carry out classroom observation. It involves the use of a system of categories to record and analyze the different ways in which teachers and students use language. Various types of system exist, for example: a *category system* for coding specific events every time they occur, a *sign system* for coding the events that occur within a predetermined period, and a *rating system* for estimating the frequency of specific events.
 Ellis 2008: Long 1980b

Interaction Hypothesis
also **IH**
the claim by Long that language competence is the result not only of INPUT, but also of interaction between a learner's input and OUTPUT. The Interaction Hypothesis is an amalgam of emergent theoretical positions which have come to form part of a recognizable and coherent research tradition which began in the 1980s. It comprises (1) MODIFIED INPUT, (2) NEGOTIATION OF MEANING, (3) *forced output* (see OUTPUT HYPOTHESIS) and (4) FEEDBACK to learner ERRORS. The over-arching claim of the hypothesis is that interaction in the L2 furthers acquisition as well as the exchange of information (i.e., there is focus on form as well as focus on meaning). There is general consensus that these four aspects of L2 interaction jointly contribute to acquisition in some way. It is less clear if they do so incrementally (each one adding value to the other) or whether they contribute to different aspects of interlanguage development. For example, it was found that interactionally modified input led to better acquisition of vocabulary than pre-modified input which in turn led to better acquisition than unmodified input. Also, it was found evidence of the superiority of output over modified and interactionally modified input in the acquisition of vocabulary. This set of findings, then, suggest an incremental contribution to vocabulary learning.

However, numerous feedback-to-error studies have shown a contribution to grammar suggesting that the hypothesis does not have a unified contribution to INTERLANGUAGE development. Moreover, because researchers in this tradition have worked almost exclusively in L2-only contexts, it is unclear what the position of the hypothesis is to the role of the L1 in acquisition.
see also FREQUENCY HYPOTHESIS, INPUT HYPOTHESIS, NOTICING HYPOTHESIS
 Ellis et al. 1994; Long 1983a, 1983b, 1996; Macaro et al. 2010; Pica et al. 1987

interactionism
another term for SOCIAL-INTERACTIONISM

interactionist position
   another term for SOCIAL-INTERACTIONISM

interactionist theory
   another term for SOCIAL-INTERACTIONISM

interactive activation
   a model of language processing which assumes that all levels of representation freely influence each other. This might mean, for example, that a listener's perception of a distorted sound at the beginning of the sequence *eel would be influenced at the time of processing by knowledge of the word *wheel* or by a context such as *He changed the *eel on the car*. An interactive account contrasts with modular accounts (see MODULARITY) which suggest that the sequence *eel must first be processed phonologically; only then can information from other levels be brought in to disambiguate it.
   Interactive activation models thus present the processing of a spoken or written word as subject simultaneously to both *bottom-up* (data driven) and *top-down* (context driven) influences. Their proponents argue that this makes all sources of information immediately available to the listener or reader, enabling an informed choice to be made as to the identity of the word. Their opponents argue that a model of this kind overloads the processor with information, making a decision more difficult.
   see also ACTIVATION, MODULARITY, BOTTOM-UP PROCESSING
   📖 Carroll 1999; Field 2004; Whitney 1998

intercultural communicative competence
   the knowledge, understanding and skills needed to communicate successfully with members of a different social group. Intercultural communicative competence recognizes the lingua franca status of English and celebrates the fact that successful bilinguals possess intercultural insights. However, many consider intercultural competence to go beyond the simple transmission and acquisition of these attributes, arguing that it involves not only the communication of culture-laden meaning (as in *pragmatic competence*, i.e., being able to use language appropriately according to context) but also its interpretation and co-construction between interlocutors. In other words, it requires the setting up of encounters between one's own culture and that of the 'other'. The argument is that shared knowledge between interlocutors is relative rather than fixed and it is in the 'third space' between culture and language that learning, through experience, takes place. Theories of intercultural competence draw from many fields including psychology and anthropology.
   Approaches to teaching intercultural competence are many, as are the controversies that surround them. In English Language Teaching particularly, the notion of a fixed target culture has been greatly undermined by the globalization of the English language and the approach of modeling according to

a native speaker widely discredited. The cultural contrast approach is also criticized for operating at too superficial a level and risking developing stereotypical views. Computer mediated communication is currently seen as a facilitator of intercultural competence as it shifts the locus of learning from the teacher and language learning material to the social participants themselves in the act of communicating.

see also COMMUNICATIVE COMPETENCE

📖 Alptekin 2002; Kern et al. 2004; Kramsch 1993; Macaro et al. 2010

interdependency principle

a term formulated by Cummins to refer to the idea that, whereas BASIC INTERPERSONAL COMMUNICATION SKILLS (BICS) develops separately in the L1 and L2, COGNITIVE ACADEMIC LANGUAGE PROFICIENCY (CALP) is common across languages, and can therefore easily be transferred from L1 use to L2 use by the learner. Cummins notes that that whereas L2 communicative skills are typically mastered by immigrant learners in about two years, it can take from five to seven years for the same learners to approach grade norms for L2 academic skills. It explains why people who are literate in their L1 find fewer problems in developing CALP in an L2 than those who are not.

The notion of interdependency is an important one because it suggests that the development of full L1 proficiency confers not only cognitive and social advantages attendant on mother tongue use but also benefits the acquisition of L2 proficiency.

see also MOTHER TONGUE MAINTENANCE

📖 Cummins 1981; Ellis 2008

interface hypothesis
also interface position, interface model, strong interface position

a theory of L2 acquisition which states although the learner possesses different kinds of L2 knowledge, these are not entirely separate, with the result that 'seepage' from one knowledge type to the other occurs. In other words, it holds that EXPLICIT KNOWLEDGE can be transformed into IMPLICIT KNOWLEDGE through the process of automatization, which is a consequence of PRACTICE. In this view, the role of practice is to allow learned language knowledge to become fluent and automatic language use.

see also NON-INTERFACE MODEL, WEAK INTERFACE MODEL

📖 Ellis 1986, 2008; Macaro et al. 2010

interference
see TRANSFER

Inter-group Model
also Inter-group Theory

a theory of L2 acquisition, proposed by Giles and Byrne, which characterizes L2 acquisition as long-term convergence and explains it in terms of attitudes relating to relationship between the learner and the target-language community. Giles and Byrne identified a number of factors that contribute to a group's 'ethnolinguistic vitality'—the key construct in the theory (see Table I.1). They then discussed the conditions under which subordinate group members (e.g., immigrants or members of an ethnic minority) are most likely to acquire native-like proficiency in the dominant group's language. These are 1) when in-group identification is weak or the L1 does not function as a salient dimension of ethnic group membership, 2) when inter-ethnic comparisons are quiescent, 3) when perceived in-group vitality is low, 4) when perceived in-group boundaries are soft and open, 5) and when the learners identify strongly with other groups and so develop adequate group identity and intra-group status. When these conditions prevail, learners experience low ethnolinguistic vitality but without insecurity, as they are not aware of the options open to them regarding their status vis-à-vis native-speaker groups. These five conditions are associated with a desire to integrate into the dominant out-group (an integrative orientation), ADDITIVE BILINGUALISM, low situational ANXIETY, and the effective use of informal contexts of acquisition. The end result is that learners will achieve high levels of social and communicative proficiency in the L2.

Variable	Description
1 Identification with own ethnic group	This concerns the extent to which learners see themselves as members of a specific group that is separate from the out-group, and also consider their L1 an important dimension of their identity.
2 Inter-ethnic comparison	This concerns the extent to which learners make favorable or unfavorable comparisons with the out-group. Learners may or may not be aware of 'cognitive alternatives'.
3 Perception of ethnolinguistic vitality	This concerns the extent to which learners see their in-group as having low or high status and as sharing or being excluded from institutional power.
4 Perception of in-group boundaries	This concerns the extent to which learners see their group as culturally and linguistically separate from the out-group (hard boundaries), or as culturally and linguistically related (soft boundaries).
5 Identification with other social groups	This concerns the extent to which learners identify with other social groups (occupational, religious, gender) and, as a consequence, whether they hold an adequate or inadequate status within their in-group.

Table I.1. Variables affecting L2 acquisition according to the Inter-group Model

Learners from minority groups will be unlikely to achieve native-speaker proficiency when their ethnolinguistic vitality is high. This occurs if (1) they identify strongly with their own in-group, (2) they see their in-group as inferior to the dominant group, (3) their perception of their ethnolinguistic vitality is high, (4) they perceive in-group boundaries as hard and closed, and (5) they do not identify with other social groups and so have an inadequate group status. In such cases, learners are likely to be aware of 'cognitive alternatives' and, as a result, emphasize the importance of their own culture and language and, possibly, engage in competition with the out-group. They will achieve low levels of communicative proficiency in the L2 because this would be seen to detract from their ethnic identity, although they may achieve knowledge of the formal aspects of the L2 through classroom study.

The Inter-group Model is very similar to the ACCULTURATION MODEL; both were designed to account for L2 acquisition in majority language settings, both attempt to specify a set of socio-psychological factors that govern how successful individual learners will be, and both use these factors to describe 'good' and 'bad' learning situations. However, whereas Schuman's model emphasizes 'contact' as the variable that mediates between social factors and L2 acquisition, Giles and Byrne see 'interaction' as crucial. The factors they identify determine to what extent learners engage in upward convergence, and they define L2 learning as long-term convergence.

Much of the work in SLA research based on Giles' accommodation framework (see ACCOMMODATION THEORY) has been directed at discovering which linguistic features are subject to convergence or divergence, and under which interactional conditions they operate. As such, the Inter-group Model integrates a macro- and microlinguistic approach to the study of L2 acquisition.

The Inter-group Model has been criticized for failing to consider the various historical and structural variables that explain why learners from minority language background make the choices they do. The concepts of ethnolinguistic vitality and ethnolinguistic group can only be properly understood by considering issues of power and domination in the majority and minority groups involve. It is also argued that by emphasizing the role of convergence in language learning, the Inter-group Model suggests that learners who identify with their mother tongue cannot be fully bilingual and thus, inadvertently, provides a theoretical justification for the language education programs that seek to weaken learners' ties to their mother tongue and their community.

see also SOCIAL IDENTITY THEORY, SOCIO-EDUCATIONAL MODEL, ACCULTURATION MODEL, LANGUAGE SOCIALIZATION

📖 Beebe & Giles 1984; Ball et al. 1984; Ellis 2008; Giles & Byrne 1982; Hall & Gudykunst 1986; Tollefson 1991

interlanguage
also **IL**

the type of language produced by second- and foreign-language learners who are in the process of learning a language. Interlanguage (IL) coined by Selinker and was intended to describe the competence of L2 learners and the source of that competence. It refers to an independent system which displays features that are neither part of the target language nor derived from the learner's first language. This is the idea that the learner's innate predisposition for acquiring language can result in the creation of a unique interim system/grammar. Various alternative terms have been used by different researchers to refer to the same phenomenon; Nemser refers to APPROXIMATIVE SYSTEM, Corder to IDIOSYNCRATIC DIALECT and *transitional competence*, and Færch et al. to *learner language*. Each of these terms has a slightly different focus. However, IL is the most commonly used one.

Selinker identified five principal cognitive processes responsible for L2 acquisition: (1) LANGUAGE TRANSFER; (2) *transfer of training* (i.e., some IL elements may derive from the way in which the learners were taught); (3) strategies of second language (see LEARNING STRATEGIES); (4) strategies of second language communication (see COMMUNICATION STRATEGIES); and (5) OVERGENERALIZATION of the target language material. INTERFERENCE (i.e., NEGATIVE TRANSFER), then, was seen as one of several processes responsible for IL. The five processes together constitute the ways in which the learner tries to internalize the L2 system. They are the means by which the learner tries to reduce the learning burden to manageable proportions and, as such, it has been suggested that they can be subsumed under the general process of *simplification*. Learners have limited processing space and, therefore, cannot cope with the total complexity of a language system, so they limit the number of hypotheses they test at any one point in time.

Selinker also noted that many L2 learners fail to reach the target language competence. That is, they do not reach the end of the IL continuum. They stop learning when their IL contains at least some rules different from those of the target language system. He referred to this as FOSSILIZATION, which occurs in most language learners and cannot be remedied by further instruction.

At a more general level, IL processes have been discussed in terms of *hypothesis testing*, which was used to explain how the L2 learner progressed along the IL continuum, in much the same way as it was used to explain L1 acquisition. Corder, for example, suggested that learners form hypotheses about the structural properties of the target language on the basis of the INPUT data they are expected to. In this view, they build a 'hypothetical grammar' which is then tested receptively and productively. Hypotheses are confirmed if learners' interpretations are plausible and their productions accepted without comment or misunderstanding. They are disconfirmed if their understanding is defective and if their OUTPUT fails to communicate and is corrected. In such cases, learners may restructure their hypotheses, providing they are sufficiently motivated to do so. One of the main problems of such accounts is that it is not clear how learners obtain the linguistic information they need to modify hypotheses during communicative exchanges.

Subsequent discussions of IL focused on its three principal features, all of which were raised by Selinker in one way or another.

1) Language-learner language is *permeable*. The L2 learner's IL system is permeable, in the sense that rules that constitute the learner's knowledge at any one stage are not fixed, but are open to amendment. In many respects this is a general feature of natural languages, which evolve over time in ways not dissimilar to the developments that take place in language-learner language. All language systems are permeable. IL differs from other language systems only in the degree of permeability, and, if the idea of fossilization is accepted, in the loss of permeability that prevents native-speaker competence being achieved by most learners.
2) Language-learner language is *dynamic*. The L2 learner's IL is constantly changing. However, he does not jump from one stage to the next, but rather slowly revises the interim systems to accommodate new hypotheses about the target language system. This takes place by the introduction of a new rule, first in one context and then in another, and so on. A new rule *spreads* in the sense that its coverage gradually extends over a range of linguistic contexts. This process of constant revision and extension of rules is a feature of the inherent instability of IL and its built-in propensity for change.
3) Language-learner language is *systematic*. Despite the VARIABILITY of IL, it is possible to detect the rule-based nature of the learner's use of the L2. He does not select haphazardly from his store of IL rules, but in predictable ways. He bases his performance plans on his existing rule system in much the same way as the native speaker bases his plans on his internalized knowledge of the L1 system.

IL theory is central to the study of SLA because of the need to understand the system in its own right. Researchers are interested in the origins of the 'grammar entries' (how they came about), how a particular structure develops or, alternatively, fossilizes, whether there are sequences of development of a structure which learners go through, and whether and how intervention or instruction impacts on IL development.

 Adjemian 1976; Corder 1967, 1971a; Ellis 1986, 2008; Færch et al. 1984; Nemser 1971; Macaro et al. 2010; Selinker 1972

interlanguage analysis
   another term for FREQUENCY ANALYSIS

interlanguage talk
also **ILT**
the language that learners receive as INPUT when addressed by other learners. Interlanguage talk (ILT) constitutes the primary source of input for many learners. In classroom contexts, ILT has been referred to as 'tutor talk'. ILT, not surprisingly, tends to be less grammatical then FOREIGNER TALK, but it is characterized by more INTERACTIONAL MODIFICATIONS associated with the negotiation of meaning.
 Ellis 2008; Flanigan 1991

inter-learner variation
see VARIABILITY

interlingual error
see ERROR ANALYSIS

internalized language
also **I-language**
language viewed as an internal property of the human mind or a computational system in the human brain. According to Chomsky, traditional approaches to grammar focus on **E-language** (**externalized language**). They base their conclusions on samples of language that have been understood independently of the properties of the mind. By contrast, studies of I-language treat language as a product of the human mind and ask what type of knowledge it is that enables the individual language user to construct grammatically correct sentences. As such, I-language approach makes use of native-speaker intuitions about what is grammatical and ungrammatical in order to investigate the abstract principles that underlie particular grammars.
 Ellis 2008; Field 2004

internal variation
see VARIABILITY

International Corpus of Learner English
also **ICLE**
a computerized corpus of argumentative essays on different topics written by advanced learners of English (i.e., university students of English in their second or third years). It is made up of a set of sub-corpora from learners with different L1 backgrounds, including Asian languages (Chinese, Japanese) and European languages (French and Russian).
 Ellis 2008

interpersonal competence
knowledge required of learners who plan to use the L2 primarily in face-to-face contact with other speakers. As with ACADEMIC COMPETENCE, vocabu-

lary is the most important level of language knowledge for these learners to acquire, although the domains of vocabulary involved are likely to be very different. Knowledge which enables them to participate in listening and speaking activities merit the highest priority for interpersonal contexts; they must be able to process language rapidly 'online' (without the opportunity to review or revise text that is possible in reading and writing), as well as possess strategies for achieving clarification and negotiation of meaning during the course of face-to-face interaction. Depending on the situation, the level of language to be used may be formal or informal. Writing and reading activities are required in some interpersonal situations, but speaking and listening are much more likely to play dominant roles in interpersonal production and interpretation.
 Saville-Troike 2006

intra-learner variation
see VARIABILITY

intralingual error
see ERROR ANALYSIS

intrinsic motivation
see MOTIVATION

introversion
see EXTROVERSION

intuitive style
see REFLECTIVE STYLE

K-L

kinaesthetic learner
a learning style that favors learning through carrying out a physical activity involving bodily movement, rather than learning by listening or watching.
see also AUDITORY LEARNER, VISUAL LEARNER
📖 Ellis 2008; Reid 1987; Richards & Schmidt 2010

L1
an abbreviation for FIRST LANGUAGE

L2
an abbreviation for SECOND LANGUAGE

L2 = L1 hypothesis
also **identity hypothesis**
a hypothesis which claims that L2 acquisition is either identical or very similar to L1 acquisition. The similarity may be evident at the level of product (i.e., in the kind of language produced by the two kinds of learner) or process (i.e., the mechanisms responsible for acquisition). The similarities in learner language in L1 and L2 acquisition are perhaps most pronounced in the early stages of development. There is evidence of a SILENT PERIOD, of the use of formulas, and of structural and semantic simplification in both types of acquisition. However, there are also obvious differences. Whereas all L1 learners necessarily pass through a silent period, many L2 learners—especially adults—do not. Many L2 learners appear to make greater use of formulaic sequences (see FORMULAIC LANGUAGE) than L1 learners in the early stages of acquisition. Also, L2 learners are able to produce some longer and less propositionally reduced utterances from the beginning. A correct characterization of early L1 and L2 acquisition might be to say that L2 learner language displays many of the features of L1 learner language plus some additional ones. The process by which individual morphemes are acquired displays both similarities and difference. For example, both L1 and L2 learners omit pronouns and they both overgeneralize individual pronouns. The substitution of noun for pronouns also occurs in both types of acquisition. However, L1 learners commonly substitute their own name in place of the first person singular

pronoun for example, 'Lwindi eating' (= I am eating), which has not been attested in L2 acquisition, except by very young children.

The similarities between L1 and L2 acquisition are, perhaps, strongest in syntactical structures. The evidence from studies of negation (and also interrogatives) suggests that learners pass through a remarkably similar sequence of acquisition for these structures. However, the sequences in the two types of acquisition are not identical. For example, children acquiring German as L1 begin with the verb in final position (e.g., *wurst hier schnitt* (= *sausages here cut*), whereas L2 learners begin with a canonical order derived from their L1, which in the case of Romance language learners results in an SVO word order.

Differences between the L1 and L2 acquisition of vocabulary can be expected given that L2 learners are equipped with a developed conceptual system to anchor for the acquisition of word forms, whereas L1 learners are faced with the dual task of developing a conceptual system and acquiring lexical forms. Also, L2 learners do not go through an extensive period of pre-verbal development. However, there are also similarities. Both sets of learners face difficulties in extracting lexical units from the speech stream. Also, L2 learners are faced with acquiring at least some new meanings as there is no one-to-one correspondence between the lexical meanings of their L1 and L2.

Similarities are also evident in the acquisition of phonology, despite the fact that L2 learners are known to transfer features from their L1. It is claimed that sequence of development for the acquisition of closed syllable structure is essentially the same for L1 and L2 learners. It is also noted that although many L1 children do not seem to pass through an epenthesis stage, moving directly from consonant deletion to the target form, some precocious children do manifest epenthesis, possibly because, like adult L2 learners, they are more aware of their listener's needs and seek to make their meaning clear by avoiding consonant deletion.

L2 learners appear to tackle the problem of learning a language in similar ways to L1 learners. These similarities are most clearly evident in **informal learning** situations when learners are attempting to engage in unplanned language use. But there are also differences in the ways in which L2 learners go about cracking the code, and these become most evident in **formal learning** situations. Informal learning typically takes place in contexts where the INPUT is not consciously structured and the primary focus is on message conveyance, while formal learning occurs in contexts where the input is usually carefully organized and the primary focus is on form. Informal learning involves IMPLICIT KNOWLEDGE, while formal learning is likely to involve at least some EXPLICIT KNOWLEDGE of L2 rules. Formal and informal learning can also be differentiated in the kind of memory learners rely on. Adult L2 learners have access to a more developed memory capacity than L1 learners and when they can use it (or are required to use it, as in many pedagogic learning activities), differences between the language they produce and that produced by L1 learners occur. However, when they are not able to use it, they will produce language that resembles young children's. It was found that when adults were unable to utilize their memory capacity to process relative clauses, they behave in the same way as L1 learners. It was argued that when the memory process depends on features of syntax, the same restrictions apply to the L1 and adult L2 learner, but where the memory process is minimally dependent on language, the adult L2 learner exploits his general memory capacity. In other words, the identity hypothesis receives support, but when they rely on learning procedures of a general kind it does not.

Another obvious source of difference between L1 and L2 acquisition lies in the fact that L2 learners have access to a previously acquired language, in some cases to several. There is clear evidence to show that this results in differences between L2 and L1 acquisition—for example, in the case of the acquisition of German word order rules.

The evidence suggests that the hypothesis is partially supported. Given the immense cognitive and affective differences between very young children and adults, the similarities in the language they produce are striking. However, there are also significant differences which have been shown to exist.

📖 Abrahamsson 2003; Clahsen 1988; Ellis 2008; Singleton 1999

L2 learner
an abbreviation for SECOND LANGUAGE LEARNER

LAD
an abbreviation for LANGUAGE ACQUISITION DEVICE

language acquisition device
also **LAD**

a hypothetical mental organ hypothesized by Chomsky to refer to children's putative 'innate' ability to learn their native (first) languages. All children throughout the world seem to be able to learn and master their native language in a relatively straightforward manner, regardless of the context in which the child is developing (e.g., rich/poor, literate/illiterate, etc.). The main factors necessary for language acquisition in children seem to be a healthy brain and exposure to linguistic INPUT. The reason for proposing the LAD stemmed from the following observations by Chomsky which contributed to his development of the nativist or innate view of language acquisition (see NATIVISM, INNATENESS HYPOTHESIS). First, all neurologically healthy children pass through similar stages of developmental progress with respect to how their L1 develops; BABBLING precedes the ONE-WORD STAGE, which is then followed by the TWO-WORD STAGE, etc. This observation seems to be independent of which L1 is being learned by the child and the socio-economic, linguistic and cultural circumstances surrounding the child's development. Second, children seem capable of learning their L1 despite the fact that much of the natural language input that they are exposed to is not itself perfectly grammatical (i.e., people make performance errors when they talk, see POVERTY OF THE STIMULUS). Finally, children acquire their L1s despite the fact that they receive no NEGATIVE EVIDENCE—an indication of what is not grammatically possible in their L1. These observations, in conjunction with work in neuroscience demonstrating that language knowledge and processing seems to be under the jurisdiction of specific brain regions (e.g., Broca and Wernicke's areas) led Chomsky to propose that language acquisition in children must be innate and that there must be some sort of center, or 'device' in the child's developing brain which facilitates linguistic development, hence the LAD. The LAD in the child's brain therefore consists of innate knowledge about what language could possibly consist of and enables them to develop their competence in their L1.

In recent years, Chomsky himself has seemingly abandoned his claims for the LAD in favor of an even stronger claim: He now believes that so much information about the nature of human language is already present in our brains at birth that all the child has to do is to 'set a few switches' to the correct values for the language being acquired. This is his *parameter-setting model*, and it too is deeply controversial.

 Chomsky 1957, 1965; Macaro et al. 2010; Trask 2005

language aptitude

a term that has been used to identify those ability characteristics that influence how well individuals can learn a second language, not including INTELLIGENCE, MOTIVATION, interest, etc. Carroll is the name associated most with studies of second language learning aptitude. He is the originator of what Skehan called the 'standard four component view of language aptitude':

1) *Phonemic coding ability*. This is an ability to discriminate among foreign sounds and to encode them in a manner such that they can be recalled later. This would certainly seem to be a skill involved in successful second language learning.
2) *Grammatical sensitivity*. This is the ability to recognize the functions of words in sentences. It does not measure an ability to name or describe the functions, but rather the ability to discern whether or not words in different sentences perform the same function. It appears logical that skill in being able to do this helps in learning another language.
3) *Inductive language learning ability*. This is the ability to infer, induce, or abduct rules or generalizations about language from samples of the lan-

guage. A learner proficient in this ability is less reliant on well-presented rules or generalizations from a teacher or from materials.
4) *Memory and learning* (rote learning ability). Originally this was phrased in terms of associations: the ability to make and recall associations between words and phrases in a native and a second language. It is not clear whether this type of association plays a major role in language learning, but memory for language material is clearly important. Some linguists suggest that second language learning is much more an accomplishment of memory for text than of the analysis of text. That is, much more is memorized than is broken into parts and subjected to rule formation and/or generalizations.

Skehan questioned the appropriateness of separating grammatical sensitivity and inductive language-learning ability. He suggested that these be combined into one ability: language analytic ability. These four (or three) abilities seem to be reasonable predictors of second language learning success in that a person who is excellent in one or more of these abilities would seem to be at an advantage in learning a second language. Various attempts have been made to measure them. Perhaps the best known is Carroll and Sapon's *Modern Language Aptitude Test* (MLAT), which attempted to measure abilities that seemed to be involved in language learning. These attributes are measured independently of the language being studied and via decontextualized instruments. This test consists of five subtests:

- *Part One: Number Learning*: The student is taught, on tape, the Kurdish number system from 1 to 4, plus the 'tens' and 'hundreds' forms of these numbers, then tested by hearing numbers which are combinations of these elements, e.g., 312, 122, 41, etc. The test aims at measuring associative memory.
- *Part Two: Phonetic Script*: This sub-test measures phonemic coding ability. The student learns a system of phonetic notations for some English phonemes. He is then tested on this learning, e.g., 'Underline the word you hear: Tik; Tiyk; Tis; Tiys'.
- *Part Three: Spelling Clues*: This is a high speed test that measures both native language vocabulary and phonemic coding ability. The student is given clues to the pronunciation of a word (e.g., 'ernst' for 'earnest') and is then asked to choose a synonym from a list of alternatives.
- *Part Four: Words in Sentences*: This tests grammatical sensitivity. In a typical item, two sentences are presented, with one word in the first sentence underlined. In the second sentence five words are underlined. The student has to decide which of the underlined words in the second sentence fulfills the same function as the underlined word in the first sentence.

- *Part Five: Paired Associates*: The student studies a written Kurdish-English vocabulary list, practices the stimulus-response pairs seen, and is then tested by means of multiple-choice items. This is a test of associative memory.

The MLAT was considered to be independent of a specific foreign language, and therefore predictive of success in the learning of any language. There have been translations and adaptions of the MLAT or parts of it into French, Hungarian, Italian and Japanese, and we have also seen the development of other measures, identified with such interesting acronyms as EMLAT, PLAB, DLAB, VORD and CANAL-FT. The general rationale underlying all of these measures is not that different from what was used in the development of the MLAT or the earlier prognosis tests, and the major focus has been on the prediction of achievement in the language.

Even though the MLAT and other measures claimed to measure language aptitude, it soon became apparent that they probably reflected the general intelligence or academic ability of a student in any instructional setting. At best, they appeared to measure ability to perform focused, analytical, context-reduced activities that occupy a student in a traditional language classroom. They hardly even began to tap into the kinds of LEARNING STRATEGIES and STYLES that recent research has shown to be crucial in the acquisition of COMMUNICATIVE COMPETENCE in context-embedded situations. Learners can be successful for a multitude of reasons, many of which are much more related to motivation and determination than to so-called 'native' abilities.

There is now a new wave underway, where it is proposed that interest should not be on the prediction of success, but rather the identification of underlying processes, and that attention should be directed towards cognitive factors linked to specific language-learning processes or phases.

see also PERSONALITY, ANXIETY, WILLINGNESS TO COMMUNICATE, LEARNER BELIEFS

📖 Becker 1991; Brown 2007; Carroll & Sapon 1959; Dörnyei & Skehan 2003; Gass & Selinker 2008; González 2008; Skehan 1998, 1989a

language-as-subject
also LAS
the traditional way of teaching a new language where it is treated as the object of instruction, just as subject matter is in history, geography, math, etc. The teacher will explain things and decides what to learn and how to do it; the students are given grammar rules; errors are corrected; and the students are expected to produce grammatically correct sentences from the start. Language-as-subject is the opposite of IMMERSION, where the new language is acquired without recourse to any of the traditional teaching techniques.

📖 Piske & Young-Scholten 2009

language classroom

a setting where the target language is taught as a subject only and is not commonly used as medium of communication outside the classroom. In this sense, it includes both foreign language classrooms (e.g., Japanese classrooms in the United States or English classes in China) and second language classrooms where the learners have no contact with the target language outside the language classroom (e.g., ESL classes in a francophone area of Canada).

Two contextual aspects are of potential importance in language classroom settings. One concerns the learning situation to be found in the classroom. The other is the level of support which parents give to the foreign/second language program. With regard to the classroom learning situation, the role of relationships between teacher and student are likely to be crucial. In the case of traditional approaches to language teaching, where the target language is perceived primarily as an object to be mastered by learning about its formal properties, the teacher typically acts as a 'knower/informer' and the learner as an 'information seeker'. In the case of innovative approaches where the emphasis is on the use of the target language in 'social behavior' a number of different role relationships are possible, depending on whether the participants are 'playing at talk', as in role play activities, or have a real-life purpose for communicating, as in information gap activities; the teacher can be 'producer' or 'referee' and the learner 'actor' or 'player'. The nature of these classroom roles is likely to influence the level and type of proficiency that develops.

Parents may play an active role by monitoring their children's curricular activities. They may also play a more indirect role by modeling attitudes conducive to successful language learning. It is argued that parents' influence on proficiency is mediated through the students' MOTIVATION.

📖 Burstall 1975; Corder 1977b; Ellis 2008; Gardner & Clement 1990; Gardner & Smythe 1975; Macaro et al. 2010

language distance

the relative degree of similarity between two languages. Language distance is used to describe a set of criteria that researchers use in order to see how similar or different languages are to one another. It is linked to the notion of language universals (features of languages which are common to all) and language typology (the categorization of different languages). Corder suggested a **language distance hypothesis**. Children learning any language will take approximately the same amount of time to master its oral form; however the learning of second languages takes different amounts of time. The extent to which the L1 and the L2 are similar will determine how easy it is to learn an L2 and how long it will take. This hypothesis has, to some extent, contributed to the establishment of criteria for the length of different second language courses. The problem however lies in the interpretation of 'similar-

ity' and how one, as a consequence, might go about grouping the world's languages. For example, is English more similar to Mandarin than French because they share relatively simple morphologies or are they distant because of their very different writing systems? In other words, if typological factors allow languages to be members of different groups, which typological differences should be considered as causing the greatest problems. Thus, the general consensus seems to be that while one cannot deny language distance as a potential variable in SLA, it cannot be considered in isolation from other variables sufficiently to allow policy or pedagogical decisions to be made on the basis of language typology alone.
 Corder 1981; Macaro et al. 2010

language distance hypothesis
see LANGUAGE DISTANCE

language education
a broad term adopted for the study of any type of (mostly second) language learning. It is less concerned with theories of second language acquisition, more with providing an overview of language teaching and learning from an historical, policy, or pedagogical methodology perspective. In other words it is concerned with language learning in its socio-political and cultural context rather than an abstracted understanding of how the human mind processes language, although it certainly does not exclude the later. There is some disagreement as to whether language education rather than SLA should form the basis of Language Teacher Education, that is the theories and research evidence (e.g., on teacher beliefs, decision making and action) that inform the language teaching profession whether at novice or experienced level.
 Macaro et al. 2010

language faculty
our biological ability to use language. Human beings are the only creatures on earth that use language, and many linguists and others have concluded that we must therefore have some kind of specific biological endowment for language, one which is totally absent, or nearly so, from all other living species: our language faculty (the Swiss linguist Ferdinand de Saussure used the term *langage* for this, but his label is now little used).
To be sure, this conclusion has been challenged from two directions. On the one hand, some experimenters have attempted to teach other species, usually apes, to use some simplified version of a human language (most often a version of a sign language) and, in spite of serious problems with their methodology and interpretations, a few observers are now prepared to accept that these creatures do indeed exhibit a (severely limited) capacity for using language—though critics of this conclusion are numerous and vigorous. On the other hand, psychologists like Jean Piaget and Jerome Bruner have argued

that our language faculty, while admittedly real, is not at all an individual and distinctive part of our biological inheritance, but merely one more manifestation of our general all-purpose cognitive abilities.

Nevertheless, the majority view among linguists at present is that our language faculty is real, that it is at least largely distinct from all of our other cognitive abilities, and that it must be the biological result of some kind of distinctive evolution within the brains of our ancestors. This is the belief that underlies a number of celebrated attempts at giving an account of our language-using abilities, including the GENETIC HYPOTHESIS OF LANGUAGE, Chomsky's INNATENESS HYPOTHESIS, Bickerton's BIOPROGRAM HYPOTHESIS, and even the search for UNIVERSAL GRAMMAR.

A constant theme in these investigations is the issue of MODULARITY. Chomsky and others have long argued that our language faculty must consist of a number of specialized and largely independent subcomponents which interact in specific ways to produce our overall linguistic behavior. More recently, however, some people have begun to question whether our language faculty as a whole should itself be regarded as a distinctive part of our mental equipment. They suggest instead that various aspects of language use may have entirely separate evolutionary origins, and that what we call our language faculty is probably an epiphenomenon; that is, a purely superficial unity which in fact results from the interaction of diverse structures and processes within our brains, many of which are in no way confined to language behavior. These debates will doubtless continue for some time. The study of all the biological aspects of our language faculty is sometimes called BIOLINGUISTICS.

📖 Jackendoff 1993; Pinker 1994b; Sampson 1997; Steinberg 1993; Trask 2005

language instinct

the powerful tendency of children to acquire language. Any physically normal child who is adequately exposed to a language will learn it perfectly, and a child exposed to two or three languages will learn all of them. A hearing child normally learns the surrounding spoken language. A deaf child exposed to a sign language will learn that. Children exposed only to a PIDGIN will turn that pidgin into a real language: a CREOLE. A group of children exposed to no language at all will invent their own and use it. In the 1990s, the Canadian psycholinguist Steven Pinker coined the felicitous term language instinct to denote this remarkable aspect of our biological endowment. Our language faculty, we now strongly suspect, is built into our genes, and learning a first language may not be so different from learning to see: at birth, our visual apparatus is not working properly, and it requires some exposure to the visible world before normal vision is acquired.

Not infrequently, the term language instinct is applied more specifically to

the GENETIC HYPOTHESIS OF LANGUAGE and/or to the related INNATENESS HYPOTHESIS.
 Aitchison 1989; Pinker 1994b; Trask 2005

language learning strategies
another term for LEARNING STRATEGIES

language proficiency
the degree of skill with which a person can use a language, such as how well a person can read, write, speak, or understand language. This can be contrasted with *language achievement*, which describes language ability as a result of learning. Proficiency is not concerned with the length of time that an individual has taken to reach that level, nor the learning environment he has had experience of. The notion of proficiency is not one which is dependent on any particular syllabus or course content. Proficiency tests of English have been developed in order to provide information about an individual which may be usable across international contexts—for example for entrance to English-speaking universities. Typical proficiency tests are the Test of English as a Foreign Language, and the International English Language Testing System, both of which test the four skills of speaking, writing, listening and reading. Other terms are often used synonymously with proficiency, for example 'achievement', 'success' 'competence' 'ability' and 'skill' are all terms which have been used in studies which in fact were testing proficiency. Moreover, 'proficient' is sometimes used as synonymous, with high attainment, rather than as a relative measure, as in the Council of Europe's three levels of 'basic user', 'independent user' and 'proficient user'. Disagreement also exists as to what proficiency measures should be taking into account. For example, to what extent should a test of English proficiency take into account awareness of the target culture given that there are now so many world 'Englishes' and, as a corollary, whether there is an inherent test bias in relation to the cultural background of the test taker.
 VanPatten & Benati 2010; Macaro et al. 2010; Richards & Schmidt 2010

language socialization
the practice by which novices in a community are socialized both to the language forms and, through language, to the values, behaviors, and practices of the community in which they live. Thus, it entails socialization through the use of language and socialization to use language. As such, it affords a promising way of examining the complex relationship between social behavior and language learning. The theory proposes that in the process of learning to become a member of a community, learners learn the L2, and, conversely, that part of learning an L2 is becoming a member of the community that speaks it. One clear implication of such a theory is that language learning will be facilitated if socialization takes place and impeded if it does not.

see also ACCULTURATION MODEL, INTER-GROUP MODEL, SOCIO-EDUCATIONAL MODEL, SOCIAL IDENTITY THEORY
📖 Ellis 2008; Schieffelin & Ochs 1986

language transfer
another term for TRANSFER

language universal
another term for TYPOLOGICAL UNIVERSALS

languaging
a term coined by Swain to refer to the role that language production (oral or written) plays in making meaning when learners are faced with some problem. Languaging is a dynamic never-ending process of using language to make meaning. The particular type of languaging that Swain investigated was languaging about language. She emphasized that this constitutes one of the principal ways in which advanced levels of language learning can be achieved. Languaging is not just a facilitator of learning; rather in languaging, we see learning taking place. Swain illustrated how languaging works for learning by examining in detail the responses of two learners to the reformulated version of a story they had jointly written. She showed how one of these learners developed an understanding of why *in 19th century Japan and *in 19th century were erroneous through METATALK and how, consequently, this learner was able to avoid these errors when rewriting the original story. Swain argued that such languaging about language serves two functions: (1) it articulates and transforms learners' thinking into an artificial form and (2) it provides a means for further reflection on this form.
see also METATALK
📖 Ellis 2008; Swain 2006

LAS
an abbreviation for LANGUAGE-AS-SUBJECT

late bilingual
see EARLY BILINGUAL

lateralization
also cerebral dominance
the assigning of specified neurological functions to the left hemisphere of the brain, and certain other functions to the right hemisphere. According to this view one of the hemispheres of the brain has or develops a special responsibility for language. In most human beings, language appears to be particularly associated with the left hemisphere. Evidence comes from:

- *Brain damage.* When the left hemisphere is damaged by an accident, a stroke or invasive surgery, it often has a serious impact upon the victim's language.
- *Commisurotomy.* In this operation, the corpus callosum joining the two hemispheres was severed to reduce the effects of epilepsy. Patients who underwent the operation could name objects in their right field of vision (connecting with the left hemisphere) but not those in their left field of vision.
- *Wada injections* of sodium amytol were once used to deactivate one side of the brain prior to surgery, in order to ascertain which hemisphere was the dominant one for language. It was usually the left one.
- DICHOTIC LISTENING. When different messages are presented to the two ears, the right ear (the ear that links to the left hemisphere) usually overrides the left. The right ear appears to be dominant for speech generally but the left for music, rhythm and intonation.

Neurological research has shown that as the human brain matures, certain functions are assigned, or 'lateralized', to the left hemisphere of the brain, and certain other functions to the right hemisphere. Intellectual, logical, and analytic functions appear to be largely located in the left hemisphere, while the right hemisphere controls functions related to emotional and social needs. (see LEFT-BRAIN DOMINANCE). It is argued that lateralization is a slow process that begins around the age of 2 and is completed around puberty. During this time the child is presumably neurologically assigning functions little by little to one side of the brain or the other; included in these functions, of course, is language. It has been found that children up to the age of puberty who suffer injury to the left hemisphere are able to relocalize linguistic functions to the right hemisphere, to 'relearn' their first language with relatively little impairment.

The hypothesis has been linked to the notion of a CRITICAL PERIOD HYPOTHESIS. First language acquisition, it is argued, has to take place during the period of lateralization if complete command of L1 is to be achieved. If acquisition is delayed, the result may be the inadequate mastery observed in cases of language deprivation. It is contended that 'plasticity' of the brain prior to puberty enables children to acquire not only their first language but also a second language, and that possibly it is the very accomplishment of lateralization that makes it difficult for people to be able ever again to easily acquire fluent control of a second language, or at least to acquire it with authentic (nativelike) pronunciation. However, the plasticity hypothesis has been challenged by evidence that a degree of left-hemisphere lateralization exists from birth. Furthermore, recent studies have identified cases of infants who have not recovered some aspects of their linguistic competence after left-brain damage, and of adults who seem to have recovered their language by relocating it to their right hemisphere.

In addition, we now have more evidence about right-hemisphere damage. While damage to the left hemisphere affects primary language functions such as syntax and lexis, damage to the right appears to affect the processing of discourse. It also seems that, while phoneme-level processing is chiefly the prerogative of the left hemisphere, the processing of suprasegmental features, especially prosody, takes place on the right. One current view of the lateralization issue is thus that the left hemisphere specializes in more rapid language operations, and the right in those connected to higher-level meaning processes. This division of functions makes sense when the brain has to deal with two closely associated processes such as processing phonemes (left side) and prosody (right side). It also accords with evidence from modern imaging techniques showing that language is much more widely distributed in the brain than the original lateralization hypothesis supposed.

It may be that the human brain is more flexible than once believed, even in adulthood when the critical period is long over. In the exceptional circumstances of simultaneous translation, some professionals appear to distribute their two operating languages between the two hemispheres—usually reserving the left for the native language and the right for the second. In this way, they keep their two languages apart and manage to cope with the lack of synchronicity between the incoming auditory signal and the outgoing translation. Again, the key seems to be the need to keep two closely associated operations distinct.

It was once believed that lateralization might be peculiar to human beings and afford an explanation of why language is unique to our species. However, an enlarged left hemisphere has been found to occur in other species, including birds. Frogs have a dominant hemisphere which appears to be associated with croaking. This suggests that, across species, the larger side of the brain has special functions related to vocalization and the processing of rapid auditory stimuli.

see also LEFT-BRAIN DOMINANCE

Aitchison 1998; Brown 2007; Deacon 1997; Dingwall 1998; Field 2004; Guiora et al. 1972a; Lenneberg 1967; Obler & Gjerlow 1999; Scovel 1969; Springer & Deutsch 1997

law of effect
see CLASSICAL CONDITIONING

learnability hypothesis
the idea, attributed to Pienemann, that a second or foreign language learner's acquisition of linguistic structures depends on how complex these structures are from a psychological processing point of view, defined as the extent to which linguistic material must be reordered and rearranged when mapping semantics and surface form. The psycholinguistic processing devices ac-

quired at one stage are a necessary building block for the following stage. This implies a TEACHABILITY HYPOTHESIS as well, since structures cannot be taught successfully if the learner has not learned to produce structures belonging to the previous stage.
see also PROCESSABILITY THEORY
📖 Richards & Schmidt 2010

learner corpora
sets of oral/or written data collected from a large number of learners and converted into electronic form to facilitate computer-based analyses by means of concordancing programs. One of the best known learner corpora is the INTERNATIONAL CORPUS OF LEARNER ENGLISH.
📖 Ellis 2008

learner beliefs
also **learner belief systems**
ideas learners have concerning different aspects of language, language learning and language teaching, that may influence their ATTITUDES and MOTIVATIONS in learning and have an effect on their LEARNING STRATEGIES and learning outcomes. Language learners form 'mini theories' of L2 learning which shape the way they set about the learning task. These theories are made up of beliefs about language and language learning. Three different approaches to investigating learner beliefs can be distinguished. According to the *normative approach*, beliefs are seen as preconceived notions, myths or misconceptions, which can be studied by means of Likert-style questionnaires such as the Belief About Language Learning Inventory—BALLI. The *metacognitive approach* views learners' metacognitive knowledge about language learning as theories in action; these are examined by means of the content analysis of learner self-reports in semi-structured interviews. Finally, the *contextual approach* views learner beliefs as varying according to context; it involves collecting a variety of data types and diverse means of data analysis. It is argued that the contextual approach is superior because rather than viewing beliefs as a mental trait, it takes into account the experience-based nature of beliefs. A fourth approach can also be identified—*metaphor analysis*. This entails analyzing the metaphors used by learners to describe their learning and constitutes an indirect means of identifying beliefs.
Research does not show a strong relationship between beliefs and learning/proficiency. However, it is perhaps not surprising that the relationship between beliefs and proficiency is weak, as the fact that learners hold a particular belief is no guarantee they will act on it; conflicts with other strongly held beliefs, situational constraints, or personal reasons may prevent them. If beliefs do impact on learning it is likely that they do so indirectly by influencing the kinds of learning strategies learners employ.

see also LEARNING STYLES, LEARNING STRATEGIES, PERSONALITY, MOTIVATION, ANXIETY, WILLINGNESS TO COMMUNICATE, INTELLIGENCE, LANGUAGE APTITUDE
📖 Barcelos 2003; Ellis 2008; Horwitz 1987a; Hosenfeld 1978; Kramsch 2003; Richards & Schmidt 2010; Wenden 1999

learner belief systems
another term for LEARNER BELIEFS

learner-instruction matching
an attempt to ensure that the teaching style is suited to the learner. It is based on the assumption that learners have different LEARNING STYLES and that they will learn most effectively if the instruction matches their particular learning style. Educational research based on learner-instruction matching is sometimes referred to as **aptitude-treatment interaction**.
📖 Ellis 2008

learner uptake
another term for UPTAKE

learning strategies
also **language learning strategies, LLSs**
specific methods of approaching a problem or task, modes of operation for achieving a particular end, planned designs for controlling and manipulating certain information. According to Oxford, language-learning strategies (LLSs) are operations employed by the learner to aid the acquisition, storage, retrieval, and use of information; they are specific actions taken by the learners to make learning easier, faster, more enjoyable, more self-directed, more effective, and more transferable to new situations. LLSs are contextualized 'battle plans' that might vary from moment to moment, or from one situation to another, or even from one culture to another. They vary within an individual. Each of us has a number of possible options for solving a particular problem, and we choose one—or several in sequence—for a given problem in learning a second language.
LLSs are perhaps best defined in terms of a set of characteristics that figure in most accounts of them (however, arguments continue as to how define learning strategies):

- Strategies refer to both general approaches and specific actions or techniques used to learn an L2.
- Strategies are problem-oriented—the learner deploys a strategy to overcome particular learning and communication problem.

- Learners are generally aware of the strategies they use and can identify what they consist of if they are asked to pay attention to what they are doing/thinking.
- Strategies involve linguistic behavior (such as requesting the name of an object) and non-linguistic (such as pointing at an object so as to be told its name).
- Linguistic strategies can be performed in the L1 and in L2.
- Some strategies are behavioral while others are mental. Thus, some strategies are directly observable, while others are not.
- In the main, strategies contribute indirectly to learning by providing learners with data about the L2 which they can then process. However, some strategies may also contribute directly (e.g., memorization strategies directed at specific lexical items or grammatical rules).
- Strategy use varies considerably as a result of both the kind of task the learner is engaged in and individual learner preferences.

Based on her synthesis of previous research and on factor-analytic, questionnaire-based studies of LLSs among adult learners, Oxford developed one of the most widely accepted classification taxonomies in the language learning area. Oxford's model of language-learning strategies consists of *six* categories: 'memory strategies', 'cognitive strategies', 'compensation strategies', 'metacognitive strategies', 'affective strategies', and 'social strategies'. Each of these is defined below and also illustrated with examples.

Memory strategies are specific devices (mnemonics) used by learners to make mental linkages that will allow new information, most often vocabulary, to enter and remain in LONG-TERM MEMORY. Examples of memory strategies are 'to make associations with what has already been learned, to draw pictures to help remember new words, and to repeatedly pronounce or write new words in order to remember them'. Although memory strategies could easily be viewed as cognitive strategies, their purpose is limited to memorization and involves mostly surface processing. Prior research shows that memory strategies operate differently from many cognitive strategies in terms of frequency of use.

Cognitive strategies are more limited to specific learning tasks and involve more direct manipulation of the learning material itself. They help learners process and use the language for learning or for accomplishing a task involving the language, e.g., 'watch TV in English, listen to radio/CDs in English, use English computer programs, and find similarities between first and second languages'. Compared with memory strategies, the purpose of cognitive strategies is not simply memorization but instead deeper processing and use of the language (for deep and surface processing). This category is commonly used for research on second language learning.

Compensation strategies are intended to make up for missing knowledge while listening, reading, speaking, or writing. For example, 'use gestures or body language (for speaking), rephrase (for speaking or writing), ask for help (for listening, reading, speaking, or writing) and make guesses based on the context' (for listening and reading). (The last strategy could also be listed as a cognitive strategy, but it is included here as a compensation strategy because it makes up for a gap in knowledge) .

Metacognitive strategies 'Meta' means 'above' or 'beyond', so metacognitive means 'beyond' the cognitive. Metacognitive is a term used in INFORMATION PROCESSING to indicate an 'executive' function, strategies that involve planning for learning, thinking about the learning process as it is taking place, monitoring of one's production or comprehension, and evaluating learning after an activity is completed, e.g., 'organize time for learning, check one's progress, and analyze one's mistakes and try not to make them again'. This category is widely used in the second language field.

Affective strategies help the learner deal with his own emotions, MOTIVATIONS, and ATTITUDES while (or about) learning English. Examples of such strategies are 'taking risks; try to relax when feeling anxious about learning, and reward oneself for succeeding'. This category, sometimes combined with social strategies, is often involved in strategy work in second language learning.

Social strategies refer to how learners interact with other people in the context of learning languages and related culture. Social strategies include, among others, 'ask someone to speak slowly, practice with others and show interest in learning about the culture of English-speaking countries'. This category, sometimes combined with affective strategies, is often part of strategy research.

These six categories (which underlie the **Strategy Inventory for Language Learning (SILL)** used by Oxford and others for a great deal of research in the learning strategy field) were further divided into *direct* and *indirect* strategies. **Direct strategies** (i.e., memory strategies, cognitive strategies, compensation strategies) are those that directly involve the target language in the sense that they require mental processing of the language, whereas **indirect strategies** (i.e., metacognitive strategies, affective strategies, social strategies) provide indirect support for language learning through focusing, planning, evaluating, seeking opportunities, controlling anxiety, increasing cooperation and empathy and other means.

In more recent years, strategy research has been evolving a theory of language learning strategies that seeks to confirm or disconfirm a number of questions that have arisen. Such research involves (1) the adequacy of categorizing strategies into the above divisions, (2) the psychological assumptions underlying the postulation of strategic options, (3) the relationship of strategy research to current language teaching paradigms, (4) intercorrelations among, and relationships between, the many strategies that have been identified, and (5) the adequacy of various measures of strategy use and awareness. Whereas research into learning strategies was popular in general educational research in the 1980s, it declined dramatically in the 1990s, with researchers turning their attention to a related concept, SELF-REGULATION (i.e., the degree to which individuals are active participants in their own learning). it is claimed that researchers should do the same in SLA, as the study of self-regulation offers a broader perspective and shifts the focus from the product (strategies) to the process. It is argued that an approach based on self-regulation provides a more satisfactory way of empowering learners than traditional strategy training as the real goal should be that of assisting learners to achieve self-regulation not to use specific strategies.

Learning strategies contrast with COMMUNICATION STRATEGIES, which pertain to the employment of verbal or nonverbal mechanisms for the productive communication of information.

see also LEARNING STYLES, PERSONALITY, MOTIVATION, ANXIETY, WILLINGNESS TO COMMUNICATE, LEARNER BELIEFS, INTELLIGENCE, LANGUAGE APTITUDE, COMMUNICATION STRATEGIES

📖 Brown 2007; Dörnyei 2005; Ellis 2008; Oxford 1990a, 2001; Tseng et al. 2006

learning styles

the characteristic cognitive, affective, and physiological behaviors that are relatively stable indicators of how learners perceive, interact with, and respond to the learning environment. Learning style is a consistent way of functioning, that reflects underlying causes of behavior. Learning styles, therefore, reflect the totality of psychological functioning. They can be distinguished from abilities (such as LANGUAGE APTITUDE) in that they constitute preferences that orient a learner to how they approach the learning task rather than capacities that determine how well they learn. Whereas abilities relate linearly to language achievement (e.g., the greater the aptitude, the higher the achievement), learning styles are typically bipolar, with both styles affording advantages and disadvantages for learning.

Learning style is sometimes distinguished from **cognitive style**, which refers to the stable, pervasive way in which people process information. This manifests itself in activity in specific contexts and thus is intermingled with other affective, physiological, and behavioral factors. The totality is learning style. In fact, learning style cannot be clearly distinguished from other individual different factors such as PERSONALITY and MOTIVATION. The distinction between cognitive and learning styles is helpful, however, as it helps to resolve a contradiction in the literature. On the one hand cognitive styles are seen as relatively fixed but on the other hand learning styles are often seen as mutable, changing according to experience, and potentially trainable.

Several different learning styles are often referred to:

- field dependence/independence (see FIELD DEPENDENCE STYLE)
- inductive/deductive
- synthetic/analytic
- reflective/ impulsive (see REFLECTIVE STYLE)
- TOLERANT OF AMBIGUITY
- left-brain/right-brain (see LEFT-BRAIN DOMINANCE)
- visual, auditory, and kinesthetic (see PERCEPTUAL LEARNING STYLES)

Differences in learning style are thought to affect how learners approach learning tasks and may affect success on those tasks. However, there are few general conclusions that can be drawn from the research on learning styles. Learners clearly differ enormously in their preferred approach to L2 learning, but it is impossible to say which learning style works best. Quite possibly, it is learners who display flexibility who are most successful, but there is no real evidence yet for such a conclusion. One of the major problems is that the concept of learning style is ill-defined, apparently overlapping with other INDIVIDUAL DIFFERENCES of both an affective and a cognitive nature. It is unlikely that much progress will be made until researchers know what it is they want to measure.

see also ANXIETY, WILLINGNESS TO COMMUNICATE, LEARNER BELIEFS, INTELLIGENCE, LANGUAGE APTITUDE

📖 Brown 2007; Dörnyei 2005; Ellis 1994a, 2008; Keefe 1979a; Little & Singleton 1990; Holec 1987; Rayner 2000; Willing 1987

learning theory

a theory that extensive exposure to linguistic INPUT is sufficient to enable an infant to recognize recurrent syntactic forms and patterns. The theory effectively treats language as no different from other forms of learned behavior. It is supported by evidence from computer modeling, where a system of FEEDBACK ensures that a connection which produces a correct outcome is strengthened and a connection which leads to a wrong outcome is weakened. In this way, computer programs have been 'trained' to produce correct *past simple* forms.

see also BEHAVIORISM, CONNECTIONISM, EMPIRICISM, PARALLEL DISTRIBUTED PROCESSING

📖 Field 2004

left-brain dominance

a style that favors logical, analytical thought, with mathematical and linear processing of information. The left-brain style is distinguished from **right-brain dominance**, which perceives and remembers visual, tactile, and auditory images; it is more efficient in processing holistic, integrative, and emotional information. Torrance lists several characteristics of left- and right-brain dominance. (see Table L.1).

Left-brain dominance	Right-brain dominance
• Intellectual	Intuitive
• Remembers names	Remembers faces
• Responds to verbal instructions and explanations	Responds to demonstrated, illustrated, or symbolic instructions
• Experiments systematically and with control	Experiments randomly and with less restraint
• Makes objective judgments	Makes subjective judgments
• Planned and structured	Fluid and spontaneous
• Prefers established, certain information	Prefers elusive, uncertain information
• Analytic reader	Synthesizing reader
• Reliance on language in thinking and remembering	Reliance on images in thinking and remembering
• Prefers talking and writing	Prefers drawing and manipulating objects
• Prefers multiple-choice tests	Prefers open-ended questions
• Controls feelings	More free with feelings
• Not good at interpreting body language	Good at interpreting body language
• Rarely uses metaphors	Frequently uses metaphors
• Favors logical problem solving	Favors intuitive problem solving

Table L.1. Left- and right-brain characteristics

With reference to second language acquisition, it is argued that that left-brain-dominant second language learners are better at producing separate words, gathering the specifics of language, carrying out sequences of operations, and dealing with abstraction, classification, labeling, and reorganization. Right-brain-dominant learners, on the other hand, appear to deal better with whole images (not with reshuffling parts), with generalizations, with metaphors, and with emotional reactions and artistic expressions.
see also LATERALIZATION
📖 Brown 2007; Torrance 1980; Stevick 1982

Levelt' s model of speech production

Levelt proposed that speech production could be accounted for in terms of four overlapping operations: (1) *conceptualization*, (2) *formulation*, (3) *articulation*, and (4) *self-monitoring*. Conceptualization is concerned with planning the message content. It draws on background knowledge, knowledge about the topic, about the speech situation and on knowledge of patterns of discourse. The conceptualizer includes a monitor, which checks everything that occurs in the interaction to ensure that the communication goes to plan. This enables speakers to self-correct for expression, grammar and pronunciation. After conceptualization, the formulator finds the words and phrases to express the meanings, sequencing them and putting in appropriate grammatical markers (such as inflections, auxiliaries, artifacts). It also prepares the sound patterns of the words to be used: L1 errors of pronunciation very commonly involve switching sounds between words that are separated from each other; such switches suggest that the pronunciation of words must be prepared in batches prior to pronunciation. The third process is articulation. This involves the motor control of the articulatory organs; in English: the lips, tongue, teeth, alveolar palate, velum, glottis, mouth cavity and breath. Self-monitoring is concerned with language users being able to identify and self-correct mistakes.

All of this happens very fast and, to be successfully, deepens on automation. That is, to some degree in conceptualization, to a considerable extent in formulation and almost entirely in articulation. Automation is necessary since humans do not have enough attention capacity to consciously control the three types of process.

Psycholinguistic models of speech production such as Levelt's enable us to recognize that whereas some variability is socially motivated some is not. In part, variability reflects the tension between the amount of effort needed to access words from the lexicon, execute a grammatical encoding, and then assign a phonological coding, and the availability of planning time. Production involves a constant trade-off of the competing demands on memory and control mechanism. The result will be systematic differences in language use in accordance with opportunities available for pre-task and online planning and monitoring.

This model has been used in studies that have investigated the effects of planning on L2 performance.

📖 De Bot 1992; Bygate 2001; Ellis 2008; Levelt 1989

Lexicalization Hypothesis

a hypothesis that addresses the role that the L1 plays in learners' ability to infer the meanings of L2 words. It states that learners will find it easier to infer the meanings of unknown L2 words that have equivalent L1 forms.
📖 Ellis 2008

lexical preference principle
also **LPP**

the principle by which second language learners are said to rely on lexical items (words) to grasp a particular semantic intention when that same intention is also coded grammatically. Example: -s = third-person singular but so

does *the dog* in *The dog barks a lot*. In this case, the LPP predicts that language learners get 'third-person singular' from *the dog* and not *-s*.
 Piske & Young-Scholten 2009

library language
a second language that functions as a tool for further learning, especially when books or journals in a desired field of study are not commonly published in the learner's L1.
 Saville-Troike 2006

linguistic competence
see COMMUNICATIVE COMPETENCE

linguistic relativity
a theory of the relationship between speech and thought associated with Edward Sapir and Benjamin Whorf, and sometimes termed the **Sapir-Whorf Hypothesis**, or, for the sake of simplicity, **Whorfian Hypothesis**.
The term is often used to cover two distinct theories:

- *linguistic relativity*: a view that each language has categories and distinctions which are unique to it;
- *linguistic determinism*: a view that the way in which we perceive and categorize the world is shaped by the language we speak, i.e., language determines thought.

The hypothesis arose from anthropological work among speakers of Polynesian, North American Indian and Eskimo languages. The researchers adopted the questionable assumption that concepts not represented in the languages they studied were absent from the world view of the people who spoke them. Today's view is that all human beings have access to basic concepts, but that languages differ in whether they codify (give form to) a particular concept or not. Thus, English codifies many more types of *walking* than most languages (*walk, stroll, amble, loiter, wander, scurry, march*, etc.); but speakers of other languages are still capable of recognizing the concepts involved.
A major test for linguistic determinism was found in the fact that languages divide up the color spectrum differently. If it could be shown that we do not all perceive the spectrum in the same way, it would suggest that our perception of the real world is indeed shaped by the way in which our language classifies and subcategorizes it. In fact, research suggests that *focal points* (prototypes) for particular colors are not only shared by speakers of the same language, but are also shared across languages. There is agreement on 'typical values' for colors even where a language possesses fewer color terms than English.

Directly opposed to linguistic relativity is a widely held view that LANGUAGE UNIVERSALS underlie the way in which languages encode reality. Some researchers would see these universals as deriving from the similar life experiences that human beings share across cultures. Others might attribute them to the fact that all human beings possess similar cognitive faculties and thus similar ways of viewing the world and organizing information.

So, while some aspects of language seem to provide us with potential cognitive mindsets, we can also recognize that through both language and culture, some universal properties bind us all together in one world. The act of learning to think in another language may require a considerable degree of mastery of that language, but a second language learner does not have to learn to think, in general, all over again. As in every other human learning experience, the second language learner can make positive use of prior experiences to facilitate the process of learning by retaining that which is valid and valuable for second culture learning and second language learning.

 Brown 2007; Field 2004; Palmer 1981; Ungerer & Schmid 1996

linguistic universals
another term for TYPOLOGICAL UNIVERSALS

LLSs
an abbreviation for LANGUAGE LEARNING STRATEGIES

LTM
an abbreviation for LONG-TERM MEMORY

local error
see ERROR ANALYSIS

locutionary act
see SPEECH ACT

logical problem of language acquisition
a term used by researchers in the Chomskyan tradition (see CHOMSKYAN THEORY) to refer to the gap between what can logically be learned from the available INPUT and what actually is learned. How is it possible for children to achieve the FINAL STATE of L1 development with general ease and complete success, given the complexity of the linguistic system which they acquire and their immature cognitive capacity at the age they do so? This question forms the logical problem of language learning. The 'problem' as it has been formulated by linguists relates most importantly to syntactic phenomena. Most linguists and psychologists assume this achievement must be attributed to innate and spontaneous language-learning constructs and/or processes (see INNATENESS HYPOTHESIS). The notion that innate linguistic

logical problem of language acquisition 215

knowledge must underlie language acquisition was prominently espoused by Noam Chomsky, who subsequently formulated a theory of UNIVERSAL GRAMMAR which has been very influential in SLA theory and research. This view has been supported by arguments such as the following:

1) Children's knowledge of language goes beyond what could be learned from the input they receive. This is essentially the poverty-of-the-stimulus argument (see POVERTY OF THE STIMULUS). According to this argument, children often hear incomplete or ungrammatical utterances along with grammatical input, and yet they are somehow able to filter the language they hear so that the ungrammatical input is not incorporated into their L1 system. Further, children are commonly recipients of simplified input from adults, which does not include data for all of the complexities which are within their linguistic competence. In addition, children hear only a finite subset of possible grammatical sentences, and yet they are able to abstract general principles and constraints which allow them to interpret and produce an infinite number of sentences which they have never heard before. Even more remarkable, children's linguistic competence includes knowledge of which sentences are not possible, although input does not provide them with this information, i.e., input 'underdetermines' the grammar that develops. Almost all L1 linguistic input to children is POSITIVE EVIDENCE, or actual utterances by other speakers which the children are able to at least partially comprehend. Unlike many L2 learners, children almost never receive any explicit instruction in L1 during the early years when acquisition takes place, and they seldom receive any NEGATIVE EVIDENCE, or explicit correction (and often fail to recognize it when they do).

2) Constraints and principles cannot be learned. Children's access to general constraints and principles which govern language could account for the relatively short time it takes for the L1 grammar to emerge, and for the fact that it does so systematically and without any 'wild' divergences. This could be so because innate principles lead children to organize the input they receive only in certain ways and not others. In addition to the lack of negative evidence mentioned above, constraints and principles cannot be learned in part because children acquire a first language at an age when such abstractions are beyond their comprehension; constraints and principles are thus outside the realm of learning processes which are related to general INTELLIGENCE. However, some scholars approach this capacity in children as a 'paradox of language acquisition'.

3) Universal patterns of development cannot be explained by language-specific input. Linguistic input always consists of the sounds, words, phrases, sentences, and other surface-level units of a specific human language. However, in spite of the surface differences in input (to the point

that people who are speaking different languages cannot understand one another), there are similar patterns in child acquisition of any language in the world. The extent of this similarity suggests that language universals are not only constructs derived from sophisticated theories and analyses by linguists, but also innate representations in every young child's mind.

If we extend the logical problem from L1 acquisition to SLA, we need to explain how it is possible for individuals to achieve multilingual competence when that also involves knowledge which transcends what could be learned from the input they receive. In other words, L2 learners also develop an underlying system of knowledge about that language which they are not taught, and which they could not infer directly from anything they hear. However, in several important respects L1 and L2 acquisition are fundamentally different; the arguments put forth for the existence of an innate, language-specific faculty in young children do not all apply to L2 learners since they are not uniformly successful, they are typically more cognitively advanced than young children, they may receive and profit from instruction and negative evidence, and they are influenced by many factors which seem irrelevant to acquisition of L1.

Thus, it is widely accepted that there is an innate capacity involved in L1 acquisition by young children (although many do not agree with Chomsky's particular formulation of its nature), but there is less certainty about the continued availability of that capacity for acquiring an L2.

 Chomsky 1957, 1965; Ellis 2008; Jackendoff 1997; Saville-Troike 2006

longitudinal study
see CROSSSECTIONAL STUDY

long-term memory
also **LTM**

a store for permanent information, including world knowledge, the lexicon and general linguistic competence. In many accounts, long-term memory (LTM) is distinguished from a SENSORY MEMORY store of very brief duration, and from a limited-capacity WORKING MEMORY (WM) which holds currently relevant information and handles cognitive operations. LTM supplies information to WM when it is required and receives information from WM that is destined for long-term storage.

An item of information (e.g., a phone number or a name that we want to remember) can be consolidated and transferred from WM to LTM by *rehearsal*—by repeating it silently in our minds. Similarly, the more often we retrieve a particular item of information from LTM, the easier it becomes to access it and the less likely it is to be lost. Information that is rarely retrieved may decay, as in language ATTRITION. Some accounts suggest that this is due to the loss of *retrieval cues* linked to the information sought.

LTM would appear to involve multiple memory systems, each with different functions. A distinction is made between two particular types of knowledge: DECLARATIVE KNOWLEDGE (knowledge that) and PROCEDURAL KNOWLEDGE (knowledge how). In a classic account of how *expertise* is acquired, information is received into LTM in declarative form and gradually becomes proceduralized as WM makes more and more use of it. A novice first draws on declarative knowledge in the form of a series of steps to which conscious attention (control) has to be given. In time, some of these steps become combined (composed), and the process becomes more and more automatic until it comes to form procedural knowledge.

Two types of declarative memory are generally recognized:

- *episodic memory* stores events; it is specific in terms of time and place;
- *semantic memory* stores generalized world knowledge.

The second may develop from the first. Imagine that a child stores in episodic memory a set of encounters with real-world entities that adults label *dog*. From these experiences, it can extrapolate a set of common features (or possibly a *prototype*); it thus forms a category in semantic memory which serves to identify the whole class of dogs. An alternative, *exemplar-based* view (see DUAL-MODE SYSTEM) would minimize the role of semantic memory and suggest that we identify examples of a category like *dog* by relating them to many previous encounters with entities that have received this label, all of them stored episodically as individual events.

Semantic memory in LTM is sometimes represented as schematic in form. A schema is a set of interrelated features associated with an entity or concept. For example, the schema for *penguin* might include: black and white, Antarctic, ice floe, fish, and paperback publisher. Schematic information strongly influences the way in which we process incoming information, and is sometimes critical to the understanding of a text.

The ease with which a memory is retrieved from LTM is determined by how strongly encoded it is and by how precise are the available cues. Effective remembering may depend upon activating the same cues at retrieval as were originally encoded with the memory (the encoding specificity hypothesis). When subjects are asked to memorize the second words of some two-word compounds (e.g. *strawberry jam*), the first word (*strawberry*) provides a powerful cue in later recall. However, the same does not occur if a different cue such as *traffic* is used.

see also SCHEMA THEORY

Cohen et al. 1993; Field 2004; Kellogg 1995

218 LPP

LPP
an abbreviation for LEXICAL PREFERENCE PRINCIPLE

majority language
see MINORITY LANGUAGE

malapropism
see TIP OF THE TONGUE

markedness
a linguistic concept related to how common or typical feature is. Generally speaking, something that is more common or ubiquitous is considered less marked or unmarked, while something less common or less natural is considered marked or more marked. In addition, something unmarked or less marked may be considered the default form of the feature. Markedness can be used to make crosslinguistic comparisons (what happens around the world with languages) or what happens within a single language.

For examples, the adjectives 'old' and 'young' can be considered unmarked and marked respectively, because whereas 'old' can be used to ask about a person's age: *How old is she?* (= what is her age), 'young' cannot, except in some very special sense: *How young is she?* (= is she as young as she makes out?).

Some markedness relations are hierarchical. According to surveys of world languages, subject relative clauses are the most common and are the least marked. Object of comparisons are the least common and are the most marked. Other features of language that exist in binary opposition to each other are often considered to exist in a marked relationship. For example, masculine gender is less marked/unmarked relative to feminine or neuter gender. In sound systems, voiceless consonants such as *s, t,* and *k* are considered less marked/unmarked compared to their voiced counterparts *z, d,* and *g*. And, as one final example, in semantics, the term *lion* is considered unmarked and can refer to any kind of lion (it is the default form of the word) while *lioness* can only refer to female lions. This is so because lioness entails the addition of a suffix to *lion*. Note that other derivatives and phrases are based on lion and not lioness: *lion-like, pride of lions*, and so on.

Markedness has been shown to be relevant to both L1 and L2 acquisition. In general, learners have more difficulty with more marked elements of

language in an L2 (regardless of whether the same elements exist in their L1 or not). Returning to the example of relative clauses, research has shown that subject and object relative clauses are easier to acquire compared to genitive and object of prepositions. By 'easier to acquire' what is normally meant is that the less marked clauses appear sooner in learner OUTPUT and learners make fewer errors with them. More marked items may take longer to appear: Learners may make more errors with them, or the marked items may simply not appear at all (depending on the structure or feature in question).
see also ABSOLUTE NON-IMPLICATIONAL UNIVERSALS
📖 Ellis 2008; VanPatten & Benati 2010

Markedness Differential Hypothesis
also MDH, Markedness Theory
an accounting of relative degrees of difficulty of learning a language by means of principles of UNIVERSAL GRAMMAR. The Markedness Differential Hypothesis (MDH) was advanced by Eckman which makes use of MARKEDNESS to explain why some L1 forms are transferred while others are not. It claims that learners transfer target-language features that are less marked than equivalent features in their L1 but do not transfer those that are more marked. More specifically, those areas of difficulty that a second language learner will have can be predicted on the basis of a comparison of the native language (NL) and the target language (TL) such that:

1) those areas of the TL that are different from the NL and are relatively more marked than in the NL will be difficult;
2) the degree of difficulty associated with those aspects of the TL that are different and more marked than in the NL corresponds to the relative degree of markedness associated with those aspects;
3) those areas of the TL that are different from the NL but are not relatively more marked than the NL will not be difficult.

The MDH constitutes an attempt to reformulate the CONTRASTIVE ANALYSIS HYPOTHESIS (CAH) to take account of markedness factors. It differs from the CAH in a number of important ways: it seeks to explain (1) not only where learning difficulty will occur, but also the relative degree of difficulty; (2) where differences between the native and the target languages will not result in difficulty; and (3) why certain structures are typically acquired before other structures.
📖 Eckman 1977; Ellis 2008

Markedness Theory
another term for MARKEDNESS DIFFERENTIAL HYPOTHESIS

MDH
an abbreviation for MARKEDNESS DIFFERENTIAL HYPOTHESIS

meaningful learning
see SUBSUMPTION

meaningful learning model
another term for SUBSUMPTION

mean length utterance
also **MLU**
the average number of morphemes produced per utterance—not always recognizable as sentences. In language acquisition research, mean length utterance (MLU) is a measure of the linguistic complexity of children's utterances, especially during the early stages of first language learning. It is measured by counting the average length of the utterances a child produces, using the morpheme rather than the word as the unit of measurement. MLU is a more reliable measure than age, due to great variations in the rate at which infants acquire language. MLU is generally not considered to be a good index of development in second language learning.
see also T-UNIT
 Field 2004; Hudson 2000; Richards & Schmidt 2010

memory
the mental capacity to store information, either for short or long periods. Early research into memory led to a multi-store model consisting of: SENSORY MEMORY, SHORT-TERM MEMORY and LONG-TERM MEMORY. The flow of information between these different stores is often represented as controlled by a central executive.
 Field 2004

memory strategies
see LEARNING STRATEGIES

mentalism
also **mentalist theory**
the theory that a human being possesses a mind which has consciousness, ideas, etc., and that the mind can influence the behavior of the body. Chomsky's attack on Skinner's theory of language learning led to a reassertion of mentalist views of first language acquisition. In place of the empiricist approach of behaviorists (see EMPIRICISM), Chomsky stressed the active contribution of the child and minimized the importance of imitation and reinforcement. He claimed that the child's knowledge of his mother tongue was

derived from a UNIVERSAL GRAMMAR (UG) which specified the essential form that any natural language could take.

In summary, mentalist views of L1 acquisition posited the following:

1) Language is a human-specific faculty.
2) Language exists as an independent faculty in the human mind, i.e., although it is part of the learner's total cognitive apparatus, it is separate from the general cognitive mechanisms responsible for intellectual development.
3) The primary determinant of L1 acquisition is the child's acquisition device (see LANGUAGE ACQUISITION DEVICE), which is genetically endowed and provides the child with a set of principles about grammar.
4) The acquisition device atrophies with age.
5) The process of acquisition consists of hypothesis-testing, by which means the grammar of the learner's mother tongue is related to the principles of UG.

see also INNATENESS HYPOTHESIS, NATIVISM, MODULARITY, LANGUAGE ACQUISITION DEVICE

 Chomsky 1959; Ellis 1986; Lenneberg 1967; Richards & Schmidt 2010; Saville-Troike 2006

metacognition
see COGNITION

metacognitive strategies
see LEARNING STRATEGIES

metalinguistic awareness
another term for METALINGUISTIC KNOWLEDGE

metalinguistic feedback
see FEEDBACK

metalinguistic knowledge
also metalanguage awareness
knowledge of the forms, structures and other aspects of a language, which a learner arrives at through reflecting on and analyzing the language. Metalinguistic knowledge refers to one's ability to consider language not just as a means of expressing ideas or communicating with others, but also as an object of inquiry. Thus, making puns suggests an ability to think about language as opposed to only using it for expressive purposes. Similarly, judging whether a given sentence is grammatical in one's native language or translat-

ing from one language to another requires thinking about language as opposed to engaging in pure use of it.

The main interest in SLA has centered on whether metalinguistic knowledge predicts better acquisition of the rule-system of the L2 than no metalinguistic knowledge. The theory would explain this mainly in terms of the difference between first language acquisition and SLA. Very young children rely less on metalinguistic knowledge of their L1, and have no knowledge of terms, yet manage, in overwhelming numbers, to learn to speak it perfectly well. In contrast, L2 learners post-critical period (see CRITICAL PERIOD HYPOTHESIS) mostly do not. It is therefore hypothesized that possessing metalinguistic knowledge might act as a short-cut to learning.

The debate is alive among practitioners some of whom argue that knowing the terminology helps to understand the patterns they are exposed to, while others see learning metalanguage, at least for some learners, as a difficult undertaking, especially when one considers the opaqueness of some of the terminology (e.g., 'indirect object pronoun').

📖 Bialystok 1988; Gass & Selinker 2008; Macaro et al. 2010; Richards & Schmidt 2010

metatalk

a term which refers to (1) the talk that learners employ to establish what kind of activity to make of a task and also what operations to employ in performing it and (2) the talk that arises when learners focus explicitly on language in the course of accomplishing a task.

see also LANGUAGING

📖 Ellis 2008

microgenesis

a term which refers to how development takes place over the course of a particular interaction in a specific sociocultural setting. In SOCIOCULTURAL THEORY, the microgenetic method has been used by researchers to investigate how learning takes place within the course of an interaction. Four key characteristics of the microgenetic method are as follows:

1) individuals are observed through a period of change
2) observations are conducted before, during, and after the period of change
3) observations during the period of transition are conducted regularly
4) observed behaviors are analyzed intensively, using both qualitative and quantitative methods, in order to identify the processes that arise in the developmental change.

📖 Ellis 2008; Lavelli et al. 2004

minimalism
also minimalist approach, minimalist program, MP
a theory of grammar introduced by Chomsky (see CHOMSKYAN THEORY) in 1995 as an advance on GOVERNMENT AND BINDING THEORY while remaining within the general paradigm of the principle and parameters model of UNIVERSAL GRAMMAR. Minimalism attempted to develop a more economical account of the principles that underline the syntax of all languages by formulating a number of 'guidelines' that provide for a more 'minimal' representation of innate knowledge of syntax. This goal is motivated in part by the desire to minimize the acquisition burden faced by children and account for the fact that children will acquire any language they are exposed to.
 Chomsky 1995; Richards & Schmidt 2010

minimalist approach
another term for MINIMALISM

minimalist program
another term for MINIMALISM

minimal terminable unit
another term for T-UNIT

minority language
a long-established language spoken as a mother tongue by people in some part of a country in which the national or official language is something else. We commonly tend to assume that everybody in, say, France speaks French. In fact, virtually all adults in France *do* speak French—but not always as their first language. In various regions of the country, the first language of all or most local people is Alsatian German, Dutch, Breton, Basque, Catalan, Occitan or Corsican. Each of these is the mother tongue in its region, and people who learn one of these as their first language in early childhood may not even begin learning French until later in life, especially after beginning formal education. Such languages are called minority languages, and minority languages are not confined to France. Alongside Spanish, Spain has Galician, Basque and Catalan; alongside German, Germany has Frisian and Wendish (the second is a Slavic language); alongside English, Britain has Welsh and Scots Gaelic; alongside English, the USA has Navaho, Hopi, Lakota, and dozens of other indigenous languages. Russia and China each have over a hundred minority languages, and countries with no minority languages are in fact a rarity—though Iceland and Portugal may be two cases.
In contrast to the minority language, the **majority language** is the language spoken by the wider community, society and/or country and is the language most often used for educational, business and governance. Examples

of majority languages are English in the USA and French in France.
see also HERITAGE LANGUAGE, IMMIGRANT LANGUAGE
📖 Trask 2005

mistake
see ERROR

MLU
an abbreviation for MEAN LENGTH UTTERANCE

modified input
discourse addressed to second language learners and young children that has been adapted or 'simplified' to make comprehension easier, such as by using comprehension checks, clarification requests and self-repetitions. Among those characteristics of modified input are (1) slower rate and clearer articulation, (2) increased use of high frequency vocabulary, less slang, fewer idioms (3) simplified syntax (e.g., short sentences, repetition, fewer clauses), (4) discourse adjustments (e.g., clearer connections between pronouns and their antecedents), and (5) alterations in prosody (e.g., increased acoustic stress on content words), among others.
Modified input contrasts with **premodified input**, which is modified to make it more comprehensible prior to the learner being required to process it. Graded readers provide learners with premodified input.
CHILD-DIRECTED SPEECH, FOREIGNER TALK, and TEACHER TALK are three main types of modified input.
see also MODIFIED OUTPUT
📖 Ellis 2008; Macaro et al. 2010; Richards & Schmidt 2010

modified output
the process of rephrasing or reformulating one's original utterance. Modified output occurs when learners modify a previous utterance. This may occur following FEEDBACK or as a result of self-monitoring. It may involve repair of an initial error or some other change. Modified output is believed to benefit L2 development through its role in stretching learners' linguistic abilities, testing hypotheses, and automatizing production.
see also MODIFIED INPUT
📖 Ellis 2008; Mackey 2007

modularity
a view that each level of language processing operates independently of the others. A modular system is one which consists of several largely independent components which interact in such a way that the whole system performs some task or tasks successfully. Since the early 1980s, the concept of modularity has become prominent in linguistics and cognitive science in at least

two ways. An issue of controversy has been the extent to which the mind should be viewed as *modular* or *unitary*. That is, should we see the mind as a single, flexible organism, with one general set of procedures for learning and storing different kinds of knowledge and skills? Or, is it more helpfully understood as a bundle of modules, with distinctive mechanisms relevant to different types of knowledge?

Discussion of modularity is much influenced by Fodor. He views the mind as composed of a set of central systems which handle generalized operations such as attention or memory. (The opposing view here is **holism**, the belief that the mind is essentially a seamless whole, with no specialized subparts.) These are supplied with information by input systems which process sensory information and language. The input systems are modular and each has specific functions. Fodor characterizes the systems as:

- *Domain specific*. Input via the ears is processed as simple auditory input in the case of music or the noise of traffic, but is recoded phonologically by the speech module if it takes the form of speech.
- *Mandatory*. We cannot help hearing an utterance as an example of speech.
- *Fast*. The processes are highly automatic.
- *Informationally encapsulated*. A module receives information from other modules and passes it on, but its immediate operation is not affected by information contained elsewhere. So, while engaged in processing a spoken word we cannot use context to identify the word more quickly (this does not preclude the use of contextual information at a later, post-perceptual stage).
- *Localized*. Input systems are part of the hard-wiring of the brain; there is a fixed neural architecture for each.

The modular view has consistently found support from within linguistics, most famously in the further debate between Chomsky and the child development psychologist, Jean Piaget. Piaget argued that language was simply one manifestation of the more general skill of symbolic representation, acquired as a stage in general cognitive development; no special mechanism was therefore required to account for first language acquisition. Chomsky's general view is that not only is language too complex to be learned from environmental exposure (his criticism of Skinner), it is also too distinctive in its structure to be 'learnable' by general cognitive means. In fact, Chomsky has been arguing that the human language faculty is modular: that it must consist of a fairly large number of semi-autonomous units, each of which is responsible for certain particular aspects of our linguistic competence. This belief is strongly reflected in Chomsky's theory of grammar, the GOVERNMENT-AND-BINDING THEORY, which posits a number of specialized grammatical modules; each of these has its own requirements, and all must be satisfied for a sentence to be well formed.

The possible role of an innate, specialist language module in SLA has been much discussed in recent years. If such innate mechanisms indeed exist, there are four logical possibilities:

1) They continue to operate during SLA, and make key aspects of SLA possible, in the same way that they make first-language learning possible.
2) After the acquisition of the first language in early childhood, these mechanisms cease to be operable, and second languages must be learned by other means.
3) The mechanisms themselves are no longer operable, but the first language provides a model of a natural language and how it works, which can be 'copied' in some way when learning a second language.
4) Distinctive learning mechanisms for language remain available, but only in part, and must be supplemented by other means. (From a UNIVERSAL GRAMMAR point of view, this would mean that universal grammar was itself modular, with some modules still available and others not.).

see also INTERACTIVE ACTIVATION, UNIVERSAL GRAMMAR
Field 2004; Fodor 1983; Mithcell & Myles 2004; Swinney 1979; Trask 2005; Wingfield & Titone 1998

Monitor Hypothesis
also Monitor Theory

a theory proposed by Krashen which distinguishes two distinct processes in second and foreign language development and use. According to Krashen, 'learning' and 'acquisition' (see ACQUISITION-LEARNING HYPOTHESIS) are used in very specific ways in second-language performance. The Monitor Hypothesis states that learning has only one function, and that is as a monitor or editor and that learning comes into play only to make changes in the form of our utterance, after it has been produced by the acquired system. Acquisition initiates the speaker's utterances and is responsible for fluency. Thus, the Monitor is thought to alter the output of the acquired system before or after the utterance is actually written or spoken, but the utterance is initiated entirely by the acquired system.

However, the Monitor cannot be used at all times. There are three conditions that must be met, although Krashen claimed that, whereas these are necessary conditions, they are not necessarily sufficient because the Monitor may not be activated even when all three conditions have been satisfied. The three conditions for Monitor use are as follows:

1) *Time*. Learners need time to consciously think about and use the rules available to them in their learned system.
2) *Focus on form*. Although time may be basic, one must also be focused on form. Learners must be paying attention to how they are saying something, not just to what they are saying.
3) *Know the rule*. In order to apply a rule, one has to know it. In other words, one has to have an appropriate learned system in order to apply it.

Needless to say, the pressures and demands of conversing in the second language in real time do not often allow for such monitoring to take place. Krashen's Monitor Hypothesis has been criticized for that reason, and also for the fact that attempts to test its predictions have been unsuccessful, for example in studies comparing learners' performance when given more time or being made to focus on form, or checking whether learners who are able to explain the rules perform better than learners who do not.

Krashen used the concept of the Monitor in order to explain individual differences in learners. He suggests that it is possible to find Monitor 'over-users' who do not like making mistakes and are therefore constantly checking what they produce against the conscious stock of rules they possess. Their speech is consequently very halting and non-fluent. On the other hand, Monitor 'under-users' do not seem to care very much about the errors they make, and for them, speed and fluency are more important. Such learners rely exclusively on the acquired system and do not seem able or willing to consciously apply anything they have learned to their output. In between the two are the supposed 'optimal' Monitor users, who use the Monitor Hypothesis when it is appropriate, that is, when it does not interfere with communication.

The problem with such claims, even though they might have some intuitive appeal, is that they are at present impossible to test empirically: how do we know when a learner is consciously applying a rule or not, or, in other words, whether the source of the rule that has been applied is the acquired system or the learned system?

Ellis 1986; McLaughlin 1987; Mithcell & Myles 2004

monitoring
a general term used to describe the mental processes involved in verifying that what one has spoken, written or even temporarily rehearsed (i.e., practiced before speaking) is correct. There is a clear distinction between monitoring and **checking** where the former relies on learner-internal resources and the latter is a recourse to external sources such as dictionaries or glossaries. Krashen's MONITOR THEORY was used as a means of differentiating between the learned system and the acquired system whereby only the conscious

learned system could monitor speech production. There is a continued interest in the role of ATTENTION in the monitoring process.
📖 Kormos 2000; Macaro 2003; Macaro et al. 2010

Monitor Model
one of the most controversial theoretical perspectives in SLA in the last quarter of the twentieth century which was proposed by Stephen Krashen in a host of articles and books. Krashen's hypotheses have had a number of different names. In the earlier years the 'Monitor Model' and the 'Acquisition-Learning Hypothesis' were more popular terms; in recent years the 'Input Hypothesis' has come to identify what is really a set of five interrelated hypotheses:

1) ACQUISITION-LEARNING HYPOTHESIS
2) MONITOR HYPOTHESIS
3) NATURAL ORDER HYPOTHESIS
4) INPUT HYPOTHESIS
5) AFFECTIVE FILTER HYPOTHESIS.

see also MULTIDIMENSIONAL MODEL, COMPETITION MODEL, VARIABLE COMPETENCE MODEL, CAPABILITY CONTINUUM PARADIGM, SOCIO-PSYCHOLINGUISTIC MODEL, NATIVIZATION MODEL, ACCULTURATION MODEL, FUNCTIONALIST MODEL
📖 González 2008; Krashen 1977,1981,1982,1985,1992, 1997

Monitor Theory
another term for MONITOR HYPOTHESIS

monolingualism
a term which refers to speakers or speech communities who know and use only one language—their L1. It can be characterized as a failure to learn an L2 and may be associated with a strong ETHNIC IDENTITY and negative attitudes towards the target-language center.
📖 Ellis 2008

morpheme studies
an approach to SLA introduced by Dulay and Burt that focuses on the sequence in which specific English grammatical morphemes are acquired. In the early 1970s, SLA researchers took interest in the acquisition of English morphemes. Work on child FIRST LANGUAGE (L1) ACQUISITION in English studied 14 morphemes and found that children, regardless of the homes they were raised in, acquired these morphemes in the same order. L2 researchers wanted to know whether this was true for English L2 and whether or not the L2 order(s) matched the L1 order. They studied morphemes such as plural

-*s*, third-person -*s*, possessive -*s*, contracted copular -*s* (*he's coming*), past tense regular -*ed*, and progressive -*ing*, among others. By the late 1980s, dozens of morpheme studies had been conducted using a variety of techniques. It is fair to say that, overall, the results suggest that L2 learners, regardless of their L1s, acquire these English morphemes in a predictable order. These are now referred to as ACQUISITION ORDERS. However, why an order exists the way it does and just what these orders reflect is still unclear. Also, there has been some controversy about what the morpheme studies overlook, such as underlying meaning attributed to some morphemes by learners.

The morpheme studies have been subject to some stringent criticisms in addition to the doubts about using accuracy order as a basis for discussing acquisition. One criticism is that the method of scoring morphemes does not take account of misuse in inappropriate contexts. Another criticism is that the use of rank order statistics hides meaningful differences, but Krashen's grouping of features into a 'natural order' (see NATURAL ORDER HYPOTHESIS) goes some way to overcoming that objection. Other objections are that the research has been restricted to a small set of morphemes, that the morphemes studies constitute a rag-bag of disparate features (the acquisition of articles and third pearson -*s*, for instance, pose the learner very different tasks, as one involves semantic considerations and the other is a purely formal feature), and that the research has lacked theoretical motivation.

Although with one or two exceptions the morpheme studies ceases in the early 1980s, interest in the natural order did not. Researchers switched attention from description to explanation by focusing on the factors that accounted for the accuracy order.

📖 Dulay & Burt 1974c; Ellis 2008; Saville-Troike 2006; VanPatten & Benati 2010

morphology development

By the time a child is two-and-a-half years old, he is going beyond TELEGRAPHIC SPEECH forms and incorporating some of the inflectional morphemes that indicate the grammatical function of the nouns and verbs used. The first to appear is usually the -*ing* form in expressions such as *cat sitting* and *mommy reading book*. The next morphological development is typically the marking of regular plurals with the -*s* form, as in *boys* and *cats*. The acquisition of the plural marker is often accompanied by a process of OVERGENERALIZATION. The child overgeneralizes the apparent rule of adding -*s* to form plurals and will talk about *foots* and *mans*. When the alternative pronunciation of the plural morpheme used in *houses* (i.e., ending in [-əz]) comes into use, it too is given an overgeneralized application and forms such as *boyses* or *footses* can be heard. At the same time as this overgeneralization is taking place, some children also begin using irregular plurals such as *men* quite appropriately for a while, but then try out the general rule on the forms, producing expressions like some *mens* and two *feets*, or even two *feetses*. Not long after, the use of the possessive inflection -*'s* occurs in expressions such as *girl's dog* and *Mummy's book*.

At about the same time, different forms of the verb 'to be', such as *are* and *was*, begin to be used. The appearance of forms such as *was* and, at about the same time, *went* and *came* should be noted. These are irregular past-tense forms that we would not expect to hear before the more regular forms. However, they do typically precede the appearance of the -*ed* inflection. Once the regular past-tense forms (*walked, played*) begin appearing in the child's speech, the irregular forms may disappear for a while, replaced by overgeneralized versions such as *goed* and *comed*. For a period, the -*ed* inflection may be added to everything, producing such oddities as *walkeded* and *wented*. As with the plural forms, the child works out (usually after the age of four) which forms are regular and which are not.

Finally the regular -*s* marker on third-person-singular present-tense verbs appears. It occurs initially with full verbs (*comes, looks*) and then with auxiliaries (*does, has*).

 Yule 2006

motherese
another term for CHILD DIRECTED SPEECH

mother talk
another term for CHILD DIRECTED SPEECH

mother tongue maintenance
a type of bilingual education which takes two forms. In the weaker form, pupils are given classes in their mother tongue, directed at developing formal language skills, including full literacy. In the stronger form, pupils are educated through the medium of their mother tongue. Examples of the former are the programs for Punjabi established in Bradford, UK and for Italian in Bedford for ethnic minority children living in those cities. Examples of the latter are the programs for the seven main language groups in Uzbekistan, and the Finnish-medium classes for Finnish migrant workers in Sweden. Mother tongue maintenance programs are based on *enrichment theory*, according to which high levels of BILINGUALISM are seen as a cognitive and social advantage. This contrasts with DEFICIT THEORY, which views bilingualism as a burden and as likely to result in cognitive disadvantage. The results of research strongly suggest that ADDITIVE BILINGUALISM (the goal of mother tongue maintenance) confers linguistic, perceptual, and intellectual advantages.

There is also evidence that mother tongue maintenance setting, particularly those of the strong kind, result in considerable educational success. They are characterized by positive organizational factors (e.g., appropriate cultural content in teaching materials), positive affective factors (e.g., low ANXIETY, high internal MOTIVATION, and self-confidence in the learners), success in developing full control of the L1, and a high level of proficiency in the L2.

Mother tongue maintenance provides support for L2 learning in two main ways. First, ensuring that L2 is an additional rather than a replacement language result in learners developing a positive self-identity. Mother tongue maintenance then is more likely to result in the positive ATTITUDEs needed for successful L2 development. The second way involves a consideration of INTERDEPENDENCY PRINCIPLE.

see also SUBMERSION, IMMERSION, SEGREGATION, DUAL LANGUAGE EDUCATION
📖 Cummins 1979; Ellis 2008; Fitzpatrick 1987; Skuttnab-Kangas 1988; Tosi 1984

motivation

in general, the driving force in any situation that leads to action. In SLA, motivation refers to the effort which learners put into learning an L2 as a result of their need or desire to learn it. Various theories of motivation have been proposed over the course of decades of research. Three different perspectives emerge:

1) From a *behavioral* perspective, motivation is seen in very matter of fact terms. It is quite simply the anticipation of reward. Driven to acquire positive reinforcement, and driven by previous experiences of reward for behavior, we act accordingly to achieve further reinforcement. Skinner, Pavlov, and Thorndike put motivation at the center of their theories of human behavior. In a behavioral view, performance in tasks—and motivation to do so—is likely to be at the mercy of external forces: parents, teachers, peers, educational requirements, job specifications, and so forth.

2) In *cognitive* terms, motivation places much more emphasis on the individual's decisions, the choices people make as to what experiences or goals they will approach or avoid, and the degree of effort they will exert in that respect. Some cognitive psychologists see underlying needs or drives as the compelling force behind our decisions. Ausubel, for example, identified six needs undergirding the construct of motivation:
   a) The need for exploration, for seeing the other side of the mountain, for probing the unknown
   b) The need for manipulation, for operating—to use Skinner's term—on the environment and causing change
   c) The need for activity, for movement and exercise, both physical and mental
   d) The need for stimulation, the need to be stimulated by the environment, by other people, or by ideas, thoughts, and feelings
   e) The need for knowledge, the need to process and internalize the results of exploration, manipulation, activity, and stimulation, to re-

solve contradictions, to quest for solutions to problems and for self-consistent systems of knowledge
f) Finally, the need for ego enhancement, for the self to be known and to be accepted and approved of by others, i.e., 'self-system'
3) A *constructivist* view of motivation places even further emphasis on social context as well as individual personal choices. Each person is motivated differently, and will therefore act on his environment in ways that are unique. But these unique acts are always carried out within a cultural and social milieu and cannot be completely separated from that context. Several decades ago, Abraham Maslow viewed motivation as a construct in which ultimate attainment of goals was possible only by passing through a hierarchy of needs, three of which were solidly grounded in community, belonging, and social status. Motivation, in a constructivist view, is derived as much from our interactions with others as it is from one's self-determination.

Motivation is something that can, like self-esteem, be *global*, *situational*, or *task-oriented*. Learning a foreign language requires some of all three levels of motivation. For example, a learner may possess high global motivation but low task motivation to perform well on, say, the written mode of the language. Motivation is also typically examined in terms of the **intrinsic** and **extrinsic** motives of the learner. Those who learn for their own self-perceived needs and goals are intrinsically motivated, and those who pursue a goal only to receive an external reward from someone else are extrinsically motivated. Finally, studies of motivation in second language acquisition often refer to the distinction between integrative and instrumental orientations of the learner. **Instrumental motivation** occurs when a learner has a functional goal (such as to get a job or pass an examination), and **integrative motivation** occurs when learner wishes to identify with the culture of the L2 group. It does not affect language learning directly; rather its effect is mediated by the learning behavior that it instigates.
It is important to note that instrumentality and integrativeness are not actually types of motivation as such, but rather are more appropriately termed *orientations*. That is, depending on whether a learner's context or orientation is (1) academic or career related (instrumental), or (2) socially or culturally oriented (integrative), different needs might be fulfilled in learning a foreign language. The importance of distinguishing orientation from motivation is that within either orientation, one can have either high or low motivational intensity. One learner may be only mildly motivated to learn within, say, a career context, while another learner with the same orientation may be intensely driven to succeed in the same orientation.

see also LEARNING STYLES, LEARNING STRATEGIES, PERSONALITY, ANXIETY, WILLINGNESS TO COMMUNICATE, LEARNER BELIEFS, INTELLIGENCE, LANGUAGE APTITUDE, SELF-REGULATION
📖 Ausubel 1968; Brown 2007; Dörnyei 2005; Ellis 2008; Gardner & Lambert 1972; Keller 1983; Maslow 1970; Williams & Burden 1997

MP
an abbreviation for MINIMALIST PROGRAM

Multicompetence Theory
a theory most closely associated with the work of Cook who defines multicompetence as the compound state of a mind with two grammars to contrast with *monocompetence*, the state of mind with only one grammar. He maintains that language knowledge of the L2 user is different from that of the monolingual. He has consolidated research in first and second language acquisition to show that the multicompetent individual approaches language differently in terms of metalinguistic awareness; multicompetence has an effect on other parts of cognition resulting in a greater metalinguistic awareness and a better cognitive processing; and that multicompetent speakers think differently from monolinguals, at least in some areas of linguistic awareness.

According to Multicompetence Theory, second language acquisition involves not the learning of one language but the gradual development of two or more languages in the same mind. Multicompetence Theory is as much a philosophical statement as a theory of language acquisition. It argues that we wrongly conceive of monolingualism as the default position given that the majority of human beings are, to some extent, bilingual (see BILINGUALISM) or multilingual (see MULTILINGUALISM). This therefore has implications for the importance that we attach to the native speaker (for which read monolingual) as the model for second language learners to aspire to. Language teachers' over-arching objective should therefore be the creation of bilinguals not monolinguals of a second language. From a psycholinguistic perspective, multicompetence offers a variation on the theory of INTERLANGUAGE where any given psychological state in a learner is on a continuum between the L1 and native speaker-like L2 competence. Rather, the L1 and the L2 are in a constant state of inter-dependence. Support for this proposition can be found in evidence that: L2 speakers have a different type of knowledge of their L1 than monolinguals; that, in fact, learning an L2 can affect the L1; that in bilinguals CODE SWITCHING can occur without problems; that bilinguals are more cognitively flexible; that there is no separation in the mental lexicon between one or more languages; and that L2 processing cannot isolate (switch off) L1 processing.
📖 Cook 1992, 2007; Kumaravadivelu 2006; Macaro et al. 2010

Multidimensional Model

a cognitive approach to SLA, proposed by Meisel, Clahsen, and Pienemann, which claims that learners acquire certain grammatical structures in developmental sequences, and that those sequences reflect how learners overcome processing limitations. Further, it claims that language instruction which targets developmental features will be successful only if learners have already mastered the processing operations which are associated with the previous stage of acquisition. The Multidimensional Model resembles Andersen's work on OPERATING PRINCIPLES in a number of respects. First, it is based on the painstaking analysis of naturally occurring learner speech. Second, it also sees the regularities in learner language as the product of cognitive processes that govern the linguistic operations learners are able to handle. However, the model constitutes a considerable advance on the idea of operating principles in that it relates the underlying cognitive processes to stages in the learner's development, explaining how one stage supersedes another. Also, the model provides an account of inter-learner variation.

The model makes the following general claims:

1) Learners manifest developmental sequences in the acquisition of a number of grammatical structures, such as word order and some grammatical morphemes.
2) Learners also display individual variation, both with regard to the extent to which they apply developmental rules and to the extent to which they acquire and use grammatical structures that are not developmentally constrained.
3) Developmental sequences reflect the systematic way in which learners overcome processing constraints. These constraints are of a general cognitive nature and govern production.
4) Individual learner variation reflects the overall orientation to the learning task, which in turn is the product of socio-psychological factors.
5) Formal instructions directed at developmental features will only be successful if learners have mastered the prerequisite processing operations associated with the previous stage of acquisition. However, formal instruction directed at grammatical features subject to individual variation faces no such constraints.

As shown in Figure M.1, the model has two principal axes, the *developmental* and the *variational*. The former are acquired sequentially as certain processing strategies are mastered. The latter are required at any time (or not at all), depending on the learner's social and effective attitudes. This allows for learners to be grouped both in terms of their stage of development and in terms of the kind of simplification they engage in. For example, Figure M.1 shows two learners (A and B) at stage 5, two at stage 4 (C and D), and two others at stage 3 (E and F), reflecting their progress on the developmental axis. It also shows differences between the learners at each level. For example, learner B produces more standard-like language than A. It is argued that progress on one axis or dimension is independent of progress on the other. It is theoretically possible, therefore, for a learner who practices elaborative simplification to use more target-like language overall than a learner who is 'developmentally' far more advanced. Learner F, for example, is only at stage 3, but uses more standard-like constructions than learner A, who is at stage 5.

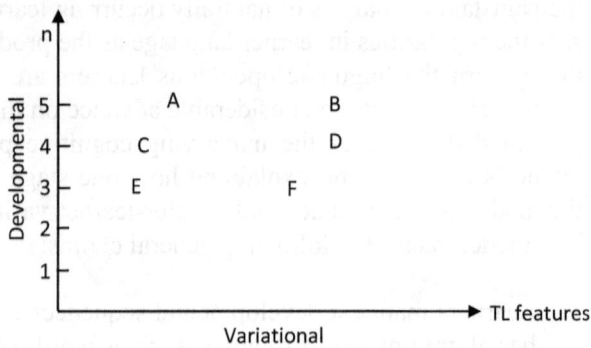

Figure M.1. The two axes of the Multidimensional Model

The identification of developmental patterns is of no value to theory construction unless a principled explanation for them can be found. It is in this respect that the Multidimensional Model offers most to SLA research. It explains why learners pass through the stages of development they do, and also, on the basis of this, affords predictions regarding when other grammatical structures (those that have not yet been investigated) will be acquired. In other words, the model has both explanatory and predictive power.

The Multidimensional Model also has a socio-psychological dimension that accounts for the simplification strategies employed by individual learners. This is described in terms of a continuum reflecting learners' orientations towards the learning task. At one end is *segregative orientation*, which arises when there is a lack of interest in contact with native speakers, discrimination on the part of native speakers, and a general lack of either INSTRUMENTAL or INTEGRATIVE MOTIVATION. At the other end is *integrative orientation*, which is evident in learners with either a strong desire to assimilate into L2 culture or in those with no desire to acculturate (see ACCULTURATION) but with a strong instrumental need to learn the L2. The socio-psychological dimension of the model echoes social theories of L2 acquisition. It explains the extent to which individual learners conform to target-language norms. The learner's orientation, however, has no effect on the general sequence of progression along the developmental axis.

The Multidimensional Model is, thus, powerful not only because it provides a satisfactory explanation of observed development in learner-language, but because it also constitutes a predictive framework.

There are, however, several problems with the model. There is no account of how or why learners overcome the processing constraints. There is also a difficulty in identifying formulaic chunks of language and of establishing *a priori* which features are variational and, therefore, not subject to the constraints that govern developmental features. If a learner, supposedly at stage 2, produces an utterance like 'where does he lives?', which belongs to stage 5, to what extent does this falsify the theory? It is very easy to immunize the theory by claiming that such an utterance is a 'formula' and thus not subject to processing constraints. A similar argument can be made for variational features. Another problem concerns the operational definition of 'acquisition'. Finally, the Multidimensional Model only provides an explanation of acquisition in terms of learner production. It tells us nothing about how learners come to comprehend grammatical structures, nor does it inform about how comprehension and production interact. In particular, the theory does not address how learners obtain INTAKE from INPUT and how this is then used to reconstruct internal grammars. It is in this respect that the theory is most limited.

One of the pedagogical implications drawn from the research related to the Multidimensional Model is the TEACHABILITY HYPOTHESIS that learners can only be taught what they are psycholinguistically ready to learn.

see also COMPETITION MODEL, VARIABLE COMPETENCE MODEL, CAPABILITY CONTINUUM PARADIGM, MONITOR MODEL, ACCULTURATION MODEL, NATIVIZATION MODEL, SOCIO-PSYCHOLINGUISTIC MODEL, PROCESSABILITY THEORY

📖 Ellis 2008; Larsen-Freeman & Long 1991; Meisel et al. 1981; Saville-Troike 2006

multilingualism

the use of three or more languages by an individual or within a speech community. Frequently, multilingual people do not have equal control over all the languages they know and also use the languages for different purposes.

see also BILINGUALISM

📖 Ellis 2008

N

native language
    see FIRST LANGUAGE

Native Language Magnet Model
    the concept that an L2 learner initially perceives L2 phonemes in terms of the learner's L1 by the 'magnet' effect of the established L1 phonemic system. The Magnet Model also suggests that perception determines production, therefore L2 phonetic production will be affected by L1 TRANSFER until the L2 phonemic system is established.
    📖 Piske & Young-Scholten 2009

native speaker
    also **NS**
    someone who speaks a language from very early childhood, and is thus expected to be fluent in the language without formal instruction. In contrast, a **non-native speaker** (also **NNS**) is a language user for whom a language is not their first language.
    📖 Piske & Young-Scholten 2009

nativism
    a term associated with Noam Chomsky who developed the theory that all humans are born with an innate capacity and a knowledge system specifically designed for language and language acquisition. This contrasts with those who hold that language is purely a result of someone's interaction with the environment (see below). Under linguistic nativism, a normally functioning human being is said to be born with UNIVERSAL GRAMMAR that constrains the shape of the language he will be exposed to as a child. Thus, even though the child does interact with the environment, Universal Grammar will restrain the hypotheses the child can make about language. For example, under nativism, the child is prohibited from making unconscious rules that are predicated on the serial ordering of words (A comes before B). Instead, the child must make unconscious rules that are predicated on syntactic structures that exist in certain relationships to each other (A can only replace A-like structures or occupy a place in a sentence designated for A-like structures).

Linguistic nativism contrasts with what might be called **general nativism**, in which children are not born with something like Universal Grammar but are born with something like processing constraints that are tied to structural distance among elements. Syntactic structure emerges because of these processing constraints.

Opposite nativism are the positions that claim all language emerges from a person's interaction with the environment and is a result of more general cognitive capacities. An example of non-nativism would be SKILL THEORY or the now-defunct BEHAVIORISM. Under these positions, children acquire language not because they are born with any innate capacity or knowledge, but because they interact with the environment in particular ways and the general mechanisms of cognition and learning take care of language acquisition just as they would the learning of anything else.

The one argument that seems to bolster linguistic nativism is the POVERTY OF THE STIMULUS. According to this argument, people (including children by the age of 5) come to know much more about language than what they could gather from the linguistic environment around them. Because people only hear impossible in the language they have learned. Because people only hear possible sentences, how do they know what is impossible? For example, how do they know that *Should I've done it? is not a possible contraction of have in English when all they've heard are the possible contractions with have? Nativists argue that people can do this because they are hardwired to rule out certain possibilities, that Universal Grammar provides them with what is impossible in language more generally.

see also INNATENESS HYPOTHESIS

📖 Pinker 1994b; Smith 1999; VanPatten & Benati 2010

Nativization Hypothesis
another term for NATIVIZATION MODEL

Nativization Model
also **Nativization Hypothesis, Nativization Theory**
a theory that, when linguistic INPUT is not available or not accessible, children fall back on an innate biological capacity for language and construct a language for themselves following universal norms. Nativization Model was developed by Andersen who built on Schumann's ACCULTURATION MODEL, in particular by providing a cognitive dimension which Schumann does not consider. For Schumann, SLA can be explained simply in terms of INPUT and the general function the learner wants to use the L2 for. He is not concerned with the learner's internal processing mechanisms. Andersen, to a much greater extent, is concerned with learning processes. According to Nativization Model, L2 acquisition consists of two general processes, 'nativization' and 'denativization'. *Nativization* consists of assimilation; learners make the input conform to their own internalized view of what constitutes the L2 sys-

tem. That is, they simplify the learning task by forming hypotheses based on knowledge that they already process (L1 knowledge and knowledge of the world). In Andersen's terms, they attend to an 'internal norm'. The result is the kind of PIDGINIZATION evident in early language acquisition and documented in Schumann's work. *Denativization* involves accommodation; learners accommodate to an 'external norm'; that is, they adjust their INTERLANGUAGE systems to make them fit with the input, making use of inferencing strategies. Denativization is apparent in **depidignization** (the elaboration of a PIDGIN language which occurs through the gradual incorporation of forms from an external source) and also in later first and second language acquisition. Subsequently, Andersen has recognized that nativization and denativization are not two separate 'forces' but aspects of the same overall process of acquisition. Andersen's later work is an attempt to develop Nativization Model by further specifying the processes, cognitive OPERATING PRINCIPLES, and COMMUNICATIVE STRATEGIES that fit within it.

The Nativization Model, like Acculturation Model, focuses on the power mechanisms of SLA. It provides explanations of why L2 learners, unlike first language learners, often fail to achieve a native-like competence. L2 learners may be cut off from the necessary input as a result of SOCIAL DISTANCE, or they may fail to attend to it as a result of PSYCHOLOGICAL DISTANCE. These models also indicate that SLA involves processes of a very general kind, which are also found in the formation and elaboration of pidgin languages. The notions of 'internal' and 'external norms' are elegant devices for explaining why early and late interlanguage systems are so very different. Characterizing SLA as the gradual transition from an internal to an external norm explains the developmental sequence which has been observed in SLA, and the switch that learners make from reliance on simplifying to reliance on inferencing strategies.

However, neither model sheds light on how L2 knowledge is internalized and used. In other words, there is no specification of the learner's assembly mechanism. Although Nativization Model does consider internal factors, there is no discussion of how these operate. In particular, it will need to consider whether intake is controlled by the way the input is shaped in interaction involving the learner and other speakers or whether it is controlled by the structure of the internal processing mechanisms themselves. Andersen's 'internal' and 'external norms' suggest that the internal mechanisms play a crucial part, but this not elaborated upon. And neither Schumann nor Andersen pays attention to the potentially facilitating effects of input/interaction. In short, what is missing from these models is an account of the role of the interaction between situation and learner.

see also MULTIDIMENSIONAL MODEL, COMPETITION MODEL, VARIABLE COMPETENCE MODEL, CAPABILITY CONTINUUM PARADIGM, MONITOR MODEL, SOCIO-PSYCHOLINGUISTIC MODEL, FUNCTIONALIST MODEL

Andersen 1979a, 1980, 1990; Ellis 1986, 2008; Field 2004

Nativization Theory

another term for NATIVIZATION MODEL

naturalistic language acquisition

an acquisition situation in which the learner receives no instruction. Naturalistic is a term that one often sees or hears in relationship to learners who acquire language without any classroom instruction. In fact, it refers to language acquisition which takes place in *natural settings*. Thus, immigrants to a country who do not enroll in language courses and basically learn the language 'on the streets' or 'on the job' are referred to as naturalistic learners. Naturalistic language acquisition contrasts with **instructed language acquisition**, which refers to language acquisition that takes place as a result of attempts to teach the L2—either directly through formal instruction or indirectly by setting up the conditions that promote natural acquisition in the classroom. Naturalistic as a term now alternates with the term nonclassroom (as in nonclassroom vs. classroom), largely because some professionals objected to the idea that classrooms were being tagged as 'unnatural' under the earlier distinction of naturalistic versus classroom.

see also FORM-FOCUSED INSTRUCTION
Ellis 2008; VanPatten & Benati 2010

Natural Order Hypothesis

a hypothesis which is associated with Steven Krashen and forms part of his MONITOR MODEL. According to the Natural Order Hypothesis children acquiring their first language acquire linguistic forms, rules, and items in a similar order. For example, in English children acquire progressive *-ing*, plural *-s*, and active sentences before they acquire third person *-s* on verbs, or passive sentences. This is said to show a natural order of development. In second language and foreign language learning grammatical forms may also appear in a natural order, though this is not identical with the ORDER OF ACQUISITION in first language learning.

Although there is evidently some truth in such a statement, it has been criticized for being too strong. It ignores well-documented cases of LANGUAGE TRANSFER, or of individual variability. Not only are such cases ignored; there is no place for them in Krashen's theory. Krashen's Natural Order Hypothesis has also been criticized for being based almost exclusively on the MORPHEME STUDIES with their known methodological problems, and which, in any case, reflect accuracy of production rather than acquisition sequences.

Krashen 1977, 1981, 1982, 1985, 1992, 1997; Mithcell & Myles 2004; Richards & Schmidt 2010

negative evidence

a term which is related to the type of FEEDBACK that language learners get, and specifically refers to information that a learner's utterance is ill-formed in some way. Negative evidence comes in two types: 'direct' and 'indirect'. **Direct negative evidence** refers to feedback in which the learner is explicitly told his utterance is incorrect in some way. Examples include 'No. We don't say it that way. We say . . .' and 'You mean *talked*. You forgot to put the past tense marker on'. Direct negative evidence happens largely in classrooms but not exclusively.

Indirect negative evidence refers to conversational interactions in which the person speaking with the learner implicitly points out something is wrong (see NEGOTIATION OF MEANING). In other words, unlike error correction, which is direct negative evidence, the term indirect is used because the intent of the speaker is not to correct the learner but to confirm, query, and so on, as part of the communicative act and yet what the interlocutor says can act as evidence for how something should be said. Here are some of the most commonly researched types of indirect negative evidence (appearing in italics) (where NNS = non-native speaker and NS = native speaker).

- Confirmation check: used to verify what one heard
  NNS: He grabbed by the craws.
  NS: *The claws? You mean with its hands?*
  NNS: Yes, yes.

- Clarification request: asking the person to clarify
  NNS: I can find no [ruddish].
  NS: *I'm sorry. You couldn't find what?*

- RECAST : restating what the person says as part of the normal interactional flow
  NNS: And so he buy a car.
  NS: *He bought a car!*
  NNS: Yes, he bought a car.
  NS: Wow, how nice.

Unlike direct negative evidence, indirect negative evidence does not normally interrupt the flow of communication and is focused on meaning. In both L1 and SLA, researchers have questioned whether negative evidence—in particular indirect negative evidence—is either necessary or beneficial to language acquisition. In L1 research, negative evidence is widely viewed as being unhelpful and certainly not necessary for language growth in the child. In SLA circles, it is not clear what the role of negative evidence is. Although there is some consensus that direct negative evidence does not advance acquisition, researchers dispute the role of indirect negative evidence. The research suggests it may be useful for lexical growth as well as other aspects of meaning-making (e.g., pragmatics), but it is far from clear whether negative evidence of any kind is useful for the growth of the formal properties of language (e.g., syntax, morphology).

The argument for indirect negative evidence is that it brings acquisitional problems into the learner's focal awareness during communication, thus increasing the salience of a grammatical or lexical form. There are several arguments against indirect negative evidence, the two most important being that (1) indirect negative evidence is haphazard and not frequent enough to be important (i.e., interlocutors just do not provide enough negative evidence, and it is not consistently provided), and (2) learners do not always perceive indirect negative evidence as an indication that they did something wrong.

see also POSITIVE EVIDENCE

📖 Piske & Young-Scholten 2009; VanPatten & Benati 2010

negative transfer

see TRANSFER

negotiation of form

a term referring to REPAIR that occurs when there is no communication difficulty (i.e., when the problem is entirely linguistic). Such repairs are uncommon in conversational interaction (although sometimes learners do request them), but have been shown to be very common in some classroom contexts.

see also NEGOTIATION OF MEANING

📖 Ellis 2008

negotiation of meaning

an attempt made in conversation to clarify a lack of understanding. Negotiation of meaning is triggered when there is a mismatch between a speaker's intended message and what the listener interprets as the intended meaning. The purpose of negotiation is to resolve the perceived mismatch, and such negotiations can occur in just about any kind of interaction. Even natives speaking to other natives may say something like *What're you getting at?* because they are not quite sure what the other person's intention is. Such negotiations are usually the result of pragmatic problems or a lack of background knowledge.

Negotiation of meaning is a term attributed to Michael Long and now widely used in the interactional research literature. It stems from Long's conviction that MODIFIED INPUT was necessary but not sufficient for L2 acquisition. Originally using the term 'modified interaction', Long proposed that negotiation of meaning occurred when teacher-learner interaction (or non-native speaker vs. native speaker interaction) broke down, or when one participant in the interaction sensed that a breakdown may have occurred. In order that the speaker's meaning might be co-constructed a number of negotiation moves were possible:

- a clarification request—*I'm sorry could you explain that?*
- a comprehension check—*Do you understand? Is that clear?*
- a confirmation signal—*Oh, right, you mean X*

Negotiation of meaning is deemed important not just for communicative reasons but potentially for acquisitional reasons. Negotiation of meaning provides indirect NEGATIVE EVIDENCE, clues to the learner that he did something wrong. Thus, interaction potentially provides useful FEEDBACK about vocabulary, syntax, and so on. However, researchers are not in agreement about the role that indirect negative evidence plays. Nonetheless, negotiation of meaning is important for maximizing comprehension on the part of the learner. Not all miscommunications are a result of what learners do wrong; they can result when learners do not understand someone else. Thus, negotiation helps to ensure comprehension. With increased comprehension, there are increased chances for acquisition, because acquisition is a by-product of comprehension to a certain degree.

see also NEGOTIATION OF FORM
 Long 1981; Macaro et al. 2010; VanPatten & Benati 2010

neurobiological SLA

a *neuropsychological* account of L2 acquisition which aims to correlate cognitive operations (such as noticing and noticing the gap) with neural functioning. Researchers attempt to show the locations in the brain and the neural circuits that are linked to the formation and consolidation of memories for language. That is, neurobiological SLA starts with the brain and moves on to language. Neural mechanisms are examined and theoretical arguments developed for how they might be involved in language.

see also NEUROLINGUISTICS SLA
 Ellis 2008

neuroimaging

the use of techniques for identifying which parts of the brain are activated when learners are asked to perform a language task. One method for achieving this is by *magnetic resonance imaging* (MRI), which is a static recording technique. It was formerly referred to as magnetic resonance tomography. It is a non-invasive method used to render images of the inside of the brain. It can provide very clear images. Another method is *electroencephalography* (EEG) which measures the electrical activity generated by the brain when metal electrodes are placed on the scalp. It records brain waves generated by the different lobes in the two hemispheres. A development of this technique is the measurement of *event-related potentials* (ERPs). Measurements are again obtained from placing electrodes on the scalp but these are averaged over many events from the same stimulus in order to eliminate disturbances due to unwanted activity such as blinking and head movements. The advantage of ERPs is that they provide clear evidence of temporal events in the brain but they provide only poor evidence of which regions of the brain are involved. *Position emission tomography* (PET) registers physiological changes in brain cells. It involves injecting water molecules tagged with radioactive isotopes into the body. It produces a map of the functional processes in the brain and has shown that when the brain is damaged in one area as a result of APHASIA, changes in other more distant areas also occur. *Functional magnetic resonance imaging* (fMRI) is another dynamic imaging technique which identifies changes in regional blood oxygen levels in cortical areas. These latter two methods provide good spatial resolution.

On the face of it, these techniques afford an excellent method for identifying both the parts of the brain and the neural pathways involved in performing different language tasks. However, there are a number of problems as follows:

1) The tasks used are often not linguistic tasks (i.e., are not part of natural language use) hence to do not involve the normal linguistic processes involved in understanding and producing messages.
2) The language tasks used often result in activation in several cortical regions making it difficult to determine which of the activated areas serves which component of the task.
3) The activation pattern revealed by the imaging technique used need to be interpreted and interpretation depends on the baseline and the statistical procedures used.
4) Different neuroimaging techniques can reveal very different results.
5) There is likely to be substantial noise in the images obtained as a result of multiple unintended secondary processes.
6) The evidence that neuroimaging provides often conflicts with that from other sources (e.g., aphasia studies).
7) The results obtained are averaged with the result that inter-individual variation is lost.

 Ellis 2008; Paradis 2004

neurolinguistics
a field of study that involves the role of brain functioning in language comprehension, production, and storage. Neurolinguistics includes research into how the structure of the brain influences language learning, how and in which parts of the brain language is stored, and how damage to the brain affects the ability to use language (see APHASIA).
see also NEUROLINGUISTICS SLA
 VanPatten & Benati 2010; Richards & Schmidt 2010

neurolinguistics SLA
a *neuropsychological* account of L2 acquisition which draws on research that has examined how damage to different parts of the human brain (as a result of some traumatic experience, natural ageing, or genetic deficiency) affects a person's ability to use a previously learned L2. This damage is of two kinds. In the case of APHASIA, the damage results in a loss of procedural ability to use the L2 (i.e., learners cannot automatically and accurately access all aspects of their IMPLICIT KNOWLEDGE of the L2 for purposes of communication). As a result there may be a failure in comprehending L2 messages or in producing spontaneous sentences that are grammatically correct. In the case of *amnesia*, learners' *declarative memory* (see LONG-TERM MEMORY) is affected, making it difficult for them to access their EXPLICIT KNOWLEDGE of the L2. In such cases, learners experience difficulty locating the specific word they want but are still able to produce utterances that are grammatical.
see ADAPTIVE CONTROL OF THOUGHT MODEL, NEUROBIOLOGICAL SLA
📖 Ellis 2008

NL
an abbreviation for NATIVE LANGUAGE

NNS
an abbreviation for NON-NATIVE SPEAKER

no access view
another term for FUNDAMENTAL DIFFERENCE HYPOTHESIS

non-implicational universal tendencies
a term referring to features which strongly tend to be found in languages. For example:

- *Phonology*. Languages tend to have fricatives. That is, not all but certainly almost all languages have at last one fricative, a [-sonorant, +continuant] phonemes, whose major allophones is such as [f, v, ð, θ, s, z, x, ɣ] (the latter pair are voiceless and voiced velar fricatives).
- *Morphology*. Languages tend to have adjectives. That is, not all but certainly most languages have in addition to nouns and verbs a class of morphemes which describes or modifies nouns within the noun phrase and which can be compared in constructions like 'this one is bigger (than that one)'. In a number of languages, in fact, the adjectives are relatively few and appear to be a closed class.
- *Syntax*. An important universal syntactic tendency concerns the basic or typical word order of sentences. Among subject (S), verb (V), and object

(O) there are six possibilities of word order of which three are common and three are uncommon, as follows:
1) SOV, about 44% of languages
2) SVO, about 33% of languages
3) VSO, 18% of languages
4) VOS
5) OSV }, about 5% of languages
6) OVS

Thus, in 95% of languages, those of the SOV, SVO, and VSO types, subjects precede objects.
see also ABSOLUTE NON-IMPLICATIONAL UNIVERSALS, ABSOLUTE IMPLICATIONAL UNIVERSALS, IMPLICATIONAL UNIVERSAL TENDENCIES
📖 Hudson 2000

non-interface hypothesis
also **non-interface position, non-interface model**
a theory of L2 acquisition which emphasizes the distinctiveness of EXPLICIT and IMPLICIT KNOWLEDGE and which claim that one type of knowledge cannot be converted directly into the other type. It concerns that fact that there is no interface (the crossover) between aspects of a second or foreign language that are taught/learned explicitly and consciously (e.g., grammatical constructions or vocabulary items) and the subconscious or automatic second language acquisition process. In its most extreme form, advocated by Stephen Krashen, there is no possibility of learning becoming acquisition or vice versa. Consciously learned language knowledge does not lead to acquisition and can only be used as a 'monitor' or corrective mechanism.
see also INTERFACE MODEL, WEAK INTERFACE MODEL, MONITOR MODEL
📖 Ellis 2008; Krashen 1982, 1985; Macaro et al. 2010

non-interface model
another term for NON-INTERFACE HYPOTHESIS

non-interface position
another term for NON-INTERFACE HYPOTHESIS

non-native language
see FOREIGN LANGUAGE

non-native speaker
see NATIVE SPEAKER

Noticing Hypothesis

the hypothesis developed by Schmidt that INPUT does not become INTAKE for language learning unless it is noticed, that is, consciously registered. By noticing, learners first perceive some kind of external feature and allow WORKING MEMORY to attend to it, spotlight it and process it to varying levels of intensity thereby bringing about a change in LONG-TERM MEMORY. It is only if these preliminary stages have been gone through that learners can compare what they have attended to and spotlighted to their previous knowledge and 'notice a gap'. According to the hypothesis, since the outside world and long-term memory are mediated by working memory processing, then nothing can be learned without noticing it first, at least to some degree. By this account subliminal or subconscious learning is impossible. Schmidt proposes that noticing is influenced by the frequency that a feature occurs in the input, the salience of that feature, the developmental readiness of the learner to that feature, and the demands of the task which may or may not allow sufficient ATTENTION to spotlight the feature and then process it. Critics of the hypothesis have pointed out that to notice (in this way) everything about an L2 would be impossible and that some learning must take place without conscious effort and that perhaps it is more the metalinguistic aspects of an L2 that are learned only by noticing.

Schmidt distinguished a strong and weak form of the Noticing Hypothesis. The strong form, which reflects his earlier position, states that there is no learning whatsoever from input that is not noticed, while the weak form, indicative of his later position, allows for representation and storage of unattended stimuli in memory but claims that people learn about the things they attend to and do not learn much about the things they do not attend to. On the second issue, Schmidt argued that attention needs to be specifically directed.

see also FREQUENCY HYPOTHESIS, INPUT HYPOTHESIS, INTERACTION HYPOTHESIS

 Ellis 2008; Macaro et al. 2010; Schmidt 1990, 1994, 1995a, 2001; Truscott 1998

Noun Phrase Accessibility Hierarchy

another term for ACCESSIBILITY HIERARCHY

NPAH

an abbreviation for ACCESSIBILITY HIERARCHY

NS

an abbreviation for NATIVE SPEAKER

O

obligatory occasion analysis
a method for identifying contexts that require the obligatory use of a specific grammatical feature in samples of learner language and calculating the accuracy with which the feature is actually supplied in these contexts. The basic procedure is as follows: First, samples of naturally occurring learner language are collected. Second, obligatory occasions for the use of specific target language (TL) features are identified in the data. In the course of using the L2, learners produce utterances which create obligatory occasions for the use of specific target-language features, although they may not always supply the features in question. Thus, if a learner says: *My sister visited us yesterday* or **my father arrive yesterday*, obligatory occasions for the use of past *-ed* have been created in both utterances. Third, the percentage of accurate use of the feature is then calculated by establishing whether the feature in question has been supplied in all the contexts in which it is required. A criterion level of accuracy can then be determined in order to provide an operational definition of whether a feature has been acquired. Usually, the level is set at 80-90 percent, below 100 percent, to take account of the fact that even adult native speakers may not achieve complete accuracy.

One problem with obligatory occasion analysis is that it takes no account of when a learner uses a feature in a context for which it is not obligatory in the TL. For example, the learner who says **I studied last night and now I understood better* has overgeneralized the past tense, using it where the TL requires the present tense. Clearly, acquisition of a feature such as past tense requires mastering not only when to use it but also when not to use it. To take account of over-use as well as misuses a procedure known as **target-like use analysis** has been suggested. It is designed to take into account the incorrect use of specific grammatical features in contexts that do not require them in the target language (e.g., **Mary and Peter likes travelling*), as well as non-suppliance in contexts that require the feature (e.g., **Simon eat an apple every day*). Both obligatory occasion and target-like use analysis are target-language-based—that is, like ERROR ANALYSIS, they seek to compare learner language and the TL—and thus reflect the *comparative fallacy*. That is, they ignore the fact that learners create their own unique rule system in the process of learning an L2.

see also TARGET-LIKE USE ANALYSIS

📖 Bley-Vroman 1983; Ellis 2008

off-line tasks

those tasks which are used to measure learner knowledge and often involve paper-and-pencil-type tests. They are the most generally used tasks to get at what learners know and are ubiquitous in the L2 literature. Some classic off-line tasks include *grammaticality judgment* tests in which learners indicate whether they believe a sentence is possible or not in a given language, *truth value judgments* in which learners determine which of two sentences logically follows or fits with something they just read, *cloze tests* in which learners fill in missing gaps in a text, and *sentence combining tests*, among others. Off-line tasks are distinguished from ON-LINE TASKS.

📖 VanPatten & Benati 2010

one-word stage
also **holophrastic stage**

the period in FIRST LANGUAGE ACQUISITION when children can produce single terms for objects. Between twelve and eighteen months, children begin to produce a variety of recognizable single-unit utterances. This period, traditionally called the one-word stage, is characterized by speech in which single terms are uttered for everyday objects such as 'milk', 'cookie', 'cat', 'cup' and 'spoon'. Other forms such as [ʌ sæ] may occur in circumstances that suggest the child is producing a version of *What's that*, so the label 'one-word' for this stage may be misleading and a term such as 'single-unit' would be more accurate. We sometimes use the term holophrastic (meaning a single form functioning as a phrase or sentence) to describe an utterance that could be analyzed as a word, a phrase, or a sentence.

While many of these holophrastic utterances seem to be used to name objects, they may also be produced in circumstances that suggest the child is already extending their use. An empty bed may elicit the name of a sister who normally sleeps in the bed, even in the absence of the person named. During this stage, then, the child may be capable of referring to *Karen* and *bed*, but is not yet ready to put the forms together to produce a more complex phrase.

see also TWO-WORD STAGE, TELEGRAPHIC SPEECH

📖 Yule 2006

on-line tasks

moment-by-moment measures of what learners are doing with language. On-line tasks tend to measure underlying processes (such as the interface between the learner's grammar and the *parsing* mechanisms). Classic examples

of on-line tasks include (1) the *moving-window technique*, in which learners read bits and pieces of a sentence on a computer screen, advancing through the sentence as they push a button, and (2) *eye-tracking*, in which the movement of people's pupils is tracked while they read a sentence on a computer screen. In both moving-window and eye-tracking, the measurement that is recorded is the time it takes learners to read a particular part of a sentence that is of interest to the researcher. Longer reading times (measured in milliseconds) generally indicate longer processing time and a point at which people are resolving a linguistic dilemma while reading.
see also OFF-LINE TASKS
📖 VanPatten & Benati 2010

Ontogeny Phylogeny Model
a model that shows the relationship between TRANSFER and developmental processes over time. This model is intended to capture the basic patterns of INTERLANGUAGE (IL) and captures phonological relationships between L1 and L2 as well as universals. Major states these relationships as follows: L2 increases, L1 decreases, and U [universals] increases and then decreases. At the early stage, the learner only has a first language and a 'dormant' U (except those parts of U that are operational in the L1). It is stated that U refers to the universals of language that are not already part of the L1 or L2 system. There are four corollaries to the Ontogeny Phylogeny Model; namely, the 'chronological', 'stylistic', 'similarity', and 'markedness' corollaries. The first is intended to capture second language development; the second, contextual variation (e.g., formal, casual speech); the third, similarity/dissimilarity in language; and the fourth, issues of MARKEDNESS in language. As can be seen below, each corollary specifies the relationship between the three constructs: L1, L2, and U.

- Chronological corollary: IL develops chronologically in the following manner: (a) L2 increases, (b) L1 decreases, and (c) U increases and then decreases.
- Stylistic corollary: IL varies stylistically in the following manner: as style becomes more formal, (a) L2 increases, (b) L1 decreases, and (c) U increases and then decreases.
- Similarity corollary: In similar phenomena, IL develops chronologically in the following manner: (a) L2 increases slowly, (b) L1 decreases slowly, and (c) U increases slowly and then decreases slowly. Thus, the role of L1 is much greater than U, compared to less similar phenomena. By implication, the less similar the phenomena (i.e., the more dissimilar), the more important the role of U is compared to L1.
- Markedness corollary: In marked phenomena, IL develops chronologically in the following manner: (a) L2 increases slowly, (b) L1 decreases [at a

normal rate] and then decreases slowly, and (c) U increases rapidly and decreases slowly. Thus, except for the earliest stages, the role of U is much greater than L1, compared to less-marked phenomena.

As can be seen, this model is concerned not only with interlanguage development (chronological), but also with issues of variation which is captured through the stylistic corollary, and linguistic relationships, such as similarity and markedness.
📖 Major 2001; Gass & Selinker 2008

operant conditioning
 also **instrumental conditioning, instrumental learning**
a learning theory proposed by Skinner within the context of BEHAVIORIST PSYCHOLOGY. Operant conditioning refers to conditioning in which the organism (in this case, a human being) emits a response, or operant (a sentence or utterance), without necessarily observable stimuli; that operant is maintained (learned) by REINFORCEMENT (e.g., a positive verbal or nonverbal response from another person, getting what they want, receiving praise, getting people to interact with them). If a child says 'want milk' and a parent gives the child some milk, the operant is reinforced and, over repeated instances, is conditioned. According to Skinner, verbal behavior, like other behavior, is controlled by its *consequences*—the events or stimuli (i.e., the *reinforcers*) that follow a response and that tend to strengthen behavior or increase the probability of a recurrence of that response. When consequences are rewarding, behavior is maintained and is increased in strength and perhaps frequency. When consequences are punishing, or when there is a total lack of reinforcement, the behavior is weakened and eventually extinguished. According to Skinner, reinforcers are far stronger aspects of learning than is mere association of a prior stimulus with a following response, as in the classical conditioning model. We are governed by the consequences of our behavior, and therefore Skinner felt we ought, in studying human behavior, to study the effect of those consequences. And if we wish to control behavior, say, to teach someone something, we ought to attend carefully to reinforcers.

Skinner is called a neobehaviorist because he added a unique dimension to behavioristic psychology. The classical conditioning of Pavlov was, according to Skinner, a highly specialized form of learning utilized mainly by animals and playing little part in human conditioning. Skinner called Pavlovian conditioning RESPONDENT CONDITIONING since it was concerned with respondent behavior—that is, behavior that is elicited by a preceding stimulus. Today virtually no one would agree that Skinner's model of verbal behavior adequately accounts for the capacity to acquire language, for language development itself, for the abstract nature of language, or for a theory of meaning. A theory based on conditioning and reinforcement is hard-pressed to explain the fact that every sentence you speak or write—with a few trivial exceptions—is novel, never before uttered either by you or by anyone else! These novel utterances are nevertheless created by very young children as they literally 'play' with language, and that same creativity continues on into adulthood and throughout one's life.

see also COGNITIVISM

📖 Brown 2007

operating principles

a term coined by Slobin to describe various learning strategies employed by children during L1 acquisition. Whereas the COMPETITION MODEL was designed to account for sentence interpretation, operating principles have been formulated to explain why certain linguistic forms typically appear in learners (L1 and L2) production before others. The idea of operating principles is not incompatible with the competition model, however, as they shed light on the general ideas of 'cue reliability' and 'cue availability'. They are based on the general assumption that those features that are easily attended to and easily processed will be the first to be learned and thus to be used in production. Slobin has attempted to describe the universal principles that guide children in the process of L1 acquisition. These principles are conceived as the operating principles by which children extract and segment linguistic information in order to build a grammar of the language they are learning. Slobin's operating principles include:

- Pay attention to the ends of words.
- Words can be modified phonologically.
- Pay attention to the order of morphemes and words.
- Avoid interrupting or rearranging units.
- Underlying semantic relations should be clearly marked.
- Avoid exceptions.
- The use of grammatical markers is meaningful and systematic.

Operating principles in L2 acquisition have been investigated by Andersen. He sought an explanation for how learners create and restructure their INTERLANGUAGE systems as a product of participating in verbal interaction with more proficient speakers. It resulted in the NATIVIZATION MODEL. Andersen's principles are based on those of Slobin, but are then adapted to the learning of second languages. However, he claims that his principles are not simply a translation to L2 learning, but rather 'macroprinciples', each one of which corresponds to a group of principles in Slobin's framework:

- *The one-to-one principle*: an interlanguage system should be constructed in such a way that an intended underlying meaning is expressed with one clear invariant surface form (or construction). For example, learners of

German initially maintain an SVO word order in all contexts, in spite of the fact that German word order is not so consistent.
- *The multifunctionality principle*: (a) where there is clear evidence in the INPUT that more than one form marks the meaning conveyed by only one form in the interlanguage, try to discover the distribution and additional meaning (if any) of the new form; (b) where there is evidence in the input that an interlanguage form conveys only one of the meanings that the same form has in the input, try to discover the additional meanings of the form in the input. For example, the one-to-one principle means that learners of English will often start with just one form for negation (e.g. *no the dog; he no go*), but once this form has been incorporated into their interlanguage, they are able to notice other forms and differentiate the environment in which they occur.
- *The principle of formal determinism*: when the form-meaning relationship is clearly and uniformly encoded in the input, the learner will discover it earlier than the other form-meaning relationships and will incorporate it more consistently within his interlanguage system. In short, the clear, transparent encoding of the linguistic feature in the input forces the learner to discover it. For example, if we consider the example of English negation above, the learner will be driven from the use of a single form to the use of multiple forms because the distribution of such forms in English is transparent (e.g., *don't* is used in preverbal environments, *not* with noun phrases, adverbs, etc.).
- *The principle of distributional bias*: if both X and Y can occur in the same environments A and B, but a bias in the distribution of X and Y makes it appear that X only occurs in environment A and Y only occurs in environment B, when you acquire X and Y, restrict X to environment A and Y to environment B. For example, in Spanish, punctual verbs (e.g., *break*) occur mainly in the preterite form, and verbs of states (e.g., *know*) mainly in the imperfect form, making the preterite much more common in the input. Second language learners of Spanish reproduce this bias, and acquire the preterite form earlier.
- *The relevance principle*: if two or more functors apply to a content word, try to place them so that the more relevant the meaning of a functor is to the meaning of the content word, the closer it is placed to the content word. If you find that a notion is marked in several places, at first mark it only in the position closest to the relevant content word. For example, Andersen's research on the second language acquisition of Spanish verb morphology broadly supports the prediction that aspect should be encoded before tense, as it is most relevant to the lexical item it is attached to (the verb), and that tense would be next since it has wider scope than aspect, but is more relevant to the verb than subject-verb agreement, which would be last.

Optimality Theory   255

- *The transfer to somewhere principle*: a grammatical form or structure will occur consistently and to a significant extent in the interlanguage as a result of transfer if and only if (1) natural acquisitional principles are consistent with the first language structure or (2) there already exists within the second language input the potential for (mis)generalization from the input to produce the same form or structure. Furthermore , in such transfer preference is given in the resulting interlanguage to free, invariant, functionally simple morphemes that are congruent with the first and second languages (or there is congruence between the first language and natural acquisitional processes) and to morphemes which occur frequently in the first and/or the second language. For example, unlike English learners of French who follow English word order for the placement of French clitic (i.e. unstressed) object pronouns and produce sentences like *Camille lit le* (target: *Camille le lit*; Camille **it** reads), French learners of English do not follow the French word order for clitic placement (i.e., they never produce *Camille it reads* in English as a second language). This is because no model for such transfer is available in the input, whereas French provides a model for post-verbal placement of objects in the case of lexical noun-phrases (as in *Camille lit **le journal***; Camille reads **the newspaper**).
- *The relexification principle*: when you cannot perceive the structural pattern used by the language you are trying to acquire, use your native language structure with lexical items from the second language. For example, Japanese learners of English sometimes use Japanese SOV word order in English in the early stages, with English lexical items.

Operating principles clearly afford only a limited account of how learners acquire an L2. They have been criticized in both L1 and L2 acquisition research on a number of grounds. It has been argued that they are difficult to test and are not mutually exclusive. Also, it is not clear how many principles are needed to explain acquisition.

see also ASPECT HYPOTHESIS, MULTIDIMENSIONAL MODEL, PROCESSABILITY THEORY, CONNECTIONISM, PERCEPTUAL SALIENCY APPROACH, ADAPTIVE CONTROL OF THOUGHT MODEL

📖 Andersen 1979a, 1980, 1983b, 1984a, 1984b, 1990, 1991; Dulay & Burt 1974d; Ellis 2008; Larsen-Freeman 1975; Slobin 1973, 1985a; Mithcell & Myles 2004

Optimality Theory
also OT

a linguistic theory which considers constraints rather than rules as central to grammar. The central idea behind Optimality Theory (OT) is that surface forms of language reflect resolutions of conflicts between competing underlying constraints. A surface form is 'optimal' if it incurs the least serious violations of a set of constraints, taking into account their hierarchical ranking. So for example, in phonology, there may be a conflict in the ranking of syllable onset alongside morpheme boundaries which will affect how a word is pronounced. Violations must be minimal and languages differ in the ranking of constraints, which may account for errors in the INTERLANGUAGE of L2 learners. OT also allows for the incorporation of general principles of MARKEDNESS into language-specific analyses.

While OT has been generally developed within a generative phonology and/or computational linguistics framework, a number of researchers have attempted to apply it to issues arising in SLA studies.

📖 Eckman 2004; Escudero & Boersma 2004; Macaro et al. 2010; Prince & Smolensky 1993

OT

an abbreviation for OPTIMALITY THEORY

other-directed learners

see SILENT PERIOD

output

language produced by a language learner, either in speech or writing.
see also INPUT, OUTPUT HYPOTHESIS

Output Hypothesis
also Comprehensible Output Hypothesis

the hypothesis that successful second language acquisition requires not only COMPREHENSIBLE INPUT, but also *comprehensible output*, language produced by the learner that can be understood by other speakers of the language. Output hypothesis attributed to the work of Merrill Swain is part of the general interaction research tradition (see INTERACTION HYPOTHESIS) which also includes MODIFIED INPUT and NEGOTIATION OF MEANING both of which Swain claimed were necessary but not sufficient for acquisition. Swain's basic premise is that 'forcing' (pushing) learners to speak in the L2 (i.e., putting them in a situation where they have to construct an utterance which they know may be wrong) furthers acquisition, and is in direct contrast to Krashen's (see also INPUT HYPOTHESIS) claim that output is the result of acquisition not its cause. Swain proposed that production, especially *pushed output*, may encourage learners to move from semantic (top-down) to syntactic (bottom-up) processing. Whereas comprehension of a message can take place with little syntactic analysis of the input, production forces learners to pay attention to the means of expression especially if they are pushed to produce messages that are concise and socially appropriate. Learners can fake it, so to speak, in comprehension, but they cannot do so in the same way in production. Production requires learners to process syntactically; they have to pay some attention to form.

According to Swain 'forced output' furthers acquisition because:

1) It encourages *noticing*—learners may notice the gap between what they want to say and what they believe they know. In other words, the noticing function relates to the possibility that when learners try to communicate in their still-developing target language, they may encounter a linguistic problem and become aware of what they do not know or know only partially. Such an encounter may raise their awareness, leading to an appropriate action on their part.
2) It encourages *hypothesis testing*—which in turn may result in either a communication breakdown, 'forcing' the learner to reformulate the utterance, or simply in useful FEEDBACK from a native speaker. Put differently, the hypothesis-testing function of output relates to the possibility that when learners use their still-developing target language, they may be experimenting with what works and what does not work. Moreover, when they participate in negotiated interaction and receive negative feedback, they are likely to test different hypotheses about a particular linguistic system.
3) It operates as a *metalinguistic* function—encouraging learners to think about linguistic information. The metalinguistic function of output relates to the possibility that learners may be consciously thinking about language and its system, about its phonological, grammatical, and semantic rules in order to guide them to produce utterances that are linguistically correct and communicatively appropriate.

Whereas modified input and negotiation of meaning may only result in learners focusing on the messages being exchanged in interaction, all these three functions of output serve to focus the learner on form as well as meaning.
It is suggested that production has seven roles:

1) It serves to generate better input through the feedback that learners' efforts at production elicit;
2) It forces syntactic processing (i.e., it obliges learners to pay attention to grammar);
3) It allows learners to test hypotheses about the target-language grammar;
4) It helps to automatize existing L2 knowledge;
5) It provides opportunities for learners to develop discourse skills, for example by producing 'long turns';
6) It is important for helping learners to develop a personal voice by steering conversations onto topics they are interested in contributing to;
7) It provides the learner with auto-input in the sense that learners can attend to the input provided by their own productions.

(1), (3), (6), and (7) constitute indirect ways that output can contribute to acquisition, through the input that learners secure for themselves by their efforts to speak. The other roles, however, suggest that production can contribute more directly and centrally to acquisition. In effect, there would seem to be two basic arguments relating to the contribution of production. The first is that production enables learners to practice what they already know, thus helping them to automatize their discourse and linguistic knowledge. Roles (4) and (5) belong here. The second argument relates to (2)—the central idea that production engages syntactic processing in a way that comprehension does not.

The comprehensible output hypothesis in L2 acquisition constitutes an important addition to work on the role of interaction in L2 acquisition. It is becoming clear that output contributes to language acquisition. What is not yet clear, however, is whether output assists learners to acquire new linguistic forms or only to automatize use of partially acquired forms (i.e., to eliminate INTERLANGUAGE variants when the target language variant is already part of a learner's interlanguage). Further work is also needed to establish whether (and under what conditions) the MODIFIED OUTPUT in repaired UPTAKE constitutes acquisition.

Ellis 2008; Kumaravadivelu 2006; Macaro et al. 2010; Richards & Schmidt 2010; Skehan 1998a; Swain 1985, 1995

overcorrection
another term for HYPERCORRECTION

overextension
in language acquisition, the use of a lexical item to refer to a wider range of entities than is normal in adult usage. For example, the word *duck* might be extended to many more types of bird than the adult concept would admit. Or, the word *ball* is extended to all kinds of round objects, including a lampshade, a doorknob and the moon. Overextension can involve up to a third of an infant's early words and is common up to the age of about 2 years 6 months. The child's reasons for including items within a concept often seem to be based upon similarities of shape; but size (e.g., the word *fly* was first used for the insect and then came to be used for specks of dirt and even crumbs of bread), texture (e.g., the expression *sizo* was first used by one child for scissors, and then extended to all metal objects), sound and movement are also important defining features. Other overextensions reflect similarity of function or association with the same event (e.g., *nap* to refer to a *blanket*). Some overextensions involve a whole series of loosely linked common features called by Vygotsky a *chain complex*. An infant was found to apply the term *quah = quack*) to a duck on a pond, then extend it to any liquid including milk in a bottle, to a coin with an eagle on it and from that to all round coin-like objects.

Although overextension has been well documented in children's speech production, it is not necessarily used in speech comprehension. One two-year-old used *apple*, in speaking, to refer to a number of other round objects like a tomato and a ball, but had no difficulty picking out the *apple*, when asked, from a set of round objects including a ball and a tomato.

Several reasons have been suggested for overextension. The child may simply have unformed impressions of the world and thus be unable to recognize similarities between items. Or, it may be using an approximate word for a concept for which it does not yet have a term. Or, it may be actively engaged in forming concepts: imposing patterns upon its experience and learning by trial and error which items are classed together. One version of this last view suggests that the child is trying to assemble a range of exemplars in order to form a *prototype* for a particular concept.

The opposite phenomenon, **underextension**, also occurs, but rather less frequently. It may be the result of a word being acquired in a way that is too dependent upon context. A child might apply *white* to snow but not to a blank page or *deep* to a swimming pool but not to a puddle.

see also OVERGENERALIZATION

Aitchison 2003; Clark 2001; Field 2004; Kuczaj 1999; Neisser 1987; Yule 2006

overgeneralization

a process common in both first and second language learning, in which a learner extends the use of a grammatical rule of a linguistic item beyond its accepted uses, generally by making words or structures follow a more regular pattern. One example is overgeneralization of inflections. Children recognize the use of *-ed* to mark past tense but extend it to all past forms including those that should be irregular. This often happens after the child has already mastered the correct irregular form. In a process known as U-SHAPED DEVELOPMENT, the child abandons accurate forms such as *went* and *brought* and adopts *goed* and *bringed*. Examples such as these provide important evidence that children do not simply parrot the words of adults but are actively engaged in a process of rule formulation and adjustment.

One account, the *rule-and-memory model* (see DUAL-MODE SYSTEM), represents the phenomenon in terms of a tension between a desire to apply a general rule and a memory for specific exceptions. Gradually, through exposure to multiple examples, memory comes to prevail over the rule in the case of irregular forms. An alternative, *connectionist* view (see CONNECTIONISM) would be that verb forms are represented by means of a set of mental connections rather than by the child forming rules. Since there are strong connections between many verb roots and past tense forms in *-ed*, competition determines that there is a phase in development when this is the dominant (because most statistically probable) form. Computer programs have modeled precisely this learning process.

The child may also overgeneralize standard sentence patterns in its repertoire. It seems that the child learns to recognize syntactic patterns by associating them with prototypical verbs: *give*, for example, as an exemplar of the pattern Verb + Noun Phrase + Noun Phrase (*gave* + *Mary* + *a present*). Other verbs are then tried out with the pattern, sometimes mistakenly. Researchers are interested in how the child seems to avoid overgeneralization in some instances, apparently recognizing that these verbs are inappropriate for a given pattern.

One type of overgeneralization that has been much studied involves a double auxiliary, as in *Why did you did scare me?* or a double tense marking as in *What did you brought?* It is explained in terms of the child having imperfectly acquired the movement rules which in CHOMSKYAN THEORY permit the formation of inverted questions, negatives, etc.

see also OVEREXTENSION

 Aitchison 1998; Field 2004; Marcus 1996; Tomasello & Brooks 1999

over-indulgence
another term for OVER-USE

overshadowing
a term which refers to a situation where two cues are associated with an outcome. Research has shown that in such cases the more subjectively salient of the two cues overshadows the weaker. As overshadowing continues overtime, *blocking* results (i.e., learners learn to selectively attend to only the more salient of the two cues). Blocking is, in fact, the result of an automatically learned inattention. An example of blocking can be found in learners who acquire adverbials to express temporal reference but fail to acquire tense and aspectual (i.e., do not progress beyond the basic variety). The L1 contributes to overshadowing and blocking by making those L2 forms that are similar to L1 forms more salient. Learners know from their L1 that adverbials can express temporal meanings and how effective such devices are in communicating temporality. Thus, the high salience of these features prevents them from attending to tense and aspect markings.

see also CONNECTIONISM, EMERGENTISM, COMPETITION MODEL

 Ellis 2008; N. Ellis 2006a, 2006b, 2006c

overt prestige
see COVERT PRESTIGE

over-use
also **over-indulgence**
a term referring to the use of an L2 features more frequently than the same feature is used by native speakers. The over-use or over-indulgence of certain grammatical forms in L2 acquisition can occur as a result of intralingual processes such as OVERGENERALIZATION. For example, L2 learners have often been observed to overgeneralize the regular past tense inflection to irregular verbs in L2 English (e.g., *costed*). Similarly, learners may demonstrate a preference for words which can be generalized to a large number of contexts. Over-use can also result from TRANSFER—often as a consequence of the AVOIDANCE or underproduction of some difficult structure.
 Ellis 2008: Levenston 1971

P

paralinguistic features
those features of communication which are non-verbal, that is, do not refer to words/phrases themselves and their meanings and therefore cannot be linguistically segmented. Prosodic features, a sub-category of paralanguage, involve conscious or unconscious aspects of speech which give additional meaning to the words and utterances themselves, for example, intonation, word stress, word pitch, rhythm, loudness and so on. Another category of paralanguage is what we might call body language and encompasses communicative signals such as gestures, coughing, crying, clearing one's throat and facial expressions. Both prosodic features and gestures have been the subject of considerable research in second language acquisition contexts. An obvious rationale for such research is that many of the features of both sub-categories are language or culture specific and therefore may be difficult for L2 learners to acquire.
📖 Macaro et al. 2010

Parallel Distributed Processing Model
also **PDP Model**
a cognitive theory of L2 acquisition which is based on the notion that information is processed simultaneously at several levels of attention. Parallel Distributed Processing (PDP) Model is one type of connectionist model of language processing, and it is sometimes used as a synonym for CONNECTIONISM. As you read the words on this page, your brain is attending to letters, word juncture and meaning, syntactic relationships, textual discourse, as well as background experiences (schemata) that you bring to the text. A child's (or adult's) linguistic performance may be the consequence of many levels of simultaneous neural interconnections rather than a serial process of one rule being applied, then another, then another, and so forth.
In this model, knowledge is seen not as 'patterns' or 'rules', nor is there any distinction drawn between DECLARATIVE and PROCEDURAL KNOWLEDGE. Instead, what learners 'know' is characterized as a labyrinth of interconnections between 'units' that do not correspond to any holistic concepts of the kind we normally recognize (e.g., a real-life person or object or, where language is concerned, a word or grammatical feature). Performance (i.e.,

INFORMATION PROCESSING) involves the activation of the requisite interconnections; learning arises when, as a result of experience, the strength of the connections (i.e., 'weights') between units is modified. PDP constitutes a unified model of cognition, straddling the traditional COMPETENCE/PERFORMANCE distinction.

The main properties of a PDP are as follows:

1) Processing is carried out in parallel rather than serially. It is argued that multiple constraints govern language processing, with semantic and syntactic factors constantly interacting without it being possible to say that one set is primary. It is also argued that if each word can help constrain the syntactic role, and even the identity, of every other word, processing must take place not serially but simultaneously on different levels.
2) A PDP model consists of 'units' or 'nodes' connected in such a way that the activation of one unit can inhibit or excite others in varying degrees. The nature of these units varies, depending on what kind of behaviors is being modeled. In some cases the units stand for hypotheses about, for example, the syntactic roles of words in a sentence, while in other cases they stand for goals and actions, and in still others for aspects of things. Units have output values which they can pass on to other units in the system. Also, in many PDP models, the units are organized into different 'levels', such that any one unit excites or inhibits other units at both its own level and other levels. The resulting network is highly complex and is thought to mirror the neural structure of the brain.
3) Knowledge is viewed in terms of the microstructure rather than macrostructure of cognition, i.e., as connection strength rather than as generalized 'patterns' or 'rules'. In this model, the patterns themselves are not stored. Rather, what is stored is the connection strengths between units that allow these patterns to be recreated.
4) Processing is activated by INPUT which stimulates one or more units and, of course, their connections with other units. Thus, in computer simulations of PDP models, selected input in the form of 'training sets' is fed into the computer, often in successive runs.
5) Learning is a by-product of information processing; as a result of responding to input, the association strengths among units are spontaneously modified. Learning consists of discovering the right connection strengths from input. Interconnection strengths do not have to be built into the models by the researcher, but are divided through experience. The models, therefore, are dynamic, interactive and self-organizing systems.
6) This process of adjusting connection strengths is governed by 'learning rules' such as the 'Hebb rule', which states: Adjust the strength of the connection between units A and B in proportion to the product of their

simultaneous activation. A number of complex learning rules have been identified.
7) PDP models can go beyond the input by means of 'spontaneous generalization'. The models can extract 'regularities' in the patterns of interconnections: these resemble higher order rules. However, PDP networks do not learn 'rules'; rather they learn to act as though they knew them.
8) PDP models display 'emergent properties'. That is, they represent learning as a gradual process involving a series of stages. They behave like language learners in that they produce incorrect as well as target-like constructions. Importantly, these incorrect responses are generated by the network itself.

The main point of criticism of the PDP Model is that, although referring to cognitive views on mental processing, they are actually deeply rooted in BEHAVIORISM. The process of learning, as described by the PDP Model, is strictly based on the environmental influence and not innate knowledge.
📖 Brown 2007; Ellis 2008; Plunkett 1988; McClelland et al.1986; MacWhinney 1989

parameter resetting
see PRINCIPLES AND PARAMETERS

parameter setting
see PRINCIPLES AND PARAMETERS

Parameter Setting Model
a theory of L2 acquisition proposed by Flynn which is based on the theory of UNIVERSAL GRAMMAR (UG) and assumes that adult L2 learners have continued access to this (see COMPLETE ACCESS VIEW). Their task is to discover how each principle is realized in the L2 (i.e., what parameter settings are needed). Flynn argued that the essential faculty for language evidenced in L1 acquisition is also evident in L2 acquisition. However, Flynn also acknowledged a crucial role for the L1. In cases where the L1 and L2 parameter settings are the same, learning is facilitated because these L2 learners are able to consult the structural configuration established for the L1 in the construction of the L2 grammar. Where the L1 and L2 parameter settings are different, the learner has to assign new values and, although this is not problematic according to Flynn, it does add to the learning burden. Flynn hypothesized that where the L1 and L2 have identical settings, the pattern of acquisition of complete sentence structures (of the kind that UG principles typically address) will correspond to the later stages of L1 acquisition. She also hypothesized that where the L1 and L2 have different settings, the pattern of acquisition will correspond to the early stages of L1 acquisition, as the learners need to first discover the relevant structural configuration in the L2.

Flynn's Parameter Setting Model rests on assumption that adult L2 learners have access to the same language faculty as L1 learners (in the case of L2 acquisition, 'parameter setting' is frequently 'PARAMETER RESETTING'). As such, it rejects the claim advanced by other theorists that age is a significant factor in L2 learning. Flynn and Manuel explicitly addressed the age issue and concluded that it is possible to argue for a monolithic critical period in L2 learning. They presented three arguments in favor of this position. First, like L1 learners, L2 learners possess grammatical knowledge that could not have been learned purely on the basis of INPUT. Second, L2 learners possess knowledge that is structure-dependent (i.e., a knowledge of language relies on knowing structural relationships in a sentence rather than looking at it as a sequence of words). Third, they exhibit the same infinite productivity of new sentences as L1 learners. In essence, Flynn and Manuel are asserting that the logical problem of L1 and L2 acquisition are the same (see LOGICAL PROBLEM OF LANGUAGE ACQUISITION).
📖 Ellis 2008; Flynn 1984, 1987; Flynn & Manuel 1991

paraphasia
a type of error resulting from APHASIA and involving the substitution, transposition or addition of a unit of language. In *phonemic paraphasia*, a word might be substituted which bears a phonological resemblance to the target word, while in *semantic paraphasia*, the substituted word might be linked to the target by meaning.
📖 Field 2004

parsing
also **syntactic parsing**
a stage in the processing of written or spoken language at which a syntactic structure is assembled from a string of words. For example, the moment a listener hears 'The man . . .', that listener immediately projects a determiner phrase (DP) while simultaneously tagging it as 'subject of sentence'. If the listener hears 'reduced' next, then that listener most likely tags the word as 'verb', 'past tense', thus projecting a verb phrase and confirms that 'the man' is the subject of the verb. However, if the listener next encounters 'to tears', then the listener's parsing mechanism stops and reanalyzes 'The man reduced to tears . . .' as a reduced relative clause that is the subject of a sentence. If a verb comes next, say, 'told', then the listener's parser projects a new verb phrase with 'The man reduced to tears' as the subject of 'told'. And so the analysis progresses as each word is encountered. Parsing, then, is this moment-by-moment (real-time) process of tagging words with syntactic roles, projecting syntactic structure, and making sense of the sentence.

Parsing research in SLA has been minimal to date but is taking on increasing importance, the question being whether L2 learners come to resolve ambiguity the same way native speakers do. For example, in Italian the sentence

Giovanni escriveva a Stefano cuando era negli Stati Uniti 'Giovanni wrote to Stefano while he was in the United States' is ambiguous as to who was in the United States: Giovanni or Stefano. Because Italian is a null subject language, the verb *era* can be either bare (have a null subject) or not (have an overt subject, in this case *lui*). Thus, the sentence can also be *Giovanni escriveva a Stefano cuando lui era negli Stati Uniti*. The question becomes how native speakers interpret null and overt subjects in the embedded clause. Research has shown that they overwhelmingly tend to link null subjects with the subject of the first clause (in this case, null subject = Giovanni) but tend to link overt subjects with nonsubjects of the first clause (in this case, *lui* = Stefano). Research on this particular feature (interpretation of null and overt subjects) has shown that even very advanced speakers of Italian L2 do not resolve ambiguity like native speakers.

A good deal of research has been conducted on ambiguous relative clauses and what they 'attach to' during parsing. For example, in *Someone shot the maid of the actor who was on the balcony*, if asked 'Who was on the balcony, the maid or the actor?', native speakers of English tend to say the actor (i.e., they 'attach' the relative clause to 'the actor'). But given the exact same sentence in Spanish, Spanish speakers tend to say the maid was on the balcony (they 'attach' the relative clause to 'the maid'). Research on L2 learners of Spanish and French have shown that in the case of relative clauses, L2 learners parse such sentences using L1 preferences but by very advanced stages can become indistinguishable from native speakers.

see also GARDEN PATH SENTENCES

📖 Field 2004; VanPatten & Benati 2010

partial access view

a view which claims that adult L2 learners have access to parts of UNIVERSAL GRAMMAR (UG) but not others. For example, functional features that are not realized in the first language (such as strong Infl or gender, for English first language learners of other languages which possess these features), cannot be acquired. Partial access position draws on the distinction between principles that have parameters and those that do not. It is argued that learners have access to linguistic principles but not to the full range of parametric variation. This view makes two assumptions. One is that adult learners will not manifest 'wild grammars' (i.e., they will not produce impossible errors) because they are constrained by UG principles. The other is that they will not to be able to acquire the L2 values of parameters when these differ from L1. For example, they have access to only those UG parameters operative in their L1. However, they may be able to switch to the L2 parameter setting with the help of direct instruction involving error correction. In other words, L2 acquisition is partly regulated by UG and partly by general LEARNING STRATEGIES. Within this view, second language grammars are UG-constrained, that is, they do not violate principles and parameters, but learners might not be able to reset parameters, and therefore operate with first language settings for some parts of the new language.

see also DUAL ACCESS VIEW, COMPLETE ACCESS VIEW, NO ACCESS VIEW
📖 Ellis 2008; Mithcell & Myles 2004; Schachter 1988

pattern matching
another term for PATTERN RECOGNITION

pattern recognition
also **pattern matching**
the establishment of a one-to-one match between, on the one hand, a set of features drawn from a stimulus and held temporarily in a sensory store; and, on the other, a stored representation in the mind. Pattern recognition enables us to identify familiar patterns (e.g., letter shapes) with a high degree of *automaticity*, and to impose patterns upon unfamiliar forms (as when users of the Latin alphabet are exposed over time to signage in the Greek or Russian ones).

Approaches to pattern recognition offer different accounts of how a pattern is stored in LONG-TERM MEMORY. They include:

- *Template matching theories*: where the pattern is matched with an exact counterpart in long-term memory. This would appear to entail storing all possible variants of the pattern—a very inefficient solution since, in order to recognize, say, the letter E, one would have to store it not only in all possible fonts but also in all possible sizes. The solution is to assume a two-stage process, where a stimulus is *normalized*, with non-essential features edited out, before being matched to the template.
- *Feature analysis theories*: where the pattern is broken into constituent parts; and is identified as a combination of those features. For example, a small number of distinctive features (lines, curves, etc.) would allow us to identify all the letters of the alphabet. There is evidence that the visual cortex in mammals is so organized as to detect the presence of simple features within a complex pattern.
- *Prototype theories*: where the pattern is compared on a 'best fit' basis with an idealized example of the pattern in long-term memory.

📖 Anderson 2009; Field 2004; Kellogg 1995; Lund 2001

Pavlovian reinforcement
another term for CLASSICAL CONDITIONING

PDP Model
another term for PARALLEL DISTRIBUTED PROCESSING MODEL

peer pressure
encouragement, often among children, to conform to the behavior, attitudes, language, etc., of those around them. Peer pressure is a particularly important variable in considering child-adult comparisons. The peer pressure children encounter in language learning is quite unlike what the adult experiences. Children usually have strong constraints upon them to conform. They are told in words, thoughts, and actions that they had better 'be like the rest of the kids'. Such peer pressure extends to language. Adults experience some peer pressure, but of a different kind. Adults tend to tolerate linguistic differences more than children, and therefore errors in speech are more easily excused. If adults can understand a second language speaker, for example, they will usually provide positive cognitive and affective feedback, a level of tolerance that might encourage some adult learners to 'get by'. Children are harsher critics of one another's actions and words and may thus provide a necessary and sufficient degree of mutual pressure to learn the second language.
📖 Brown 2007

peer reviewing
a practice connected with L2 writing which has received considerable research attention. There are a number of claimed advantages of fellow students reading the written output of L2 learners including the following: It provides an alternative readership to the teacher; it is less threatening and less evaluative in nature; it encourages a focus on communication rather than accuracy; it may be pitched more at the level of the learner. Results, in terms of furthering the skill of writing, or more thorough revisions, however, have so far been mixed. Peers appear to respond to surface errors just as much as teachers and are not always able to give as effective advice as teachers. Students do not always feel confident that peer comments are valid. Thus, when studies have compared peer reviewing with teacher feedback it appears that writers are more likely to revise as a result of teacher feedback than peer feedback.
see also FEEDBACK
📖 Macaro et al. 2010; Paulus 1999; Tsui & Ng 2000

perceptual strategy
any of several rough principles which listeners may use in interpreting utterances. A perceptual strategy is essentially a kind of principled guess about how the words we are hearing fit into a syntactic structure. In the last several decades, practitioners of PSYCHOLINGUISTICS have proposed a number of such strategies, and the reality of these strategies is supported by varying amounts of experimental evidence. One of these is the *principle of late closure*, which says 'if possible, put the next word into the phrase you are currently processing'. By this principle, if you hear *Susie decided gradually to*

get rid of her teddy-bears, you will associate *gradually* with *decided*, and not with *to get rid of her teddy-bears*. Another proposed strategy is the *canonical sentoid strategy*, by which the first string of words that could possibly be a sentence is assumed to be a sentence. It is this strategy which makes GARDEN-PATH SENTENCES so difficult to interpret: when you hear *The horse shot from the stable fell down*, you naturally take *The horse shot from the stable* as a complete sentence and are left floundering by the continuation, even though the whole utterance has a perfectly straightforward interpretation.
📖 Trask 2005

performance
see COMPETENCE

perlocutionary act
see SPEECH ACT

personal function
see SYSTEMIC LINGUISTICS

personality
those aspects of an individual's behavior, attitudes, beliefs, thought, actions and feelings which are seen as typical and distinctive of that person and recognized as such by that person and others. Personality factors such as SELF-ESTEEM, INHIBITION, ANXIETY, RISK TAKING and EXTROVERSION, are thought to influence second language learning because they can contribute to MOTIVATION and the choice of LEARNING STRATEGIES.
Personality is typically measured by means of some kind of self-report questionnaire. A number of language-specific questionnaires have been developed by SLA researchers. These have been used to measure particular dimensions of personality such as risk-taking or extroversion. Also researchers have made use of general personality questionnaires such as *Eysenck Personality Inventory* and the *Myers-Briggs Type Indicator*. One of the problems with this multiplicity of measurement instruments is that it is very difficult to draw general conclusions, as it is difficult to identify to what extent the constructs being measured are the same or different.
see also LEARNING STYLES, WILLINGNESS TO COMMUNICATE, LEARNER BELIEFS, INTELLIGENCE, LANGUAGE APTITUDE
📖 Ellis 2008; Eysenck & Eysenck 1964; Myers & Briggs 1976; Richards & Schmidt 2010

phonological awareness
the extent to which a pre-literate individual is capable of recognizing the individual phonemes which constitute a spoken word. The ability to divide a word into its constituent phonemes cannot be taken for granted, especially since phonemes in natural speech vary greatly. Adult Portuguese illiterates

have proved weak at tasks which involve analyzing the phonemic structure of words (though they performed better at classifying syllables and rimes). This suggests that awareness of the phoneme as a unit may not pre-date learning to read, and indeed may be the product of literacy.

Some scholars argue for a reciprocal relationship. There is evidence that the ability to combine separate phonemes into syllables is a predictor of progress in early reading. On the other hand, progress in early reading seems to pave the way for the ability to delete an initial or final sound from a word rather than vice versa.

📖 Field 2004; Goswami & Bryant 1990; Perfetti 1985, 1999

phonological perception

the perception by an infant of the phonological system of its first language, as evidenced in signs of use. There are several views on the extent to which a newly born infant is attuned to speech. An *articulatory learning theory* suggests that an infant has no perceptual capacity at birth and that the phonological system is entirely acquired through exposure to INPUT. An *attunement theory* has it that the infant is born with the capacity to perceive certain fundamental sounds, which enables it to identify some of those which feature in the target language (TL). A strong *nativist* view (see NATIVISM) holds that the infant is endowed with the capacity to distinguish the speech sounds of all human languages but later loses it for sounds which are not relevant to the TL. Finally, a *maturational nativist view* envisages a biologically determined program for both perception and production.

Not enough is known about the precise relationship between perception and production in phonological development. It may be that problems in distinguishing certain sounds influence the order in which phonemes are acquired. For example, in English /f/ and /r/ appear late, and one possible explanation is that they are easily confused with /θ/ and /w/. The cause does not lie in the infant's hearing, which is fully developed at this point; rather, its brain may not yet be able to process these distinctions.

An insight into the relation between perception and production is provided by the *fis phenomenon*. Assume that a child pronounces the adult word *fish* as [fɪs]. If an adult imitates the child's pronunciation, the child can recognize that it is wrong but cannot put it right. This does not necessarily show that the child has a precise representation in its mind of the adult form; but it does show that it has a representation that is distinct from the form that it produces. Hence a suggestion that the infant might possess two distinct lexicons: one for perception and one for production. In its current form, this theory assumes that there is actually a single lexicon (containing elements of word meaning) but that it has separate *phonological registers* for input and OUTPUT.

Many studies have shown that the development of auditory perception begins much earlier than might be supposed. Important research areas include:

- *Categorical perception.* Experimenters have demonstrated that infants as young as four months distinguish stops by means of sharply defined boundaries and can also distinguish vowels and liquids. However, the infants do not appear to recognize category boundaries for fricatives. This finding may be significant, as, across languages, fricatives tend to emerge late.
- *Critical period.* The issue here is whether there is a *critical period* (see CRITICAL PERIOD HYPOTHESIS) during which infants are particularly sensitive to the phonology of their target language. It appears that infants can distinguish between sounds which are not contrastive in the language they are acquiring, whereas most adults cannot. Initial evidence suggested that infants lost the ability to make these distinctions as early as nine months. However, later findings have indicated that children of four years old can still make certain 'robust' non-native distinctions, and that adults remain capable of distinguishing sounds which are entirely absent in the native language (e.g., for English-speakers, different Xhosa clicks). Discriminatory ability may thus be lost to different degrees, reflecting the extent to which L2 phonemes are distinct from those in the first language.
Jusczyk's *WRAPSA model* offers an account based upon focus of attention rather than complete loss of discriminatory ability. It suggests that we continue to perceive all the contrasts in the signal but that certain features are given special 'weighting'. Our perception of sounds does not change but the way we distribute our attention is determined by the language we acquire.
- *Phoneme awareness.* Children find it difficult to distinguish *minimal pairs* (*mend/send, road/wrote*) before about two years six months. This suggests that early words are represented holistically rather than in terms of the phonemes that constitute them. It is unclear exactly when the child develops an awareness of phonemes. One view is that we only come to recognize phonemic segments as a result of learning to read alphabetically. Another theory is that perception vocabulary remains holistic for a while but that production vocabulary is specified in terms of phonemes and/or the articulatory gestures associated with them.
- *Rhythm.* Infants appear to pick up the rhythm patterns of their mother's speech even while in the womb. The child then may exploit rhythmic properties of the speech signal in order to locate word boundaries in connected speech. English-acquiring infants develop an awareness of the *strong-weak pattern* which characterizes much of the English lexicon and may use it as the basis for identifying potential words.
- *Syllable.* It may also be that a unit of phonological processing is available to the infant, the best candidate being the syllable. Infants display sensitivity to syllable structure at a very early age—probably as a result of no-

ticing the steady-state sequences in the speech stream which correspond to the vowels at the center of each syllable.
- *Normalization.* The adult voices to which the infant is exposed vary greatly in pitch, speech rate, accent, etc. Studies have tested the infant's capacity to compensate for these features when extracting phonological information. Once a given phoneme distinction has been achieved, infants show that they are able to sustain it even when the phonemes are uttered by different voices. Infants also appear capable of making the distinction between /bɑ/ and /wɑ/ which, for adults, depends upon assessing the speech rate of the talker.

see also PHONOLOGICAL PRODUCTION
📖 Field 2004; Goodman & Nusbaum 1994; Ingram 1989

phonological production

the acquisition by an infant of the phonological system of its first language, as evidenced in signs of use. An infant's first productions are purely reflexive, consisting of wailing, laughter, gurgling, etc., in response to immediate sensations. Its first speech-like productions take the form of BABBLING, which begins at between six and ten months and is characterized by a limited range of sounds resembling adult consonant-vowel (CV) syllables. There is disagreement as to whether babbling is unrelated to later phonological development or whether it is a precursor of speech. At a later stage, babbling adopts intonation contours which seem to mimic those of adults. Intonation thus appears to be acquired independently of phoneme development.

The question has been raised of whether there is a universal order of phoneme acquisition. It is difficult to determine when a particular phoneme has been 'acquired': it may be used accurately in certain contexts but not in others. Furthermore, the ability to recognize a phoneme may precede its emergence in production by quite a long period. That said, findings suggest that, whatever the ambient language, infants do indeed acquire certain sounds early on: namely, nasal consonants, labials, stops and back vowels. Some scholars have concluded that such forms must be innate (see INNATENESS HYPOTHESIS); however, the phenomenon could equally be due to early limitations on the child's perceptual system or to the child employing the easiest articulatory gestures first. Some evidence for innateness comes from the fact that sounds which are universally infrequent (such as English /æ/ tend to emerge late. An alternative suggestion is that the order in which phonemes are acquired may reflect their frequency in the INPUT to which the child is exposed. However, the evidence is unclear, and it is noteworthy that the omnipresent /ð/ in English emerges late.

Children develop systematic ways of reducing adult words to forms which match their production capacities. They might consistently voice unvoiced sounds (*paper* = [beːbəː]) or replace fricatives by stops (*see* = [tiː]). A common feature is the simplification of consonant clusters (*train* = [ten]). Analogy seems to play a part, with sets of similar words showing similar pronunciation features. But there are often anomalies, termed *idioms*: single words which continue to be pronounced wrongly when the rest of a set has been acquired phonologically. There are also *chain shifts* (if *truck* is pronounced *duck*, it may cause *duck* to become *guck*).

see also PHONOLOGICAL PERCEPTION

📖 Field 2004; Fletcher & Garman 1986; Fletcher & MacWhinney 1995; Ingram 1989, 1999; Menn & Stoel-Gammon 1995

Piagetian stages of development
another term for COGNITIVE DEVELOPMENT

pidgin
a term which refers to a language with a markedly reduced grammatical structure, lexicon and stylistic range, compared with other languages, and which is the native language of no one. Structures which have been reduced in this way are said to be pidginized. Pidgins are formed by two mutually unintelligible speech communities attempting to communicate, each successively approximating to the more obvious features of the other's language. Such developments need considerable motivation on the part of the speakers, and it is therefore not surprising that pidgin languages flourish in areas of economic development, as in the pidgins based on English, French, Spanish and Portuguese, in the East and West Indies, Africa and the Americas (where they were often referred to as *trade languages*). Some pidgins have become so useful that they have developed a role as auxiliary languages, and been given official status by the community (e.g., Tok Pisin). These cases are called *expanded pidgins* because of the way they have added extra features to cope with the needs of the users. Pidgins become creolized (see CREOLE) when they become the mother tongue of a community.

📖 Crystal 2008

pidginization
a process by which non-native speakers develop a linguistic system in contact language situations to effect communication. The result is a PIDGIN, a linguistic system with reduced vocabulary and reduced grammar when compared to the two languages that come into contact to form it. Pidgins exist all around the world, with some of the most studied ones being in the Pacific and Caribbean Islands (e.g., Tok Pisin which is a pidgin in Papua New Guinea). Pidgins often exhibit commonalities as they develop, regardless of the languages that come into contact. Some of these commonalities include subject-verb-object word order, lack of relative clauses, reduction of closed

syllables, reduction of verbal inflections with words often taking the place of inflections, reduced inventory of phonemes (sounds), among others.

John Schumann applied the concept of pidginization to SLA in the mid-1970s when he asserted that some learners, who do not get beyond the very basic level of acquisition, may speak a kind of pidgin as a result of two languages coming into contact. His famous research subject, Alberto, was an immigrant from Costa Rica who lived in Massachusetts but had limited contact with English speakers. During the course of Schumann's research, Alberto had not advanced beyond the earliest stages of negation (e.g., *no like beer, I no like beer, He don't like beer*) and, for example, showed evidence of nonmarking of past tense (e.g., *Yesterday my country change the president*). Schumann concluded that Alberto, compared to the other research subjects, showed little development over time and was speaking a pidgin-like version of English largely, because Alberto was engaged in the communication of purely denotative referential information and not integrative and expressive information. In other words, Alberto was not using language to become part of a society or culture, one of the aspects that Schumann claimed fostered pidginization.

Pidginization applied to SLA hit its apex in the late 1970s and early 1980s but has since fallen out of favor for various theoretical and practical reasons.
📖 Schumann 1978b; VanPatten & Benati 2010

pivot grammar

an attempt within the NATIVIST HYPOTHESIS to trace a consistent pattern in an infant's early two-word utterances (see TWO-WORD STAGE). Pivot grammar was introduced into language acquisition studies of the 1960s, to refer to a primitive word-class thought to characterize the early two-word combinations produced by children. It was commonly observed that the child's first two-word utterances seemed to manifest two separate word classes, and not simply two words thrown together at random. Consider the following utterances: *my cap; that horsie; bye-bye Jeff; Mommy sock*. Linguists noted that the words on the left-hand side seemed to belong to a class that words on the right-hand side generally did not belong to. That is, *my* could co-occur with *cap, horsie, Jeff,* or *sock*, but not with *that* or *bye-bye*. *Mommy* is, in this case, a word that belongs in both classes. The first class of words was called 'pivot', since they could pivot around a number of words in the second, 'open' class. Thus, the first rule of the GENERATIVE GRAMMAR of the child was described as follows:

Sentence → pivot word + open word

This analysis is no longer popular, for several reasons (e.g., it fails to relate to the analysis of adult grammatical structures, ignores the semantic structure of such sentences, and seems to apply to only certain types of sentence in

certain children). For example, in the utterance *Mommy sock*, which nativists would describe as a sentence consisting of a pivot word and an open word, Bloom found at least three possible underlying relations: agent-action (*Mommy is putting the sock on*), agent-object (*Mommy sees the sock*), and possessor-possessed (*Mommy's sock*). By examining data in reference to contexts, Bloom concluded that children learn underlying structures, and not superficial word order. Thus, depending on the social context, *Mommy sock* could mean a number of different things to a child. Those varied meanings were inadequately captured in a pivot grammar approach.
📖 Bloom 1971; Brown 2007; Crystal 2008

planned discourse
see VARIABLE COMPETENCE MODEL

planned focus-on-form
see FOCUS ON FORM

POS
an abbreviation for POVERTY OF THE STIMULUS

positive evidence
utterances in the surrounding language heard by the learner which serve to inform the learner about what is grammatical and acceptable in that language. Positive evidence stands in contrast to NEGATIVE EVIDENCE and explicit information (e.g., telling a learner how something works in a language). Positive evidence is, essentially, the INPUT that learners hear in communicative settings, in both L1 and L2 situations. It contains any and all utterances that learners might hear from more proficient or native speakers of the language. It can also be input that learners get from written texts (in the L2 context, of course, given that child L1 learners do not read). Some people refer to it as primary linguistic data. It is called positive because it does not contain direct negative FEEDBACK, such as error correction. According to theories of acquisition that work with UNIVERSAL GRAMMAR, only positive evidence can be used by the language learning mechanism; that is, the language learning mechanism cannot make use of negative evidence. The language learning mechanism also cannot make use of explicit information such as rules provided to the learner. In short, what the language learning mechanism needs is samples of language from the communicative environment. Positive evidence is also implicated in the POVERTY OF THE STIMULUS situation, meaning that learners come to know far more about language than what is evident in the language they are exposed to.
📖 Long 1996; Piske & Young-Scholten 2009; VanPatten & Benati 2010

positive transfer
see TRANSFER

poverty of the stimulus
also **POS**

a term referring to the notion that view the INPUT available to learners as an inadequate source of information for building a grammar because the input is so impoverished that it is insufficient to explain learning. The stimulus can be considered impoverished on several grounds: (1) input is degenerate (e.g., it contains ungrammatical sentences), (2) input underdetermines the grammar that needs to be constructed, and (3) the input to children does not typically contain NEGATIVE EVIDENCE. The best example comes from knowledge about what is disallowed in a language. For example, speakers of English know that *I've done it* is a fine sentence but that the contraction of *I've* is disallowed in the question **Should I've done it?* One can only say *Should I have done it?* How does a person come to know that *I've* (and contractions more generally) is allowed in some instances and disallowed in others? No one teaches a child this, and negative evidence on grammar and syntax is virtually absent or at best haphazard in interactions with child L1 learners. And yet every speaker of English comes to know what is disallowed with contractions. What makes the poverty of the stimulus (POS) particularly interesting is that learners only get POSITIVE EVIDENCE in the input; that is, they only get examples of what languages allow. Thus, the input underdetermines the grammatical and syntactic knowledge that a speaker comes to have about a language.

In addition, people do not always speak in complete sentences. They also create false starts, they make what looks like surface grammatical errors as they change the nature of a sentence in the middle of speaking it, they slur, they abbreviate, they chop words, and so on. Spoken language does not look like well-written prose, for example. Thus, when we say the input to children is impoverished, there is a POS: The input does not always look good, and it only contains positive evidence.

POS is the bedrock of UNIVERSAL GRAMMAR (UG), which says that people are born with an innate specification for language; that is, certain principles about language come hardwired at birth. These principles are what constrain language and serve as the internal and unseen 'negative' information that guides speakers into what is allowed and disallowed in a language. In the case of contractions, we begin with the concept that UG allows movement of constituents in a language. *I should have done it* and *Should I have done it* are related in that the *should* has moved from one position in the sentence to another in order to form the question version. What UG contains, though, is also the concept that movement leaves traces. When the *should* moves it leaves behind its trace, where it originated from. Imagine a small *t* standing for trace so that in the speaker's mind the question has this structure: Should

I *t* have done it? This trace blocks contraction; it literally occupies the space, and thus *I* and *have* cannot merge to form a contraction. Therefore, UG contains two things that are relevant in this instance: the possibility of movement, and traces left behind by movement. Such an explanation means, then, that anyone born with normal capabilities for language has access to this information, and this is what helps the speaker come to know what is disallowed.

The POS has been applied to SLA as well.

see also LOGICAL PROBLEM OF LANGUAGE ACQUISITION

📖 Ellis 2008; Schwartz 1993, 1998; VanPatten & Benati 2010; White 1989, 2003, 2007

Power Law of Practice

a term stating that the logarithm of the reaction time and/or the error rate for a particular task decrease linearly with the logarithm of the number of practice trials taken, i.e., practice improves performance but with a gradually diminishing effect.

📖 Ellis 2008

practice

see CONSCIOUSNESS RAISING

pragmatic competence

the knowledge that speaker-hearers use in order to engage in communication, including how speech acts are successfully performed. Pragmatic competence is normally distinguished from LINGUISTIC COMPETENCE. Both are seen as relating to 'knowledge', and are therefore distinct from actual performance.

📖 Ellis 2008

pre-emption

in UG-based SLA studies, the term is used to refer to the prevention of the development of an INTERLANGUAGE form that cannot be disconfirmed purely on the basis of POSITIVE EVIDENCE.

📖 Ellis 2008

premodified input

see MODIFIED INPUT

preparatory act

see HEAD ACT

priming

an increase in the speed with which a word is recognized, which results from having recently seen or heard a word that is closely associated with it.

Shown the word *doctor*, a subject recognizes words such as *nurse* or *patient* more rapidly than usual—always provided they are presented soon afterwards. *Doctor* is referred to as the 'prime' and *patient* as the 'target'. The sight of the word *doctor* is said to prime *patient*.

Exposure to the prime is represented as *activating* (or bringing into prominence) a range of associated words. These words then become easier to identify because they are already foregrounded in the mind. The process, known as *spreading activation*, is highly *automatic* and not subject to conscious control. Most priming effects are relatively short-lived, and *decay* quite quickly, thus ensuring that too many lexical items are not activated simultaneously.

Priming effects have given rise to a research method which measures *reaction time* (how long it takes to recognize a word) in order to establish which words are most closely associated with a given prime. The experiments often involve a *lexical decision task*, where the subject is asked to press a button when he/she sees an actual word rather than a non-word. A comparison is then made between reaction times for targets which are associated with the prime and those for targets which are not.

Experiments often make use of *cross-modal priming*, where the prime is a spoken stimulus and the target is a visual stimulus on a computer screen. The logic for this is that it enables experimenters to tap into an abstract mental representation of the word which is independent of modality.

Several types of priming can be distinguished:

- *Repetition priming* involves repeating a recently-encountered word. This effect is surprisingly long lived: priming effects have been reported after a delay of several hours. The effects are stronger for low-frequency words than for more common ones, a phenomenon known as *frequency attenuation*. Repetition priming provides evidence of the way a reader traces patterns of coherence in a text by means of recurrent words.
- *Form-based priming* involves words which are orthographically similar. It has proved difficult to demonstrate that, for example, *spring* primes *string*. One explanation is that the two words are in competition with each other to form a match with what is in the stimulus, and thus reduce (*inhibit*) each other's activation.
- *Semantic priming* involves words which are semantically related. Strong effects have been recorded with words that fall into the same lexical set (*chair-table*), antonyms (*hot-cold*), words which share functional properties (*broom-floor*) and superordinate-hyponym pairs (*bird-robin*). However, the strength of the effect may depend on the strength of the associa-

tion: the co-hyponyms *cat* and *dog* are strongly associated but the similar co-hyponyms *pig* and *horse* are not.

📖 Field 2004; Harley 2001

Principles and Parameters
a nativist theory of first language acquisition which reflects the current thinking of Noam Chomsky. Chomsky takes the view that infants are born with an innate UNIVERSAL GRAMMAR (UG). This consists of a set of universal *principles* which characterize all (or nearly all) languages and a set of *parameters*, features which differentiate languages, usually on binary lines. A simple example of a parameter is the distinction between *pro-drop* languages which permit the omission of a subject pronoun and languages where the subject pronoun is obligatory (compare Italian *capisco* with English *I understand*). **Parameter setting** (the process by which children determine what setting of a parameter is appropriate for the one they are learning) is often represented on a + or - basis (e.g., + or - pro-drop).
A child is thus innately endowed with knowledge about language in general which gives it a head start in cracking the code of speech. However, it is also endowed with a set of choices which have to be made in relation to the language to which it is exposed.
Examples of innate principles are:

- *Structure dependency*: the structure of all languages consists of hierarchically organized phrases.
- *The Projection Principle*: syntactic structure is determined by entries in the lexicon (the choice of the verb *give* entails the use of a particular syntactic pattern).
- *The Subjacency Principle*: any constituent of a sentence that is moved (for example, to form a question or negative) can only cross one major boundary (a *bounding node*). Where such a major boundary falls is, however, determined by a language-specific parameter.
- *Binding Principles*: unlike most pronouns, an *anaphor* (the term is used here for reflexives such as 'himself' and reciprocals such as 'each other') can only refer to an antecedent within the same sentence.

Examples of parameters set in response to the ambient language are:

- *The Null Subject* (or pro-drop) *Parameter*: whether the language does/does not oblige the speaker to express a pronoun subject.
- *The Head Parameter*: whether the head (major constituent) falls at the beginning or at the end of a standard phrase.

- *Bounding Parameters*: restrictions on the way in which constituents can be moved (e.g., in forming negatives and interrogatives).
- the *Adjacency Parameter*: in effect, whether a transitive verb has to be followed immediately by its direct object or not. Compare English *I like music a lot* with French *J'aime beaucoup la musique*.
- *The Branching Parameter*: whether the hierarchical structure of a sentence as shown in a *tree diagram* branches towards the left or towards the right. There are marked differences between *right-branching languages* like English which standardly place the direct object after the verb and *left-branching* ones like Japanese where the object occurs before the verb.

A further parameter in which there has been much interest concerns *preposition stranding*. English accepts both *pied-piping* (*About what were you talking?*) and *stranding* (*What were you talking about?*). However, there are some quite complex restrictions on stranding, and native speakers disagree about the acceptability of sentences such as *What meeting did she phone after?* There are wide variations between languages as to whether they permit stranding or not.

Many attempts have been made to test the Principles and Parameters hypothesis empirically. A problem here lies in the fact that UG relates to an individual's competence and not to their performance. An established procedure is therefore to ask subjects to make *grammaticality judgments*, i.e., to indicate whether for them, as users of the language, a sentence is grammatically acceptable or not. This method has been used to trace similarities between native speakers of a given language, to compare responses across languages whose parameters are said to be different and to compare the judgments made by monolinguals with those made by bilinguals or learners of a second language.

Attention has focused on the process of parameter setting. One issue is whether both parameters are neutral at the outset or whether one is the default or *unmarked* one. The degree of MARKEDNESS depends on whether a feature is a part of the 'core' or the 'periphery'. The core features of a language are those that are governed by UG, while peripheral features are those that are not. Core features are considered unmarked because they require minimal evident for acquisition, whereas peripheral features are considered marked because they require much more substantial evidence. The degree of markedness of a feature can also vary within the core, depending on the parameter setting involved. Parameter settings can be ordered according to how marked they are. Some observational evidence suggests that infants acquiring their first language start off with an unmarked setting which has to be 'reset' if it is not appropriate. For example, English-acquiring infants often omit pronoun subjects in their early productions, suggesting 'pro-drop' as a default setting. However, the 'pro-drop' example illustrates the dangers of using empirical data from language acquisition to support conclusions about UG. The data relates to the infants' productions (i.e., to their performance); it is by no means clear to what extent this reflects the underlying competence which they have derived from inherited UG. The absence of a subject pronoun may reflect a cognitive inability to process more than two words rather than any preferential parameter setting.

Parameter setting also has important implications for research into second language acquisition. In second language acquisition, parameter-setting is more appropriately considered to be **parameter resetting**. When a learner acquires a language whose settings are different from those of their L1, they have to reset established parameters because learners already have parameter-settings initially established for their first language.

 Ellis 1997; Chomsky 1965; Cook & Newson 2007; Crain & Lillo-Martin 1999; Field 2004; O'Grady 1997; Radford 1990; Richards & Schmidt 2010; White 2003

private speech
audible speech not addressed to an addressee. Private speech can take a number of forms including imitation, vicarious response, i.e., response that a classroom learner produces to questions the teacher has addressed to another learner and mental rehearsal. Young children frequently resort to talking to themselves, even when they are in the company of of others. This self-directed speech can take the form of questions that they ask themselves, instructions regarding what to do or not to do, and evaluations of their performance. It is similar to the language used by conversationalists who are very familiar to one another—that is, it is paratactic and consists largely of comments (new information) on unstated topics. Such talk seems to function as a proxy for social talk and serves the same basic purpose of enabling the child to obtain control over the mental functioning needed to perform an activity.

Adults as well as children employ private speech. According to the principle of continuous access, adults continue to have access to the knowing strategies they have used previously. In difficult situations adults are able to reactivate developmentally primitive strategies as a way of achieving SELF-REGULATION. When faced with performing a new function, the adult learner is able to revert back to private speech in order to achieve self-regulation. When an individual finds himself faced with a difficult task, he externalizes the inner order so that he may regulate himself. Private talk by adult learners is seen as the means by which new linguistic forms are manipulated and practiced and thus come to move from the interpsychological to intrapsychological plane. It lies between social and inner speech.

Because private speech is intended for the speaker, not the listener, it is not constrained by the same norms that affect social speech. In L2 learners this is evident in two ways. First, they may resort to the use of their L1 in self-directed speech. Second, if they use the L2, they may not employ target language forms even if they have internalized these. Thus, what are apparent errors may simply be the private forms that learners use in their struggle to maintain control over a task. The notion of deviance cannot be easily applied to private speech. Such a perspective suggests that to evaluate the accuracy of learners' productions, it is important to distinguish whether the talk that arises in the performance of a task is social or private.

There is little clear evidence as yet that private speech contributes to language acquisition. Investigating the contribution of private speech to L2 development is obviously problematic. A major problem is deciding what constitutes private speech in a corpus of language use.

see also INNER SPEECH
 Ellis 2003, 2008; Ohta 2001b

proactive inhibition
also **proactive interference**
the way in which previous learning prevents or inhibits the learning of new habits. L2 learners are hypothesized to experience difficulty in learning target-language forms that are different from first-language forms. According to BEHAVIORIST LEARNING THEORY, INTERFERENCE is the result of what was called proactive inhibition. L2 learning involves developing new habits wherever the stimulus-response links of the L2 differ from those of the L1. In order to develop these new habits, the learner has to overcome proactive inhibition. By contrast, **retroactive inhibition** (also **retroactive interference**) is the effect of later learning on earlier learning. For example, children learning English may learn irregular past-tense forms such as *went*, *saw*. Later, when they begin to learn the regular *-ed* past-tense inflection, they may stop using *went* and *saw* and produce *goed and *seed.
 Brown 2007; Ellis 1986, 2008; Richards & Schmidt 2010

proactive interference
another term for PROACTIVE INHIBITION

procedural knowledge
see ADAPTIVE CONTROL OF THOUGHT MODEL

Processability Theory
a reorientation of the MULTIDIMENSIONAL MODEL that extends its concepts of learning and applies them to teaching second languages, with the goal of determining and explaining the sequences in which processing skills develop in relation to language learning. Processability Theory, coined by Piennemann and a further development of his TEACHABILITY HYPOTHESIS, posits that the human brain has a linguistic processor which has constraints in its ability to perform certain processing routines. These constraints and limitations are related to the nature of grammatical features of a given language. The combination of limitations on processing, and the features of the

language, predict the *route* that acquisition of that language will follow. This notion of route implies that structures only become learnable when the previous steps on this acquisitional path have been acquired.

Processability Theory aims to clarify how learners acquire the computational mechanisms that operate on the linguistic knowledge they construct. Pienemann believes that language acquisition itself is the gradual acquisition of these computational mechanisms, that is, the procedural skills necessary for the processing of language. It is limitations in the processing skills at the disposal of learners in the early stages of learning which prevent them from attending to some aspects of the second language.

According to Pienemann, L2 learners must learn certain output processing procedures in order to string words together to make L2-like utterances. These procedures emerge over time and in a set order or stage-like fashion. Learners cannot skip any procedure or stage, and any given stage assumes the stages prior to it. In its most basic form, the theory is built on the idea that grammatical information may need to be exchanged between elements during output processing (e.g., the grammatical information that a subject is singular has to be exchanged with the verb to make sure it is in the correct form). At the same time, elements in a sentence may be syntactically close to each other or syntactically far from each other, with the grammatical information that needs to be shared having to travel shorter or longer syntactic distances (or no distance at all).

Pienemann applied his model to a range of developmental phenomena that have been observed in second language acquisition, in both morphology and syntax, and across languages (German, English, Swedish, Japanese). Here his explanation of the well-documented acquisition of word order in German will be reviewed, based on the findings of the ZISA project (Zweitspracherwerb Italienischer, Spanischer und Portugiesischer Arbeiter: *Second language development of Italian and Spanish workers*). This project worked with Italian, Spanish, Portuguese and later Turkish first language learners of German in an untutored setting (they were all migrant workers). One of the major findings was that there is a clear developmental route in the acquisition of German word order (a complex and much-studied feature of the German language), found in both naturalistic and classroom learners.

The developmental stages that Pienemann and colleagues describe are as follows:

- Stage 1: Canonical Order (SVO)
  Die kinder spielen mimt ball (= *The children play with the ball*)
  Learners' initial hypothesis is that German is SVO, with adverbials in sentence-final position.
- Stage 2: Adverb preposing
  Da kinder spielen (= *There children play*)

Learners now place the adverb in sentence initial position, but keep the SVO order (no verb-subject inversion yet).
- Stage 3: Verb separation (V-SEP)
  Aller kinder muß die pause machen (= *All children must the break have*)
  Learners place the non-finite verbal element (here *machen*) in clause-final position.
- Stage 4: Verb-second (V2)
  Dann hat sie wieder die knoch gebringt (= *Then has she again the bone brought*)
  Learners now place the finite verb element (*hat*) in sentence-second position, resulting in verb-subject inversion.
- Stage 5: Verb-final in subordinate clauses (V-Final)
  Er sagte daß er nach hause kommt (= *He said that he to home comes*)
  Learners place the finite verb (*kommt*) in clause-final position in subordinate clauses.

What causes this particular staged development and not some other? Processability Theory accounts for these stages. Pienemann suggests that Stage 1 is the result of the L2 learners organizing sentences on the basis of the 'natural' order in which events are perceived, and this is assumed to be: 'actor - action - acted upon'. The construction of sentences in Stage 1 is determined by a strategy which maps this perceptual order on to L2 words or phrases; this is therefore essentially a pre-linguistic phase of acquisition. It is a strategy referred to as the *Canonical Order Strategy*:

Actor	Action	Acted Upon
Die kinder	*spielen*	*mim ball*

With continued exposure to the L2, however, learners soon notice discrepancies between what they can produce with the Canonical Order Strategy and the INPUT. But the areas of the input in which they notice such discrepancies are themselves constrained by *perceptual saliency*: learners first notice differences at the beginnings or the ends of sentences, because it is held that these are more salient portions of the input than the middles of sentences. This means that learners will first be able to move elements from inside to outside the sentence, that is, to sentence-initial or sentence-final positions, then from outside to inside before being able to move elements within the sentence. What learners notice in the case of German word order is that adverbs as well as subjects appear in first position in sentences, and non-finite verb forms (participles, infinitives and particles) appear in sentence-final position.

This leads to the postulation of a second strategy, the *Initialisation-Finalisation Strategy*: movements of constituents to the beginnings and ends of sentences are allowed. Why does adverb fronting appear earlier than V-SEP? The answer is that V-SEP does not just involve movement to the end of the sentence, it also involves disruption of a continuous constituent, the [V + participle, infinitive, or particle]. Therefore a strategy of continuity of elements within the same constituent must be involved, delaying the acquisition of V-SEP, which violates this strategy.

Movement into sentence-internal positions is held to be less salient perceptually than movement to the end of the sentence, and so V2 will be acquired only after considerably more exposure to German. One last strategy, the *Subordinate Clause Strategy* is required to predict why V-Final is acquired as the last stage. This strategy suggests that permutations of elements in subordinate clauses which make the word order in main and subordinate clauses different will be avoided. Thus, L2 learners tend to assume that German subordinate clauses have the same word order properties as main clauses, even into advanced stages of acquisition.

An important implication of Pienemann's Processability is that teaching is constrained. Because learners cannot skip stages and the procedures must build up over time, if learners are at stage 3, they cannot successfully be taught grammatical targets at stage 6, for example, i.e., after instruction, learners will not be able to spontaneously use the procedures.

Pienemann's Processability Theory is best seen as a development of the multidimensional model, as it also seeks to explain what is known about acquisitional sequences in terms of a set of processing procedures. As Pienemann put it once we can spell out the sequence in which language processing routines develop we can delineate those grammars that are processable at different points of development. Drawing on LEVELT'S MODEL OF SPEECH PRODUCTION, he proposed that language production, whether in the L1 or the L2, could only be explained with reference to a set of basic premises: (1) speakers possess relatively specialized processing components that operate autonomously and in parallel, (2) processing is incremental (i.e., a processor can start working on the incomplete output of another processor), (3) in order to cope with non-linearity (i.e., the fact that a linguistic sequence does not match the natural order of events as in 'Before the man rode off, he mounted his horse'), speakers need to store grammatical information in memory, and thus it follows that (4) grammatical processing must have access to a grammatical memory store, which is 'procedural' rather than 'declarative' (see ADAPTIVE CONTROL OF THOUGHT MODEL). It should be clear from this account that Processability Theory is in actuality a theory of language production. However, it can lay claim to being a theory of language acquisition in that it proposes that the processing procedures are hierarchical and are mastered one at a time. It is hypothesized that processing devices will be acquired in their sequence of activation in the production process. Thus, the failure to master a low-level procedure blocks access to higher-level procedures and makes it impossible for the learner to acquire those grammatical features that depend on them.

Pienemann also addressed a number of other key issues within the compass of Processability Theory. (1) the similarity/difference between L1 and L2 acquisition, (2) variability in learner language, (3) variability in rate of development and ultimate level of attainment, and (4) the role of the L1. He noted that although the sequence of acquisition in L1 and L2 may be different (as is the case in L1/L2 acquisition of German) this does not mean that both types of acquisition are not subject to the same proceeding constraints. He argued that the differences are the result of the fact that L1 and L2 learners' initial canonical word order is subject-object-verb (SOV) whereas in L2 learners it is typically SVO. This has implications for which procedures are now required for development. Whereas L2 learners need to instantiate the category and phrasal procedures, L1 learners do not because these are implicated in the verb-end order.

To account for variability, Pienemann suggested that if learners are unable to carry out a particular processing operation, they may resort to one of several solutions to the problem this poses them. They may leave out a constituent (e.g., *Where he going?*) or utilize canonical word order (e.g., *Where he is going?*). Thus, variability arises because processability leaves a certain amount of leeway which allows the learner a range of solutions.

Variability in rate of development and ultimate level of attainment is explained with reference to *variational features*. If learners make inferior choices with regard to these features then this may impede access to processing procedures. For example, if learners select the zero copula option in equational sentences (e.g., *me good*) this has repercussions for the acquisition of question formation as they lose out on a prototypical form of inversion (i.e., *Am I good?*). Thus, the selections that learners make with regard to variational features determine rate and level of progress along the developmental axis. In this respect, Processability Theory appears to differ from the multidimensional model which claims that the developmental and variational axes of L2 acquisition are completely independent of each other.

Pienemann addressed the role of the L1 in Processability Theory. The key points he made are that an L1 feature is not transferred even if it corresponds to an L2 feature unless it is processable (i.e., constitutes a feature that is located within the learner's current processing capacity), and following on from this, that the initial state of the L2 does not correspond to the final state of the L1.

see also LEARNABILITY HYPOTHESIS

 Clahsen 1984; Clahsen & Muysken 1986; Ellis 2008; Macaro et al. 2010; Pienemann 1998, 2003, 2005a, 2005b; Pienemann et al. 2005; Mithcell & Myles 2004; Saville-Troike 2006; Towell & Hawkins 1994; VanPatten & Benati 2010

processing instruction

a type of grammar instruction whose purpose is to affect the ways in which learners attend to INPUT data. It is input-based rather than OUTPUT-based. It is designed to assist learners to construct form-function mappings in line with the target language.
📖 Ellis 2008; VanPatten 1996

production strategy

a term which refers to the utilization of linguistic knowledge in communication. They differ from COMMUNICATION STRATEGIES in that they do not imply any communication problem and in that they are generally used without conscious awareness.
📖 Ellis 2008

productivity

a general term used in linguistics to refer to the creative capacity of language users to produce and understand an indefinitely large number of sentences. It contrasts particularly with the *unproductive* communication systems of animals, and in this context is seen by some linguists as one of the design features of human language. The term is also used in a more restricted sense with reference to the use made by a language of a specific feature or pattern. A pattern is *productive* if it is repeatedly used in language to produce further instances of the same type (e.g., the past-tense affix *-ed* in English is productive, in that any new verb will be automatically assigned this past-tense form). *Non-productive* (or *unproductive*) patterns lack any such potential; e.g., the change from *mouse* to *mice* is not a productive plural formation—new nouns would not adopt it, but would use instead the productive *s*-ending pattern. *Semi-productive* forms are those where there is a limited or occasional creativity, as when a prefix such as *un-* is sometimes, but not universally, applied to words to form their opposites, e.g., happy → unhappy, but not sad → *unsad.
📖 Crystal 2008

projection

a concept related to linguistic approaches to understanding acquisition and was formalized in the **Projection Hypothesis** by Helmut Zobl. What the hypothesis predicts is that because some structures are related by MARKEDNESS, the learner may not need POSITIVE EVIDENCE from the environment to know (implicitly, of course) that something exists. The learner's internal mechanisms can 'project' it based on the data at hand.

Normally, this means that the learner's mechanisms project from marked to unmarked or lesser marked features. So, if Z is more marked than T and the two are related, once the learner acquires Z, the learner can infer that T exists even if T has not appeared in the input. We can take a concrete example from relative clauses. Relative clauses exist in a markedness relationship, and there is a well-known hierarchy that lists them from unmarked to most marked:

- *subject relative clause*: Tom is the man *who studied SLA*;
- *object relative clause*: SLA is the subject *that Tom studied*;
- *indirect object relative clause*: Tom is the guy *who I gave the SLA book to*;
- *object of preposition clause*: Tom is the guy *who I studied SLA with*;
- *genitive clause*: Tom is the guy *whose SLA book I borrowed*;
- *object of comparison clause*: Tom is the guy *who I am taller than*.

Under the Projection Hypothesis, when learners encounter and acquire genitive relative clauses, their grammars can project the existence of everything from subject relative clauses to object relative clauses if any of these have not been acquired. Note that projection is unidirectional: a grammar can only project from more marked to lesser marked. Thus, learners cannot project the existence of genitive clauses if they have acquired object clauses.

Zobl applied this concept to features related to UNIVERSAL GRAMMAR (UG); however, since his initial hypothesis the concept of markedness within UG has received little attention, largely because the theory of UG has evolved. But within non-UG related structures, such as relative clauses and certain phonological contrasts, projection remains a valid construct. It has even been exploited in some experiments on instructed SLA. Susan Gass conducted an experiment in the early 1980s in which she taught learners more marked relative clauses. When she tested the learners afterwards, she found that they had projected lesser marked relative clauses that were absent in their pretest performance. Thus, learners' grammars could be affected by teaching more marked elements of language and letting the lesser marked ones get projected by the learners' own internal capacities.

    VanPatten & Benati 2010

Projection Hypothesis
see PROJECTION

prototypicality
a term used by Kellerman to refer to perceptions that learners have regarding the structure of their own language. These perceptions lead them to treat some structures as potentially transferable and others as potentially non-transferable. A number of points emerge from Kellerman's work on prototypicality. The first is that it is possible to provide a clear operational definition of MARKEDNESS or 'prototypicality' by making use of native speakers' judgments of 'similarity'. The second is that learners have perceptions about

what is transferable from their L1 and act in accordance with these perceptions. The third is that these perceptions reflect learners' ideas about what is prototypical or semantically transparent in their L1. According to Kellerman, learners prize 'reasonableness in language' and attempt to keep their L2s transparent. L1 structures that they perceive to be working against this principle—such as idioms that are highly metaphorical or grammatical structures where meanings are not overtly encoded—are not transferred. It is also argued that learners' perceptions regarding the transferability of L1 items are not influenced by their experience with the L2.
 Ellis 2008; Kellerman 1977, 1978, 1979, 1986, 1989

psycholinguistics
an interdisciplinary field which brings together linguistics and psychology (both their theories and empirical methods) to understand the mental processes and psychological mechanisms which make it possible for humans to acquire, understand, produce and process language. The main themes in psycholinguistic research are how humans understand spoken and written language, and how we produce and acquire language. Unlike linguistics where the main focus is on understanding the structure of language and languages, in psycholinguistics, psychological techniques and methods are used to carry out studies aimed at understanding a range of issues which inform our understanding of the nature of the psychological mechanisms which allow us to acquire and use language.

There are two possible directions of study. One may use language as a means of elucidating psychological theories and processes (e.g., the role of language as it affects MEMORY, perception, attention, learning, etc.), and for this the term *psychological linguistics* is sometimes used. Alternatively, one may investigate the effects of psychological constraints on the use of language (e.g., how memory limitations affect speech production and comprehension). It is the latter which has provided the main focus of interest in linguistics, where the subject is basically seen as the study of the mental processes underlying the planning, production, perception and comprehension of speech, and investigations typically proceed by examining linguistic performance through small-scale experimental tasks. A theory-driven approach is also encountered, in which evidence to support a point of linguistic theory (often in relation to GENERATIVE GRAMMAR) accumulates using such techniques as adult grammaticality judgments. The subject now includes a large number of research domains, notably child language acquisition, second language acquisition, language processing, linguistic complexity, the relationship between linguistic and cognitive universals, the study of reading, language pathology, and species specificity.
see also DEVELOPMENTAL LINGUISTICS
 Macaro et al. 2010; Crystal 2008

psychotypology
see TRANSFER

R

rationalism
see EMPIRICISM

recast
reformulation of learners' utterances that occur naturally in interactions. Recasts usually occur when the learner has produced some kind of non-native-like utterance, and the other interlocutor (e.g., a teacher, parent or other native speaker) repeats the learner's utterance and changing only those elements needed to make it correct without changing any of the meaning, and allowing for the conversation or questioning sequence to immediately resume. For example, in the following interchange, the recast functions like a *confirmation check*, as in the following interchange between Bob, a native speaker, and Tom, a non-native speaker:

Bob: So where's Dave?
Tom: He vacation.
Bob: *He's on vacation?* [confirmation check]
Tom: Yes, on vacation.
Bob: Lucky guy

The native speaker's recast in this example is a natural reaction that shows he understood what the learner meant. Bob neither says *You said it wrong* nor tells Tom explicitly that he did something wrong. Bob's sole intent was to confirm what he heard. It was even said with a bit of rising intonation to indicate *Is this what you said?* Thus, it was a communicative event within the interaction. Unlike what teachers may do in classrooms, it was not intended as a correction.

Recasts are generally implicit in that they are not introduced by phrases such as *You mean, Use this word*, and *You should say*. However, some recasts are more salient than others in that they may focus on one word only, whereas others incorporate the grammatical or lexical modification into a sustained piece of discourse. Recasts also include translations in response to a student's use of the L1.

However, recasts are classified in research under NEGATIVE EVIDENCE, as *indirect negative evidence*. This means that they are considered subtle indi-

cators to learners that they have produced something less than target-like. The claim by proponents of recasts is that these communicative events can help focus learners' attention at a given time on something that is non-native-like and may aid in pushing acquisition along. But there is debate as to whether or not this is the case. Those who argue against any important role for recasts (and negative evidence more generally) have argued that recasts are infrequent and inconsistent, just as they are in child L1 acquisition situations. Thus, they cannot form an important part of acquisition for L2 learners.
📖 VanPatten & Benati 2010; Macaro et al. 2010; Gass & Selinker 2008

reflective style
the tendency to take a relatively long time to make a decision or solve a problem, sometimes in order to weigh options before making a decision. Reflective (R) style contrasts with **impulsive** (I) **style** which is the tendency to make quick decisions in answer to problems; sometimes, but not always, those decisions involve risk-taking or guessing. These two styles are closely related to the **systematic** and **intuitive styles**. An intuitive style implies an approach in which a person makes a number of different gambles on the basis of 'hunches' with possibly several successive gambles before a solution is achieved. Systematic thinkers tend to weigh all the considerations in a problem, work out all the loopholes, and then, after extensive reflection, venture a solution.

The implications for language acquisition are numerous. It has been found that children who are conceptually reflective tend to make fewer errors in reading than impulsive children; however, impulsive persons are usually faster readers, and eventually master the 'psycholinguistic guessing game' of reading so that their impulsive style of reading may not necessarily deter comprehension.

R/I has some important considerations for classroom second language learning and teaching. Teachers tend to judge mistakes too harshly, especially in the case of a learner with an impulsive style who may be more willing than a reflective person to gamble at an answer. On the other hand, a reflective person may require patience from the teacher, who must allow more time for the student to struggle with responses. It is also conceivable that those with impulsive styles may go through a number of rapid transitions of semigrammatical stages of SLA, with reflective persons tending to remain longer at a particular stage with larger leaps from stage to stage.

see also LEFT-BRAIN DOMINANCE, FIELD DEPENDENCE STYLE
📖 Brown 2007; Kagan 1965; Goodman 1970

regularization
a term related to OVERGENERALIZATION which is concerned with how learners in both first and second language acquisition treat irregular forms or ex-

ceptional rules. It is common in both L1 and L2 contexts for learners to regularize the irregular past tense forms, and both children and adults produce such things as *wented* and *goed* instead of *went* at a particular stage of acquisition. Although many teachers may view such things as errors, in terms of SLA they are viewed as progress. Such forms show that the regular past tense endings, which were most likely missing in an earlier stage (e.g., the learner said 'talk' instead of 'talked'), are now firmly entrenched in the learner's grammar.

Outside of SLA, regularization is an attested phenomenon of language change and historical linguistics. Much of language change over time is a result of regularization, as speakers (particularly undereducated or illiterate speakers, but not always) begin to weed out irregularities. In contemporary English, there is vacillation between such forms as *dived/dove* and *strived/strove*, for example, and it is not atypical for a native speaker to sometimes stop and check himself when trying to use the past tense or even past participle of these and other verbs. This is because languages are living things whose evolution continues with each generation of speakers. In some dialects of English, *was* has replaced *were* ('So we was walkin' down the street mindin' our own business . . .') as these speakers regularize the past tense of *be*. Although regularization is most easily exemplified in what happens to verbal inflections, regularization can and does happen in all parts of language, including syntax. Regularization is thus not surprising or unexpected in an L2 context.

📖 VanPatten & Benati 2010

regulatory function
see SYSTEMIC LINGUISTICS

rehearsal
the recycling of material in the mind, with a view to retaining it longer. There are two types. *Maintenance rehearsal* involves refreshing information within WORKING MEMORY so as to keep it available for use. *Elaborative rehearsal* involves consolidating this information with a view to transferring it to LONG-TERM MEMORY. The two types of rehearsal are responsible for position effects (i.e., the ability to recall certain words according to where they occur in a list) in word recall tasks. In the *primacy effect*, words from the beginning of a list are recalled better because they have been subject to greater elaborative rehearsal. In the *recency effect*, words from the end of the list are recalled because they are still being supported by maintenance rehearsal. The difference between the two effects is demonstrated by asking subjects to perform an *interference task* (such as counting or doing simple calculations) before the list is recalled. In these circumstances, the primacy effect is sustained, but the recency effect disappears. This suggests that the

words which feature in the recency effect are vulnerable to being dislodged by new incoming short-term information.

Maintenance rehearsal enables the listener or reader to store linguistic material short term. The purpose does not seem to be to support word recognition. Instead, we need to retain the verbatim form of an utterance in order to deal with sentences where it is difficult to impose a semantic or syntactic pattern until we reach the end. Maintenance rehearsal is critical to PARSING sentences that are long or complex, have a non-standard word order or have difficult thematic relationships (in the form, for example, of a passive verb).

Elaborative rehearsal plays an important part in learning situations (including rote learning). The greater the number of repetitions, it is believed, the greater the probability of successful storage. Evidence of this is found in an increased primacy effect when extra time is allowed for mastering a word list.

What is the form in which linguistic material is stored while it is being rehearsed? Researchers have investigated the question by asking subjects to remember lists of words—a process demanding elaborative rehearsal. They have discovered that successful recall declines when a list features words that take a long time to say. This happens regardless of whether the list is in spoken or written form, suggesting that written material is *recoded* into some kind of phonological form when it is held in store. Likewise, the phenomenon of INNER SPEECH during reading (the impression of a voice in the head) suggests that a phonological form also features in maintenance rehearsal. Rehearsal is thus generally represented as involving a phonological mechanism which handles both spoken and written INPUT (see WORKING MEMORY). It may seem odd that written material needs to be recoded. One explanation is that information stored in phonological form is more robust; another is that it interferes less with the reading process.

Because rehearsal is phonological in form, simple tasks which involve speaking aloud (reciting numbers or even just repeating the word *the*) interfere with it. This effect, known as *articulatory suppression*, is widely used in research into rehearsal.

📖 Baddeley 1997; Field 2004; Gathercole & Baddeley 1993

reinforcement

a term which is most associated with BEHAVIORISM and involves the kind of FEEDBACK learners get from their environment. In the days when language was seen as stimulus-response, the response was the reinforcement. Both L1 and L2 learners were believed to get either *positive reinforcement* or *negative reinforcement*. Positive reinforcement was continued conversation, looks of approval, verbal reactions such as 'very good' and others. Negative reinforcement was interrupted conversation or problematic comprehension on the part of the person listening to the learner, looks of disapproval, and verbal reactions such as, 'No, say it this way', among others.

Under current psychological accounts of language acquisition (which differ from linguistic accounts), *strengthening* has replaced reinforcement. Learners build up linguistic information that consists of connections between things. Each time the learner hears the same thing in the INPUT, a connection is strengthened. Each time the learner uses a connection successfully, it is strengthened. Strengthening is thus tied to frequency; more frequent linguistic items get stronger connections in the mind/brain. Less frequent items get weaker connections. This is one way in which psychologists explain REGULARIZATION, i.e., the elimination of irregular forms and rules. In the examples from past tense, forms such as *went* and *had* are highly frequent and tend to stay in the language over generations. They have strong connections in speakers' minds/brains. Such is not the case for less frequent or highly infrequent words such as the past tense of *dive*. Is it *dove* or *dived*? Native speakers of English will vacillate because the connections in the mind/brain for these forms are much weaker compared to *went* and *had*, for example.

In the L2 context, reinforcement has fallen to the wayside as a construct, but strengthening has not. Those who take psychological approaches will often talk of strong and weak connections in SLA as well as the nature of strengthening as a process.

 VanPatten & Benati 2010

repair
see UPTAKE

representational function
see SYSTEMIC LINGUISTICS

request
an attempt on the part of a speaker to get the hearer to perform or to stop performing some kind of action in the interests of the speaker. A number of general illocutionary and sociolinguistic features of request can be identified:

1) The speaker wishes the hearer to perform the request, believes the hearer is able to perform the act, and does not believe the act will be performed in the absence of the request.
2) A request can be more or less direct.
3) Requests are also subject to 'internal' and 'external' modification. Internal modification takes the form of downgrades, which are intended to mitigate the force of the act, and upgrades, which are intended to increase the degree of coerciveness of the act. External modifications consists of moves that occur either before or after the head act (i.e., the act that actually performs the request); these moves can also be classified according to whether the purpose is to downgrade or upgrade the force of the act.

4) Requests can be encoded from the speaker's perspective (e.g., *give me the book*), from the hearer's perspective (e.g., *could you give me the book?*), form a joint perspective (e.g., *let's read a book*) or from an impersonal perspective (e.g., *it would be nice to read a book*).
5) Requests are inherently imposing. For this reason they call for considerable 'face-work'. The choice of linguistic realization depends on a variety of social factors to do with the relationships between the speaker and the addressee, the perceived degree of imposition which a particular request makes on the hearer (i.e., it involves a choice of politeness strategy), and the goal of the act (e.g., requesting goods or initiating joint activity).
6) Although the main sociopragmatic categories of request can be found in different languages, there are pragmalinguistic differences relating to the preferred form of a request that is used in a particular situation. Also, crosslinguistic differences exist in the choice of other linguistic features such as internal and external modification devices.

Requests have received considerable attention in SLA research for a number of reasons. They are important in social life, they are face-threatening and, therefore, call for considerable linguistic expertise on the part of the learner, they differ cross-linguistically in interesting ways and they are often realized by means of clearly identifiable formulas. L2 learners—even beginners—appear to have few problems in understanding the illocutionary force of a request, probably because they are able to make use of situational cues. Advanced learners are able to perceive the sociolinguistic meanings encoded by different request types, although they may be oversensitive to these. With regard to production, learners begin with very simple requests and then slowly build up their repertoire, learning not only an increasing number of formal devices for performing them, but also how to mitigate their requests in accordance with the impositive load. In other words, there is clear evidence of pragmalinguistic development, although even very advanced leaners do not perform fully to target-language norms, showing a tendency to verbosity, perhaps because they are aware of the dangers inherent in making requests. There is less clear evidence of sociopragmatic development, especially in the case of adults in foreign language contexts.
see also APOLOGY
Ellis 2008; Fraser 1983; Searle 1976; Blum-Kulka et al. 1989b

resilient features

those features that are required relatively easily even when the only INPUT available to the learner is deficient. Examples are word order rules. Resilient features contrast with **fragile features**, which are acquired late, often with effort, and only when there is access to adequate input. Examples of fragile

features are plural and tense markings.
📖 Ellis 2008

respondent conditioning
another term for CLASSICAL CONDITIONING

restrictive simplification
a term which refers to learners' continued use of simplified structures such as the deletion of function words, even though they have developed knowledge of corresponding no-simplified structures. It is designed to achieve optimal results in communication by reducing the grammar in a way that makes it easy to handle. Restrictive simplification contrasts with **elaborative simplification**, which is a strategy that helps to complexity the grammatical system by formulating hypotheses (e.g., through the use of OVERGENERALIZATION) that are approximations to the actual rule and often involve overextensions of a rule. Not all learners engage in elaborative simplification.
📖 Ellis 2008

restructuring
an INTAKE process that, in terms of language development, occurs gradually in LONG-TERM MEMORY. Often associated with the work of the psychologist McLaughlin, it refers to a qualitative changes that takes place as a child learner moves from stage to stage in their development. These changes relate to both the way knowledge is represented in the minds of learners and also the strategies they employ. For example, learners may begin by representing past-tense forms as separate items and then shift to representing them by means of a general rule for past-tense formation. Thus, it is a process in which the building blocks or components of a current pattern in the brain are co-ordinated, integrated or reorganized into new units, thereby allowing the old components to be replaced by a more efficient procedure. New units become more proficient through two basic processes: *automatization* (no longer having to stop and think about what they are saying) and the *principle of economy* (discarding hypotheses that no longer match the new evidence).
One way of characterizing restructuring is in terms of Anderson's ACT theory, (see ADAPTIVE CONTROL OF THOUGHT MODEL) whereby DECLARATIVE KNOWLEDGE is reorganized into PROCEDURAL KNOWLEDGE. Another way is the progression from more *exemplar-based representations* of language (e.g., formulaic language) to more *rule-based representations* where its application to second language learning becomes more obvious (see DUAL-MODE SYSTEM). McLaughlin also gives the useful example of young children who may consider (advanced) age, appearance and behavior to be fundamental to the meaning of 'uncle', whereas older children will focus on what they understand by kinship and family relations even if the uncle is only 15 years

old. This could be said to mirror, in the L2 learning context, the transition from 'foreign' cultural conceptualizations to becoming familiar with those concepts.

Restructuring is conceptually synonymous with Ausubel's construct of SUBSUMPTION.

see also INFERENCING, INFORMATION PROCESSING THEORY, RESTRUCTURING CONTINUUM, STRUCTURING, U-SHAPED DEVELOPMENT

📖 Brown 2007; Ellis 2008; Macaro et al. 2010; McLeod & McLaughlin 1986; McLaughlin 1990b

restructuring continuum
a term referring to a view that the INTERLANGUAGE continuum is a restructuring continuum. That is, the starting point of L2 acquisition is the learner's L1, which is gradually replaced by the target language as acquisition proceeds. Such a view suggests that TRANSFER will be more evident in the early than the later stages of development. However, although such evidence strongly suggests that learners gradually restructure their interlanguage by replacing L1 features with L2 features, caution is needed. Not all ERRORs in early interlanguage are traceable to transfer—many are *intralingual* and resemble those found in L1 acquisition. In some case, transfer is only evident in the later stages of development, while in others early transfer is never eliminated.

see also ERROR ANALYSIS

📖 Corder 1978a; Ellis 2008 he

retroactive inhibition
see PROACTIVE INHIBITION

retroactive interference
another term for RETROACTIVE INHIBITION

right-brain dominance
see LEFT-BRAIN DOMINANCE

risk taking
willingness to gamble, to try out hunches about a language with the possibility of being wrong. Risk taking is an important characteristic of successful learning of a second language. Some of the negative ramifications that foster fear of risk taking both in the classroom and in natural settings are described as follows: In the classroom, these ramifications might include a bad grade in the course, a fail on the exam, a reproach from the teacher, a smirk from a classmate, punishment or embarrassment imposed by oneself. Outside the classroom, individuals learning a second language face other negative consequences if they make mistakes. They fear looking ridiculous; they fear the

frustration coming from a listener's blank look, showing that they have failed to communicate; they fear the danger of not being able to take care of themselves; they fear the alienation of not being able to communicate and thereby get close to other human beings. Perhaps worst of all, they fear a loss of identity.

The classroom antidote to such fears is to establish an adequate affective framework so that learners feel comfortable as they take their first public steps in the strange world of a foreign language. To achieve this, one has to create a climate of acceptance that will stimulate self-confidence, and encourage participants to experiment and to discover the target language, allowing themselves to take risks without feeling embarrassed.

Risk-taking variation seems to be a factor in a number of issues in second language acquisition and pedagogy. The silent student in the classroom is one who is unwilling to appear foolish when mistakes are made. SELF-ESTEEM seems to be closely connected to a risk-taking factor: when those foolish mistakes are made, a person with high global self-esteem is not daunted by the possible consequences of being laughed at. It is argued that FOSSILIZATION may be due to a lack of willingness to take risks. It is safe to stay within patterns that accomplish the desired function even though there may be some errors in those patterns.

see also INHIBITION, ANXIETY, WILLINGNESS TO COMMUNICATE, EMPATHY, MOTIVATION, ATTRIBUTION THEORY

📖 Beebe 1983; Brown 2007; Dufeu 1994

rote learning
see SUBSUMPTION

S

salience
the importance of a perceived element of INPUT. In linguistics and language acquisition, salience is used to talk about grammatical features and to what extent they catch a person's eye or ear. Salience could be a result of phonological properties. In general, features that carry stress are said to be more salient than those that do not. Thus, salience is partly tied to syllabicity as only syllables (units with a vowel) can carry stress. Somewhat related to phonological properties is the issue of location in words and sentences. Things that occur at the beginning of words and sentences are said to be more salient than things that occur in other positions. Following this, things that occur at the ends of words and sentences are more salient than things that occur in the middle. More generally, some researchers have posited that it is pausing that makes something salient. That is, a word or feature that is bounded on one or more sides by a pause is more salient than one that is not. Because the beginnings and ends of sentences are bounded on at least one side by a pause, these positions are said to be more salient. Some scholars have advocated that salience may relate to novel properties or features. That is, something that is new might receive attention or catch the eye/ear simply because it is new. At the same time, some scholars have suggested that similarity to L1 (making the feature closer to 'old stuff') may contribute to salience; for example, words that sound like L1 words may be more salient for learners.

The construct of salience has been applied in instructed SLA to written input via text enhancement. Text enhancement is a technique by which grammatical features are consistently highlighted in a text in some way by bolding, italicizing, capitalization, underlining, and other means. The idea is to make the feature more salient, thus drawing learner attention to it and increasing the likelihood that learners will notice and process it. For example, to make third-person -*s* more salient to learners, an instructor might give them reading passages that look like this:

John like*s* SLA. He think*s* it is very interesting. He read*s* books on it, and he attend*s* lectures on SLA at the university. His roommate, Bob, disagree*s*. He think*s* SLA is boring. Bob studie*s* English literature.

Thus, by consistently bolding the third-person ending in these passages, the instructor presumably is making the inflection more salient.
see also INPUT ENHANCEMENT
 VanPatten & Benati 2010

Sapir-Whorf Hypothesis
see LINGUISTIC RELATIVITY

Savant
an individual who is severely mentally impaired, but shows exceptional gifts, often in painting or music. A savant has been discovered who possesses similar gifts for language. Christopher was diagnosed as brain-damaged early in life and has to live in care; yet he is able to translate from, and communicate in, some 16 languages. This is taken by some scholars to demonstrate that there is a dissociation between linguistic and general cognitive abilities; and that language is a separate modular faculty (see MODULARITY).
see WILLIAMS SYNDROME, SPECIFIC LANGUAGE IMPAIRMENT, DOWN'S SYNDROME
 Field 2004; Smith & Tsimpli 1995

scaffolding
the support provided to learners to enable them to perform tasks which are beyond their capacity, by way of stimulating its interest in a task, orienting it towards appropriate goals, highlighting salient features of a task and demonstrating relevant strategies. The term is sometimes used in FIRST LANGUAGE ACQUISITION to refer to a form of adult INPUT which provides an infant step by step with the material upon which to build utterances. In SLA and general educational literature, scaffolding refers to the assistance that a teacher or more proficient/experienced other learner can bring to an individual's process of learning. Because some learners may not have the linguistic tools necessary to express their ideas, their interlocutors may sometimes help to build the conversation or topic by providing crucial bits of language. In this way, the more proficient speaker is providing assistance.
The term scaffolding comes from SOCIOCULTURAL THEORY (SCT), the central of which is that cognition needs to be investigated without isolating it from social context. SCT sees learning, including language learning, as dialogically based. It is argued that the language acquisition device is located in the interaction that takes place between speakers rather than inside learners' heads. That is, acquisition occurs *in* rather than *as a result of* interaction. From this perspective, then, L2 acquisition is not a purely individual-based process but shared between the individual and other persons. One of the principal ways in which this sharing takes place is scaffolding. Other terms

used to refer to much the same idea are 'collaborative dialogue' and 'instructional conversion'.

To illustrate, look at the following example (where NNS = non-native speaker and NS = native speaker):

NNS: Look.
NS: Look? At what?
NNS (pointing): That.
NS: It's a bug.
NNS: Bug.
NS: Yeah, a bug. And it's crawling very slowly.
NNS: Crawling.
NS: Yeah, crawling slowly. Maybe it's looking for food.

In this interchange, what is worth noting is how much the NS talks to fill in what the NNS cannot do. While the NNS is basically speaking in one word utterances, the NS is speaking in full sentences, fleshing out the conversational topic and providing key linguistic information, such as vocabulary, at particular points. This is what is referred to as scaffolding.

Scaffolding is closely associated with Vygotsky's concept of the ZONE OF PROXIMAL DEVELOPMENT which is 'the distance between the actual developmental level (of a child), as determined by independent problem solving, and the level of potential development' attainable through the guidance of others. The idea is that this 'other' provides the support as the learning edifice is being gradually constructed by the learner. It is not a question of simply transferring knowledge to the learner but of helping him progress up the different floors of the building by providing a process framework which guides the learner from floor level to floor level. By providing needed language, scaffolding may increase the SALIENCE of some aspects of language, for example. Learners may be getting critical data at the right time, and because they are actively engaged in the conversation, they are paying attention to both what is said and how it is said. Some might claim, however, that scaffolding could delay acquisition. Learners could use scaffolding to compensate for weaknesses in their own productive abilities and thus rely on others to 'do the work'. Either way, scaffolding appears to be a normal part of interactions.

Graham and Macaro used the terms 'high scaffolding' and 'low scaffolding' to describe the amount of teacher and researcher support and guidance provided to students during a listening strategies instruction program. The emphasis was not on telling them how to listen but in helping them to discover their own best way of listening. In practical terms scaffolding can be provided by raising awareness of current knowledge and processes, teacher modeling, teacher feedback, providing reminders and clues during tasks. As stu-

dents become more confident and proficient the scaffolding can be gradually removed leaving behind a more *autonomous* learner.
📖 Artigal 1992; Ellis 2008; Field 2004; Macaro et al. 2010; VanPatten & Benati 2010 Graham and Macaro (2008)

Schema Theory

a theory introduced by Bartlett that in comprehending language people activate relevant schemata allowing them to process and interpret new experiences quickly and efficiently. A schema (plural: schemas or schemata) is a complex knowledge structure which groups all that an individual knows about or associates with a particular concept.

As an example, an adult in Western society has a schema for *restaurant* which entails: waiters/waitresses, a meal (not a snack), a meal eaten on the premises, a main course with optional first course and dessert, menus, a bill, a chef (unseen), cutlery, glasses, napkins, etc. This begins as *episodic* knowledge based on individual experiences of restaurants, but turns into *semantic* knowledge as the individual's experience of restaurants grows.

When a reader encounters the word *restaurant*, they access this schematic knowledge. It enables them to build a richer context than a writer provides; indeed, the writer can assume that the schema is shared with the reader, and is thus spared the need to go into excessive detail. Schematic knowledge also enables the reader to anticipate events and ideas which might occur later in the text and to relate incidents in the text to what happens in normal life.

Schemas which supply background knowledge to the interpretation of a text are sometimes referred to as *content schemas*. The reader's ability to draw upon one may depend upon having a clearly established context for the text in question. A well-known experimental passage described how to use a washing machine but the schema could not be accessed without the assistance of an explanatory title.

Studies of reading and listening sometimes refer to *formal schemas*, which reflect previous experience of a text type or genre. Thus, in reading a scientific paper, we expect it to contain an abstract, a review of the literature, a presentation and analysis of data, etc. This type of schema also provides expectations about style and register.

As well as referring to long-term knowledge structures, the term 'schema' is sometimes used more specifically to refer to the *meaning representation* that a reader or listener builds up while processing a particular piece of discourse. We approach a text with certain expectations about what it will say, which we derive from the title or from the purpose of the text; these enable us to develop a text-specific schema even before we read. As we read, we revise and add to the initial schema.

Schemas vary from one language user to another, and can be modified *ad hoc* to deal with a current situation. There are said to be three ways in which they can be changed. *Tuning* involves small adjustments made temporarily in order to confront immediate needs. *Accretion* modifies a schema gradually but permanently as new information is acquired or as repeated examples of contrary evidence accumulate. Thus, a child might have to adjust its category of *duck* to exclude birds that it has come to recognize as belonging to the category *swan*. RESTRUCTURING occurs when a sudden insight or new piece of knowledge leads to a radical reorganization of existing knowledge structures.

Associated with Schema Theory are two other types of stored knowledge. A *frame* is a schema with optional slots. The frame for *ship* provides us with the information 'large means of transport, floats on sea, manned by sailors'. We then use information from the text we are reading in order to fill empty slots relating to purpose (*warship vs. ferry vs. merchant ship*), power (*diesel vs. steam vs. sail*), color, destination, etc. If the information is not provided, we fill the slots with default values. In the absence of further information, our slots for *ship* would probably be filled out with passengers, a funnel and a dark color rather than guns, sails or bright red.

A *script* is a sequence of activities associated with a stereotypical situation. A restaurant script entails a particular ritual (W = waiter, C = customer): W greets C, C asks if there is a table, W shows C to the table, W presents menu, W asks what C wants to drink, C orders first two courses of meal. Scripts provide a framework for many everyday events, and permit speakers and writers to adopt a kind of shorthand. If we read *Helen ate in a restaurant*, we can supply for ourselves the details of what happened without having to have them spelt out.

 Bartlett 1932; Field 2004; Minsky 1977; Schank & Abelson 1977

second language
see SECOND LANGUAGE ACQUISITION

second language acquisition
also **SLA**

a common term which refers to the process of learning another language after the native language has been learned. Sometimes the term refers to the learning of a third, fourth, or *n*th language. The important aspect is that SLA refers to the learning of a non-native language after the learning of the native language. The additional language is called a **second language** (**L2**), even though it may actually be the third, fourth, or tenth to be acquired. It is also commonly called a **target language** (**TL**), which refers to any language that is the aim or goal of learning. The scope of SLA includes *informal L2 learning* that takes place in naturalistic contexts, *formal L2 learning* that takes place in classrooms, and L2 learning that involves a mixture of these settings and circumstances. For example, informal learning happens when a child from Japan is brought to the US and picks up English in the course of playing and attending school with native English-speaking children without any specialized language instruction, or when an adult Guatemalan immigrant in Canada learns English as a result of interacting with native English speakers or with co-workers who speak English as a second language. Formal learning occurs when a high school student in England takes a class in French, when an undergraduate student in Russia takes a course in Arabic, or when an attorney in Colombia takes a night class in English. A combination of formal and informal learning takes place when a student from the USA takes Chinese language classes in Taipei or Beijing while also using Chinese outside of class for social interaction and daily living experiences, or when an adult immigrant from Ethiopia in Israel learns Hebrew both from attending special classes and from interacting with co-workers and other residents in Hebrew. Some might prefer the term **second language studies (SLS)** as it is a term that refers to anything dealing with using or acquiring a second/foreign language.

In trying to understand the process of second language acquisition, we are seeking to answer three basic questions:

1) *What* exactly does the L2 learner come to know?
2) *How* does the learner acquire this knowledge?
3) *Why* are some learners more successful than others?

There are no simple answers to these questions—in fact, there are probably no answers that all second language researchers would agree on completely. In part this is because SLA is highly complex in nature, and in part because scholars studying SLA come from academic disciplines which differ greatly in theory and research methods. The multidisciplinary approach to studying SLA phenomena which has developed within the last half-century has yielded important insights, but many tantalizing mysteries remain. New findings are appearing every day, making this an exciting period to be studying the subject. The continuing search for answers is not only shedding light on SLA in its own right, but is illuminating related fields. Furthermore, exploring answers to these questions is of potentially great practical value to anyone who learns or teaches additional languages.

SLA has emerged as a field of study primarily from within linguistics and psychology (and their subfields of applied linguistics, PSYCHOLINGUISTICS, SOCIOLINGUISTICS, and social psychology), as a result of efforts to answer the *what, how,* and *why* questions posed above. There are corresponding differences in what is emphasized by researchers who come from each of these fields:

- Linguists emphasize the characteristics of the differences and similarities in the languages that are being learned, and the linguistic COMPETENCE

(underlying knowledge) and linguistic PERFORMANCE (actual production) of learners at various stages of acquisition.
- Psychologists and psycholinguists emphasize the mental or cognitive processes involved in acquisition, and the representation of language(s) in the brain.
- Sociolinguists emphasize VARIABILITY in learner linguistic performance, and extend the scope of study to COMMUNICATIVE COMPETENCE (underlying knowledge that additionally accounts for language use, or PRAGMATIC COMPETENCE).
- Social psychologists emphasize group-related phenomena, such as identity and social motivation, and the interactional and larger social contexts of learning.

Applied linguists who specialize in SLA may take any one or more of these perspectives, but they are also often concerned with the implications of theory and research for teaching second languages. Each discipline and subdiscipline uses different methods for gathering and analyzing data in research on SLA, employs different theoretical frameworks, and reaches its interpretation of research findings and conclusions in different ways.

It is no surprise, then, that the understandings coming from these different disciplinary perspectives sometimes seem to conflict in ways that resemble the well-known Asian fable of the three blind men describing an elephant: one, feeling the tail, says it is like a rope; another, feeling the side, says it is flat and rubbery; the third, feeling the trunk, describes it as being like a long rubber hose. While each perception is correct individually, they fail to provide an accurate picture of the total animal because there is no holistic or integrated perspective. Ultimately, a satisfactory account of SLA must integrate these multiple perspectives
📖 Gass & Selinker 2008; Saville-Troike 2006

second language development
also **SLD**
an alternative to SECOND LANGUAGE ACQUISITION, where language learning is seen as a number of dynamically interrelated processes in the mind of the second language/bilingual learner and involves both gain (ACQUISITION) and loss (ATTRITION).
📖 Piske & Young-Scholten 2009

second language learner
also **L2 learner**
a neutral term typically used to refer to an individual acquiring a second language after the age at which the individual is assumed to have established the basics (syntactic and phonological competence) of their first language, held by many to be around age five. The term BILINGUALISM is also used in

reference to young children's acquisition of an additional language. However, application of this term varies, from its use only to refer to the simultaneous acquisition of two languages from birth, to its use to refer to the acquisition of an additional language at any age (see SIMULTANEOUS BILINGUALISM).
 Piske & Young-Scholten 2009

second language learning
see FOREIGN LANGUAGE LEARNING

second language studies
see SECOND LANGUAGE ACQUISITION

segregation
an educational setting where the L2 learner is educated separately from the majority or a politically powerful minority, who speak the target language as their mother tongue. Segregation forces a monolingual policy on the relatively powerless. Immigrants or migrant workers who are educated in special schools, centers, or units designed to cater for their language needs constitute an example of segregation in a majority setting. Bantu education in Namibia prior to independence is an example of segregation in a setting where a powerful minority spoke the official language (Afrikaans) as a mother tongue.

It is argued that segregation settings produce poor results. The overall aim of education in these setting is the development of a limited proficiency—sufficient to meet the needs of the majority or powerful minority and to ensure their continued political and economic control. Although some support for L1 development is provided, this is also usually limited. Negative L2-related factors include the poor quality of L2 instruction and the lack of opportunity to practice the L2 in peer-group contexts.

However, the case against segregation is not clear-cut. In certain situations, the provision of separate educational facilities may have beneficial effects. For example, short-term programs for refugee populations newly arrived in the United States or European countries can help them adjust socially, affectively, and situationally to the demands of their new country. It can also be argued that the maintenance of minority languages requires at least some segregation. The advantages of segregation are also recognized by minority communities themselves, as illustrated by their attempts to set up separate schools for their children.

Segregation also has some advantages where L2 learning is concerned. In particular, because the learners are likely to be at the same level of development, it is possible to tailor INPUT to their level. Where the learners have different L1s, the L2 is likely to serve as a language of classroom communication and not just as a learning target. This is likely to broaden the functions that it typically serves. For these reasons, segregation may facilitate the development of 'survival skills' in the L2. Segregated language education that

is designed to meet the needs of a minority language group and is requested by them may help them both develop basic L2 skills quickly and also maintain their own L1.
see also SUBMERSION, IMMERSION, MOTHER TONGUE MAINTENANCE
📖 Baker 2006; Ellis 2008; Skuttnab-Kangas 1988, 2000

selective adaptation
the adjustment of a language user's categories (especially perceptual categories) as a result of repeated exposure to a stimulus. When a listener is exposed repeatedly to the same sound, their acoustic feature detectors become fatigued. Their perceptual boundaries then become shifted in a way that disfavors the sound being heard. For example, extended repetition of the syllable /ba/ desensitizes a listener to the features which characterize /b/, and, straight afterwards, they manifest a perceptual bias in favor of /p/.
📖 Field 2004

selective attention
a term which refers to how people attend to the stimuli around them. We are constantly bombarded by stimuli, both visual and auditory, and yet we keep from going crazy. This is because we have built-in filters so that when we focus on a task, we do not attend to unnecessary stimuli such as the buzzing of fluorescent lights overhead, traffic noise on the streets, and so on. However, even when focused on a task, we do not attend to and pick up all the information we have focused on. We select certain bits of information depending on a variety of factors, while other bits of information fall to the wayside. When approaching a traffic light, for example, we focus on the color of the light as well as the flow of traffic and may ignore the fact that a building on the right has a broken window even though the building is clearly within our peripheral vision. In short, in our daily lives selective attention is the norm. We filter out what we do not need at a given moment.
Some scholars working with cognition applied to SLA have used the construct of selective attention to discuss what learners do when processing language. Clearly, learners do not process all of the linguistic data that confront them at a given time. If so, acquisition would be much quicker than it is—in fact, almost instantaneous. As they do with everything else, learners focus on particular things depending on tasks, demands, prior knowledge, and a variety of other factors. They selectively attend to linguistic data. At this point, those working within a cognitive framework cannot predict what elements of language learners select and which ones go unattended, so the potential for spotting problems in language acquisition is limited. Under several accounts, early-stage learners selectively attend to vocabulary and chunks of the language that help them grasp meaning as quickly as possible, while ignoring grammatical devices that do not immediately aid them in getting meaning. How selective attention can be applied to later stages of acquisition is un-

clear. Selective attention is also used as a rationale for focus on form and grammatical intervention in classrooms. If learners are selectively attending to stimuli and filtering out linguistic data, then perhaps instruction can bring those data into the attentional realm.

see also ATTENTION, NOTICING

 VanPatten & Benati 2010

self-efficacy
> see ATTRIBUTION THEORY

self-esteem
> a term referring to the evaluation which individuals make and customarily maintain with regard to themselves; it expresses an attitude of approval or disapproval, and indicates the extent to which individuals believe themselves to be capable, significant, successful and worthy. In short, self-esteem is a personal judgment of worthiness that is expressed in the attitudes that individuals hold toward themselves. It is a subjective experience which the individual conveys to others by verbal reports and other overt expressive behavior.
>
> People derive their sense of self-esteem from the accumulation of experiences with themselves and with others and from assessments of the external world around them. Three general levels of self-esteem have been described in the literature to capture its multidimensionality:
>
> 1) **General self-esteem** (also **global self-esteem**) is said to be relatively stable in a mature adult, and is resistant to change except by active and extended therapy. It is the general or prevailing assessment one makes of one's own worth over time and across a number of situations. In a sense, it might be analogized to a statistical mean or median level of overall self-appraisal.
> 2) **Situational self-esteem** (also **specific self-esteem**) refers to one's self-appraisals in particular life situations, such as social interaction, work, education, home, or on certain relatively discretely defined traits, such as intelligence, communicative ability, athletic ability, or personality traits like gregariousness, empathy, and flexibility. The degree of specific self-esteem a person has may vary depending upon the situation or the trait in question.
> 3) **Task self-esteem** relates to particular tasks within specific situations. For example, within the educational domain, task self-esteem might refer to one subject-matter area. In an athletic context, skill in a sport—or even a facet of a sport such as net play in tennis or pitching in baseball—would be evaluated on the level of task self-esteem. Specific self-esteem might encompass second language acquisition in general, and task self-esteem might appropriately refer to one's self-evaluation of a particular

aspect of the process: speaking, writing, a particular class in a second language, or even a special kind of classroom exercise.

see also INHIBITION, ANXIETY, RISK TAKING, WILLINGNESS TO COMMUNICATE, EMPATHY, MOTIVATION, ATTRIBUTION THEORY
 Brown 2007; Coopersmith 1967

self-monitoring
the process of checking one's own language productions to ensure that they are: (a) accurate in terms of syntax, lexis and phonology; (b) appropriate in terms of register; (c) at an acceptable level of speed, loudness and precision; (d) likely to be clear to the listener/reader; and (e) likely to have the desired rhetorical impact. It seems unlikely that a speaker can focus on all these criteria simultaneously. Indeed, many speech errors (possibly over half) are not repaired. It is difficult to say whether a particular error has not been detected or whether the speaker felt that it was not worth interrupting the flow of speech to deal with it. However, the balance of evidence suggests that self-monitoring is selective. Research has found that speakers are more aware of errors that are closely linked to the prevailing context or to the task in hand. Speakers also identify with the listener in that they are more likely to correct an error that is likely to impair understanding than one that is not.

Furthermore, the attention committed to self-monitoring seems to fluctuate during the course of an utterance: errors are detected and repaired much more often when they occur towards the end of a clause. This finding suggests that the weight of attention during the early part of the unit of utterance is directed towards executing the speech plan, but that, once the plan is running, the speaker has spare attentional capacity for evaluating the output.

Evidence from repairs indicates two different points at which self-monitoring occurs. A speaker engages in pre-articulatory editing, when they check if their speech plan has been correctly assembled before putting it into effect. They also scan their speech while it is being uttered. Editor theories propose that the first kind of self-monitoring takes place at each successive stage of planning (syntactic, lexical, phonological, articulatory). However, this would impose an enormous processing burden. Other scholars have concluded that the pre-articulatory editor does not operate at all levels of planning but only at a late stage before production. This view is supported by evidence from experiments in which subjects are coaxed into uttering taboo words.

Levelt suggests that the two types of self-monitoring involve similar processes, two *perceptual loops*. In the first, the speaker attends to *internal speech* (a 'voice in the head' in the form of a *phonetic plan* which is the outcome of speech planning). In the second, they attend to *overt speech*. Both operations feed in to the same speech comprehension system as is used for processing the speech of others. This account faces the objection that the errors detected in a speaker's own speech are often different in kind from

those detected in the speech of others. However, this may be due to the different goals of the speaker, who wishes to ensure that the forms of language produced conform to a plan, and the listener, for whom errors of form are secondary to the extraction of meaning.
📖 Field 2004; Levelt 1989

self-motivating strategies

strategies used by learners to increase or protect their existing MOTIVATION. This is a rather new area in educational psychology, but research during the past decade has shown that learners' self-motivating capacity is a major factor contributing to success. Self-motivating strategies may play a role in empowering learners to be more committed and enthusiastic language learners. Even under adverse conditions in certain classrooms and without any teacher assistance, some learners are more successful at staying committed to the goals they have set for themselves than others are. It is assumed that they apply certain self-management skills to overcome environmental distractions or distracting emotional or physical needs/states; in fact, they motivate themselves.

Self-motivating strategies are made up of five main classes, which are listed below with two typical example strategies for each:

1) *Commitment control strategies* for helping to preserve or increase the learners' original goal commitment:
   a) Keeping in mind favorable expectations or positive incentives and rewards (e.g., a film director fantasizing about receiving an Oscar).
   b) Focusing on what would happen if the original intention failed.
2) *Metacognitive control strategies* for monitoring and controlling concentration, and for curtailing unnecessary procrastination:
   a) Identifying recurring distractions and developing defensive routines.
   b) Focusing on the first steps to take.
3) *Satiation control strategies* for eliminating boredom and adding extra attraction or interest to the task:
   a) Add a twist to the task (e.g., reordering certain sequences or setting artificial records and trying to break them).
   b) Use your fantasy to liven up the task (e.g., treating the task as a game, creating imaginary scenarios).
4) *Emotion control strategies* for managing disruptive emotional states or moods, and for generating emotions that will be conducive to implementing one's intentions (these strategies are similar to AFFECTIVE (learning) STRATEGIES):
   a) Self-encouragement
   b) Using relaxation and mediation techniques.

5) *Environmental control strategies* for eliminating negative environmental influences and exploiting positive environmental influences by making the environment an ally in the pursuit of a difficult goal;
   a) Eliminating negative environmental influences (such as sources of interference: e.g., noise, friends; and environmental temptations, e.g., a packet of cigarettes).
   b) Creating possible environmental influences (e.g., making promise or a public commitment to do or not to do something, asking friends to help you or not to allow you to do something).

Thus, raising learners' awareness of self-motivation strategies, in particular drawing attention to specific strategies that are especially useful in a given situation, may have a significant empowering effect on the students.
 Cohen & Dörnyei 2002; Corno & Kanfer 1983; Dörnyei 2001b; Kuhl 1987

self-regulation
the ability to monitor one's learning and make changes to the strategies that one employs. It involves both the ability to exercise control over one's attitudinal/motivational state and to engage in self-critical reflection of one's actions and underlying belief systems. The basic assumption underlying the notion of motivational self-regulation is that students who are able to maintain their MOTIVATION and keep themselves on-task in the face of competing demands and attractions should learn better than students who are less skilled at regulating their motivation.
 Ellis 2008

semilingualism
a term sometimes used for people who have acquired several languages at different periods of their lives, but who have not developed a native-speaker level of proficiency in any of them. This issue is regarded as controversial by many linguists.
 Richards & Schmidt 2010

sensitive period
see CRITICAL PERIOD HYPOTHESIS

sensory memory
a briefly retained record of a stimulus in its raw form. Sensory memory is divided into:

- **Iconic memory**. A short-lived imprint on the mind of an exact visual image—including the image of words encountered in reading. The trace may be retained for about a quarter of a second without being categorized (e.g., matched to letters). An alternative view is that the image is pro-

cessed for about half a second, enabling perceptual faculties at different levels to determine first location (e.g., letter order) and then identity.
- **Echoic memory**. A short-lived verbatim memory of a piece of speech. Echoic memory may last for at least 2 seconds. It has been suggested that it consists of two phases—a sensory one of about a quarter of a second and a longer one with the information categorized phonetically, which lasts another 3-4 seconds. Echoic memory appears to last rather longer than iconic. Recall of the last digit in a list is significantly better when the list is presented in spoken form than when it is presented in written—suggesting that we do indeed retain a brief 'echo' of what has just been said.

📖 Ellis 2008; Field 2004; Kellogg 1995

sequential bilingualism
see SIMULTANEOUS BILINGUALISM

short-term memory
a memory store in which information is briefly retained for the purpose of a current piece of processing. The information may come from external sources (e.g., a visual or spoken stimulus) or may have been withdrawn from the more permanent store in LONG-TERM MEMORY. The term WORKING MEMORY is often preferred to short-term memory because it emphasizes the fact that this component of memory does not simply store information but also processes it.
📖 Field 2004

sign language
a language employed by those with impaired hearing, whose modality is the use of gesture rather than sound. Sign language is based on three components: the place where the sign is made, the shape and angle of the hand(s), and the movement of the hand(s).

Historically, many sign languages evolved naturally within the communities that use them. This has given rise to a distinctive American Sign Language (ASL), British Sign Language (BSL), Australian Sign language and so on. It has also meant that Sign is an independent linguistic system. It is not simply a translation of speech into gesture in the way that writing is a translation of speech into script. ASL and BSL differ from standard dialects of English in a number of ways, particularly in the way they mark syntactic relations. They do not employ suffixed inflections: there are no specific signs for *–ed*, *-ing*, etc. They do not have articles and sometimes modify a lexical sign in situations where English would use function words.

Current thinking stresses the importance of equipping children early with a means of self-expression in the form of Sign. Fluent signers thus acquire competence in a first language which has no spoken or written form. When they later acquire English as a second language, they have to master not only a different linguistic system but also two new modalities (speech and writing).

Sign is of psycholinguistic interest for a number of reasons:

- *Sign originally developed naturally and independently.* The situation has been compared with the way in which CREOLEs develop from PIDGINs. The outcome of both processes is a fully-fledged language which appears to have been acquired on the basis of incomplete INPUT. This lends support to NATIVIZATION THEORY, which holds that, in the absence of linguistic input, an innate biological program drives the acquisition process.

  Concrete evidence of how Sign develops was obtained when Nicaragua set up its first educational program for deaf learners in 1980, with instruction based on lip-reading. Lacking any formal sign system, the learners communicated with each other outside the classroom by means of simple miming gestures (*homesigns*) which they had used at home to hearing relatives. Gradually these developed into a set of signs which the whole community shared and recognized.

  Some ten years later, a new intake of deaf students arrived, learned the sign system of the older ones and greatly amplified it with a number of syntactic features including markers of word class and verb agreement and a procedure for pronoun reference. Thus, a new sign language emerged in two generations of learners, just as the CREOLIZATION model would predict.

  There is some evidence that there may be a critical period (see CRITICAL PERIOD HYPOTHESIS) for sign language acquisition. Those who acquire Sign young appear to make fewer mistakes of form while they are learning. An older age of acquisition seems to limit ultimate attainment, with a greater likelihood of grammatical inaccuracy and of problems in sentence recall.

- *Sign uses a different modality from that of conventional languages.* If it could be shown that the acquisition of Sign is markedly different from that of speech, it would challenge the notion that language acquisition is supported by a universal innately acquired mechanism. It would also suggest that language is part of general cognitive processing (and thus affected by the modality in which it operates) rather than a separate modular faculty (see MODULARITY). The current state of evidence indicates certain strong similarities between the acquisition of signing by children of deaf parents and the acquisition of spoken language, but there are also differences. Both hearing and deaf children babble vocally; but there is said to be a higher incidence of manual BABBLING among deaf children with deaf parents. There is evidence that many deaf children acquire their first sign words earlier than children acquiring spoken language; however, this may be due to the fact that signing demands less precise motor control than speaking. Whereas hearing children manifest a sudden VOCABULARY SPURT at a certain stage in their development, vocabulary acquisition among signers tends to be more gradual. On the other hand, there are some striking similarities in the content of these early vocabularies, which are nearly identical across the two groups. There are also similarities in the way in which conceptual meanings (e.g., the notion of *dog*) become overgeneralized (see OVERGENERALIZATION). One might expect that signs which are *iconic* (i.e., related in some visual way to the entity they refer to) would be easier to master than those which are purely symbolic; but they do not appear to be acquired ahead of others.

There appears to be a relatively consistent order of acquisition for the forms of signing just as there is in phonology, though there is some variation. Of the three aspects of sign form, hand position is mastered the most readily and hand shape gives the most difficulty.

The resemblances between the two acquisition routes become particularly striking at the TWO-WORD STAGE. Deaf children learn to combine words just as their hearing peers do. They appear to discover the same semantic relationships—and do so in roughly the same order.

- *Sign has a different linguistic structure from English.* If children have been taught Sign first, they effectively come to English as a second language. When they write, their errors of syntax and spelling are often indistinguishable from those of a foreign learner. Their writing manifests features which may derive from structural differences between Sign and English. They often have serious difficulties with function words (articles, pronouns, prepositions, auxiliary verbs) and with inflectional suffixes. In reading, they are easily fazed by non-standard word orders (*Mary was contacted by John*). Word order is flexible in Sign; but signers seem to expect English to adhere quite strictly to its standard SVO (Subject-Verb-Object) sequence. In sum, there is some evidence that performance in the second language (English) is constrained by TRANSFER from the first (Sign) despite the difference of modalities. On the other hand, some of these errors are also found with non-signing deaf learners.

📖 Bonvillian 1999; Field 2004; Klima & Bellugi 1979; Strong 1988

silent period

just as children acquiring their first language go through a period in which they hear language but do not yet produce it, many language learners also experience a period of time in which they are unable or reluctant to speak. In the case of L1 acquisition, children go through a lengthy period of listening to people talk to them before they produce their first words. This silent period is necessary, for the young child needs to discover what language is and what it does. In the case of L2 acquisition, the silent period refers to the early stages of SLA during which learners may not produce any language at all or produce the most minimal language. The silent period is a term made popular by Steven Krashen in the early 1980s. It is readily observable in child L2 learners and less so in older learners, largely because the communicative demands made on older learners from the beginning is greater (e.g., they may have to use the L2 on the job, they are in classrooms that demand production, people may simply expect adults to talk). According to Krashen, the language learner is building up competence during the silent period by actively listening and processing the INPUT data around him. The learner need not be speaking to be acquiring language. Transferred into language pedagogy under the *Natural Approach*, the recommendation was to allow learners to have a silent period in the early stages of classroom learning. Thus, students should not be forced to speak until they are ready to do so. Presumably, early forced speaking would raise the learner's levels of ANXIETY and other negative emotions, perhaps inhibiting acquisition more generally. In addition, the idea was that by forcing learners to speak before they are ready, they would learn to rely on L1 rules to produce utterances as a communicative strategy (see COMMUNICATIVE STRATEGIES). This strategy, too, might impede language acquisition more generally.

Of course, not all learners go through a silent period. Many learners—particularly classroom learners—are obliged to speak from the beginning. But even when production is not required, some learners opt for it. Saville-Troike suggested that the reason may lie in differences in the learners' social and cognitive orientation. She distinguished **other-directed** and **inner-directed learners**. The former approach language as an interpersonal, social task, with a predominant focus on the message they wish to convey, while the latter approach language learning as an intrapersonal task, with a predominant focus on the language code. She suggested that while other-directed learners do not typically go through a silent period, inner-directed learners do.

📖 Ellis 2008; Saville-Troike 1988; VanPatten & Benati 2010

simultaneous bilingualism
also **infant bilingualism, bilingual first language acquisition**
the acquisition of two languages from birth both as first languages, for example, before a child is three years old. If the child first acquires one language, then the other, the child is said to have acquired **sequential bilingualism** (also called **consecutive bilingualism, successive bilingualism**). Some researchers differentiate between childhood bilingualism and adolescent or adult bilingualism. The first process follows a path similar to the one a child follows in learning one first language while the second follows a different path. One reasonably common pattern observed in simultaneous bilingualism is the case where one parent speaks one language to a child, while the other

parent speaks a different language (known as *one parent, one language*). Sequential bilingualism can occur in contexts where the child speaks one language in the home environment, but upon starting pre-school or kindergarten is exposed to a second language.

see also BILINGUALISM, COMPOUND BILINGUALISM, EARLY BILINGUALISM, ADDITIVE BILINGUALISM

📖 Baker 2006; Brown & Attardo 2005; Macaro et al. 2010

situational ethnicity
see ACCULTURATION

situational self-esteem
see SELF-ESTEEM

skill-acquisition theory
another term for SKILL-LEARNING THEORY

skill-building hypothesis
another term for SKILL-LEARNING THEORY

skill-learning theory
also **skill-acquisition theory, skill-building hypothesis, skill theory**

a theory which is based on the view that language learning, like other kinds of skill, is characterized by a progression from an initial DECLARATIVE KNOWLEDGE stage involving controlled processing, to a final PROCEDURAL KNOWLEDGE stage where knowledge is automatic. Skills are learned as a result of appropriate 'practice'. Practice, however, needs to be skill-related. So, the development of skill in listening requires practice in processing INPUT while the development of speaking requires practice in oral production. According to this view, procedural knowledge is unidirectional; that is, automatization of different skills, such as listening, does not directly assist automatization of a different skill, such as speaking. However, automatization of one skill may have an indirect effect on a different skill by improving and strengthening declarative knowledge which is bi-directional (i.e., can be utilized in the development of different skills).

According to skill-acquisition theories, L2 learners achieve proceduralization through extensive practice in using the L2. However practice is a relatively crude concept, especially when applied to language learning. The traditional view is that practice involves the process of repeatedly and deliberately attempting to produce some specific target feature. It was this view that led to the use of the mechanical drills found in the audiolingual and oral-situational methods of language teaching. What was missing from this view, was recognition of the importance of practice directed at behavior rather than structures. It was shown that that practice is often not effective in enabling learners to use new structures autonomously—practice does not make perfect. This is because practicing a structure in a mechanical way reifies the structure by decontextualizing it and thus does not affect LONG-TERM MEMORY or lead to any change in behavior. To change behavior (i.e., develop automatic processes) it is necessary to provide practice of the actual behavior itself. In the case of language learning, behavior must entail attempts to communicate. Thus, for practice to work for the development of the speaking skill it must involve learners producing the target structure in the context of communicative activity. According to this view, then, communicative practice serves as a device for proceduralzing knowledge of linguistic structures that have been first presented declaratively. Instruction that incorporates such practice can be seen as an attempt to intervene directly in the process by which declarative knowledge is proceduralized.

There can be little doubt that language learning, in part at least, does involve skill-learning in the sense that practice aids the process by which L2 knowledge is automatized—as also claimed by the emergentist theories (see EMERGENTISM). However, skill-acquisition theories are problematic in two related respects. First, they provide no explanation for the orders and sequences of acquisition. It is argued that the route followed by L2 learners is not convincingly explained by such approaches. Second, it is difficult to accept that acquisition of all L2 features begins with declarative knowledge. This implies a role for metalinguistic awareness in L2 acquisition.

see also ADAPTIVE CONTROL OF THOUGHT MODEL, COGNITIVE THEORY

Anderson 1983; Ellis 1988b, 2008; Dekeyser 1998; McLaughlin 1987; Mithcell & Myles 2004

skill theory
another term for SKILL-LEARNING THEORY

SLA
an abbreviation for SECOND LANGUAGE ACQUISITION

SLD
an abbreviation for SECOND LANGUAGE DEVELOPMENT

SLI
an abbreviation for SPECIFIC LANGUAGE IMPAIRMENT

slips of the ear
a processing error in which one word or phrase is heard as another, as in hearing *great ape* when the utterance was *gray tape*. Slips of the ear provide insights into how the speech signal is processed and how words are recognized in connected speech. The data can be analyzed at phoneme level, with the proviso that it is difficult to determine to what extent top-down lexical

effects (the knowledge of whole words that nearly fit the signal) may have led to a particular interpretation. With consonants, three types of error occur: *deletions* where no consonant is heard, *additions* where a consonant is inserted for which there are no cues in the signal and *substitution* where the reported consonant resembles the target one. Most consonant errors are word-initial. Since words are processed *online*, a mistake in this position is more likely to lead to a wrong match at word-level. Plosives are the most liable to be misinterpreted—supporting the findings of *confusability* studies. So far as vowels are concerned, those in stressed syllables are much less prone to misinterpretation than those in unstressed.

Slips of the ear are useful in providing insights into how listeners determine where word boundaries lie in connected speech. When listeners misplace boundaries, they tend to insert them between a weak syllable and a strong—suggesting that segmentation is influenced by the predominant *strong-weak pattern* which characterizes English rhythm. This finding from naturalistic slips of the ear is supported by similar evidence from slips induced by the *faint speech* method, which involves playing anomalous sentences at a level just above the subject's hearing threshold. What both sources of data show is the vulnerability of weakly stressed function words, which may be misheard or attached to preceding strong ones.

Although there is a well-established corpus of slips of the ear, there are some problems in relying upon it as data. The slips are not usually audio-recorded, which means that the written record we have is dependent upon the observer's analysis of the situation and limited in terms of contextual information. It is difficult to determine if any part was played by ambient *noise*, regional accent or by context (the absence of disambiguating information or the presence of misleading information). A major question is how representative the slips are, and how many others may have occurred without the listener heeding them. It is also possible that some apparent slips of the ear may in fact have originated in SLIPS OF THE TONGUE. Finally, it is not always easy to determine with certainty the cause of a slip. These difficulties are admitted by researchers, but the corpus is large enough for some general conclusions to be reached.

see also TIP OF THE TONGUE

📖 Aitchison 2003; Bond 1999; Field 2004; Yule 2006

slips of the tongue
also SOT

a speech error in which a sound or word is produced in the wrong place. This produces expressions such as *a long shory stort* (instead of 'make a long story short'), *use the door to open the key*, and *a fifty-pound dog of bag food*. Slips of this type are sometimes called **spoonerisms** after William Spooner, an Anglican clergyman at Oxford University, who was renowned for his tongue-slips. Most of the slips attributed to him involve the interchange of two initial sounds, as when he addressed a rural group as *noble tons of soil*, or described God as *a shoving leopard to his flock*, or in this complaint to a student who had been absent from classes: *You have hissed all my mystery lectures*.

Most everyday slips of the tongue, however, are not as entertaining. They are often simply the result of a sound being carried over from one word to the next, as in *black bloxes* (for 'black boxes'), or a sound used in one word in anticipation of its occurrence in the next word, as in *noman numeral* (for 'roman numeral'), or *a tup of tea* ('cup'), or *the most highly played player* ('paid'). The last example is close to the reversal type of slip, illustrated by *shu flots*, which may not make you *beel fetter* if you are suffering from a *stick neff*, and it is always better to *loop before you leak*. The last two examples involve the interchange of word-final sounds and are much less common than word-initial slips.

It has been argued that slips of this type are never random, that they never produce a phonologically unacceptable sequence, and that they indicate the existence of different stages in the articulation of linguistic expressions. Although the slips are mostly treated as errors of articulation, it has been suggested that they may result from 'slips of the brain' as it tries to organize linguistic messages.

see also TIP OF THE TONGUE, SLIPS OF THE EAR
📖 Yule 2006

SLS

an abbreviation for SECOND LANGUAGE STUDIES

social constructivism

see CONSTRUCTIVISM

social distance

a term which refers to the cognitive and affective proximity of two cultures that come into contact within an individual. *Distance* is obviously used in a metaphorical sense to depict dissimilarity between two cultures. On a very superficial level one might observe, for example, that people from the United States are culturally similar to Canadians, while US natives and Chinese are, by comparison, relatively dissimilar. We could say that the social distance of the latter case exceeds the former.

John Schumann described social distance as consisting of the following parameters:

1) *Dominance*. In relation to the target language (TL) group, is the L2 (second language learning) group politically, culturally, technically, or economically dominant, nondominant, or subordinate?

1) *Integration.* Is the integration pattern of the L2 group assimilation, ACCULTURATION, or preservation? What is the L2 group's degree of enclosure—its identity separate from other contiguous groups?
2) *Cohesiveness.* Is the L2 group cohesive? What is the size of the L2 group?
3) *Congruence.* Are the cultures of the two groups congruent—similar in their value and belief systems? What are the attitudes of the two groups toward each other?
4) *Permanence.* What is the L2 group's intended length of residence in the target language area?

Schumann used the above factors to describe hypothetically 'good' and 'bad' language learning situations, and illustrated each situation with two actual crosscultural contexts. His two hypothetical 'bad' language learning situations:

- The TL group views the L2 group as dominant and the L2 group views itself in the same way. Both groups desire preservation and high enclosure for the L2 group, the L2 group is both cohesive and large, the two cultures are not congruent, the two groups hold negative attitudes toward each other, and the L2 group intends to remain in the TL area only for a short time.
- The second bad situation has all the characteristics of the first except that in this case, the L2 group considers itself subordinate and is considered subordinate by the TL group.

The first situation, according to Schumann, is typical of Americans living in Riyadh, Saudi Arabia. The second situation is descriptive of Navajo Indians living in the southwestern part of the United States.

A 'good' language learning situation, according to Schumann's model, is one in which the L2 group is nondominant in relation to the TL group, both groups desire assimilation (or at least acculturation) for the L2 group, low enclosure is the goal of both groups, the two cultures are congruent, the L2 group is small and noncohesive, both groups have positive attitudes toward each other, and the L2 group intends to remain in the target language area for a long time. Under such conditions social distance would be minimal and acquisition of the target language would be enhanced. Schumann cites as a specific example of a 'good' language learning situation the case of American Jewish immigrants living in Israel.

Schumann's hypothesis was that the greater the social distance between two cultures, the greater the difficulty the learner will have in learning the second language, and conversely, the smaller the social distance (the greater the social solidarity between two cultures), the better will be the language learning situation.

📖 Brown 2007; Ellis 2008; Schumann 1976

social identity
see SOCIAL IDENTITY THEORY

Social Identity Theory
a theory formulated by Peirce and Norton which claims that learners' social identities affect how successful they will be in learning an L2. Norton defined **social identity** as the relationship between the individual and the larger social world, as mediated through institutions such as families, schools, workplaces, social services, and law courts. It contrasts with both 'cultural identity' (the relationship between individuals and members of a group who share a common history, a common language, and similar ways of understanding the world) and ETHNIC IDENTITY (the relationship between the individual and members of the race to which the learner belongs). Norton expressed a preference for the term social identity because she believed that this term best captures the heterogeneous and dynamic nature of identity in the learners she investigated. In fact, her theory is concerned with the relationship between power, identity, and language learning.

The theory seeks to address three general questions: (1) under what conditions do language learners speak? (2) how can we encourage learners to become more communicatively competent? (and 3) how can we facilitate interaction between learners and target-language speakers? Answers to these questions are provided by three central propositions:

1) Social identity is multiple, contradictory, and dynamic. That is, each person possesses a number of different identities, some of which may be in opposition. Identities are modified, abandoned, or added to at any time depending on circumstances.
2) L2 learners need to invest in a social identity that will create appropriate opportunities for them to learn the L2. They need to be prepared to struggle to establish such an identity.
3) L2 learners need to develop an awareness of the right to speak. This requires that they understand how the rules of speaking are socially and historically constructed to support the interests of a dominant group within society. In other words, identity construction has to be understood in relation to larger social processes.

Implicit in this view of social identity, L2 use, and L2 learning is the idea of 'ownership' of the language being learned. Norton challenged the view that native speakers own the language and asserted that learners need to see themselves as legitimate speakers of it. Thus, Norton challenged the traditional notions of 'native speaker' and 'non-native speaker'.

Norton's theory was developed to account for under-privileged learners in a majority language setting. However, it can also help to account for a different kind of learner—privileged, short-stay learners in a majority setting.

The importance of Norton's theory is that it provides a non-deterministic account of how social factors influence L2 acquisition by attributing 'agency' to the learner. It is capable of explaining why some learners are successful and others less so. However, it is also limited in scope in a number of ways. It deals exclusively with learners learning an L2 in a majority setting and it is therefore not clear to what extent it can explain L2 learning in foreign language settings. It addresses how learning opportunities are created but has nothing to say about how these opportunities actually result in acquisition. Indeed, at times, Norton is guilty of uncritically equating learning opportunities with learning. Norton did not provide any evidence to show what the learners she investigated actually learned as a product of the identities they assumed. Nor does she show that learners who achieved the right to speak learned more rapidly than those who do not.

see also INTER-GROUP MODEL, SOCIO-EDUCATIONAL MODEL, ACCULTURATION MODEL, LANGUAGE SOCIALIZATION

Ellis 2008; Norton 1997, 2000; Peirce 1995

social-interactionism
also **interactionism, interactionist position, interactionist theory, social-interactionist theory**
approaches to language acquisition which emphasize the parts played by the child's environment, its social instincts, its pragmatic needs and its relationship with the carer. Those who take this position do not necessarily deny the existence of an innately endowed capacity for language (see INNATENESS HYPOTHESIS). But they maintain that genetic factors, if they exist, are insufficient on their own to ensure that language develops. Nor is simple exposure to language enough. What is important is the interaction, both linguistic and non-linguistic, which derives from the child's need to communicate.

It is argued that CHILD DIRECTED SPEECH (CDS) is not as impoverished as Chomsky suggests. The modifications that are made to adult speech (slow rate, repetitions, set phrases, simple syntax and heightened intonation patterns) appear to assist the child in decoding what is said. In response to the *nativist* assertion (see NATIVISM) that children do not receive FEEDBACK on ill-formed utterances (see NEGATIVE EVIDENCE), social-interactionists claim that correction is often indirect. Without specifically correcting a child, parents show puzzlement, recast utterances or give responses that exemplify the correct form. There is also evidence that carers grade their language sensitively, increasing sentence length and complexity as the child gets older in response to evidence of the child's linguistic development.

A child's language does not develop faster in proportion to the level of INPUT by the carer. But there appears to be a correlation between speed of acquisition and the pragmatic content of CDS—in particular, the extent to which, through questions, directives, acknowledgements and references to the child's activities, the adult invites interaction by the child.

Social-interactionist views stress the importance of the infant's relationship to its environment. One aspect is the familiarity of certain objects and events which ensures that there is a repetitive and even a ritualistic quality to much of the language that is used. Interaction with the principal carer (especially in the form of play) also follows predictable sequences; and it is through play that semantic relationships such as the agent/object distinction are said to become manifest. The carer plays an important role in interpreting new events as they arise.

📖 Bruner 1983, 1985; Cattell 2000; Ellis 2008; Field 2004; Halliday 1975; Owens 2001

social-interactionist theory
another term for SOCIAL-INTERACTIONISM

social strategies
see LEARNING STRATEGIES

sociocultural theory
an approach established by the Russian psychologist Vygotsky which claims that interaction not only facilitates language learning but is a causative force in acquisition. Further, all of learning is seen as essentially a social process which is grounded in sociocultural settings. These settings include schools, family life, peer groups, work places, and so on. Socioculturalists claim that the most important cognitive activities in which people engage are shaped by these environments. The theory considers language and, by extension, SECOND LANGUAGE ACQUISITION (SLA) as contextually situated and is concerned with situated language as it relates to internal processes. This paradigm, despite the label 'sociocultural', does not seek to explain how learners acquire the cultural values of the L2 but rather how knowledge of an L2 is internalized through experiences of a sociocultural nature. In SLA research sociocultural theory has been used as a framework for analyzing tasks and activities. Given the same task, not all students will interpret it in the same way and consequently their behavior in relation to that task will vary with its interpretation. It has also been used as a way to describe how learners regulate their learning behaviors through meta-comments about the language task and through interacting with others.

There are a number of concepts that are different from more traditional approaches to SLA; namely, 'mediation' and 'regulation', 'internalization', and the 'zone of proximal development'. *Mediation* is the most important of these, because sociocultural theory rests on the assumption that human activity (including cognitive activity) is mediated by what are known as symbolic artifacts (higher-level cultural tools) such as language and literacy and by material artifacts. These artifacts mediate the relationship between humans and the social and material world around us. To think of this in more concrete terms, one can consider how humans have developed tools to ease what might otherwise be an arduous process. If one wanted to put strands of wool together to create material, one could hold the strands taut and interweave other pieces of wool. But, over time, humans have developed tools to mediate the weaving process; namely, a loom with all of its component parts (e.g., the reed, the heddles) and a shuttle. Within sociocultural theory, humans use symbols as tools to mediate psychological activity and to control our psychological processes. This control is voluntary and allows us to attend to certain things, to plan, and to think rationally. The primary tool that humans have available is language and it is a tool that allows us to connect to our environment (both physical and social). Language gives humans the power to go beyond the immediate environment and to think about and talk about events and objects that are far removed both physically and temporally.

Regulation is a form of mediation. As children learn language, they also learn to regulate their activities linguistically. There are three stages of development on the way to self-regulation. The first stage involves the use of objects as a way of thinking (object-regulation). One can think of parents using objects (e.g., pieces of candy) to help children with the abstract concept of counting. A second stage is known as other-regulation whereby learning is regulated by others rather than objects. Finally, self-regulation, the final stage occurs when activities can be performed with little or no external support. This occurs through internalization of information (addition without the use of pieces of candy, although some external support is required in the case of more complex mathematical manipulations).

Another concept central to sociocultural theory is what is referred to as *internalization*. This is the process that allows us to move the relationship between an individual and his environment to later performance. One way internalization occurs is through imitation, which can be both immediate and intentional and delayed, as seen, for example, in early child language research by, in which imitation/practice was observed by children when they were alone in bed. This is also known as PRIVATE SPEECH. The items focused on by learners in these imitation/private speech situations are controlled by the learner and not necessarily by the teacher's agenda.

Another concept that is associated with sociocultural theory is known as the **zone of proximal development** (**ZPD**), which is defined as the distance between the actual developmental level as determined by independent problem solving and the level of potential development as determined through problem solving under adult guidance or in collaboration with more capable peers. What this means is that learning results from interpersonal activity; it is interpersonal activity that forms the basis for individual functioning. This clearly embodies the social nature of learning and underscores the importance of collaborative learning as it shapes what is learned.

In sum, in this view, human cognition results from the full context (historical, social, material, cultural) in which experiences take place. Thus, the experiences we have, and the interactions we engage in, are crucial in the development of cognition. Language is a tool (a symbolic artifact) that mediates between individuals and their environment.

see also INNER SPEECH, CONSTRUCTIVISM, SCAFFOLDING

Couchlan & Duff 1994; Gass & Selinker 2008; Kramsch 2002; Lantolf 2000a, 2004; Lantolf & Appel 1994; Macaro et al. 2010; Saville-Troike 2006; Tarone & Swain 1995; VanPatten & Benati 2010; Vygotsky 1987

Socio-educational Model

a model of L2 learning developed by Gardner which posits that the social and cultural milieu in which learners grow up determines the attitudes and motivational orientation they hold towards the target language, its speakers, and its culture. These in turn influence learning outcomes. Unlike INTERGROUP MODEL and ACCULTURATION MODEL, which were designed to account for the role that social factors play in natural setting, in particular majority language contexts, Gardner's model was developed to explain L2 learning in classroom settings, in particular the foreign language classroom. The model seeks to interrelate four aspects of L2 learning: (1) the social and cultural milieu, (2) individual learner differences, (3) the setting, and (4) learning outcomes. As such, it goes beyond purely social factors and is more comprehensive than the other two models—it is not just a matter of learning new information but of acquiring symbolic elements of a different ethnolinguistic community.

The strength of Gardner's model is that it explains how setting is related to PROFICIENCY—one of the primary goals of any social theory of L2 acquisition—by positing a series of intervening variables (ATTITUDES, MOTIVATION, self-confidence) and by trying to plot how these are interrelated and how they affect learning. In this respect, it provides the most detailed account of how social factors influence proficiency currently available.

Missing from the model is any account of how particular settings highlight different factors that influence attitudes, motivation, and achievement, although Gardner recognizes the need to pay close attention to the social milieu in order to identify alternative factors. Also missing from the model is any reference to the concept of INTERLANGUAGE development and how this takes place through the process of social interaction. Gardner's model only considers ultimate proficiency, measured mainly by language tests of various kinds. It does not consider the kinds of developmental patterns. Nor does it consider the social aspects of VARIABILITY in learner language. The model, therefore, cannot explain why learners develop in the way they do.

see also SOCIAL IDENTITY THEORY, LANGUAGE SOCIALIZATION, SOCIOCULTURAL THEORY, SOCIAL-INTERACTIONISM

📖 Ellis 2008; Gardner 1979, 1983, 1985

sociolinguistic competence
see COMMUNICATIVE COMPETENCE

sociolinguistics
a branch of linguistics which studies all aspects of the relationship between language and society. Sociolinguists study such matters as the linguistic identity of social groups, social attitudes to language, standard and non-standard forms of language, the patterns and needs of national language use, social varieties and levels of language, the social basis of BILINGUALISM and MULTILINGUALISM, and so on. An alternative name sometimes given to the subject (which suggests a greater concern with sociological rather than linguistic explanations of the above) is the *sociology of language*. Any of the branches of linguistics could, in principle, be separately studied within an explicitly social perspective, and some use is accordingly made of such terms as *sociophonetics* and *sociophonology*, when this emphasis is present, as in the study of the properties of accents. In Hallidayan linguistics (see SYSTEMIC LINGUISTICS), the term *sociosemantics* has a somewhat broader sense, in which the choices available within a grammar are related to communication roles found within the speech situation, as when a particular type of question is perceived in social terms to be a threat.

The term overlaps to some degree with *ethnolinguistics* and *anthropological linguistics*, reflecting the overlapping interests of the correlative disciplines involved—sociology, ethnology and anthropology. The study of dialects is sometimes seen as a branch of sociolinguistics, and sometimes differentiated from it, under the heading of *dialectology*, especially when regional dialects are the focus of study. When the emphasis is on the language of face-to-face interaction, the approach is known as *interactional sociolinguistics*. *Sociological linguistics* is sometimes differentiated from sociolinguistics, particularly in Europe, where the term reflects a concern to see language as an integral part of sociological theory. Also sometimes distinguished is *sociohistorical linguistics*, the study of the way particular linguistic functions and types of variation develop over time within specific languages, speech communities, social groups and individuals.

📖 Crystal 2008

sociolinguistic variables
a linguistic feature that varies in accordance with factors such as age, sex, social class, and ethnic membership. For example, Labov illustrates how

variation in /r/ in the speech of New Yorkers reflects the social class of a speaker.
📖 Ellis 2008, Labov 1972

sociopragmatic failure
a term used by Thomas which occurs when a learner performs the wrong ILLOCUTIONARY ACT for the situation and constitutes a deviation with regard to appropriateness of meaning. An example is a learner who apologizes where a native speaker would thank someone.
📖 Ellis 2008; Thomas 1983

Socio-psycholinguistic Model
a VARIABILITY theory of L2 acquisition developed by Preston which envisages INTERLANGUAGE development, like other kinds of language change, as involving both 'change from above' and 'change from below'. In the case of general language change, the former involves linguistic responses to straightforward social pressures and is accompanied by awareness of features that are prestigious or stigmatized, while the latter involves changes that are not conscious and which usually arise spontaneously in the speech of members of the working class. In the case of interlanguage, the VERNACULAR STYLE can be influenced both from above (when forms enter through the learner's careful style) and from below (when they enter directly into the vernacular style). Forms that enter from above are odd and require more effort and attention to maintain. Examples are English third person singular -*s* and noun plurals. The distinction between these two types of change is necessary to account for the finding that the direction of stylistic shifting varies with some features (such as articles showing greater accuracy in the vernacular and others (like third person -*s*) greater accuracy in the careful style.

Preston's model rests on the idea of the learner's knowledge of the L2 as 'a complex variation space', which can be accounted for in terms of (1) planning, (2) depth, and (3) stability. The concept of *planning* is envisaged as a continuum. Preston, however, sees planning not just as something that learners do when using their knowledge, but as actually reflected in the knowledge system itself. He talks of the planned and unplanned sides of learner system in a distinction that seems very close to Bialystok's ideas of *analyzed* and *unanalyzed knowledge* (see BIALYSTOK'S THEORY OF L2 LEARNING). Learners will vary as to which side—or type of knowledge—is most fully represented in their interlanguage systems.

The *depth* dimension of the model is an attempt to take account of the social uses that learners make of their variable systems. Thus, there are likely to be different frequencies of use that reflect gender, class, age, genres, relationships, etc. These differences reflect the attempts of learners to use their knowledge functionally for social purpose. Learners, like native speakers, will use forms symbolically for these purposes.

Stability is a characteristic of both the surface structure of the learner's interlanguage system and also of the way this system is used to convey social meanings. In the case of the former, a stable system is one where there is an absence of variation because no new forms are entering the system and existing forms have become categorical. In the case of the latter, stability is evident when continued association of a given feature with a given social manning halts or slows the development of that feature. When this kind is found, FOSSILIZATION may occur.

Preston raised the interesting possibility that learners will differ in the extent to which the variability of their systems is a product of the planning or the depth dimensions. He noted that where there is no real community of learners and no previous accretion of symbolic depth, change will be more linguistically determined along the shallow, surface plane of the model proposed here. Thus classroom learners are more likely to manifest planning than social variability, although even these learners are likely to assign some symbolic value to the developing forms.

Preston further addressed the nature of the L2 grammar that learners develop from a sociolinguistic perspective. He proposed that learners develop grammars consisting of variable rules that account for their choice of linguistic forms in accordance with social factors (responsible for external variation) and linguistic context (responsible for internal variation). A key feature of this later modeling of linguistic competence is that some features may be 'weaker' than others. Preston argued that the elements of linguistic competence may be 'less there'. He proposed that those features that are learned as part of the vernacular are more deeply entrenched than those features that are learned post-vernacular. In other words, he conceived of grammars that have post-vernacular areas in which the constructions are 'there' in competence but weaker. Finally Preston acknowledged that an elaborated psycholinguistic model of learner variability would also need to incorporate a memory and processing component.

Preston's theory constitutes, thus, a real attempt to integrate psycholinguistic and sociolinguistic perspectives. However, it is not clear and does not appear to provide an explanation of the nature of the form-function networks that learners construct at different stages of development.

see also COMPETITION MODEL, VARIABLE COMPETENCE MODEL, CAPABILITY CONTINUUM PARADIGM, MONITOR MODEL, ACCULTURATION MODEL, NATIVIZATION MODEL, FUNCTIONALIST MODEL

📖 Ellis 2008; Preston 1989, 2002

SOT

an abbreviation for SLIPS OF THE TONGUE

specific language impairment
also **SLI**

a condition in which a child who appears otherwise normal fails to acquire language like its peers. These children sometimes have restricted vocabularies or make relatively basic errors of grammar. They may show problems of comprehension as well as problems of production: finding it difficult to follow the utterances of others or to put thoughts into words. In particular, they seem to have difficulty in sustaining a contextual framework for a conversation. What is striking is that this linguistic deficit cannot be clearly linked to low intelligence or cognitive impairment. It appears to affect language but not other faculties.

Some researchers believe that the condition provides convincing evidence that language is *modular* (see MODULARITY) and distinct from other forms of cognition. Others take the view that the underlying causes are most likely cognitive or perceptual.

Early research into specific language impairment (SLI) sought a link with hearing difficulties caused by *otitis media with effusion* (OME), a disorder of the middle ear which causes some hearing loss. This view is no longer generally held, and more recent scholars have suggested that SLI may result from a deficit in the child's ability to recognize recurring patterns such as inflections in the language it encounters.

Those who adopt a *nativist* view (see NATIVISM) maintain that innate grammatical components within UNIVERSAL GRAMMAR are defective or absent in SLI sufferers. An important study of three generations of a family suggested that about half of them suffered severely from SLI and thus that the condition might be genetic. These individuals performed quite well on general *grammaticality judgment* tasks but their language lacked many important inflectional markings such as number, gender and verb endings. The initial conclusion drawn (the *feature-blindness hypothesis*) was that their representation of grammar lacked an important component which enables others to recognize and acquire inflectional morphology. However, it was later suggested that SLI sufferers adopt a strategy of learning exemplar by exemplar instead of recognizing that inflectional marking can be derived by rule. This means that they have difficulty in using inflections because the process of retrieving them makes heavy demands on memory. A strong version of this hypothesis is, however, difficult to square with evidence that SLI sufferers sometimes overgeneralize inflectional endings (*goed*), showing that they have some awareness of the system.

A contrary view attributes the absence of inflections in the language of SLI sufferers to inadequate perception. It finds a cause in the low SALIENCE of grammatical morphemes, which (in English) are weakly stressed and short in duration. English-speaking children suffering from SLI have been compared with Italians whose language has more perceptible inflectional markings.

The Italian children showed a more extensive use of inflection and a preference for the more salient feminine articles *la* and *una* rather than the masculine *il* and *un*.

However, there are some reservations about the perceptual account. First, SLI appears to affect written as well as spoken language (though it could be that children simply do not write inflections because they do not perceive them). Second, no correlation has been established between the perceptual prominence of a feature and the likelihood that it will be absent from the speech of an SLI sufferer. If anything, the appearance of a particular inflection or functor seems to be determined by its grammatical function: final *-s* is more likely to be used for a noun plural than to mark possession or present simple third person. Children with SLI also have difficulty with inflections and functors that are not phonologically weak, such as irregular past tense forms and direct object pronouns. Finally, there is the argument that, if a perceptual deficit affects the recognition of certain inflectional features, there should be an impact upon wider syntactic knowledge (e.g., the recognition of word classes).

A third possibility is that SLI may not be a unitary disorder but the result of a combination of several different forms of language impairment which are present to different degrees in different sufferers. Clinically based accounts have suggested a number of subtypes representing the symptoms which appear to co-occur in cases of SLI and of *autism* (i.e., a condition characterized by a withdrawal from linguistic interaction with others).

see also DOWN'S SYNDROME, WILLIAMS SYNDROME

Bishop 1997; Field 2004; Fletcher 1999; Gopnik 1990; Gopnik et al. 1997

specific self-esteem
another term for SITUATIONAL SELF-ESTEEM

Speech Accommodation Theory
another term for ACCOMMODATION THEORY

speech act
an utterance as a functional unit in communication. The term speech act is derived from the work of the Austin in the 1930s, and now used widely in linguistics, to refer to a theory which analyzes the role of utterances in relation to the behavior of speaker and hearer in interpersonal communication. In speech act theory, there are three types of acts that utterances can be said to perform: a **locutionary act**, an **illocutionary act**, and a **perlocutionary act**. A *locutionary act*, or locution, refers simply to the act of saying something that makes sense in the language. In other words, that follows the grammatical rules of language. An *illocutionary act* is one that is performed through the medium of language: stating, warning, wishing, promising, and so on. And finally, a *perlocutionary act* refers to an act performed by making an

utterance which intrinsically involves an effect on the behavior, beliefs, feelings, etc., of a listener. Examples of perlocutionary acts include frightening, surprising, misleading, deterring, convincing, insulting and persuading. A distinction may be drawn between the intended and the actual perlocutionary effect of an utterance (e.g., a speaker may intend to persuade X to do Y, but instead succeed in getting X to do Z).
Several categories of speech act have been proposed:

- *Directives*—speakers try to get their listeners to do something, e.g., begging, commanding, requesting
- *Commissives*—speakers commit themselves to a future course of action, e.g., promising, guaranteeing
- *Expressives*—speakers express their feelings, e.g., apologizing, welcoming, sympathizing
- *Declarations*—the speaker's utterance brings about a new external situation, e.g., christening, marrying, resigning
- *Representatives*—speakers convey their belief about the truth of a proposition, e.g., asserting, hypothesizing

A speech act which is performed indirectly is sometimes known as an *indirect speech act*, such as the speech act of requesting above. Indirect speech acts are often felt to be more polite ways of performing certain kinds of speech act, such as requests and refusals. The verbs which are used to indicate the speech act intended by the speaker are sometimes known as *performative verbs*. The criteria which have to be satisfied in order for a speech act to be successful are known as *felicity conditions*.
The study of speech acts in INTERLANGUAGE has concentrated on illocutionary meanings or language functions. The questions that have addressed are (1) To what extent and in what ways do learners perform illocutionary acts in the L2 differently from native speakers of the target language? Are there differences in the form of the illocutionary act and/or the appropriateness of its use on a particular occasion? and (2) How do learners learn to perform different illocutionary acts?
see also REQUEST, APOLOGY
 Crystal 2008; Finch 2005; Searle 1975

speech community
a term which describes any regionally or socially definable human group which can be identified by the use of a shared spoken language or language variety. It can vary in size from a tiny cluster of speakers to whole nations or supranational groups (e.g., a village, a region, a nation)
 Crystal 2008; Richards & Schmidt 2010

stereotype 333

speech event
a term describing a communicative exchange made meaningful by culturally specific structures of participants, genres, codes and other elements. Usage in a language is organized through the higher-level patterning of speech events. Examples of highly structured speech events are debates and interviews. Much less structured are conversations.
📖 Crystal 2008

speech planning
in some contexts of language use, speakers have the opportunity to plan their speech, while in others they have to use the language more spontaneously. Speech planning influences the choices of linguistic form. For example, L2 learners may use a target-language form in planned language use but an INTERLANGUAGE form in unplanned language use. Speech planning is sometimes investigated by studying 'temporal variables' (e.g., speech rate and pause length).
📖 Ellis 2008

spoonerisms
see SLIPS OF THE TONGUE

stabilization
see FOSSILIZATION

stage theory of development
another term for COGNITIVE DEVELOPMENT

Standard Theory
see GENERATIVE THEORY

state anxiety
see ANXIETY

stereotype
a term referring to a linguistic variable which is a widely recognized characterization of the speech of a particular group, which may or may not reflect accurately the speech of those it is supposed to represent. Our cultural milieu shapes our worldview in such a way that reality is thought to be objectively perceived through our own cultural pattern, and a differing perception is seen as either false or strange and is thus oversimplified. If people recognize and understand differing worldviews, they will usually adopt a positive and open-minded ATTITUDE toward cross-cultural differences. A closed-minded view of such differences often results in the maintenance of a stereotype—an

oversimplification and blanket assumption. A stereotype assigns group characteristics to individuals purely on the basis of their cultural membership.
The stereotype may be accurate in depicting the typical member of a culture, but it is inaccurate for describing a particular individual, simply because every person is unique and all of a person's behavioral characteristics cannot be accurately predicted on the basis of an overgeneralized median point along a continuum of cultural norms. To judge a single member of a culture by overall traits of the culture is both to prejudge and to misjudge that person. Worse, stereotypes have a way of potentially devaluing people from other cultures.
Sometimes our oversimplified concepts of members of another culture are downright false. Americans sometimes think of Japanese as being unfriendly because of their cultural norms of respect and politeness. Asian students in the perception of American students in the United States are too often lumped together under the misguided notion that many countries and cultures in Asia share much in common. Even in the TESOL literature, common stereotypes of Asian students are depicted: They (1) are obedient to authority, (2) lack critical thinking skills, and (3) do not participate in classroom interaction. Such attitudes need to be replaced by a critical awareness of the complex nature of cultural understanding.
Both learners and teachers of a second language need to understand cultural differences, to recognize openly that people are not all the same beneath the skin. Language classrooms can celebrate cultural differences, and even engage in a critical analysis of the use and origin of stereotypes.
📖 Abrams 2002; Crystal 2008; Kumaravadivelu 2003

stimulus-appraisal system
a theory of MOTIVATION involving learners assessing the emotional relevance of stimuli on the basis of their novelty, pleasantness, and relevance to their goals or needs, their ability to cope, and compatibility with their self and social image. The stimulus-appraisal system has been seen as having a neurobiological basis.
📖 Ellis 2008; Schumann 1997

strategic competence
see COMMUNICATIVE COMPETENCE

Strategy Inventory for Language Learning
see LEARNING STRATEGIES

strong interface position
another term for INTERFACE HYPOTHESIS

structuralism
also **structuralist linguistics**
the dominant linguistic model of the 1940s and 1950s, in which the linguist's task was to identify the structural characteristics of human languages by means of a rigorous application of scientific observation of the language, and using only publicly observable responses for the investigation.
📖 Brown 2007

structuralist linguistics
see STRUCTURALISM

structured input
INPUT that has been specially designed to expose learners to exemplars of a specific linguistic feature. It constitutes a technique in FORM-FOCUS INSTRUCTION.
📖 Ellis 2008

structuring
an INTAKE process which refers to the complex process that governs the establishment of mental representations of the target language (TL), and their evolution in the course of INTERLANGUAGE (IL) development. The notion of mental representation is at the heart of the process of internalization of language. It refers to how the L2 system is framed in the mind of the learner. It combines elements of 'analysis' and 'control' proposed by Bialystok. *Analysis* is connected to language knowledge, and *control* is connected to language ability. As learners begin to understand how the L2 system works, and as their mental representations of the system become more explicit and more structured, they begin to see the relationships between various linguistic categories and concepts. Control is the process that allows learners direct their attention to specific aspects of the environment or a mental representation as problems are solved in real time. In other words, the intake process of structuring helps learners construct, structure and organize the symbolic representational system of the TL by gradually making explicit the implicit knowledge that shape their IL performance. It also guides the gradual progress the learners make from *unanalyzed knowledge*, consisting of prefabricated patterns and memorized routines, to *analyzed knowledge*, consisting of propositions in which the relationship between formal and functional properties of the TL become increasingly apparent to the learners (see BIALYSTOK'S THEORY OF L2 LEARNING).
see also RESTRUCTURING, INFERENCING
📖 Bialystok 1990, 2002; Kumaravadivelu 2003; Rivers 1991

subjacency

a syntactic term related to what is called *movement*. In syntactic theory, phrases are said to move from particular locations in a sentence to a position 'higher up' in the sentence. For example, the verb kicked normally requires two arguments: an agent (the kicker) and a theme (the kickee). In English, these are usually realized as subjects and objects, respectively. In addition, subjects normally precede verbs in English while objects normally follow: *John kicked the ball*. When asking a Wh-question about this particular event, we might say *What did John kick?* Intuitively, we know that *what* is an object in this sentence, and we can state the question another way: *John kicked what?* Clearly, these two forms of questions are related, and *what* is the object of the verb in each one. What syntacticians say is that in the *What did John kick?* version, the *what* has moved out of its normal position to occupy a position higher up in the sentence. This is called Wh-movement.

However, there are restrictions on movement that keep phrases from traveling too far from their origin ('too far' meaning how many syntactic boundaries they cross). For example, *Who did Mary say that the man saw?* is fine but **Who did Mary meet the man who saw* is not fine. Hidden within the structure of these two sentences are syntactic boundaries, and in the bad sentence, there are too many for the Wh-phrase to travel from its position behind the verb. It must remain 'subjacent' to the verb, hence the term subjacency. Such movements are called subjacency violations. (The concept of subjacency has evolved over the years within *syntax*, but the general point about crossing syntactic boundaries has not.)

Subjacency has been an important focus of research within SLA. A number of studies have examined to what extent L2 learners can come to know about subjacency violations. Although from a theoretical perspective all languages are capable of allowing phrases to move, not all languages actually do move phrases around. In Chinese, for example, *Who did Mary see?* is not a possible sentence. It can only be said as *Mary saw who?* with the Wh-phrase remaining in its position by the verb. The question of interest to SLA scholars is what happens with speakers of Chinese when they learn English. Clearly, they must learn that Wh-phrases can move in order to form questions, but do they acquire the abstract knowledge related to subjacency? Do they come to learn that *Who did Mary meet the man who saw?* is not permissible in English? This is an important test case for the question of parameters and parameter resetting (see universal grammar) in SLA as L1 TRANSFER can be ruled out as an intervening variable in the case of Chinese learners of English L2. A general review of the literature would yield a number of studies and analyses on this matter, and it would appear that learners can indeed acquire the subtle aspects of syntax related to subjacency, although not all do.

📖 VanPatten & Benati 2010

submersion

a term which refers to educational settings where L2 learners are required to learn in classrooms where most of the students are native speakers so that few adjustments take place. Submersion program is a program where linguistic minority children with a low-status mother tongue are forced to accept instruction through the medium of a foreign majority language with high status, in classes where some children are native speakers of the language of the instruction, where the teacher does not understand the mother tongue of the minority children, and where the majority language constitutes a threat to their mother tongue—a subtractive learning situation (see ADDITIVE BILINGUALISM).

More specifically, right from the beginning L2 learners are taught with native speakers. This can create communication problems and insecurity in the learners. If L1 support is provided, it is of the 'pull-out' kind, which stigmatizes the L2 child and also deprives learners of the opportunity to progress in content subjects. Both the content and language teachers are typically monolingual and thus unable to communicate with the learners in their L1. In some areas, the learners are actively discouraged from speaking in their L1. The students' low academic performance may reflect the low expectations that teachers often have of the students, particularly those from certain ethnic groups (e.g., Mexican American students in the United States). Reading material and subject-matter instruction in the L1 are not available, resulting in increased insecurity in the learners. Parental involvement in the school program is actually limited. There are often problems with learners' social and emotional adjustment to school. For many learners, the disjunction between L1 use in the home and L2 use at school constitutes a painful experience.

Submersion is common in Britain and the United States, where ethnic minority children are educated in mainstream classroom.

see also IMMERSION

📖 Baker 2006; Cohen & Swain 1979; Ellis 2008; Rodriguez 1982; Skuttnab-Kangas 1988

subsumption
also **meaningful learning model**

the process of relating and anchoring new material to relevant established entities in cognitive structure (see MEANINGFUL LEARNING). David Ausubel contended that learning takes place in the human organism through a meaningful process of relating new events or items to already existing cognitive concepts or propositions—hanging new items on existing cognitive pegs. Meaning is not an implicit response, but a clearly articulated and precisely differentiated conscious experience that emerges when potentially meaningful signs, symbols, concepts, or propositions are related to and incorporated within a given individuals cognitive structure on a nonarbitrary and substantive basis. It is this relatability that, according to Ausubel, accounts for a number of phenomena: the acquisition of new meanings (knowledge), retention, the psychological organization of knowledge as a hierarchical structure, and the eventual occurrence of forgetting.

The cognitive theory of learning as put forth by Ausubel is perhaps best understood by contrasting **rote learning** and **meaningful learning**. In the perspective of rote learning, the concept of meaningful learning takes on new significance. Ausubel described rote learning as the process of acquiring material as discrete and relatively isolated entities that are relatable to cognitive structure only in an arbitrary and verbatim fashion, not permitting the establishment of meaningful relationships. That is, rote learning involves the mental storage of items having little or no association with existing cognitive structure. Most of us, for example, can learn a few necessary phone numbers and ZIP codes by rote without reference to cognitive hierarchical organization.

On the other hand, meaningful learning, or subsumption, may be described as a process of relating and anchoring new material to relevant established entities in cognitive structure. As new material enters the cognitive field, it interacts with, and is appropriately subsumed under, a more inclusive conceptual system. The very fact that material is subsumable, that is, relatable to stable elements in cognitive structure, accounts for its meaningfulness. If we think of cognitive structure as a system of building blocks, then rote learning is the process of acquiring isolated blocks with no particular function in the building of a structure and no relationship to other blocks. Meaningful learning is the process whereby blocks become an integral part of already established categories or systematic clusters of blocks.

Any learning situation can be meaningful if (1) learners have a meaningful learning set—that is, a disposition to relate the new learning task to what they already know—and (2) the learning task itself is potentially meaningful to the learners—that is, relatable to the learners' structure of knowledge. The second method of establishing meaningfulness—manufacturing meaningfulness—is a potentially powerful factor in human learning. We can make things meaningful if necessary and if we are strongly motivated to do so. Students cramming for an examination often invent a mnemonic device for remembering a list of items; the meaningful retention of the device successfully retrieves the whole list of items.

The distinction between rote and meaningful learning may not at first appear to be important since in either case material can be learned. But the significance of the distinction becomes clear when we consider the relative efficiency of the two kinds of learning in terms of retention, or LONG-TERM MEMORY. We cannot say, of course, that meaningfully learned material is never forgotten. But in the case of such learning, forgetting takes place in a much more intentional and purposeful manner because it is a continuation of the very process of subsumption by which one learns; forgetting is really a second or 'obliterative' stage of subsumption, characterized as memorial reduction to the least common denominator. Because it is more economical and less burdensome to retain a single inclusive concept than to remember a large number of more specific items, the importance of a specific item tends to be incorporated into the generalized meaning of the larger item. In this obliterative stage of subsumption, the specific items become progressively less identifiable as entities in their own right until they are finally no longer available and are said to be forgotten. It is this second stage of subsumption that operates through **cognitive pruning** procedures. Pruning is the elimination of unnecessary clutter and a clearing of the way for more material to enter the cognitive field, in the same way that pruning a tree ultimately allows greater and fuller growth. Using the building-block analogy, one might say that, at the outset, a structure made of blocks is seen as a few individual blocks, but as 'nucleation' begins to give the structure a perceived shape, some of the single blocks achieve less and less identity in their own right and become subsumed into the larger structure. Finally, the single blocks are lost to perception, or pruned out, to use the metaphor, and the total structure is perceived as a single whole without clearly defined parts.

An important aspect of the pruning stage of learning is that subsumptive forgetting, or pruning, is not haphazard or chance—it is systematic. Thus, by promoting optimal pruning procedures, we have a potential learning situation that will produce retention beyond that normally expected under more traditional theories of forgetting.

Subsumption theory provides a strong theoretical basis for the rejection of conditioning models of practice and repetition in language teaching. In a meaningful process like second language learning, mindless repetition, imitation, and other rote practices in the language classroom have no place. The Audiolingual Method, which emerged as a widely used and accepted method of foreign language teaching, was based almost exclusively on a behavioristic theory of conditioning that relied heavily on rote learning. The mechanical 'stamping in' of the language through saturation with little reference to meaning is seriously challenged by subsumption theory. Rote learning can be effective on a short-term basis, but for any long-term retention it fails because of the tremendous buildup of interference.

The notion that forgetting is systematic also has important implications for language learning and teaching. In the early stages of language learning, certain devices (definitions, paradigms, illustrations, or rules) are often used to facilitate subsumption. These devices can be made initially meaningful by assigning or 'manufacturing' meaningfulness. But in the process of making language automatic, the devices serve only as interim entities, meaningful at a low level of subsumption, and then they are systematically pruned out at later stages of language learning. We might thus better achieve the goal of COMMUNICATIVE COMPETENCE by removing unnecessary barriers to automaticity. A definition, mnemonic device, or a paraphrase, for example, might

be initially facilitative, but as its need is minimized by larger and more global conceptualizations, it is pruned.
📖 Anderson & Ausubel 1965; Ausubel 1963, 1964, 1965, 1968; Brown 1972, 2007; Smith 1975

subtractive bilingualism
see ADDITIVE BILINGUALISM

successive bilingualism
another term for SEQUENTIAL BILINGUALISM

symmetrical bilingualism
see BALANCED BILINGUALISM

sympathy
see EMPATHY

syntactic parsing
another term for PARSING

systematic style
see REFLECTIVE STYLE

systematic variation
see VARIABILITY

systemic linguistics
a model for analyzing language in terms of the interrelated systems of choices that are available for expressing meaning, developed by Halliday in the late 1950s. Basic to the approach is the notion, ultimately derived from the anthropologist Malinowski, that language structures cannot be idealized and studied without taking into account the circumstances of their use, including the extralinguistic social context. From this functional view, language acquisition needs to be seen as the mastery of linguistic functions. Learning one's mother tongue is learning the uses of language, and the meanings, or rather the meaning potential, associated with them. The structures, the words and the sounds are the realization of this meaning potential. Learning language is learning how to mean. To relate this notion to the question about what language learners essentially acquire, in Halliday's view it is not a system of rules which govern language structure, but rather 'meaning potential'—what the speaker/hearer can (what he can mean, if you like), not what he knows'. The process of acquisition consists of mastering certain basic functions of language and developing a meaning potential for each. Halliday describes the evolution of the following pragmatic functions in early L1 acquisition

(he calls them functions of language as a whole), which are universal for children:

1) The **instrumental function** (also called *I want function*) serves to manipulate the environment, to cause certain events to happen. Sentences like *This court finds you guilty, On your mark, get set, go!* or *Don't touch the stove* have an instrumental function; they are communicative acts that have a specific perlocutionary force; they bring about a particular condition.
2) The **regulatory function** (also called *do as I tell you function*) of language is the control of events. While such control is sometimes difficult to distinguish from the instrumental function, regulatory functions of language are not so much the 'unleashing' of certain power as the maintenance of control. *I pronounce you guilty and sentence you to three years in prison* serves an instrumental function, but the sentence *Upon good behavior, you will be eligible for parole in 10 months* serves more of a regulatory function. The regulations of encounters among people—approval, disapproval, behavior control, setting laws and rules—are all regulatory features of language.
3) The **representational function** (also called *I've got something to tell you function*) is the use of language to make statements, convey facts and knowledge, explain, or report—that is, to 'represent' reality as one sees it. *The sun is hot, The president gave a speech last night*, or even *The world is flat* all serve representational functions, although the last representation may be highly disputed.
4) The **interactional function** (also called *me and you function*) of language serves to ensure social maintenance. *Phatic communion*, Malinowski's term referring to the communicative contact between and among human beings that simply allows them to establish social contact and to keep channels of communication open, is part of the interactional function of language. Successful interactional communication requires knowledge of slang, jargon, jokes, folklore, cultural mores, politeness and formality expectations, and other keys to social exchange.
5) The **personal function** (also called *here I come function*) allows a speaker to express feelings, emotions, personality, 'gut-level' reactions. A person's individuality is usually characterized by his use of the personal function of communication. In the personal nature of language, cognition, affect, and culture all interact.
6) The **heuristic function** (also called *tell me why function*) involves language used to acquire knowledge, to learn about the environment. Heuristic functions are often conveyed in the form of questions that will lead to answers. Children typically make good use of the heuristic function in

their incessant 'why' questions about the world around them. Inquiry is a heuristic method of eliciting representations of reality from others.
7) The **imaginative function** (also called *let's pretend function*) serves to create imaginary systems or ideas. Telling fairy tales, joking, or writing a novel are all uses of the imaginative function. Poetry, tongue twisters, puns, and other instances of the pleasurable uses of language also fall into the imaginative function. Through the imaginative dimensions of language we are free to go beyond the real world to soar to the heights of the beauty of language itself, and through that language to create impossible dreams if we so desire.

These seven different functions of language are neither discrete nor mutually exclusive. A single sentence or conversation might incorporate many different functions simultaneously. Yet it is the understanding of how to use linguistic forms to achieve these functions of language that comprises the crux of second language learning. A learner might acquire correct word order, syntax, and lexical items, but not understand how to achieve a desired and intended function through careful selection of words, structure, intonation, nonverbal signals, and astute perception of the context of a particular stretch of discourse.
One application of Halliday's model to the study of SLA comes with seeing L2 learning as a process of adding multilingual meaning potential to what has already been achieved in L1. It is argued that second language acquisition is largely a matter of learning new linguistic forms to fulfill the same functions (as already acquired and used in L1) within a different social milieu.
📖 Halliday 1973; Brown 2007; Saville-Troike 2006

T

tandem learning
a term which takes its name from the idea that speakers of different languages may work closely together (i.e., 'in tandem') to learn one another's language and culture through a reciprocal exchange of language. Ideally, both partners should benefit equally from the exchange. Partners are responsible for establishing their own learning goals and deciding on methods and materials. Tandem learning may take place in face-to-face situations or by telephone or on-line, synchronously or asynchronously. Forms of tandem learning may also be called 'language exchange' or 'language buddies', or other terms which convey the reciprocal and autonomous nature of the learning.
📖 Macaro et al. 2010

target language
see SECOND LANGUAGE

target-like use analysis
see OBLIGATORY OCCASION ANALYSIS

task
an activity which is designed to help achieve a particular learning goal. Various definitions of task exist. However, the essential characteristics are as follows:

1) There is a primary focus on meaning (as opposed to from).
2) There is some kind of gap (information, opinion, or reasoning), which needs to be filled through performance of the task.
3) Learners need to use their own linguistic resources to perform the task.
4) There is a clearly defined communicative outcome other than the display of correct language.

Tasks can involve any of the four language skills either in isolation or in various combinations. However, SLA researchers have been predominantly concerned with speaking tasks. Tasks, or rather the performance of them, create opportunities for learning, which can be assessed in relation to some

theory of L2 acquisition. Thus, one of the goals of SLA research has been to identify the design features and methods of implementation that influence how tasks are performed and thereby, hypothetically, afford opportunities for learning.
 Ellis 2008

task-induced variation
a blanket term used to refer to the variability in language use evident when learners are asked to perform different tasks. Ultimately, it is traceable to other sources (such as *linguistic* and *situational contexts*).
 Ellis 2008

task self-esteem
see SELF-ESTEEM

teachability hypothesis
the idea that the teachability of language is constrained by what the learner is ready to acquire. The teachability hypothesis predicts that instruction can only promote language acquisition if the INTERLANGUAGE of the L2 learner is close to the point when the structure to be taught is acquired in the natural setting so that sufficient processing prerequisites are developed. Teachability hypothesis is closely related to Pienemann's work on PROCESSABILITY THEORY and the development of OUTPUT processing procedures. According to the theory, learners develop the ability to produce certain kinds of grammatical structures over time in a hierarchical order. What this means is that learners progress from stage 1 to stage 2 to stage 3 and so on, with each stage implying the learner has traversed the stages below it—but not necessarily the stages above it. Thus, if we collect data and find evidence of stage 3 behavior in a learner, we can infer he has passed through stages 1 and 2 but we cannot infer that he is at stage 4.

Each stage is marked by particular processing procedures, and a learner must have acquired the processing procedure for each stage before going on to the next stage. The theory holds that learners cannot skip stages and thus cannot acquire processing procedures for which they are not ready. Thus, a learner cannot skip stage 4 and go from stage 3 to stage 5. That learner cannot skip the processing procedures of stage 4 to acquire those at stage 5.

This restriction on staged development and that the processing procedures for each stage are hierarchically ordered has implications for language teaching. Because learners cannot skip stages, they cannot learn and spontaneously produce grammatical structures for which they are not ready in terms of processing procedures. Teachability, then, refers to the idea that the effects of instruction are also constrained. Instruction in grammar can only make a difference if the learner is at the point at which he would naturally acquire the processing procedure needed to produce the grammatical structure in

question. In his research, Pienemann offers evidence that this is so. Learners taught structures that were too far beyond their current level of processing ability did not acquire the structures in question. In some cases, learners backslid (i.e., regressed to a previous stage), suggesting they were cognitively overloaded by the processing demands of the new structure.
 Ellis 2008; Kumaravadivelu 2006; Pienemann 1985; VanPatten & Benati 2010

teacher talk

that variety of language sometimes used by teachers when they are in the process of teaching. L2 teacher talk can be viewed as a special register, analogous to FOREIGNER TALK. Studies of teacher talk, like those of foreigner talk, have sought to describe its phonological, lexical, grammatical, and discoursal properties. The research indicates that teachers modify their speech when addressing L2 learners in the classroom in a number of ways and also that they are sensitive to their learners' general proficiency level. Many of these modifications are the same as those found in foreigner talk but some seem to reflect the special characteristics of classroom settings—in particular the need to maintain orderly communication.
see also CARETAKER SPEECH
 Chaudron 1988; Ellis 2008

telegraphic speech

strings of words (lexical morphemes without inflectional morphemes) in phrases produced by two-year-old children. Between two and two-and-a-half years old, the child begins producing a large number of utterances that could be classified as 'multiple-word' speech. The salient feature of these utterances ceases to be the number of words, but the variation in word-forms that begins to appear. This stage is described as telegraphic speech. The term derives from the written style used in the days when pay-by-the-word telegrams were a common method of communication (*Send Check Brighton*), and is still used to describe any elliptical written style (e.g., in newspaper headlines or want-ads). This stage is characterized by strings of words (lexical morphemes) in phrases or sentences such as *this shoe all wet*, *cat drink milk* and *daddy go bye-bye*. The child has clearly developed some sentence-building capacity by this stage and can get the word order correct. While this type of telegram-format speech is being produced, a number of grammatical inflections begin to appear in some of the word-forms and simple prepositions (*in*, *on*) are also used.

By the age of two-and-a-half years, the child's vocabulary is expanding rapidly and the child is initiating more talk while increased physical activity includes running and jumping. By three, the vocabulary has grown to hundreds of words and pronunciation has become closer to the form of adult language.

see also TWO-WORD STAGE, TELEGRAPHIC SPEECH
📖 Crystal 2008; Yule 2006

TESOL
Teachers of English to Speakers of Other Languages. The acronym can be used to refer both to the US-based organization of that name and to describe the teaching of English in situations where it is either a second language or a foreign language. In British usage this is more commonly referred to as ELT, i.e. English Language Teaching.
📖 Richards & Schmidt 2010

TG
an abbreviation for TRANSFORMATIONAL GRAMMAR

tip of the tongue
also TOT
a state in which a language user is aware of the existence of a particular word (perhaps a search for the word has been triggered by a *meaning code*) but cannot retrieve it from the lexicon. Studies of this phenomenon have shown that speakers generally have an accurate phonological outline of the word, can get the initial sound correct and mostly know the number of syllables in the word. This experience also mainly occurs with uncommon words and names. It suggests that our 'word-storage' system may be partially organized on the basis of some phonological information and that some words in the store are more easily retrieved than others.

When we make mistakes in this retrieval process, there are often strong phonological similarities between the target word we are trying to say and the mistake we actually produce. For example, speakers produced *secant*, *sextet* and *sexton* when asked to name a particular type of navigational instrument (*sextant*). Other examples are *fire distinguisher* (for 'extinguisher') and *transcendental medication* (instead of 'meditation'). Mistakes of this type are sometimes referred to as **malapropism**s after a character called Mrs. Malaprop (in a play by Sheridan) who consistently produced 'near-misses' for words, with great comic effect. Another comic character known for his malapropisms was Archie Bunker, who once suggested that *We need a few laughs to break up the monogamy*.

The TOT state demonstrates that it is possible to hold the meaning of a word in one's mind without necessarily being able to retrieve its form. This has suggested to commentators that a lexical entry falls into two distinct parts, one relating to form and one to meaning, and that one may be accessed without the other. In assembling speech, we first identify a given word by some kind of abstract meaning code and only later insert its actual phonological form into the utterance we are planning.
📖 Field 2004; Yule 2006

TL
an abbreviation for TARGET LANGUAGE

tolerance of ambiguity
another term for AMBIGUITY TOLERANCE

top-down processing
see BOTTOM-UP PROCESSING

topic familiarity
in SLA, a term which is most often associated with research on listening and reading comprehension. How familiar one is with a topic relates to SCHEMA THEORY, that is the complex set of mental structures in which information connected with a topic is stored. As the listener or reader of a text makes first contact with the meaning of that text through words or phrases it contains, the familiarity with the topic, triggered by those words and phrases, will be activated. The extent of activation, and the effectiveness of that activation, will depend on a number of factors which so far have been under-explored in the literature: the modality of the text (listening is more likely to involve initial levels of activation than reading); culturally linked familiarity, how the knowledge of the topic is structured; interest in the topic; learner characteristics and so on. A number of studies have suggested that, if one is familiar with a topic, comprehension is facilitated and this has led to a possible practitioner belief that all selected texts should be familiar to the learners. However, this approach may not necessarily develop comprehension skills when, 'in the real world' the topic is unfamiliar. Similarly, some authors have advocated the use of 'advance organizers' (see GRAPHIC ORGANIZERS) where topic familiarity is stimulated by the teacher in order to facilitate comprehension. Again, this may or may not develop comprehension skills in the long term. Comprehension problems may arise when anomalies in the text are not detected by the learner, that is, when later in-text evidence, which is contradictory, is ignored and initial (imprecise) topic familiarity is not monitored and moderated.
📖 Macaro et al. 2010; Tsui & Fullilove 1998

TOT
an abbreviation for TIP OF THE TONGUE

trait anxiety
see ANXIETY

transfer
also **language transfer**
the effect of one language on the learning of another. Two types of language

transfer may occur. **Positive transfer** is transfer which makes learning easier, and may occur when both the native language and the target language have the same form. For example, both French and English have the word *table*, which can have the same meaning in both languages. **Negative transfer** is the use of a native-language pattern or rule which leads to an error or inappropriate form in the target language. Negative transfer can be referred to as **interference**, in that previously learned material interferes with subsequent material—a previous item is incorrectly transferred or incorrectly associated with an item to be learned. For example, a French learner of English may produce the incorrect sentence *I am here since Monday* instead of *I have been here since Monday*, because of the transfer of the French pattern *Je suis ici depuis lundi* ('I am here since Monday').

The term transfer is closely associated with *behavioristic theories* (see BEHAVIORISM) of L2 learning. According to behaviorist theories of language learning, the main impediment to learning was interference from prior knowledge (PROACTIVE INHIBITION). In effect, the behaviorist accounts of transfer, as reflected in the CONTRASTIVE ANALYSIS HYPOTHESIS in particular, overpredict both the transferability of specific items (i.e., they fail to explain when they are transferred and when they are not), and transfer load (how much is transferred). However, it is now widely accepted that the influence of the learner's native language cannot be adequately accounted for in terms of habit formation. Transfer is not simply a matter of interference or of falling back on the native language. Nor is it just a question of the influence of the learner's native language, as other, previously acquired second language can also have an effect. This suggests that the term L1 transfer is inadequate. It is argued that a superordinate term that is theory-neutral is needed (see CROSSLINGUISTIC INFLUENCE). Increasingly, researchers have thought to identify the conditions that promote and inhibit transfer, (i.e., constraints on transfer). It is argued that constraints can involve general cognitive capacities including 'perception and memory' and 'principles of language either totally or partially independent of other human capacities', i.e., they can be cognitive or linguistic. A number of constraints have been identified: (1) social factors (the effect of the addressee and of different learning contexts on transfer), (2) MARKEDNESS (the extent to which specific linguistic features are special in some way, (3) PROTOTYPICALITY (the extent to which a specific meaning of a word is considered core or basic in relation to other meanings of the same word, (4) LANGUAGE DISTANCE and **psychotypology** (the perceptions that speakers have regarding the similarity and difference between languages), and (5) developmental factors (constraints relating to the natural processes of INTERLANGUAGE development). Nonstructural factors such as the nature of the tasks a learner is performing and individual learner differences (e.g., PERSONALITY and age) also constrain L1 transfer. Some of these factors are clearly external in nature, for example social factors, whereas

others are equally clearly internal, for example developmental factors. Other constraints, however, have both an external and internal dimension—for example, markedness and language distance/psychotypology.
see also COMMUNICATIVE INTERFERENCE, ERROR ANALYSIS
📖 Brown 2007; VanPatten & Benati 2010; Richards & Schmidt 2010

transformational-generative grammar
another term for TRANSFORMATIONAL GRAMMAR

transformational grammar
see GENERATIVE THEORY

transitional constructions
the interim language forms that learners use while they are still learning the grammar of a language. For example, before learners master the rule for English negatives, they operate with interim rules (such as 'no' + verb).
see also FIRST LANGUAGE ACQUISITION
📖 Ellis 2008

triglossia
see DIGLOSSIA

T-Unit
also **minimal terminable unit**
a measure of the linguistic complexity of sentences, defined as the shortest unit which a sentence can be reduced to, and consisting of one independent clause together with whatever dependent clauses are attached to it. The T in T-Unit stands for 'minimal terminal unit' and was introduced as a term by Hunt to measure the development of sentences in the writing of primary and secondary school children. According to Hunt, each T-Unit contains one independent clause and its dependent clauses. In his terms, they are the shortest units into which a piece of discourses can be cut without leaving any sentence fragments as residue. Hunt found that the mean length of T-Unit (MLTU), obtained by dividing the number of T-Units into the total number of words in the writing sample, was a reliable measure of syntactic complexity and that gradual lengthening occurred from grade to grade. Examples of two types of T-Units are given below:

1) There was a little boy next door who had a red bicycle. [S (S)] = 1 T unit.
2) There was a little boy next door, and he had a red bicycle. (S + S) = 2 T units.

In example 1, a clause (in this case a relative clause) is embedded in an independent main clause, giving the sentence one T-Unit. In example 2, two (it could be more) independent clauses (with subjects and finite verbs) are conjoined giving the sentences two T-Units.

T-Units have been widely used in SLA research to track the development of syntactic complexity and accuracy in second language learners, in both oral and written production. Measures include words per T-Unit (usually as mean), correct T-Units (and number of words) and clauses per T-Unit. T-Unit analysis has been criticized for the artificial way in which it breaks up coordinated clauses and thereby ignores what might be sophisticated rhetorical structure in adult second language writers.

📖 Bardovi-Harlig 1992; Hunt 1965, 1970; Macaro et al. 2010; Richards & Schmidt 2010

turn-taking

in a conversation, conventions in which participants allow appropriate opportunities for others to talk, or 'take the floor'. Turn-taking is the set of practices through which conversation is organized and is therefore an important aspect of CONVERSATION ANALYSIS. Patterns of turn-taking were first described following a study of the use of English in telephone conversations and group talk, although turn-taking mechanisms may vary between cultures or between languages. In English-speaking societies, turn-taking usually means that in a conversation one participant speaks at a time. The first speaker, A, speaks and then stops. The next speaker, B, speaks and then stops, so there is a conversational pattern that looks like this: A-B-A-B-A-B.

Rules that govern turn-taking constitute a *local management system*. In this system, speakers compete over a scarce resource, namely, the control of the *floor*. The floor here refers to the right to speak and be listened to. The speakers share the floor by taking turns to utilize it. The minimal units by which turns are shared are called *turn-construction units*, and they are made up of sentences, clauses or phrases. They are identified in part by prosodic features such as intonation. The end of such a unit marks the point at which speakers may change. This point is known as the *transition relevance place*. The transition relevance place does not mean that speakers must or will change at that point. It simply means that it is possible, at that point, for speakers to change.

There are rules that govern speaker change or how the floor is shared in the course of an interaction. This has to do with speaker selection. When A is the current speaker and B is the next speaker:

1) If A selects B in the current turn, then A must stop speaking and B must speak next. Transition occurs at the first transition relevance place after B's selection.
2) If A does not select B, then any (other) party may self-select, the first speaker gaining rights to the floor then makes a contribution.

3) If A has not selected B, and no other party self-selects, A may (but need not) continue speaking. In other words, he may claim the right to the next turn constructional unit but does not have to.

The pattern then repeats itself. These rules mean that generally only one person speaks at a time. Overlaps can occur as competing first starts. Alternatively, they may occur where a transition relevance place has been misprojected, such as where a tag or address term has been appended.
Conversation analysts may be interested in cases where turn-taking appears to break down, as this may indicate something important is happening in the conversation. They may also examine how participants orient to such breakdowns and attempt to repair them. In addition, an analysis of turn allocation in conversation can reveal a lot about the relative power of speakers and can therefore be utilized in *critical discourse analysis*.
📖 Baker & Ellece 2011; Levinson 1983; Sacks et al. 1974

two-word stage
a period in FIRST LANGUAGE ACQUISITION beginning at around 18-20 months when children produce two terms together as an utterance. Depending on what we count as an occurrence of two distinct words used together, the two-word stage can begin around eighteen to twenty months, as the child's vocabulary moves beyond fifty words. By the time the child is two years old, a variety of combinations, similar to *baby chair, mommy eat, cat bad*, will usually have appeared. The adult interpretation of such combinations is, of course, very much tied to the context of their utterance. The phrase *baby chair* may be taken as an expression of possession (= this is baby's chair), or as a request (= put baby in chair), or as a statement (= baby is in the chair), depending on different circumstances.
Whatever it is that the child actually intends to communicate through such expressions, the significant functional consequences are that the adult behaves as if communication is taking place. That is, the child not only produces speech, but receives FEEDBACK confirming that the utterance worked as a contribution to the interaction. Moreover, by the age of two, whether the child is producing 200 or 300 distinct 'words', he will be capable of understanding five times as many, and will typically be treated as an entertaining conversational partner by the principal CAREGIVER.
see also ONE-WORD STAGE, TELEGRAPHIC SPEECH, PIVOT GRAMMAR
📖 Yule 2006

typological universals
also **language universals, linguistic universals**
principles of language valid for all languages. Within the framework of UNIVERSAL GRAMMAR, universals are abstract principles that apply to all languages. These are generally derived by deduction as scholars examine how a

language behaves and then posit generalizations that can later be checked against other languages. In the framework of linguistic typology, however, universals are less abstract and are based on readily observable data. Such universals are determined by surveying world's languages and then arriving at a conclusion about what might constitute a universal. Typological universals are identified by examining a representative sample of natural languages in order to identify features that are common to all or most of these languages. A typological approach to linguistic analysis involves a crosslinguistic comparison of specific features such as articles, word order or relative clause construction. It provides a basis for identifying both which features are rare in a particular language (e.g., the use of inversion after initial adverbials in English), and also which features are common.

Various kinds of commonalities have been identified. There are a number of unrestricted or *absolute* universals, which are exemplified in all languages. For example, all languages have nouns and verbs and vowels and consonants. However, there are probably few such universals, universal *tendencies* being much more common. A specific feature may be found in a large number of languages, but be missing from some.

Cutting across the distinction between absolute universals and universal tendencies is the distinction between *implicational* and *non-implicational* universals. Frequently, crosslinguistic comparisons demonstrate that there are connections between two or more features, such that the presence of one feature implies the presence of another or others. Implicational universals take the form of 'if/then' statements. These can be 'simple' or 'complex'. A simple implicational universal involves a connection between just two features. For example, if a language has a noun before a demonstrative, then it has a noun before a relative clause. A complex implicational universal involves a relationship between several features. For example, if a language is SOV, then if the adjective precedes the noun, then the genitive precedes the noun.

More specifically, the two characteristics of absoluteness and implicationalness determine universals of four types:

1) ABSOLUTE NON-IMPLICATIONAL UNIVERSALS
2) NON-IMPLICATIONAL UNIVERSAL TENDENCIES
3) ABSOLUTE IMPLICATIONAL UNIVERSALS
4) IMPLICATIONAL UNIVERSAL TENDENCIES

Typological universals are important in SLA research because research has demonstrated that L2 learners' linguistic systems seem to obey typological universals during development, and such universals may even constrain their development, especially constraining the influence of the L1. For example, learners may acquire subject relative clauses before object relative clauses but never object relative clauses before subject relative clauses. Or, they may produce more errors with object relative clauses than with subject relative clauses. Learners might have more difficulty with the production of voiced consonants at the ends of words than voiceless consonants, and we would expect words ending in voiceless consonants to be 'easier' to acquire and produce than words ending in voiced consonants.

see also UNIVERSAL GRAMMAR, MARKEDNESS

📖 Ellis 2008; Hudson 2000; VanPatten & Benati 2010

U

UG
an abbreviation for UNIVERSAL GRAMMAR

ultimate attainment
another term for FINAL STATE

unanalyzed knowledge
see BIALYSTOK'S THEORY OF L2 LEARNING

underextension
see OVEREXTENSION

Unified Model
see COMPETITION MODEL

Universal Grammar
also **UG**
a linguistic theory proposed by Chomsky which attempts to account for the GRAMMATICAL COMPETENCE of every language user, regardless of which language he speaks. The term Universal Grammar (UG) is used in two ways:

a) A mechanism which is innate in human beings and which sensitizes an infant to the features which characterize all languages, thus giving it a head start in the process of acquiring its own. Some accounts see UG as part of a *maturational* process, with awareness of the characteristics of language gradually unfolding as the child develops. Others assume that it is fully present, *hard-wired*, from the start, but that the child is not able to take full advantage of it because of its limited cognitive development.

b) The linguistic content of such a mechanism, a set of phonological, syntactic and lexical features which are shared by all languages. The content of UG falls into two categories: *principles* which are true universals, occurring in all (or nearly all) languages, and *parameters*, which are universal to the extent that they occur across languages in one form or another (see PRINCIPLES AND PARAMETERS). An example of the latter is the *pro-drop parameter* which specifies whether a language employs an obligatory subject pronoun (*She speaks English*) or is able to omit it (*Parla inglese*). Another example is seen in the fact that languages with a standard VO (verb + direct object) word order make use of certain syntactic patterns which differentiate them sharply from those with an OV (direct object + verb) order. These patterns constitute a set of '*If . . . then*' features—meaning that if a language has one, it is likely to manifest most or all of the others.

There are two broad approaches to the quest for evidence of universals. The Chomskyan approach is based upon putting to the test a detailed theoretical model. Researchers might ask adult subjects to make *grammaticality judgments*, deciding whether a particular string of words is or is not acceptable. These judgments are said to tap in to competence and are preferred to evidence of actual speech production, which would reflect PERFORMANCE. An alternative typological approach examines evidence across many languages in order to trace similarities.

There is a broad measure of agreement that the following are universal:

- some lexical categories (noun and verb);
- *structure-dependency*;
- phrases containing a head of the same type as the phrase;
- a phrase structure consisting of *Specifier*, *Head* and *Complement*.

UG theory accepts that languages may deviate to some degree from the universal pattern. A language user's competence is said to consist of a *core grammar* of universal principles and parameters and a *periphery* of features specific to the language in question, which cannot be explained by reference to UG. They might be survivals from an earlier stage of the language, loans from other languages or fixed idioms. The relationship between core grammar and periphery is best described as a cline, with central UG characteristics defined as *unmarked* and features that fall outside UG as progressively more and more *marked* (see MARKEDNESS). When acquiring a language, the child comes to recognize that some features of the target language do not conform to the criteria specified by UG, and have to be mastered by a process which is independent of the normal acquisition route.

Chomsky himself recognizes that cognitive constraints such as SHORT-TERM MEMORY restrictions may have an impact upon performance, limiting what the child is capable of achieving with its innately acquired UG. For example, the absence of a subject pronoun in much early English speech might indicate a parameter setting which initially favors a pro-drop pattern; but it might equally well indicate a cognitive inability to process more than two words. A useful distinction has been made between *language acquisition*, which is supported by UG, and *language development*, in which cognitive factors play a part.

Although UG is pretty much accepted as part of the child's L1 language making capacity, its status in SLA has been hotly debated. There are a number of logical possibilities concerning its role in SLA. One is that it is essentially the same as for L1 acquisition. Another is that it is different because L2 learners achieve variable success. A third is that it is different because L2 competence is qualitatively different from L1 competence. These positions lead to different views regarding the role of UG in L2 acquisition. These are (1) the COMPLETE ACCESS VIEW, (2) the NO ACCESS VIEW, (3) the PARTIAL ACCESS VIEW, and (4) the DUAL ACCESS VIEW.

📖 Ellis 1997; Chomsky 1965; Cook & Newson 2007; Crain & Lillo-Martin 1999; Field 2004; O'Grady 1997; Radford 1990; Richards & Schmidt 2010; White 2003

unplanned discourse
see VARIABILITY

uptake
also **learner uptake**
a student utterance that immediately follows a teacher's FEEDBACK and that constitutes a reaction in some way to the teacher's intention to draw attention to some aspect of the student's initial utterance (this overall intention is clear to the student although the teacher's specific linguistic focus may not be). Uptake is used to describe a stage in a process of potential language acquisition and is a student 'move' during interaction. It is a signal, of whatever kind, that demonstrates to the teacher or the researcher that the student has noticed an element in the interaction. If there is no uptake, then there is topic continuation, which is initiated by either the same or another student (in both cases, the teacher's intention goes unheeded) or by the teacher (in which case the teacher has not provided an opportunity for uptake).

Whereas the early research focused on addressing key theoretical issues and describing the corrective practices of teachers, later research has attempted to investigate whether corrective feedback is uptaken by learners and whether it actually assists acquisition.

There are two types of student uptake: (a) '**repair**' (i.e., the student's utterance successfully repairs the initial problem) and (b) 'needs repair' (i.e., the student's response fails to successfully repair the initial utterance and still needs repair). A number of ways students perform these two types of uptake are distinguished (see Table U.1). The needs-repair category can lead to additional feedback from the teacher and thus allows for error treatment sequences to go beyond the third turn.

Following repair, teachers often seize the moment to reinforce the correct form before proceeding to topic continuation by making short statements of approval such as, *Yes!*, *That's it!*, and *Bravo!* or by repeating the student's corrected utterance.

📖 Ellis 2008; Kim & Han 2007; Lyster 1998a; Lyster & Ranta 1997; Macaro et al. 2010

A. Repair
1) Repetition (i.e., the student repeats the teacher's feedback).
2) Incorporation (i.e., the student incorporates repetition of the correct form in a longer utterance).
3) Self-repair (i.e., the student corrects the error in response to the teacher feedback that did not supply the correct form).
4) Peer-repair (i.e., a student other than the student who produced the error corrects it in response to teacher feedback).
B. Needs repair
1) Acknowledgement (e.g., a student says 'yes' or 'no' in response to the teacher's feedback).
2) Same error (i.e., the student produces the same error again).
3) Different error (i.e., the student fails to correct the original error and in addition produces a different error).
4) Off target (i.e., the student responds by circumventing the teacher's linguistic focus).
5) Hesitation (i.e., the student hesitates in response to the teacher feedback).
6) Partial repair (i.e., the student partly corrects the initial error).

Table U.1. Types of uptake following corrective feedback

U-shaped acquisition
another term for U-SHAPED DEVELOPMENT

U-shaped development
also **U-shaped acquisition, U-shaped learning**
a process in first and second language acquisition where a syntactic feature appears to have been acquired but is later used or formed incorrectly. In U-shaped development, learners often go through three distinct phases, where they can initially manifest accurate performance, then show a decrease in their performance, which in turn is followed by a progression in learning. Viewed on a graph, with time on the *X* axis, and accuracy on the *Y*, this 'accurate, less accurate, accurate' pattern resembles a U shape, hence the term 'U-shaped function'. Often quoted is a finding that many children use the correct irregular past tense forms in English (*went, fell*) but then go on to use incorrect forms in *-ed* (*wented, goed, falled*). In due course, the correct form is restored.

Initial mastery of language may well be holistic: the child acquiring inflected words as individual units without recognizing the system that links, for example, *walked* to its stem *walk*. Similarly, irregular forms such as *broke* or *went* are probably first acquired as if they were simple items of vocabulary. However, at some stage, the child comes to recognize that morphology is

358 U-shaped learning

rule-governed. Its reaction is then to overgeneralize (see OVERGENERALIZATION) the rules it has extrapolated ('for past tense, add -*ed*'), replacing irregular forms with regularized ones. In time, evidence from adult speech leads it to restrict the application of the -*ed* rule and to reinstate the irregular forms.

A connectionist (see CONNECTIONISM) computer program has simulated the trial-and-error learning of regular and irregular past tense forms in English. The learning process manifested exactly the kind of U-shaped development that has been observed naturalistically.

McLaughlin among others presents a view of SLA where learners are acquiring a complex skill, as in other domains of cognition, which requires constant RESTRUCTURING where subskills for different tasks are integrated and become more automatic. This restructuring can often result in a U-shaped function on many features and aspects of L2 lexical and syntactic development.

📖 Field 2004; Macaro et al. 2010; McLaughlin 1987

U-shaped learning

another term for U-SHAPED DEVELOPMENT

V

variability
also **variation**

instability in learners' linguistic systems. As learners produce language, they may not be consistent in what they do. Although sometimes they might produce a form or structure accurately in a consistent manner or they might produce it inaccurately in a consistent manner, very often learners vacillate. That is, during a given time frame, they may produce something both accurately and inaccurately, and even their inaccurate productions might vary in terms of what they produce. This behavior is known as variability or variation in the INTERLANGUAGE. For example, a learner might produce the following two utterances during the same game of bingo: *No look my card* and *Don't look my card*.

There are several possible approaches that account for the apparent contradiction between variation and systematicity in learner language. The first approach is that practiced by linguists in the Chomskyan tradition, who adopt what Tarone has called a '*homogeneous competence model*'. In this approach variation is seen as a feature of performance rather than of the learner's underlying knowledge system. The type of data often preferred by researchers who operate within the homogeneous competence paradigm consist of speakers' intuitions regarding what they think is correct in the L2 rather than actual instances of language use. In effect, then, variability is either discounted in this paradigm as simply as 'slips' or 'performance errors' or, in some case explained in terms of multiple competencies.

The second approach is *sociolinguistic* in orientation. Sociolinguists such as Labov view a speaker's competence as itself inherently variable. They identify two major sources of variability. **Internal variation** arises as a result of linguistic factors that condition which specific variant of a linguistic form a speaker selects. For example, whether syllable simplification takes place, depends in part on whether the consonant cluster is integral to a content word (e.g., *mist*) or arises as a result of a grammatical inflection (e.g., *missed*), with final consonant deletion more likely in the latter than the former. **External variation** arises as a result of social factors that lead a speaker to select one form rather than another. The influence of social factors such as age, gender, and social class is evident in both different varieties of language preferred by groups of speakers (i.e., in inter-speaker variation) and also in stylistic variation within the performance of a single speaker in different social contexts (i.e., in intra-speaker variation). SLA researchers who adopt a sociolinguistic orientation prefer to work with data (often multiple sets of data) that reflect actual instances of language use. In this approach, the problem of variability is addressed by demonstrating that it is systematic. The third approach is *psycholinguistic*. Psycholinguistic processing models seek to account for the variation that results from factors that influence the learner's ability to process L2 knowledge under different conditions of use. For example, systematic differences in performance have been found to exist in learner language depending on whether it is *planned* or *unplanned*. Researchers in this tradition collect samples of language use elicited under experimental conditions. They seek to show that planning variability is systematic and to explain it in terms of mental processing. However, the distinction between the psycholinguistic and sociolinguistic approaches is not clear-cut, as sociolinguists such as Labov have evoked the notion of ATTENTION to account for the variability evident when speakers switch styles depending on the addressee. Labov appeared to view attention as a global sort of activity rather than as involving a conscious focus on the variable in question. Thus, attention can be viewed as both a psycholinguistic and sociolinguistic construct.

The following, as shown in Figure V.1, is a typology of the different kinds of formal variation that can be found in the use of natural language—including learner language. The typology addresses variation in choice of linguistic form. It excludes functional variation (i.e., variation in the choice of language function).

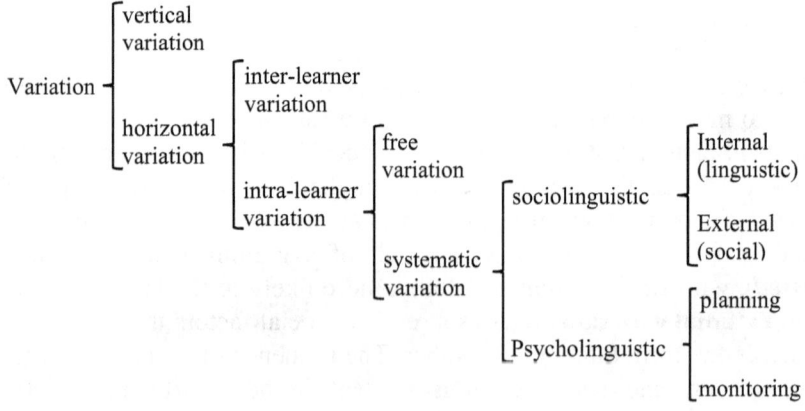

Figure V.1. *A typology of variation in the choice of linguistic form found in learner language*

A basic distinction is made between **horizontal** and **vertical variation**. Horizontal variation refers to the variation evident in learner language at a particular moment or stage in a learner's development, while vertical variation refers to the differences in learner language evident from one time to another. It reflects the development that is taking place in the learner's interlanguage. Horizontal variation is subdivided into **inter-** and **intra-learner variation**. Inter-learner variability reflects individual learner factors such as MOTIVATION and PERSONALITY, but it is also arises as a result of social factors such as social class and ethnic grouping, as the Labovian paradigm has demonstrated, and as a result of psycholinguistic factors, such as WORKING MEMORY. As these same social and psycholinguistic factors are also involved in intra-learner variation, there is clearly an interaction between individual learner factors such as sex, social class, and working memory and the situational factors involved in style shifting.

Intra-learner variation can take the form of either **free variation** or **systematic variation**. Free variation arises when linguistic choices occur randomly, making it impossible to predict when a learner will use one form as opposed to another. The existence of free variation in learner language is, however, controversial. Many sociolinguists consider that free variation does not exist or that it occurs for only a very short period of time and is of minor interest. Systematic variation occurs when it is possible to identify some factor that predisposes a learner to select one specific linguistic form over another. Systematic variation is evident in form-function analyses that demonstrate that, at any one time of development, learners' grammars reflect particular configurations of form-function mapping. That is, learners organize their linguistic system in such a way that specific forms are used to realize specific language functions. Thus, the choice of one linguistic form in preference to another is determined by the language function the learner wishes to perform. Systematic variation is conditioned by both sociolinguistic and psycholinguistic factors. Sociolinguistic accounts of variation distinguish internal and external sources. Internal variation is determined by linguistic contexts (i.e., the elements that precede and follow the variable structure in question) and other linguistic factors such as MARKEDNESS. External variation is accounted for in terms of the social factors that are configured in different situational contexts of language use that conspire to categorically or probabilistically influence the learner's choice of linguistic forms. The situational context covers a whole host of factors (e.g., time, topic, purpose, and tone). Psycholinguistic sources of variability include the means learners use to control their linguistic resources (i.e., planning and monitoring) under different conditions of language use.

see also ACCOMMODATION THEORY, PROCESSABILITY THEORY, GRADUAL DIFFUSION MODEL

Ellis 1985, 2008; Labov 1970; Macaro et al. 2010; Tarone 1983; VanPatten & Benati 2010

Variable Competence Model

a theory of L2 acquisition developed by Ellis which seeks to account for the VARIABILITY evident in learner language (INTERLANGUAGE) by positing that this reflects a competence that is itself variable (i.e., it contains variable rules or different styles). The model is based on two distinctions—one of which refers to the process of language *use*, and the other to the *product*. The theory also proposes to account for SLA within a framework of language use. In other words, it claims that the way a language is learned is a reflection of the way it is used. The product of language use comprises a continuum of discourse types ranged from entirely unplanned to entirely planned. **Unplanned discourse** is discourse that lacks forethought and preparation. It is associated with spontaneous communication, e.g., everyday conversation or brainstorming in writing. **Planned discourse** is discourse that is thought out prior to expression. It requires conscious thought and the opportunity to work out content and expression. Examples are a prepared lecture or careful writing. The *process* of language use is to be understood in terms of the distinction between linguistic knowledge (or *rules*) and the ability to make use of this knowledge (*procedures*). The language user possesses procedures for realizing the meaning potential of rules in context. In other words, the language user makes his knowledge of linguistic rules work by exploiting them in relationship to both the situational and linguistic context. He actualizes his abstract knowledge of sentences to create utterances in discourse.

If follows from this view of the process of language use that the product (i.e., the different types of discourse) is the result of either or both of following:

1) a variable competence, i.e., the user possesses a heterogeneous rule system;
2) variable application of procedures for actualizing knowledge in discourse.

The Variable Competence Model of SLA claims that both (1) and (2) occur. Furthermore, it claims that they are related.

The variability of the learner's rule system is described with reference to Bialystok's dual distinction between *automatic/nonautomatic* and *analyzed/unanalyzed* (see BIALYSTOK'S THEORY OF L2 LEARNING). The first distinction concerns the relative access that the learner has to L2 knowledge. Knowledge that can be retrieved easily and quickly is autonomous. Knowledge that takes time and effort to retrieve is nonautomatic. The second distinction concerns the extent to which the learner possesses a propositional mental representation which makes clear the structure of the knowledge and its relationship to other aspects of knowledge. Both automatic/nonautomatic and the analyzed/unanalyzed distinctions represent continua rather than dichotomies. There are degrees of automatic and analyzed knowledge.

Knowledge is activated for use by means of processes, which, again, are distinguished according to whether they are primary or secondary. Each set of processes has an external and internal representation, referred to as discourse and cognitive processes respectively. Primary processes are responsible for engaging in unplanned discourse. They draw on knowledge that is relatively unanalyzed and automatic. Secondary processes come into play in planned discourse and draw on knowledge towards the analyzed end of the continuum. An example of a primary process is *semantic simplification* (i.e., the omission of elements from a proposition in production). An example of a secondary process is MONITORING (i.e., the editing of language performance). Primary and secondary processes account for how L2 learners actualize their linguistic knowledge in discourse. They account for the variability of language-learner language by positing that both different types of knowledge and different procedures are involved in the construction of different discourse types. They also account for acquisition.

Thus, for example, early SLA is characterized by the heavy use of semantic simplification, because this is a procedure that requires little L2 knowledge. Later procedures, such as those used to reduce reliance on shared knowledge and no-verbal devices, by making explicit the relationship between one proposition and another and between each proposition and its situational context, are characteristic of later SLA. Also knowledge that to begin with is available only for use via secondary processes (because it exists only in processes and so used in unplanned as well as planned discourse.

To summarize, the Variable Competence Model proposes

1) There is a single knowledge store containing variable interlanguage rules according to how automatic and how analyzed the rules are.
2) The learner possesses a capacity for language use which consists of primary and secondary discourse and cognitive processes.
3) L2 performance is variable as a result of whether primary processes employing unanalyzed L2 rules are utilized in unplanned discourse, or secondary processes employing analyzed L2 rules are utilized in planned discourse.
4) L2 development occurs as a result of
    a) acquisition of new L2 rules through participation in various types of discourse (i.e., new rules originate in the application of PROCEDURAL KNOWLEDGE);
    b) activation of L2 rules which initially exist either in nonautomatic unanalyzed form or in an analyzed form so they can be used in unplanned discourse.

364 variation

see also MULTIDIMENSIONAL MODEL, COMPETITION MODEL, CAPABILITY CONTINUUM PARADIGM, MONITOR MODEL, SOCIO-PSYCHOLINGUISTIC MODEL, ACCULTURATION MODEL, NATIVIZATION MODEL, FUNCTIONALIST MODEL
📖 Ellis 1984a, 1986, 2008; Bialystok 1982

variation
another term for VARIABILITY

verbal deficit hypothesis
another term for DEFICIT HYPOTHESIS

vernacular style
see CAPABILITY CONTINUUM PARADIGM

vertical variation
see VARIABILITY

visual learner
a learner who finds it easier to learn things when they see them written down, rather than simply hearing them (an AUDITORY LEARNER). Visual learners tend to prefer reading and studying charts, drawings, and other graphic information.
see also AUDITORY LEARNER, KINAESTHETIC LEARNER
📖 Ellis 2008; Reid 1987; Richards & Schmidt 2010

vocabulary burst
another term for VOCABULARY SPURT

vocabulary explosion
another term for VOCABULARY SPURT

vocabulary spurt
also **vocabulary burst, vocabulary explosion**
a sudden rapid increase in the vocabulary produced by a child, which usually begins during the second half of the second year of life. At the time the spurt occurs, the child usually has a productive vocabulary of around 50 to 100 words; this may rise to as many as 350 to 500 over a relatively short period of time. While many of the new words are nouns, the spurt results in a much higher overall proportion of verbs and adjectives in the child's vocabulary than before.
The precise cause of the spurt is unknown. One explanation is that the child has suddenly become aware that language functions as a symbolic system. This might take the form of a naming insight, where the child comes to fully appreciate the link between objects and the names attached to them. A sec-

ond view links the spurt to developments in cognition, particularly in the child's ability to categorize objects. A third finds an explanation in the development of the child's articulatory skill, while a fourth suggests that there may be some kind of bottleneck which needs to be passed before referential vocabulary can expand. This last view has been supported by evidence from connectionist computer simulations of the learning of words (see CONNECTIONISM), which have manifested a spurt like that observed in real life.

However, no theory entirely fits the data, and the concept of a vocabulary spurt remains somewhat controversial. One reason is that a sudden increase in vocabulary is not universal. In some infants, vocabulary develops in a series of short bursts; in some, the development is gradual and continuous. It has also proved difficult to pinpoint the moment at which, in a given child, the increase begins; this would seem to cast doubt upon the theory of a sudden insight into the nature of language. Finally, account has to be taken of the complex relationship between comprehension and production; it may be that many of the words that feature in the spurt have been 'acquired' much earlier and stored for future use.

📖 Bates et al. 1995; Bloom 2000; Clark 2003, 2009; Dromi 1999; Field 2004

Vygotskyan

The ideas of the Russian psychologist Lev Vygotsky cover several areas:

1) *Thought and language*. For Vygotsky, thought and language are mutually supportive. Thought exists prior to language, and there is initially a separation between the two; but, during three phases of language acquisition, their different functions become established:
   Phase 1: Before the age of two, pre-linguistic thought (action schemas and images) becomes linked to pre-intellectual language in the form of BABBLING. Thought becomes verbal and speech rational.
   Phase 2: From two to seven, the child does not distinguish clearly between private thoughts and public conversation. Both are expressed externally in *egocentric speech*. Speech thus serves as a means of imposing patterns upon thought.
   Phase 3: From seven onwards, thought becomes internalized. The thinking aloud of the previous phase continues in the form of *internal speech*, the voice in the head which plays a role in reading, in writing and in the *rehearsal* of items which need to be memorized.
2) *Concept formation*. Vygotsky suggested that the way in which children learn to categorize the world around them followed three phases:
   Phase 1: The child puts together disparate objects in a heap to form a syncretic relationship. A group of objects is created at random; the group then becomes defined by its spatial proximity.
   Phase 2: The child begins to think in *complexes*, associations based upon concrete relationships between objects, rather than simply its own im-

pressions. At this stage, Vygotsky identified what he terms a *chain complex*: a child used *quah* (= quack) for a duck on a pond, then any liquid including milk, then a coin with an eagle on it, then any round coin-like object. Each new item that is added has something in common with a previous member of the category.

Phase 3: The child moves from grouping objects on the basis of maximum similarity to grouping them on the basis of a single attribute (e.g., roundedness or flatness). When a trait (or *potential concept*) has been identified, it now becomes stable and established.

3) *Cognitive and linguistic development.* Vygotsky saw human behavior as closely related to the social environment in which it developed. He suggested that, for the developing child, there was always a potential area of skill and knowledge (a ZONE OF PROXIMAL DEVELOPMENT (ZPD) just ahead of what it could currently achieve. Vygotsky argued that a child is enabled to enter the next ZPD as a result of communicative interaction with its carers, who provide step-by-step support for the learning process. The concept of a ZPD has been invoked in discussion of both first and second language acquisition.

see also COGNITIVE DEVELOPMENT, SCAFFOLDING

📖 Field 2004; Vygotsky 1934, 1962

W-Z

Wave Theory
a sociolinguistic theory developed by Bailey to account for linguistic change. It explains how old rules spread from one speech community to another and how new rules arise. It also accounts for how rules spread from one linguistic environment to another. Whereas Labov sought to account for VARIABILITY in groups of speakers by means of variable rules, Baily developed alternative means, based on a view of how language change takes place. Baily sought to show how a theory of language change can account for synchronic variability in language use. According to his Wave Theory, linguistic innovation is first introduced by one group of speakers. By the time it is taken up by a second group, the first group has introduced a second innovation. And so as old rules spread, new rules arise. The spread, or diffusion, of new rules also takes place in another way. Initially, a rule may be restricted to a specific linguistic environment and then gradually come to be used in an increasing range of environments. Linguistic environments can be distinguished according to their weight. Change originates in heavy environments (i.e., those environments that favor the use of a particular variant) and then spreads through intermediate to light environments (i.e., those environments that do not favor the use of the variant). Thus, like Labov's variable rule, the Wave Theory accounts for systematic effects of both social and linguistic factors.
The relationship between language change and synchronic variation (i.e., the variation apparent in speakers at a single point in time) is clearly evident in CREOLES.
see also ACCOMMODATION THEORY
 Bailey 1973; Ellis 2008

weak interface hypothesis
also **weak interface position, weak interface model**
a claim that EXPLICIT LEARNING of rules may have no more than a facilitating effect on language acquisition and may aid the learner to grasp COMPREHENSIBLE INPUT. As a theory of instructed language acquisition, the weak interface model is based on the distinction between IMPLICIT and EXPLICIT KNOWLEDGE. This model, developed by Ellis, claims that explicit knowledge can be converted into implicit knowledge in the case of *variational* feature

(e.g., copula 'be') but not *developmental* features (e.g., negation or third person -*s*) unless the learner has reached the stage of development that allows for the integration of the feature into the INTERLANGUAGE system. This distinction draws on MULTIDIMENSIONAL MODEL, which was based on studies of the L2 acquisition of German that had shown that whereas somewhat grammatical features appear to be constrained so that they can only be acquired in a fixed sequence, others are acquirable at any time. Weak interface model also posited a role for explicit knowledge as a facilitator of implicit knowledge by helping learners to notice linguistic forms in the INPUT and to carry out a comparison between what they have noticed and their own current interlanguage. A corollary of this model is that not all L2 knowledge originates in an explicit form—more often than not knowledge commences as implicit knowledge. Thus, the model claims that there is both a direct interface between explicit and implicit knowledge (albeit one circumscribed by developmental constraints) and an indirect interface. Later, Ellis has tended to emphasize the indirect role of this interface.

N. Ellis has also posited a connection between explicit and implicit knowledge. He described the two types of knowledge as 'dissociable but cooperative'. He described the two types of knowledge as primary; most knowledge is tacit knowledge; most learning is implicit; the vast majority of our cognitive processing is unconscious. He supported Krashen's claim that implicit and explicit knowledge are distinct and disassociated—they involve different types of representation and are substantiated in different parts of the brain. Unlike Ellis, however, he argued that explicit cannot be converted into implicit knowledge, but like Ellis he also acknowledged an indirect role for explicit knowledge as a facilitator of implicit knowledge. In particular, he considered explicit knowledge (and the consciousness it presupposes) to support and enhance the unconscious process involved in acquiring implicit knowledge. For example, he saw explicit knowledge playing a role in the initial registration of the sequences that make up constructions, which are then tuned and integrated into implicit system through subsequence implicit processing of L2 input. He proposed the following learning sequence:

external scaffold attention → internally motivated attention → explicit learning → explicit memory → implicit learning → implicit memory → automatization, and abstraction

and went to suggest that conscious and unconscious processes are dynamically involved together in every cognitive task and in every learning episode. N. Ellis's account of the two knowledge sources and their interaction, then, can also be viewed as a weak interface model, in fact, even weaker than Ellis' model.

see also INTERFACE MODEL, NON-INTERFACE MODEL, EXPLICIT MEMORY, IMPLICIT LEARNING
 Ellis 1994, 2006c; 2008; N. Ellis 1994a, 2005; Seliger 1977

weak interface model
another term for WEAK INTERFACE HYPOTHESIS

weak interface position
another term for WEAK INTERFACE HYPOTHESIS

Whorflan Hypothesis
another term for SAPIR-WHORF HYPOTHESIS

wild grammar
a term which refer to a grammar that contains rules that contravene UNIVERSAL GRAMMAR (UG). It is argued that children do not in fact construct wild grammars (that conform only with those principles of UG that are available to them at a given time and do not conform to those principles which have not yet matured) because they are constrained by UG principles.
 Ellis 2008; Goodluck 1986

Williams Syndrome
also **WS**
a genetic condition in which sufferers show signs of cognitive impairment, yet their language competence appears to be relatively unaffected. The symptoms are the reverse of those associated with SPECIFIC LANGUAGE IMPAIRMENT, where individuals of normal INTELLIGENCE fail to achieve full linguistic competence.
Williams sufferers are often talkative and highly gregarious. They exhibit major cognitive deficits in the form of poor problem-solving skills and impaired spatial reasoning, and may have IQs as low as 50. Yet their early vocabulary and speaking skills are rated as above average. They are often verbally adept at repeating information and telling stories; though they experience problems in analyzing language at thematic level.
Williams Syndrome has been linked to imbalances in brain structure, with a reduction of some areas of the brain but a sparing of the *cerebellum* and *frontal lobes*. Some scholars cite the Syndrome as evidence of a dissociation between language and other cognitive abilities, and thus as support for the notion that language is a separate, *modular* faculty (see MODULARITY). An alternative view is that the intelligence of Williams sufferers is splintered in a manner that spares the processes most critical to language development.
see also DOWN'S SYNDROME, SAVANT, SPECIFIC LANGUAGE IMPAIRMENT
 Bellugi et al. 1993; Deacon 1997; Field 2004

willingness to communicate
also WTC

an underlying continuum representing the predisposition toward or away from communicating, given the choice. A factor related to *attribution* and *self-efficacy* (see ATTRIBUTION THEORY), one that has seen a surge of recent interest in the research literature, is the extent to which learners display a willingness to communicate as they tackle a second language.

Emerging from studies and assertions about language learners' *un*willingness (shyness) to communicate, researchers have now been examining the extent to which WTC is a factor not just in second language acquisition, but one that may have its roots in a learner's first language communication patterns.

MacIntyre et al. found that a number of factors appear to contribute to predisposing one learner to seek, and another learner to avoid, second language communication. Noting that a high level of communicative ability does not necessarily correspond with a high WTC, MacIntyre et al. proposed a number of cognitive and affective factors that underlie the latter: MOTIVATION, PERSONALITY, intergroup climate, and two levels of self-confidence. The first level resembles SITUATIONAL SELF-ESTEEM, or *state communicative self-confidence*, and the second, an overall global level simply labeled *L2 self-confidence*. Both self-confidence factors assume important roles in determining one's willingness to communicate.

Work on WTC is in its infancy. It is a promising construct in several respects. It constitutes an obvious link between other, more thoroughly investigated constructs (such as learner attitudes and motivation) and language proficiency. It is a construct of obvious relevance to language teaching. It is suggested that developing WTC is the ultimate goal of instruction.

see also LEARNING STYLES, LEARNING STRATEGIES, PERSONALITY, MOTIVATION, ANXIETY, LEARNER BELIEFS, INTELLIGENCE, LANGUAGE APTITUDE

📖 Brown 2007; Dörnyei 2005; Ellis 2008; MacIntyre et al. 1998, 2002

WM

an abbreviation for WORKING MEMORY

working memory
also WM

a mental construct that accounts for how the key processes of perception, attention, and rehearsal take place. Over the past decade, there has been significant interest in the psychological construct of working memory in SLA research. In brief, working memory refers to the structures and processes that humans use to store and manipulate information. The term that preceded working memory was most often SHORT-TERM MEMORY. The major difference is that working memory focuses on the manipulation of information rather than just the storage of information, as was the case with short-term memory. Working memory is those mechanisms or processes that are involved in the control, regulation, and active maintenance of task-relevant information in the service of complex cognition, including novel as well as familiar, skilled tasks.

There are a number of models of working memory but the one that has figured strongly in SLA is that of Baddeley and Hitch. This identifies three key components. The 'phonological loop' holds information briefly in a phonological form which allows for articulatory rehearsal (i.e., where the phonological string is repeated in inner speech to prevent it from decaying). Rehearsal occurs within a limited time span (about 2 seconds) and is an optional process. The 'visual sketchpad' is used in the temporary storage and manipulation of spatial and visual information. The 'central executive' is the most important component. It serves a variety of functions, including selective attention to specific stimuli while ignoring others, temporary activation of material in LONG-TERM MEMORY, and resolution of potential conflicts between schemas. All three components are seen as having limited capacity. That is, they are constrained in the amount of information and processing they can handle.

Working memory capacity varies from individual to individual. So, the ability to juggle numerous language tasks also varies from individual to individual. This is generally referred to as *working memory capacity*. There are numerous ways that researchers have used to determine working memory capacity and, like all elicitation measures, there is difficulty in perfectly aligning the elicitation task with the underlying construct. It is important to note that defining the construct and measuring it are not the same. Most measures use a dual-task format combining some memory measure with a processing memory. Common among these is the *reading span task*. In these tasks, participants may read a number of sentences and are told to remember the last word of each sentence. At the end of a set of sentences (usually two to six), they are asked to write down (in order) the last word of each sentence. So that rehearsal will not take place, often they are asked to respond to the plausibility of each sentence.

Working memory research in SLA is in its infancy. As with other constructs in SLA (e.g., COMPETENCE), it is not always clear how best to measure it. Many of the differences in second language working memory research need to be understood in the context of data collection.

📖 Baddeley 1986; Baddeley & Hitch 1974; Ellis 2008; Gass & Selinker 2008; Miyake & Shah 1999

WS

another term for WILLIAMS SYNDROME

WTC

an abbreviation for WILLINGNESS TO COMMUNICATE

Zipf's law
a finding that any piece of text will contain a very small number of high-frequency word forms and a large number of low-frequency word forms. A second observation was that words with higher text frequency are shorter in length.
📖 Field 2004; Zipf 1935

zone of proximal development
see SOCIOCULTURAL THEORY

ZPD
an abbreviation for ZONE OF PROXIMAL DEVELOPMENT

References

Abrahamsson, N. (2003). Development and recoverability of L2 codes: A longitudinal study of Chinese/Swedish interphonology. *Studies in Second Language Acquisition, 25*, 313-349.

Abrams, Z. (2002). Surfing to cross-cultural awareness: Using Internet-mediated projects to explore cultural stereotypes. *Foreign Language Annals, 35*, 141-160.

Adjemain, C. (1976). On the nature of interlanguage system. *Language learning, 26*, 297-320.

Adler, R (1972). Culture shock and the cross cultural learning experience. *Readings in Intercultural Education* (Vol. 2). Pittsburgh: Intercultural Communication Network.

Aitchison, J. (1989). *The articulate mammal*. London: Unwin Hyman.

Aitchison, J. (1998). *The articulate mammal* (4th ed.) London: Routledge.

Aitchison, J. (2003). *Words in the mind* (3rd ed.). Oxford: Wiley-Blackwell.

Allen, L. (2000). Form-meaning connections and the French causative. *Studies in Second Language Acquisition, 22*, 69-84.

Alpert, R., & Haber, R. (1960). Anxiety in academic achievement situations. *Journal of Abnormal and Social Psychology, 61*, 207-215.

Alptekin, C. (2002). Towards intercultural communicative competence in ELT. *ELT Journal, 56*, 57-64.

Andersen, R. (1979a). Expanding Schumann's Pidginization Hypothesis. *Language Learning, 29*, 105-119.

Andersen, R. (1980). The role of creolization in Schumann's Pidginization Hypothesis for second language acquisition. In R. Scarcella & S. Krashen (Eds.), *Research in second language acquisition*. Rowley, MA: Newbury House.

Andersen, R. (Ed.). (1983b). *Pidginization and creolisation as language acquisition*. Rowley, MA: Newbury House.

Andersen, R. (Ed.) (1984a). *Second languages: A cross-linguistic perspective*. Rowley, MA: Newbury House.

Andersen, R. (1984b). The one-to-one principle of interlanguage construction. *Language learning, 34*, 77-95.

Andersen, R. (1990). Models, processes, principles and strategies: Second language acquisition inside and outside of the classroom. In B. VanPatten & J. Lee (Eds.), *Second language acquisition—foreign language learning*. Clevedon: Multilingual Matters.

Andersen, R. (1991). Developmental sequences: the emergence of aspect marking in second language acquisition. In T. Huebner & C. Ferguson (Eds.), *Crosscurrents in second language acquisition and linguistic theories* (pp. 305-24). Amsterdam: John Benjamins.

Andersen, R., & Shirai, Y. (1994). Discourse motivations for some cognitive acquisition principles. *Studies in Second Language Acquisition, 16*, 133-156.

Anderson, J. (1976). *Language, memory, thought*. Hillsdale, NJ: Lawrence Erlbaum Associates.

Anderson, J. (1980). *Cognitive psychology and its implications*. San Francisco: Freeman.

Anderson, J. (1983). *The architecture of cognition*. Cambridge, MA: Harvard University Press.

Anderson, J. (2009). *Cognitive psychology and its implications* (7th ed.). New York: W. H. Freeman.

Anderson, J. (1993). *Rules of the mind*. Hillsdale, NJ: Lawrence Erlbaum Associates.

Anderson, R., & Ausubel, D. (Eds.). (1965). *Readings in the psychology of cognition*. New York: Holt, Rinehart & Winston.

Atkinson, J., & Drew, P. (1979). *Order in court. The organization of verbal interaction in judicial settings*. London: MacMillan.

August, D., & Shanahan, T. (2008). *Developing reading and writing in second-language learners: Lessons from the report of the National Literacy Panel on language-minority children and youth*. New York: Routledge.

Ausubel, D. (1963). Cognitive structure and the facilitation of meaningful verbal learning. *Journal of Teacher Education, 14*, 217-221.

Ausubel, D. (1964). Adults vs. children in second language learning: Psychological considerations. *Modern Language Journal, 48*, 420-424.

Ausubel, D. (1965). Introduction to part one. In R. Anderson & D. Ausubel (Eds.), *Readings in the psychology of cognition* (pp. 3-17). New York: Holt, Rinehart & Winston.

Ausubel, D. (1968). *Educational psychology: A cognitive view*. New York: Holt, Rinehart & Winston.

Bachman, L. (1990). *Fundamental considerations in language testing*. New York: Oxford University Press.

Baddeley, A. (1986). *Working memory*. Oxford: Oxford University Press.

Baddeley, A. (1997). *Human memory: Theory and practice*. Hove: Psychology Press.

Baddeley, A., & Hitch, G. (1974). Working memory. In G. Bower (Ed.), *The psychology of learning and motivation* (Vol. 8). New York, NY: Academic Press.
Baker, C. (2006). *Foundations of bilingual education and bilingualism.* Clevedon: Multilingual Matters.
Baker, P., & Ellece, S. (2011). *Key terms in discourse analysis.* London and New York: Continuum.
Ball, P., Giles, H., & Hewstone, M. (1984). The intergroup theory of second language acquisition with catastrophic dimensions. In H. Tajfel (Ed.), *The social dimension* (Vol. 2). Cambridge: Cambridge University Press.
Balota, D. (1994). Visual word recognition: The journey from features to meaning. In M. Gernsbacher (Ed.), *Handbook of psycholinguistics* (pp. 303-58). San Diego, CA: Academic Press.
Barcelos, A. (2003). Researching beliefs about SLA: A critical review. In P. Kalaja & A. Barcelos (Eds.), *Beliefs about SLA: New research approaches.* Dordrecht: Kluwer.
Bardovi-Harlig, K. (1992). A second look at T-Unit analysis: Reconsidering the sentence. *TESOL Quarterly, 26* (2), 390-395.
Bardovi-Harlig, K. (1999b). From morpheme studies to temporal semantics: Tense-aspect research in SLA. *Studies in Second Language Acquisition, 21,* 341-382.
Bartlett, F. (1932). *Remembering.* Cambridge: Cambridge University Press.
Bates, E. (1976). *Language and context: The acquisition of pragmatics.* New York, NY: Academic Press.
Bates, E., Benigni, L., Bretherton, I., Camaioni, L., & Volterra, V. (1979). *The emergence of symbols: Cognition and communication in infancy.* New York, NY: Academic Press.
Bates, E., Bretherton, I., & Snyder, L. (1988). *From first words to grammar.* Cambridge, Cambridge University Press.
Bates, E., Dale, P., & Thal, D. (1995). Individual differences and their implications for theories of language development. In P. Fletcher & B. MacWhinney (Eds.), *The handbook of child language* (pp. 96-151). Oxford: Blackwell.
Bates, E., & Goodman, J. (1999). On the emergence of grammar from the lexicon. In B. MacWhinney (Ed.), *The emergence of language.* Mahwah, NJ: Lawrence Erlbaum Associates.
Bates, E., & MacWhinney, B. (1982). Functionalist approaches to grammar. In E. Wanner & L. Gleitman (Eds), *Language acquisition: The state of the art* (pp. 173-218). Cambridge: Cambridge University Press.
Becker, A. (1991). Language and languaging. *Language and Communication, 11,* 33-35.

Beebe, L. (1983). Risk-taking and the language learner. In H. Seliger & M. Long (Eds.), *Classroom oriented research in second language acquisition* (pp. 39-65). Rowley, MA: Newbury House.

Beebe, L., & Giles, H. (1984). Speech accommodation theories: A discussion in terms of second language acquisition. *Interactional Journal of the Sociology of Language, 46*, 5-32.

Bellugi, U., Marks, S., Bihrle, A., & Sabo, H. (1993). Dissociation between language and cognitive functions in Williams Syndrome. In D. Bishop & K. Mogford (Eds.), *Language development in exceptional circumstances* (pp. 177-189). Hove: Psychology Press.

Benson, P. (2001). *Teaching and researching autonomy in language learning*. Harlow: Longman/Pearson Education.

Berko, J. (1958). The child's learning of English morphology. *Word, 14*, 150-77.

Bialystok, E. (1978). A theoretical model of second language learning. *Language learning, 28*, 69-84.

Bialystok, E. (1979). Explicit and implicit judgments of L2 grammaticality. *Language Learning, 29*, 81-104.

Bialystok, E. (1981a). The role of linguistic knowledge in second language use. *Studies in Second Language Acquisition, 4*, 31-45.

Bialystok, E. (1982). On the relationship between knowing and using forms. *Applied linguistics, 3*, 181-206.

Bialystok, E. (1988). Levels of bilingualism and levels of linguistic awareness. *Developmental Psychology, 24*, 560-567.

Bialystok, E. (1990). *Communication strategies: A psychological analysis of second language use*. Oxford: Basil Blackwell.

Bialystok, E. (1991). Achieving proficiency in a second language: A processing description. In R. Phillipson, E. Kellerman, L. Selinker, M. Sharwood-Smith, & M. Swain (Eds.), *Foreign/second language pedagogy research*. Clevedon: Multilingual Matters.

Bialystok, E. (2002). Cognitive processes of L2 user. In V. Cook (Ed.), *Portraits of the L2 user* (pp. 145-165). Clevedon, England: Multilingual Matters.

Bialystok, E., & Ryan, E. (1985). A metacognitive framework for the development of first and second language skills. In D. Forrest-Pressley, G. Mackinnon, & T. Waller (Eds.), *Metacognitive, cognition, and human performance* (Vol. 1). New York, NY: Academic Press.

Bickerton, D. (1984). The language bioprogram hypothesis. *Behavioral and Brain Sciences, 7*, 173-221.

Bishop, D. (1997). *Uncommon understanding: Development and disorders of language comprehension in children*. Hove: Psychology Press.

Bley-Vroman, R. (1983). The comparative fallacy in interlanguage studies: The case of systematicity. *Language learning, 33*, 1-17.

Bloom, L. (1971). Why not pivot grammar? *Journal of Speech and Hearing Disorders, 36*, 40-50.

Bloom, P. (2000). *How children learn the meanings of words*. Cambridge, MA: MIT Press.

Blum-Kulka, S., House, J., & Kasper, G. (1989b). Investigating cross-cultural pragmatics: An introductory overview. In S. Blum-Kulka, J. House, & G. Kasper (Eds.), *Cross-cultural pragmatics: Request and apologies*. Norwood, NJ: Ablex.

Bonvillian, J. (1999). Sign language development. In M. Barrett (Ed.), *The development of language* (pp. 277-310). Hove: Psychology Press.

Breen, M. (1985). Authenticity in the language classroom. *Applied Linguistics, 6*, 60-70.

Brown, H. (1972). Cognitive pruning and second language acquisition. *Modern Language Journal, 56*, 218-222.

Brown, H. (2007). *Principles of language learning and teaching* (5th ed.). Pearson Education.

Brown, H. (2001). *Teaching by principles: An interactive approach to language pedagogy* (2nd ed.). White Plains, NY: Pearson Education.

Brown, R. (1973). *A first language: The early stages*. London: Allen and Unwin.

Brown, S., & Attardo, S. (2005). *Understanding language structure, interaction, and variation: An introduction to applied linguistics and sociolinguistics for nonspecialists*. Michigan: University of Michigan Press.

Bruner, J. (1983). The acquisition of pragmatic commitments. In R. Golinkoff (Ed.), *The transition from prelinguistic to linguistic communication* (pp. 27-42). Hillsdale, NJ: Erlbaum.

Bruner, J. (1985). *Child's talk: Learning to use language*. New York: Norton.

Burstall, C. (1975). Factors affecting foreign-language learning: A consideration of some recent search findings. *Language Teaching and Linguistics Abstracts, 8*, 5-25.

Burt, M., Dulay, H., & Hernandez, E. (1973). *Bilingual syntax measure*. New York: Harcourt Brace Jovanovich.

Bussmann, H. (1996). *Routledge dictionary of language and linguistics*. Translated and edited by G. Trauth and K. Kazzazi. London: Routledge.

Bygate, M. (2001). Speaking. In R. Carter, & D. Nunan (Eds.), *The Cambridge guide to teaching English to speakers of other languages* (pp. 14-20). Cambridge: Cambridge University Press.

Canale, M. (1983). From communicative competence to communicative language pedagogy. In J. Richards & R. Schmidt (Eds.), *Language and communication* (pp. 2-27). London: Longman Group, Ltd.

Caplan, D. (1992). *Language: Structure, processing and disorders*. Cambridge, MA: MIT Press.

Carroll, D. (1999). *Psychology of language* (3rd ed.). Pacific Grove, CA: Brooks Cole.

Carroll, J., & Sapon, S. (1959). *Modern language aptitude test*. New York: The Psychological Corporation.

Carroll, S. (2000). *Input and evidence: The raw material of second language acquisition*. Amsterdam: John Benjamins.

Carroll, S. (2001). *Input and evidence: The raw material of second language acquisition*. Amsterdam: John Benjamins.

Carroll, S. (2007). Autonomous induction theory. In B. VanPatten & J. Williams (Eds.), *Theories in second language acquisition: An introduction*. Mahwah, NJ: Lawrence Erlbaum Associates.

Carter, R., & Nunan, D. (Eds.). (2001). *The Cambridge guide to teaching English to speakers of other languages*. Cambridge: Cambridge University Press.

Cattell, R. (2000). *Children's language: consensus and controversy*. London: Cassell.

Cazden, C. (1972). *Child language and education*. New York: Holt, Rinehart & Winston.

Chaudron, C. (1988). *Second language classrooms: Research on teaching and learning*. Cambridge: Cambridge University Press.

Chomsky, N. (1957). *Syntactic structures*. The Hague: Mouton.

Chomsky, N. (1964). *Current issues in linguistic theory*. The Hague.

Chomsky, N. (1965). *Aspects of the theory of syntax*. Cambridge, MA: Massachusetts Institute of Technology Press.

Chomsky, N. (1981). *Lectures on Government and Binding*. Dordrecht: Foris.

Chomsky, N (1982). *Some concepts and consequences of the theory of Government and Binding*. Cambridge, MA: MIT Press.

Chomsky, N. (1995). *The minimalist program*. Cambridge, MA: MIT Press.

Clahsen, H. (1984). The acquisition of German word order: A test case for cognitive approaches to L2 development. In Andersen, R. (Ed.), *Second languages: A cross-linguistic perspective*. Rowley, MA: Newbury House, 219-42.

Clahsen, H. (1988). Critical phases of grammar development: A study of the acquisition negation in children and adults. In P. Jordens & J. Lalleman (Eds.), *Language development*. Dordrecht: Foris.

Clahsen, H. (1990). The comparative study of first and second language development. *Studies in Second Language Acquisition, 12*, 135-154.

Clahsen, H., & Muysken, P. (1986). The availability of Universal Grammar to adult and child learners—A study of the acquisition of German word order. *Second Language Research, 2*, 93-119.

Clark, E. (2001). Emergent categories in first language acquisition. In M. Bowerman & S. Levinson (Eds.), *Language acquisition and conceptual development* (pp. 379-405). Cambridge: Cambridge University Press.

Clark, E. (2003). *First language acquisition*. Cambridge: Cambridge University Press.
Clark, E. (2009). *First language acquisition* (2nd ed.) Cambridge: Cambridge University Press.
Clark, H., & Clark, E. (1977). *Psychology and language: An introduction to psycholinguistics*. New York: Harcourt Brace Jovanovich.
Cohen, A., & Dörnyei, Z. (2002). Focus on the language learner: Motivation, styles and strategies. In N. Schmitt (Ed.), *An introduction to applied linguistics*. London: Arnold; 170-187.
Cohen, A., & Macaro, E. (Eds.). (2007). *Language learner strategies: Thirty years of research and practice*. Oxford: Oxford University Press.
Cohen, A., & Swain, M. (1979). Bilingual education: The immersion model in the North American context. In J. Pride (Ed.), *Sociolinguistic aspects of language learning and teaching*. Oxford: Oxford University Press.
Cohen, G., Kiss, G., & Le Voi, M. (1993). *Memory: Current issues*. Buckingham: Open University.
Connor, U. (1996). *Contrastive rhetoric: Cross-cultural aspects of second language writing*. New York: Cambridge University Press.
Connor, U., Nagelhout, E., & Rozycki, W. (Eds.). (2008). *Contrastive rhetoric: Reaching to intercultural rhetoric*. Amsterdam/Philadelphia: John Benjamins.
Cook, V. (1992). Evidence for multi-competence. *Language Learning, 42*, 557-591.
Cook, V. (2007). The goals of ELT: Reproducing native-speakers or promoting multi-competence among second language users? In J. Cummins & C. Davison (Eds.), *International handbook on English language teaching* (Vol. 2). (pp. 237-248). Amsterdam: Kluwer.
Cook, V. (2009b). Language user groups and language teaching. In V. J. Cook, & Li Wei (Eds.), *Contemporary Applied linguistics* (Vol. 1). London: Continuum.
Cook, V., & Newson, M. (1996). *Chomsky's Universal Grammar: An introduction* (2nd ed.). Oxford: Blackwell.
Cook, V., & Newson, M. (2007). *Chomsky's Universal Grammar. An introduction* (3rd ed.). Oxford: Blackwell.
Coopersmith, S. (1967). *The antecedents of self-esteem*. San Francisco: Freeman.
Corder, S. (1967). The significance of learners' errors. *International Review of Applied Linguistics, 5*, 161-170.
Corder, S. (1971a). Idiosyncratic dialects and error analysis, *International Review of Applied Linguistics, 9*, 147-159.
Corder, S. (1973). *Introducing applied linguistics*. Harmondsworth, UK: Penguin Books.

Corder, S. (1974). Error analysis. In J. Allen & S. Corder (Eds.). *The Edinburg course in applied linguistics.* (Vol. 3). Oxford: Oxford University Press.

Corder, S. (1977b). Simple codes and the source of the learner's initial heuristic hypothesis. *Studies in Second Language Acquisition, 1,* 1-10.

Corder, S. (1978a). Language distance and the magnitude of the learning task. *Studies in Second Language Acquisition, 1,* 1-10.

Corder, S. (1981). *Error analysis and interlanguage.* Oxford: Oxford University Press.

Corno, L., Kanfer, R. (1993). The role of volition in learning and performance. *Review of Research in Education, 19,* 301-341.

Coughlan, P., & Duff, P. (1974). Same task, different activities: Analysis of of a SLA task from an activity theory perspective. In J. Lantolf & G. Appel (Eds.), *Vygotskian approaches to second language research.* Norwood, NJ: Ablex.

Crain, S., & Lillo-Martin, D. (1999). *An introduction to linguistic theory and language acquisition.* Oxford: Blackwell.

Crystal, D. (1992). *An encyclopedic dictionary of language and languages.* Cambridge, MA: Blackwell.

Crystal, D. (2008). *A dictionary of linguistics and phonetics* (6th Ed.). Malden, Mass: Blackwell.

Crystal, D., & Varley, R. (1999). *Introduction to language pathology* (4th Ed.). London: Whurr.

Cummins, J. (1979). Cognitive/academic language proficiency, linguistic interdependence, the optimum age question and some other matters. *Working Papers on Bilingualism, 19,* 121-129.

Cummins, J. (1981). Age on arrival and immigrant second language learning in Canada: A reassessment. *Applied Linguistics, 11,* 132-149.

Cummins, J. (1988). Second language acquisition within bilingual education programs. In L. Beebe (Ed.), *Issues in second language acquisition: multiple perspectives.* New York: Newbury House.

Cutler, A., & Mehler, J. (1993). The periodicity bias. *Journal of Phonetics, 21,* 103-8.

Deacon, T. (1997). *The symbolic species.* London: Penguin.

De Bot, K. (1992). A bilingual production model: Levelt's speaking model adapted. *Applied linguistics, 13,* 1-24.

De Bot, K., & Weltens, B. (1995). Foreign language attrition. *Annual Review of Applied Linguistics, 15,* 151-164.

Dc Boysson-Bardies, B., & Vihman, M. (1991). Adaptation to language: Evidence from babbling and first words in four languages. *Language 67,* 297-318.

De Guerrero, M. (2005). *Inner speech—L2: Thinking words in a second language.* New York: Springer.

DeKeyser, R. (1995). Learning second language grammar rules: An experiment with a miniature linguistic system. *Studies in Second Language Acquisition, 17*, 379-410.

DeKeyser, R. (1998). Beyond focus on form: Cognitive perspectives on learning and practicing second language grammar. In C. Doughty & J. Williams (Eds.), *Focus on form in classroom second language acquisition.* Cambridge: Cambridge University Press.

DeKeyser, R. (2003). Implicit and explicit learning. In C. Doughty & M. Long (Eds.), *Handbook of second language acquisition.* Malden, Mass: Blackwell.

Dekeyser, R., Salaberry, R., Robinson, P., & Harrington, M. (2002). What gets processed in processing instruction? *Language Learning, 52*, 805-823.

De Villiers, J., & De Villiers. P. (1978). *Language acquisition.* Cambridge, MA: Harvard University Press.

Diller, K. (Ed.). (1978). *The language teaching controversy.* Rowley, Mass: Newbury House.

Dingwall, W. (1998) The biological bases of human communicative behavior. In J. Gleason & N. Ratner (Eds.), *Psycholinguistics* (2nd ed.). (pp. 51-105). Fort Worth, TX: Harcourt Brace.

Dörnyei, Z. (2001b). *Teaching and researching motivation.* Harlow: Longman.

Dörnyei, Z. (2005). *The psychology of the language learner: Individual differences in second language acquisition.* Mahwah, NJ: Lawrence Erlbaum Associates.

Dörnyei, Z. (in press). Individual differences: Interplay of learner characteristics and learning environment. In N. Ellis & D. Larsen-Freeman (Eds.), *Language as a complex adaptive system.* Oxford: Wiley Blackwell.

Dörnyei, Z., & Skehan, P. (2003). Individual differences in second language learning. In C. Doughty & M. Long, *The handbook of second language acquisition* (pp. 589-630). Oxford: Blackwell.

Dörnyei, Z., & Ushioda, E. (in press). *Teaching and researching motivation* (2nd ed.). Harlow: Longman.

Doughty, C. (2003). Instructed SLA: Constraints, compensation, and enhancement. In C. Doughty & M. Long (Eds.), *The handbook of second language acquisition* (pp. 256-310). Oxford: Blackwell.

Doughty, C., & Long, M. (Eds.). (2003). *The handbook of second language acquisition.* Oxford: Blackwell.

Doughty, C., & Varela, E. (1998). Communicative focus-on-form. In C. Doughty & J. Williams (Eds.), *Focus-on-form in classroom second language acquisition.* Cambridge: Cambridge University Press.

Dromi, E. (1999). Early lexical development. In M. Barrett (Ed.), *The development of language* (pp. 99-131). Hove: Psychology Press.

Dufeu, B. (1994). *Teaching myself.* Oxford: Oxford University Press.

Dulay, H., & Burt, M. (1973). Should we teach children syntax? *Language Learning, 23*, 95-123.

Dulay, H., & Burt, M. (1974a). Errors and strategies in child second language acquisition. *TESOL Quarterly, 8*, 129-136.
Dulay, H., & Burt, M. (1974c). Natural sequences in child second language acquisition. *Language Learning, 24*, 37-53.
Dulay, H., & Burt, M. (1974d). A new perspective on the creative construction processes in child second language acquisition. *Language Learning, 24*, 253-278.
Duncan, S. (1973). Towards a grammar for dyadic conversation. *Semiotica, 9*, 29-46.
Eckman, F. (1977). Markedness and the contrastive analysis hypothesis. *Language Learning, 27*, 315-330.
Eckman, F. (2004). Optimality theory, markedness and second language syntax: The case of resumptive pronouns in relative clauses. *Studies in Phonetics, Phonology and Morphology, 10*, 89-110.
Ehrman, M. (1996). *Understanding second language difficulties.* Thousand Oaks, CA: Sage.
Eisenstein, M. (1980). Grammatical explanations in ESL: Teach the student, not the method. *TESL Talk, 11*, 3-13.
Elbers, L. (1982). Operating principles of repetitive babbling: A cognitive continuity approach. *Cognition 12*, 45-63.
Ellis, N. (Ed.) (1994a). Introduction: Implicit and explicit language learning—An overview. In N. Ellis (Ed.), *Implicit and explicit learning of languages.* San Diego: Academic Press.
Ellis, N. (Ed.) (1994b). *Implicit and explicit learning of languages.* San Diego: Academic Press.
Ellis, N. (1996). Sequencing in SLA: Phonological memory, chunking, and points of order. *Studies in Second Language Acquisition, 18*, 91-126.
Ellis, N. (2002a). Frequency effects in language processing: A review with implications for theories of implicit and explicit language acquisition. *Studies in Second Language Acquisition, 24*, 143-188.
Ellis, N. (2003). Constructions, chunking, and connectionism: The emergence of second language structure. In C. Doughty & M. Long (Eds.), *Handbook of second language acquisition* (pp. 33-68). Oxford: Blackwell.
Ellis, N. (2005). At the interface: Dynamic interactions of explicit and implicit language knowledge. *Studies in Second Language Acquisition, 27*, 305-352.
Ellis, N. (2006a). Language acquisition as rational contingency learning. *Applied Linguistics, 27*, 1-24.
Ellis, N. (2006b). Cognitive perspectives in SLA: The associative-cognitive CREED. *AILA Review, 19*, 100-121.
Ellis, N. (2006c). Selective attention and transfer phenomena in SLA: Contingency, cue, competition, salience, interference, overshadowing, blocking and perceptual learning. *Applied Linguistics, 27*, 164-149.
Ellis, R. (1984a). *Classroom second language development.* Oxford: Pergamon.

Ellis, R. (1985). Sources of variability in interlanguage. *Applied Linguistics, 6,* 118-131.
Ellis, R. (1986). *Understanding second language acquisition.* Oxford: Oxford University Press.
Ellis, R. (1988b). The role of practice in classroom language learning. *AILA Review, 5,* 20-39.
Ellis, R. (1994). *The study of second language acquisition.* Oxford: Oxford University Press.
Ellis, R. (1997). *SLA research and language teaching.* Oxford: Oxford University Press.
Ellis, R. (2002a). Grammar teaching: Practice or consciousness-raising. In J. Richards, & W. Renandya (Eds.), *Methodology in language teaching: An anthology of current practice* (pp. 167-174). Cambridge: Cambridge University.
Ellis, R. (2002b). Does form-focus instruction affect the acquisition of implicit knowledge? A review of the research. *Studies in second language acquisition, 24,* 223-236.
Ellis, R. (2003). *Task-based language learning and teaching.* Oxford: Oxford University Press.
Ellis, R. (2006c). Modeling learning difficulty and second language proficiency: The differential contributions of implicit and explicit knowledge. *Applied Linguistics, 27,* 431-463.
Ellis, R. (2008). *The study of second language acquisition.* Oxford: Oxford University Press.
Ellis, R., Basturkmen, H., & Loewen, S. (2002). Doing focus-on-form. *System, 30,* 419-432.
Ellis, R., & Barkhuizen, G. (2005). *Analyzing learner language.* Oxford: Oxford University Press.
Ellis, R., Tanaka, Y., & Yamazaki, A. (1994). Classroom interaction, comprehension and the acquisition of L2 word meanings. *Language Learning, 44,* 449-491.
Escudero, P., & Boersma, P. (2004). Bridging the gap between L2 speech perception research and phonological theory. *Studies in Second Language Acquisition, 26,* 551-585.
Eysenck, M. (2001). *Principles of cognitive psychology* (2nd ed.). Hove: Psychology Press.
Eysenck, H., & Eysenck, S. (1964). *Manual of the Eysenck Personality Inventory.* London: Hodder and Stoughton.
Faltis, C. (1984). A commentary on Krashen's input hypothesis. *TESOL Quarterly, 18,* 352-357.
Færch, C., Haastrup, K., & Phillipson, R. (1984). *Learner language and language learning.* Clevedon, UK: Multilingual Matters.

Felix, S. (1985). More evidence on competing cognitive systems. *Second language research, 1*, 47-72.
Field, J. (2004). *Psycholinguistics: The key concepts.* London: Routledge.
Fitzpatrick, F. (1987). *The open door: The Bradford Bilingual Project.* Clevedon: multilingual Matters.
Flanigan, B. (1991). Peer tutoring and second language acquisition in elementary school. *Applied Linguistics, 12*, 141-158.
Fletcher, P. (1999). Specific language impairment. In M. Barrett (Ed.), *The development of language* (pp. 349-371). Hove: Psychology Press.
Fletcher, P., & Garman, M. (Eds.). (1986). *Language acquisition* (2nd ed.). Cambridge: Cambridge University Press.
Fletcher, P., & MacWhinney, B. (Eds.). (1995). *The handbook of child language.* Oxford: Blackwell.
Flynn, S. (1984). A universal in L2 acquisition based on a PBD typology. In F. Eckman, L. Bell, & D. Nelson (Eds.), *Universals of second language acquisition* (PP. 75-87). Rowley, MA: Newbury House.
Flynn, S. (1987). *A parameter-setting model of L2 acquisition: Experimental studies in anaphora.* Dordrecht: Reidel.
Flynn, S., & Manuel, S. (1991). Age-dependent effects in language acquisition: An evaluation of the critical period hypothesis. In L. Eubnak (Ed.), *Point counterpoint: Universal Grammar in the second language.* Amsterdam: John Benjamins.
Fodor, J. (1983). *The modularity of mind.* Cambridge, MA: MIT Press.
Fraser, B., Tintell, E., & Walters, J. (1983). An approach to conducting research on the acquisition of pragmatic competence in a second language. In D. Larsen-Freeman (Ed.), *Discourse analysis in second language research.* Rowley, MA: Newbury House.
Gaies, S. (1983). The investigation of language classroom processes. *TESOL Quarterly, 17*, 205-218.
Gallaway, C., & Richards, B. (Eds.). (1994). *Input and interaction in language acquisition.* Cambridge: Cambridge University Press.
Gardener, H. (1993). *Multiple intelligences: The theory in practice.* New York: Basic Books.
Gardner, H. (1999). Intelligence reframed. New York: Basic Books.
Gardner, H. (2004). Changing minds. Boston: Harvard Business School Press.
Gardner, R. (1979). Social psychological aspects of second language acquisition. In H. Giles & R. St. Clair (Eds.), *Language and social psychology.* Oxford: Blackwell.
Gardner, R. (1983). Learning another language: A true social psychological experiment. *Journal of Language and Social Psychology, 2*, 219-240.
Gardner, R. (1985). *Social psychology and second language learning: The role of attitudes and motivation.* London: Edward Arnold.

Gardner, R., & Clement, R. (1990). Social psychological perspectives on second language acquisition. In H. Giles & W. Robinson (Eds.), *Handbook of language and social psychology*. Chichester: John Wiley and Sons.

Gardner, R., & Smythe, P. (1975). *Second language acquisition: A social psychological approach*. Research Bulletin 332. Department of Psychology, University of Western Ontario, Canada.

Gardner, R., & Lambert, W. (1972). *Attitudes and motivation in second language learning*. Rowley, MA: Newbury House.

Gass, S. (1988). Integrating research areas: A framework for second language studies. *Applied Linguistics, 9,* 198-217.

Gass, S., & Selinker, L. (2008). *Second language acquisition: An introductory course* (3rd ed.). New York: Routledge.

Gatbonton, E. (1978). Patterned phonetic variability in second language speech: A gradual diffusion model. *Canadian Modern Language Review, 34,* 335-347.

Gatbonton, E., Trofimovich, P., & Magid, M. (2005). Learners' ethnic affiliation and L2 pronunciation accuracy: A sociolinguistic investigation. *TESOL Quarterly, 39,* 489-511.

Gathercole, S., & Baddeley, A. (1993). *Working memory and language*. Hove: Erlbaum.

Genesee, F. (1987). *Learning through two languages: Studies of immersion and bilingual Education*. Cambridge, MA: Newbury House.

Genesee, F., Lindholm-Leary, K., Saunders, W., & Christian, D. (2006). *Educating english language learners: A synthesis of research evidence*. Cambridge: Cambridge University Press.

Gerken, L. (1994). A metrical template account of children's weak syllable omissions from multisyllabic words. *Journal of Child Language, 21,* 565-84.

Giles, H., & Byrne, J. (1982). An intergroup approach to second language acquisition. *Journal of multicultural and multilingual development, 3,* 17-40.

Giles, H., & Coupland, N. (1991). *Language: Contexts and consequences*. Keynes, UK: Open University Press.

Giles, H., & Johnson, P. (1981). The role of language in ethnic group relations. In J. Turner & H. Giles (Eds.), *Intergroup behavior*. Chicago, Ill.: University of Chicago Press.

Giles, H. & Ryan, E. (1982). Prolegomena for developing a social psychological theory of language attitudes. In E. Ryan & H. Giles (Eds.), *Attitudes towards language variation*. London: Edward Arnold.

Gleitman, L. (1990). The structural sources of verb meanings. *Language Acquisition, 1,* 3-35.

Goleman, D. (1995). *Emotional intelligence*. New York: Bantam Books.

Goleman, D. (1998). *Working with emotional intelligence*. New York: Bantam Books.

González, J. (2008). *Encyclopedia of bilingual education*. Thousand Oaks, CA: Sage.

Goodluck, H. (1986). Language acquisition and linguistic theory. In P. Fletcher & M. Garman, M. (Eds.), *Language acquisition* (2nd ed.). Cambridge: Cambridge University Press.

Goodman, J., & Nusbaum, H. (Eds.). (1994). *The development of speech perception: The transition from speech sounds to spoken words*. Cambridge, MA: MIT Press.

Goodman, K. (1970). Reading: A psycholinguistic guessing game. In H. Singer & R. Ruddell (Eds.), *Theoretical models and processes of reading*. Newark, DE: International Reading Association.

Gopnik, M. (1990). Feature blindness: A case study. *Language Acquisition, 1*, 139-64.

Gopnik, M., Dalakis, J., Fukuda, S., & Fukuda, S. (1997). Familial Language Impairment. In M. Gopnik (Ed.), *The inheritance and innateness of grammars* (pp. 111-40). New York: Oxford University Press.

Goswami, U., & Bryant, P. (1990). *Phonological skills and learning to read*, Hove: Erlbaum.

Granger, S. (1998a). The computerized learner corpus: A versatile new source of data for SLA research. In S. Granger (Ed.), *Learner English on computer*. London: Addison Wesley Longman.

Gregg, K. (1984). Krashen's monitor and Occam's razor. *Applied Linguistics 5*, 79-100.

Gregg, K. (1994). Krashen's monitor theory, acquisition theory, and theory. In R. Barasch & C. Vaughan James (Eds.), *Beyond the monitor model* (pp. 37-55). Boston: Heinle & Heinle.

Guiora, A., Beit-Hallami, B., Brannon, R., Dull, C, & Scovel, T. (1972a). The effects of experimentally induced changes in ego states on pronunciation ability in second language: An exploratory study. *Comprehensive Psychiatry, 13*.

Guiora, A., Brannon, R., & Dull, C. (1972b). Empathy and second language learning. *Language Learning, 22*, 111-130.

Hall, B., & Gudykunst, W. (1986). The intergroup theory of second language ability. *Journal of language and social psychology, 5*, 294-316.

Halliday, M. (1973) *Explorations in the functions of language*. London: Edward Arnold.

Halliday, M. (1975). *Learning how to mean: Explorations in the development of language*. London: Arnold.

Han, Z. (2004). *Fossilization in adult second language acquisition*. Clevedon: Multilingual Matters.

Hansen, L. (1984). Field dependence-independence and language testing: Evidence from six Pacific island cultures. *TESOL Quarterly, 18*, 311-324.

Hansen, J., & Stansfield, C. (1981). The relationship of field dependent-independent cognitive styles to foreign language achievement. *Language Learning, 31*, 349-367.

Harley, T. (2001). *The psychology of language.* (2nd ed.) Hove: Psychology Press.

Harris, M. & Coltheart, M. (1986). *Language processing in children and adults.* London: Routledge & Kegan Paul.

Hatch, E. (1974). Second language learning—universals? *Working Papers on Bilingualism, 3*, 1-17.

Hatch, E., & Wagner-Gough, J. (1976). Explaining sequence and variation in second language acquisition. *Language Learning, 4*, 293-316.

Hawkins, R. & Chan, C. (1997). The partial availability of UG in second language acquisition. The failed functional features hypothesis. *Second Language Research, 13*, 187-226.

Herron, C., Cole, P., York, H., & Linden, P. (1998). A comparison study of student retention of foreign language video: Declarative versus interrogative advance organizer. *Modern Language Journal, 82*, 237-247.

Hogan, R. (1969). Development of an empathy scale. *Journal of Consulting and Clinical Psychology, 33*, 307-316.

Holec, H. (1981). *Autonomy and foreign language learning.* Oxford: Pergamon.

Holec, H. (1987). The learner as manager: Managing learning or managing to learn? In A. Wenden & J. Rubin (Eds.), *Learner strategies in language learning.* Englewood Cliffs, NJ: Percentile Hall.

Horwitz, E. (1987a). Surveying students beliefs about language learning. In A. Wenden & J. Rubin (Eds.). *Learner strategies in language learning.* New York: Prentice Hall.

Horwitz, E. (2001). Language anxiety and achievement. *Annual Review of Applied Linguistics, 21*, 112-126.

Horwitz, E., Horwitz, M., & Cope, J. (1986). Foreign language classroom anxiety. *Modern Language Journal, 70*, 125-132.

Hosenfeld, C. (1978). Students' mini-theories of second language learning. *Association Bulletin, 29*, 2.

Housen, A., & Pierrard, M. (2006a). Investigating instructed second language acquisition. In A. Housen & M. Pierrard (Eds.), *Investigations in instructed second language acquisition.* Berlin: Mouton de Gruyter.

Hudson, G. (2000). *Essential introductory linguistics.* Malden, MA: Blackwell.

Hulstijn, J. (1990). A comparison between the information-processing and the analysis/control approaches to language learning. *Applied Linguistics, 11*, 30-45.

Hunt, K. (1965). *Grammatical structures written at three grade levels.* (Research Report No. 3). Urbana. IL: National Council of Teachers of English.

Hunt, K. (1970). Recent measures in syntactic development. In M. Lester (Ed.), *Readings in applied transformation grammar*. New York: Holt, Rinehart and Winston.

Hyltenstam, K. & Abrahamsson, N. (2003). Maturational constraints in SLA. In C. Doughty & M. Long (Eds.), *The handbook of second language acquisition*. Oxford: Blackwell.

Hymes, D. (1966). *On communicative competence*. Paper presented at the Research Planning Conference on Language Development among Disadvantaged Children. Yeshiva University.

Hymes, D. (1967). *On communicative competence*. Unpublished manuscript, University of Pennsylvania.

Hymes, D. (1972). On communicative competence. In J. Pride & J. Holmes (Eds.), *Sociolinguistics*. Harmondsworth, UK: Penguin Books.

Hymes, D. (1974). *Foundations in sociolinguistics: An ethnographic approach*. Philadelphia: University of Pennsylvania Press.

Ingram, D. (1989). *First language acquisition*. Cambridge: Cambridge University Press.

Ingram, D. (1999). Phonological acquisition. In M. Barrett (Ed.), *The development of language* (pp. 73-97). Hove: Psychology Press.

Jackendoff, R. (1993). *Patterns in the mind: Language and human nature*. New York, NY, Harvester Wheatsheaf.

Jackendoff, R. (1997). *The architecture of the language faculty*. Cambridge, MA: MIT Press.

James, C. (1998). *Errors in language learning and use: Exploring error analysis*. Harlow, UK: Addison Wesley Longman.

Jamieson, J. (1992). The cognitive styles of reflection/impulsivity and field independence and ESL success. *Modern Language Journal, 76*, 491-501.

Johnson, K., & Johnson, H. (Eds.). (1999). *Encyclopedic dictionary of applied linguistics*. Malden, Mass: Blackwell.

Johnson, J., Prior, S., & Artuso, M. (2000). Field dependence as a factor in second language communicative production. *Language Learning, 50*, 529-567.

Johnson, R., & Swain, M. (Eds.). (1997). *Immersion education: International perspectives*. Cambridge: Cambridge University Press.

Jusczyk, P. (1997). *The discovery of spoken language*. Cambridge, MA: MIT Press.

Kachru, B. (1986). *The alchemy of English: The spread, functions, and models of non-native Englishes*. Oxford, UK: Pergamon Institute of English.

Kagan, J. (1965). Reflection-impulsivity and reading ability in primary grade children. *Child Development, 36*, 609-628.

Kaplan, R. (1966). Cultural thought patterns in inter-cultural education. *Language Learning, 16*, 1-20.

Kaplan, R. (2005). Contrastive rhetoric. In E. Hinkel (Ed.), *Handbook of research in second language teaching and learning* (pp. 375-391). Mahwah, NJ: Lawrence Erlbaum Associates.

Kaufman, D. (2004). Constructivist issues in language learning and teaching. *Annual Review of Applied Linguistics, 24*, 303-319.

Keefe, J. (1979a). Learning style: An overview. In J. Keefe (Ed.), *Student learning styles: Diagnosing and describing programs*. Reston Va.: National Secondary School Principals.

Keenan, E., & Comrie, B. (1977). Noun phrase accessibility and universal grammar. *Linguistic Inquiry, 8*, 63-99.

Keller, J. (1983). Motivational design of instruction. In C. Reigelruth (Ed.), *Instructional design theories and models: An overview of their current status*. Hillsdale, NJ: Lawrence Erlbaum Associates.

Kellerman, E. (1977). Towards a characterization of the strategies of transfer in second language learning. *Interlanguage Studies Bulletin, 2*, 58-145

Kellerman, E. (1978). Giving learners a break: native language intuitions as a source of predictions about transferability. *Working papers on bilingualism, 15*, 59-92

Kellerman, E. (1979). Transfer and non-transfer: where are we now? *Studies in Second Language Acquisition, 2*, 37-57.

Kellerman, E. (1986). An eye for an eye: crosslinguistic constraints on the development of the L2 lexicon. In E. Kellerman & M. Sharwood-Smith (Eds.), *Cross-linguistic influence in second language acquisition*. Oxford: Pergamon.

Kellerman, E. (1989). The imperfect conditional. In K. Hyltenstam & L. Obler (Eds.), *Bilingualism across the lifespan: aspects of acquisition, maturity and loss*. Cambridge: Cambridge University Press.

Kellerman, E. (1992). *Another look at an old classic; Schachter's avoidance.* Lecture notes. Temple University Japan.

Kellerman, E. (1995). Cross-Linguistic influence: Transfer to nowhere? *Annual Review of Applied Linguistics, 15*, 125-150.

Kellerman, E., & Sharwood-Smith, M. (1986). *Cross-linguistic influence in second language acquisition.* New York: Pergamon Press.

Kellogg, R. (1995). *Cognitive psychology.* London: Sage Publications.

Kern, R., Ware, P., & Warschauer, M. (2004). Crossing frontiers: New directions in online pedagogy and research. *Annual Review of Applied Linguistics*, 243-260.

Keshavarz, M. (1999). *Contrastive analysis and error analysis* (2nd ed.). Tehran: Rahnama Press.

Kim, J., & Han, Z. (2007). Recasts in communicative EFL classes: Do teacher intent and learner interpretation overlap? In A. Mackey (Ed.), *Conversational interaction in second language acquisition*. Oxford: Oxford University Press.

Klein, W. (1991). Seven trivia of language acquisition. In L. Eubnak (Ed.), *Point counterpoint: Universal Grammar in the second language*. Amsterdam: John Benjamins.

Klima, E., & Bellugi, V. (1966). Syntactic regularities in the speech of children. In J. Lyons & R. Wales (Eds.), *Psycholinguistic papers* (pp. 183-219). Edinburgh: Edinburgh University Press.

Klima, E., & Bellugi, U. (1979). The signs of language. Cambridge, MA: Harvard University Press.

Kormos, J. (2000). The role of attention in monitoring second language speech production. *Language Learning, 50*, 343-384.

Kramsch, C. (1993). *Context and culture in language teaching*. Oxford: Oxford University Press.

Kramsch, C. (Ed.). (2002). *Language acquisition and language socialization: Ecological perspectives*. London: Continuum.

Kramsch, C. (2003). Metaphor and the subjective construction of beliefs. In P. Kalaja & A. Barcelos (Eds.), *Beliefs about SLA: New research approaches*. Dordrecht: Kluwer.

Krashen, S. (1977). The monitor model for adult second language performance. In M. Burt, H. Dulay, & M. Finocchiaro (Eds.), *Viewpoints on English as a second Language*. New York: Regents.

Krashen, S. (1981). *Second language acquisition and second language learning*. Oxford, UK: Pergamon.

Krashen, S. (1982). *Principles and practice in second language acquisition*. New York: McGraw-Hill.

Krashen, S. (1985). *The input hypothesis: Issues and implications*. London: Longman.

Krashen, S. (1986). *Bilingual education and second language acquisition theory*. In Sacramento, CA: California State Department of Education.

Krashen, S. (1992). Under what conditions, if any, should formal grammar instruction take place? *TESOL Quarterly, 26*, 409-411.

Krashen, S. (1997). *Foreign language education: The easy way*. Culver City, CA: Language Education Associates.

Krashen, S., & Scarcella, R. (1978). On routines and patterns in second language acquisition and performance. *Language Learning, 28*, 283-300

Krashen, S., & Terrell, T. (1983). *The natural approach: Language acquisition in the classroom*. London: Prentice Hall.

Kuczaj, S. (1999). The development of a lexicon. In M. Barrett (Ed.). *The development of language* (pp. 133-159). Hove: Psychology Press.

Kuhl, J. (1987). Action control: the maintenance of motivational states. In F. Halish & J. Kuhl (Eds.). *Motivation, intention, and volition*. Berlin: Springer; 279-191.

Kumaravadivelu, B. (2003). Problematizing cultural stereotypes in TESOL. *TESOL Quarterly, 37*, 709-718.

Kumaravadivelu, B. (2006). *Understanding language teaching: From method to postmethod*. Mahwah, NJ: Lawrence Erlbaum Associates.
Labov, W. (1970). The study of language in its social context. *Stadium Generale*, *23*, 30-87.
Labov, W. (1972). *Sociolinguistic patterns*. Philadelphia: University of Pennsylvania Press.
Lado, R. (1957). *Linguistics across cultures*. Ann Arbor: University of Michigan Press.
Lamb, T., & Reinders, H. (2008). *Learner and teacher autonomy: Concepts, realities and responses*. Amsterdam: John Benjamins.
Lambert, W. (1974). Culture and language as factors in learning and education. In F. Aboud & R. Mead (Eds.), *Cultural factors in learning and education. Bellingham*. Washington D.C.: Fifth Western Washington Symposium on Learning.
Lambert, W., & Tucker, G. (1972). *The bilingual education of children: The St. Lambert experiment*. Rowley, MA: Newbury House.
Lantolf, J. (Ed.). (2000a). *Sociocultural theory and second language learning*. Oxford: Oxford University Press.
Lantolf, J. (Ed.). (2000b). Second language learning as a mediated process. *Language Teaching*, *33*, 79-96.
Lantolf, J. (Ed.). (2004). Sociocultural theory and second foreign language learning. An overview of sociocultural theory. In K. Van Esch & O. St. John (Eds.), *Vygotsky's theory of education in cultural context*. Frankfurt am Main: Peter Lang.
Lantolf, J., & Appel, G. (Eds.). (1994a). *Theoretical framework: An introduction to Vygotskian approaches to second language research*. Norwood, NJ: Ablex.
Larson, D., & Smalley, W. (1972). *Becoming bilingual: A guide to language learning*. New Canaan, CN: Practical Anthropology.
Larsen-Freeman, D. (1975). The acquisition of grammatical morphemes by adult ESL students. *TESOL Quarterly*, *9*, 409-430.
Larsen-Freeman, D. (1997). Chaos/complexity science and second language acquisition. *Applied Linguistics*, *18*, 141-165.
Larsen-Freeman, D. & Long, M. (1991) *An introduction to second language acquisition research*. New York: Longman.
Lavelli, M., Pantoja, A., Hsu, H., Messinger, D., & Fogel, A. (2004). Using microgenetic designs to study change processes. In D. Teti (Ed.), *Handbook of research methods in developmental psychology*. Baltimore, Md: Blackwell Publishers.
Leki, I. (1991). Twenty-five years of contrastive rhetoric: Text analysis and writing pedagogies. *TESOL Quarterly*, *25*, 123-144.
Lenneberg, E. (1967). *Biological foundations of language*. New York: Wiley.

Lennon, P. (1990). Investigating fluency in EFL: A quantitative approach. *Language Learning, 40*, 387-417.

Lennon, P., (2000). The lexical element in spoken second language fluency. In H. Riggenbach (Ed.), *Perspectives on fluency* (pp. 25-42). The University of Michigan Press, Michigan.

Leontiev, A. (1981). *Psychology and the language learning process.* London: Pergamon.

Lesser, R., & Milroy, L. (1993). Linguistics and aphasia. Harlow: Longman.

Levelt, W. (1989). *Speaking.* Cambridge, MA: MIT Press.

Levenston, E. (1971). Over-indulgence and under-representation: aspects of mother tongue interference. In G. Nickel (Ed.), *Papers in contrastive linguistics.* Cambridge, Cambridge University Press.

Levinson, S. (1983). *Pragmatics.* Cambridge: Cambridge University Press.

Lightbown, P., & Spada, N. (2006). *How languages are learned* (3rd ed.). Oxford: Oxford University Press.

Little, D., & Singleton, D. (1990). Cognitive style and learning approach. In R. Duda & P. Riley (Eds.), *Learning styles.* Nancy, France: University of Nancy.

Loewen, S. (2005). Incidental focus on form and second language learning. *Studies in Second Language Acquisition, 27*, 361-386.

Long, M. (1977). Teacher feedback on learner error: Mapping cognitions. In H. Brown, C. Yorio, & R. Crymes (Eds.), *On TESOL '77.* Washington D.C.: TESOL.

Long, M. (1980b). Inside the black box: Methodological issues in classroom research on language learning. *Language Learning, 30*, 1-42

Long, M. (1981). Input, interaction and second language acquisition. In H. Winitz (Ed.), *Native language and foreign language acquisition.* Annals of the New York Academy of Sciences 379.

Long, M. (1982). Native speaker/non-native speaker conversation in the second language classroom. In M. Long & C. Richards (Eds.), *Methodology in TESOL: A book of readings* (pp. 339-354). Rowley, MA: Newbury House.

Long, M. (1983a). Native speaker/non-native speaker conversation and the negotiation of comprehensible input. *Applied linguistics, 4*, 126-141.

Long, M. (1983b). Native speaker/non-native speaker conversation in the second language classroom. In M. Clarke & J. Handscombe (Eds.), *On TESOL '82.* Washington D.C.: TESOL.

Long, M. (1991). Focus on form: A design feature in language teaching methodology. In K. de Bot, R. Ginsberg, & C. Kramsch (Eds.), *Foreign language research in cross-cultural perspective* (pp. 39-52). Amsterdam: John Benjamins.

Long, M. (1996). The role of the linguistic environment in second language acquisition. In W. Ritchie & T. Bhatia (Eds.), *Handbook of second language acquisition* (414-468). New York, NY: Academic Press.

Long, M. (2003). Stabilization and fossilization in interlanguage. In C. Doughty & M. Long (Eds.), *The handbook of second language acquisition* (pp. 487-535). Oxford: Blackwell.

Lorenz, K. (1961). *King Solomon's ring.* Translated by Marjorie Kerr Wilson. London: Methuen.

Lund, N. (2001). *Attention and pattern recognition.* London: Routledge.

Lyons, J. (1970). *Chomsky.* London: Fontana.

Lyster, R. (1998a). Recasts, repetition and ambiguity in L2 classroom discourse. *Studies in Second Language Acquisition, 20,* 51-80.

Lyster, R. (2004). Differential effects of prompts and recasts in form-focused instruction. *Studies in Second Language Acquisition, 26,* 399-432.

Lyster, R., & Ranta, L. (1997). Corrective feedback and learner uptake: Negotiation of form in communicative classrooms. *Studies of Second Language Acquisition, 28,* 269-300.

Macaro, E. (2003). *Teaching and learning a second language: A guide to current research and its applications.* London: Continuum.

Macaro, E. (2010). *Continuum companion to second language acquisition.* London: Continuum.

Macaro, E., Vanderplank, R., & Murphy, V. (2010). A compendium of key concepts in second language acquisition. In E. Macaro (Ed.), *Continuum companion to second language acquisition* (pp. 29-106). London: Continuum.

MacIntyre, P, Baker, S., Clement, R., & Donovan, L. (2002). Sex and age effects on willingness to communicate, anxiety, perceived competence, and L2 motivation among junior high school French immersion students. *Language Learning, 52,* 537-564.

MacIntyre, P., Dornyei, Z., Clement, R., & Noels, K. (1998). Conceptualizing willingness to communicate in a L2: A situational model of L2 confidence and affiliation. *Modem Language Journal, 82,* 545-562.

MacIntyre, P., & Gardner, R. (1989). Anxiety and second language learning: Toward a theoretical clarification. *Language Learning, 39,* 251-275.

MacIntyre, P., & Gardner, R. (1991c). Methods and results in the study of anxiety and language learning: A review of the literature. *Language Learning, 41,* 85-117.

Mackey, A. (Ed.). (2007). *Conversational interaction in second language acquisition.* Oxford: Oxford University Press.

Mackey, A., & Philp, J. (1998). Conversational interaction on second language development: Recasts, responses, and red herrings? *Modern Language Journal, 82,* 338-356.

MacWhinney, B. (2001). The competition model: The input, the context and the brain. In P. Robinson (Ed.), *Cognition and second language instruction.* Cambridge University Press, Cambridge.

MacWhinney, B. (2007b). A unified model. In N. Ellis & P. Robinson (Eds.), *Handbook of cognitive linguistic and second language acquisition*. Mahwah, NJ: Lawrence Erlbaum Associates.

Macwhinney, B., & Bates, E. (Eds.). (1989). *The crosslinguistic study of linguistic processing*. Cambridge, Cambridge University Press.

MacWhinney, B., Pleh, C., & Bates, E. (1985). The development of sentence interpretation in Hungarian. *Cognitive Psychology, 17*, 178-209.

Matsuda, P. (1997). Contrastive rhetoric in context: A dynamic model of L2 writing. *Journal of Second Language Writing, 6*(1), 45-60.

McCafferty, S., Roebuck, R., & Wayland, R. (2001). Activity theory and the incidental learning of second-language vocabulary. *Language Awareness, 10*, 289-294.

McClelland, J, Rumelhardt, D., & Hinton, G. (1986). The appeal of parallel distributed processing. In J. McClelland & D. Rumelhart (Eds.), *Parallel distributed processing: Explorations in the microstructure of cognition* (Vol. 1). Cambridge, MA: MIT Press.

Major, R. (2001). *Foreign accent: The ontogeny and phylogeny of second language phonology*. Mahwah, NJ: Lawrence Erlbaum Associates.

Marcus, G. (1996). Why do children say 'breaked'?. *Current Directions in Psychological Science, 5*, 81-5.

Markee, N., & Kasper, G. (2004). Classroom talks: An introduction. *The Modern Language Journal, 88*, 491-500.

Maslow, A. (1970). *Motivation and personality* (2nd ed.). New York: Harper & Row.

McGinn, L., Stokes, J., & Trier, A. (2005). *Does music affect language acquisition?* Paper presented at TESOL, San Antonio, TX.

McLaughlin, B. (1987). *Theories of second-language learning*. London: Arnold.

McLaughlin, B. (1990a). Conscious versus unconscious learning. *TESOL Quarterly, 24*, 617-634.

McLaughlin, B. (1990b). Restructuring. *Applied Linguistics, 11*, 113-128.

McLaughlin, B., Rossman, T., & McLeod, B. (1983). Second language learning: An information-processing perspective. *Language Learning, 36*, 109-123.

McLeod, B., & McLaughlin, B. (1986). Restructuring or automaticity? Reading in a second language. *Language Learning, 36*, 109-123.

McNeill, D. (1966). Developmental psycholinguistics. In F. Smith & G. Miller (Eds.), *The genesis of language* (pp. 15-84). MIT Press.

Meisel, J. (1991). Principles of universal grammar and strategies of language learning: Some similarities and differences between first and second language acquisition. In L. Eubank (Ed.), *Point counterpoint: Universal Grammar in the second language*. Amsterdam: John Benjamins.

Meisel, J., Clahsen, H. & Pienemann, M. (1981). On determining developmental stages in natural second language acquisition. *Studies in Second Language Acquisition, 3*, 109-135.

Menn, L., & Stoel-Gammon, C. (1995). Phonological development. In P. Fletcher & B. MacWhinney (Eds.), *The handbook of child language* (pp. 335-359). Oxford: Blackwell

Minsky, M. (1977). Frame system theory. In P. Johnson-Laird & P. Wason (Eds.), *Thinking: Readings in cognitive science.* Cambridge: Cambridge University Press.

Mitchell, R. & Myles, F. (1998). *Second language learning theories.* London: Arnold.

Mithcell, R. & Myles, F. (2004). *Second language learning theories* (2nd ed.). London. Hodder Arnold.

Miyake, A., & Friedman, N. (1998). Individual differences in second language proficiency: Working memory as language aptitude. In A. Healy & L. Bourne, (Eds.), *Foreign language learning: Psycholinguistic studies on training and retention* (pp. 339-364). Mahwah, NJ: Lawrence Erlbaum Associates.

Miyake, A., & Shah, P. (Eds.). (1999). *Models of working memory: Mechanisms of active maintenance and executive control.* Cambridge, UK: Cambridge University Press.

Mohan, B., & Lo, W. (1985). Academic writing and Chinese students: Transfer and developmental factors. *TESOL Quarterly, 19,* 515-534.

Morgan, J., & Demuth, K. (Eds.). (1996). *Signal to syntax.* Mahwah, NJ: Lawrence Erlbaum Associates.

Myers, I., & Briggs, K. (1976). *The Myers-Briggs Type Indicator, Form G.* Paolo Alto, Calif: Consulting Psychologist Press.

Myers-Scotton, C. (1989). Code-switching with English: Types of switching, types of communities. *World Englishes, 8,* 333-346.

Naiman, N., Frohlich, M., Stern, H., & Todesco, A. (1978). *The good language learner Toronto: Ontario Institute for Studies in Education.* (Reprinted by Multilingual Matters, Clevedon, UK.).

Nayar, P. (1997). ESL/EFL dichotomy today: Language politics or pragmatics? *TESOL Quarterly, 31* 9-37.

Neisser, U. (Ed.). (1987). *Concepts and conceptual development.* Cambridge: Cambridge University Press.

Nemser, W. (1971). Approximative systems of foreign language learners. *International Review of Applied Linguistics, 9,* 115-123.

Norton, B. (1997). Language, identity and the ownership of English. *TESOL Quarterly, 31,* 409-429.

Nusbaum, H., & Goodman, J. (1994). Learning to hear speech as spoken language. In J. Goodman & H. Nusbaum (Eds.), *The development of speech perception: The transition from speech sounds to spoken words* (pp. 299-338). Cambridge, MA: MIT Press.

Obler, L., & Gjerlow, K. (1999). *Language and the brain.* Cambridge: Cambridge University Press.

Ochs, E., & Schieffelin, B. (1984). Language acquisition and socialization: Three developmental stories and their implications. In R. Shweder & R. Levine (Eds.), *Culture and its acquisition.* New York: Cambridge University Press.

Odlin, T. (2003). Cross-linguistic influence. In C. Doughty & M. Long (Eds.), *The handbook of second language acquisition* (pp. 436-486). Maiden, MA: Blackwell Publishing.

O'Grady, W. (1997). *Syntactic development.* Chicago, IL: University of Chicago Press.

Ohta, A. (2001b). *Second language acquisition in the classroom: Learning Japanese.* Mahwah, NJ: Lawrence Erlbaum Associates.

Owens, R. (2001). *Language development: An introduction* (5th ed). Needham Heights, MA: Allyn & Bacon.

Oxford, R. (1990a). *Language learning strategies: What every teacher should know.* New York: Newbury House.

Oxford, R. (1999). Anxiety and the language learner: New insights. In J. Arnold (Ed.), *Affect in language learning* (pp. 58-67). Cambridge UK: Cambridge University Press.

Palmer, F. (1981). *Semantics* (2nd ed.). Cambridge: Cambridge University Press.

Paradis, M. (2004). *A neurolinguistics theory of bilingualism.* Amsterdam: John Benjamins.

Park, E. (2002). On the potential sources of comprehensible input for second language acquisition. *Working Papers in TESOL and Applied Linguistics, 2*(3), 1-21.

Paulus, T. (1999). The effect of peer and teacher feedback on student writing. *Journal of Second Language Writing, 8,* 265-290.

Pavlenko, A. (2002). Poststructuralist approaches to the study of social factors in second language learning and use. In V. Cook (Ed.), *Portraits of the L2 user* (pp. 277-302). Clevedon: Multilingual Matters.

Peirce, B. (1995). Social identity, investment and language learning. *TESOL Quarterly, 29,* 9-31.

Penfield, W., & Roberts. L. (1959). *Speech and brain mechanisms.* Princeton, NJ: Princeton University Press.

Perfetti, C. (1985). *Reading ability.* New York: Oxford University Press.

Perfetti, C. (1999). Cognitive research and the misconceptions of reading education. In J. Oakhill & R. Beard (Eds.), *Reading development and the teaching of reading* (pp. 42-58). Oxford: Blackwell.

Perude, C. (1991). Cross-linguistic comparisons: Organizational principles in learner languages. In T. Huebner & C. Ferguson (Eds.), *Crosscurrents in second language acquisition and linguistic theories*. Amsterdam: John Benjamins.

Peters, A. (1977). Language learning strategies: Does the whole equal the sum of the parts? *Language, 53*, 560-573.

Peters, A. (1983). *The units of language acquisition*. Cambridge: Cambridge University Press.

Piaget, J. (1954). *The construction of reality in the child*. New York: Basic Books.

Piaget, J. (1955). *The language and thought of the child*. New York: Meridian.

Piaget, J. (1970). *The science of education and the psychology of the child*. New York: Basic Books.

Piaget, J. (1972). *The principles of genetic epistemology*. New York: Basic Books.

Piaget, J., & Inhelder, B. (1969). *The psychology of the child*. New York: Basic Books.

Piattelli-Palmarini, M. (1980). *Language and learning: The debate between Chomsky and Piaget*. Cambridge, MA: Harvard University Press.

Pica, T. (1994b). Research on negotiation: What does it reveal about second-language learning conditions, processes, and outcomes? *Language Learning, 44*, 493-527.

Pica, T. Young, R., & Doughty, C. (1987). The impact of interaction on comprehension. *TESOL Quarterly, 21*, 737-758.

Pienemann, M. (1985). Learnability and syllabus construction. In K. Hyltenstam & M. Pienemann (Eds.), *Modeling and assessing language acquisition*. Clevedon: Multilingual Matters.

Pienemann, M. (1998). *Language processing and second-language development: Processability theory*. Amsterdam: John Benjamins.

Pienemann, M. (2003). Language processing capacity. In C. Doughty & M. Long, (Eds.), *The handbook of second language acquisition* (pp. 679-714). Oxford: Blackwell Publishing.

Pienemann, M. (2005a). An introduction to processability theory. In M. Pienemann (Ed.), *Cross-linguistic aspects of Processability Theory*. Amsterdam: John Benjamins.

Pienemann, M. (Ed.). (2005b). *Cross-linguistic aspects of Processability Theory*. Amsterdam: John Benjamins.

Pinker, S. (1994a). How could a child use verb syntax to learn verb Semantics? *Lingua, 92*, 377-410.

Pinker, S. (1994b). *The language instinct: The new science of language and mind*. London, Allen Lane/Penguin.

Pinker, S. (1999). *Words and rules*. New York: Basic Books.

Piske, T., & Young-Scholten, M. (Eds.). (2009). *Input matters in SLA*. Multilingual Matters.
Prator, C. (1967). *Hierarchy of difficulty*. Unpublished classroom lecture, University of California, Los Angeles.
Preston, D. (1989). *Sociolinguistics and second language acquisition*. Oxford: Basil Blackwell.
Preston, D. (2002). A variationist perspective on second language acquisition. In R. Kaplan (Ed.), *The Oxford handbook of applied linguistics*. New York: Oxford University Press.
Prince, A., & Smolensky, P. (1993). *Optimality theory: Constraint interaction in generative grammar*. Rutgers University Center for Cognitive Science Technical Report 2.
Radford, A. (1990). *Syntactic theory and the acquisition of English syntax*. Oxford: Blackwell.
Radford, A. (2009). *An introduction to English sentence structure*. Cambridge: Cambridge University Press.
Rayner, S. (2000). Reconstructing style differences in thinking and learning: profiling learner performance. In R. Riding & S. Rayner (Eds.), *Interpersonal perspectives on individual differences* (Vol. 1). Stamford, Conn: Ablex.
Reid, J. (1987). The learning style preferences of ESL students. *TESOL Quarterly, 21*, 87-111.
Reid, J. (1995). *Learning styles in the ESL/EFL classroom*. Boston: Heinle & Heinle.
Richards, J., & Schmidt, R. (2010). *Longman dictionary of language teaching and applied linguistics* (4th ed.). Pearson Education.
Riley, P (1981). Towards a contrastive pragmalinguistics. In J. Fisiak (Ed.), *Contrastive linguistics and the language teacher*. Oxford: Pergamon.
Rivers, W. (1991). Mental representations and language in action. *The Canadian Modern Language Review, 47*, 249-265.
Robinson, P. (1995a). Attention, memory, and the noticing hypothesis. *Language Learning, 45*, 283-331.
Robinson, P. (2001a). Individual differences, cognitive abilities, aptitude complexes and learning conditions in second language acquisition. *Second Language Research, 17*, 368-392.
Robinson, P. (2001b). Task complexity, cognitive resources, and syllabus design: A triadic framework for examining task influences on SLA. In P. Robinson (Ed.), *Cognition and second language instruction*. Cambridge: Cambridge University Press.
Robinson, P. (Ed.). (2001c). *Cognition and second language instruction*. Cambridge: Cambridge University Press.
Robinson, P. (2003). Attention and memory during SLA. In C. Doughty & M. H. Long (Eds.). *The handbook of second language acquisition* (pp. 631-679). Oxford: Blackwell.

Rodriguez, R. (1982). *Hunger of memory: The education of Richard Rodriguez.* Boston: David R. Godine.
Sacks, H., Schegloff, E., & Jefferson, G. (1974). A simplest systematics for the organization of turn-taking for conversation. *Language, 50,* 696-735.
Sajavaara, K. (1981b). Contrastive linguistics past and present and a communicative approach. In J. Fisiak (Ed.), *Contrastive linguistics and the language teacher.* Oxford: Pergamon.
Sampson, G. (1997). *Educating eve: The 'language instinct' debate.* London, Cassell.
Saville-Troike, M. (1988). Private speech: Evidence for second language learning strategies during the silent period. *Journal of Child Language, 15,* 567-590.
Saville-Troike, M. (1996). The ethnography of communication. In S. McKay & N. Hornberger (Eds.), *Sociolinguistics and language teaching.* Cambridge: Cambridge University Press.
Saville-Troike, M. (2006). *Introducing second language acquisition.* UK: Cambridge University Press.
Saxton, M. (1997). The contrast theory of negative input. *Journal of Child Language, 24,* 139-161.
Saxton, M. (2000). Negative evidence and negative feedback: immediate effects on the grammaticality of child speech. *First Language, 20,* 221-252.
Schachter, J. (1974). An error in error analysis. *Language Learning, 24,* 205-214.
Schank, R., & Abelson, R. (1977). *Scripts, plans, goals and understanding.* Hillsdale, NJ: Erlbaum.
Schegloff, E. A. & Sacks, H. (1973). Opening up closings. *Semiotica, 8,* 289-327.
Schieffelin, B., & Ochs, E. (1986). Language socialization. *Annual Review of Anthropology, 15,* 513-541.
Schmitt, N. (Ed.). (2004). *Formulaic sequences: Acquisition, processing and use.* Amsterdam: John Benjamins.
Schmidt, R. (1990). The role of consciousness in second language learning. *Applied Linguistics, 11,* 129-158.
Schmidt, R. (1994). Deconstructing consciousness in search of useful definitions for applied linguistics. *AILA Review, 11,* 11-26.
Schmidt, R. (Ed.). (1995a). Consciousness and foreign language learning: A tutorial in the role of attention and awareness in learning. In R. Schmidt (Ed.), *Attention and awareness in foreign language teaching and learning.* Honolulu: University of Hawai'i Press.
Schmidt, R. (2001). Attention. In P. Robinson (Ed.), *Cognition and second language instruction* (pp. 3-32). Cambridge: Cambridge University Press.

Schumann, J. (1986). Research on the acculturation model for second language acquisition. *Journal of Multilingual and Multicultural Development, 7*, 379-392.

Schumann, J. (1978a). The acculturation model for second-language acquisition. In R. Gingras (Ed.), *Second language acquisition and foreign language teaching* (pp. 27-50). Washington D.C.: Center for Applied Linguistics.

Schumann, J. (1978b). *The Pidginization process: A model for second language acquisition.* Rowley, MA: Newbury House.

Schumann, J. (1978c). Social and psychological factors in second language acquisition. In J. Richards (Ed.), *Understanding second and foreign language learning: Issues and approaches.* Rowley, MA: Newbury House.

Schumann, J. (1997). *The neurobiology of affect in language.* Cambridge, MA: Blackwell.

Schumann, J., Crowell, S., Jones, N., Lee, N., Schuchert, S., & Wood, L. (Eds.). (2004). *The neurobiology of learning: Perspectives from second language acquisition.* Mahwah, NJ: Lawrence Erlbaum Associates.

Schwartz, B. (1993). On explicit and negative data effecting and affecting competence and linguistic behavior. *Studies in Second Language Acquisition, 15*, 147-163.

Schwartz, B. (1998). The second language instinct. *Lingua, 106*, 133-160.

Scovel, T. (1969). Foreign accents, language acquisition, and cerebral dominance. *Language Learning, 19*, 245-254.

Scovel, T (1978). The effect of affect on foreign language learning: A review of the anxiety research. *Language Learning, 28*, 129-142.

Scovel, T. (2000). A critical review of the critical period research. *Annual Review of Applied Linguistics, 20*, 213-223.

Searle, J. (1975). Indirect speech acts. In P. Cole & J. Morgan (Eds.), *Syntax and semantics* (Vol. 3). New York, NY: Academic Press.

Searle, J. (1976). The classification of illocutionary acts. *Language in Society, 5*, 1-24.

Segalowitz, N. (2003). Automaticity and second languages. In C. Doughty & M. Long (Eds.), *The handbook of second language acquisition* (382-408). Oxford: Blackwell Publishing.

Selinker, L. (1972). Interlanguage. *International Review of Applied Linguistics, 10*, 209-231.

Selinker, L. (1992). *Rediscovering interlanguage.* London: Longman.

Selinker, L. & Lakshmanan, U. (1992). Language transfer and fossilization: The 'Multiple Effects Principle'. In S. Gass & L. Selinker (Eds.), *Language transfer in language learning* (pp. 197-216). Amsterdam: John Benjamins.

Selinker, L., & Lamendella, J. (1978). Two perspectives on fossilization in interlanguage learning. *Interlanguage Studies Bulletin, 3*, 143-191.

Sharwood-Smith, M. (1993). Input enhancement in instructed SLA: Theoretical bases. *Studies in Second Language Acquisition, 15*, 165-179.

Sharwood-Smith, M. (1996). Crosslinguistic influence with special reference to the acquisition of grammar. In P. Jordens & J. Lalleman (Eds.), *Investigating second language acquisition*. Berlin: Mouton de Gruyter.
Sinclair, J., & Coulthard, M. (1975). *Towards an analysis of discourse*. Oxford: Oxford University Press.
Singleton, D. (1999). *Exploring the second language language lexicon*. Cambridge: Cambridge University Press.
Singleton, D. (2007). The critical period hypothesis: Some problems. *Interlingüística, 17*, 48-56.
Singleton, D., & Muñoz, C. (2011). In E. Hinkel (Ed.). *Handbook of research in second language learning* (Vol. 2). Mahwah, NJ: Lawrence Erlbaum Associates.
Skehan, P. (1989a). *Individual differences in second language learning*. London: Edward Arnold.
Skehan, P. (1996). Second language acquisition research and task-based instruction. In D. Willis & J. Willis (Eds.), *Challenge and change in language teaching*. London: Heinemann.
Skehan, P. (1998a). Task-based instruction. *Annual Review of Applied Linguistics*, 18, 268-286.
Skehan, P. (1998b). *A cognitive approach to language learning*. Oxford: Oxford University Press.
Skinner, B. (1957). *Verbal behavior*. New York: Appleton-Century-Crofts.
Skuttnab-Kangas, T. (1988). Multilingualism and the education of minority children. In T. Skuttnab-Kangas & Cummins (eds.). *Minority education*. Clevedon: Multilingual Matters.
Skuttnab-Kangas, T. (2000). *Linguistic genocide in education—or worldwide diversity in human rights?* Mahwah, NJ: Lawrence Erlbaum Associates.
Slavin, R. (2003). *Educational psychology: Theory and practice*. Boston: Allyn and Bacon.
Slobin, D. (1973). Cognitive prerequisite for the development of grammar. In C. Ferguson & D. Slobin (Eds.), *Studies of child language development*. New York: Appleton-Century-Crofts.
Slobin, D. (Ed.). (1985a). *The crosslinguistic study of language acquisition* (Vols. 1-2). Hillsdale, NJ: Lawrence Erlbaum.
Smith, F. (1975). *Comprehension and learning: A conceptual framework for teachers*. New York: Holt, Rinehart & Winston.
Smith, N. (1999). *Chomsky: Ideas and ideals*. Cambridge: Cambridge University Press.
Snow, C. (1986). Conversations with children. In P. Fletcher & M. Garman (Eds.), *Language acquisition* (2nd ed.). (pp. 363-75). Cambridge: Cambridge University Press.
Snow, C. (1995). Issues in the study of input. In P. Fletcher & B. MacWhinney (Eds.), *The handbook of child language* (pp. 180-94). Oxford: Blackwell.

Spada, N., & Lightbown, P. (1999). Instruction, first language influence, and developmental readiness in second language acquisition. *Modern Language Journal, 83*, 1-22.

Speilmann, G., & Radnofsky, M. (2001). Learning language under tension: New directions from a qualitative study. *Modern Language Journal, 85*, 259-278.

Spivey, N. (1997). *The constructivist metaphor: Reading, writing, and the making of meaning.* San Diego: Academic Press.

Springer, S., & Deutsch. G. (1997). *Left brain, right brain* (5th ed.), New York: W. H. Freeman.

Stanovich, K. (1980). Toward an interactive-compensatory model of individual differences in the development of reading fluency. *Reading Research Quarterly, 16*, 32-71.

Stansfield, C., & Hansen, J. (1983). Field dependence independence as a variable in second language cloze test performance. *TESOL Quarterly, 17*, 29-38.

Steinberg, D. (1993). *An introduction to psycholinguistics.* London, Longman.

Stern, H. (1983). *Fundamental concepts of language teaching.* Oxford: Oxford University Press.

Sternberg, R. (1985). *Beyond IQ: A triarchic theory of human intelligence.* New York: Cambridge University Press.

Sternberg, R. (1988). *The triarchic mind: A new theory of human intelligence.* New York: Viking Press.

Sternberg, R. (1997). *Successful intelligence: How practical and creative intelligence determine success in life.* New York: Plume.

Sternberg, R. (2003). *Wisdom, intelligence, and creativity synthesized.* New York: Cambridge University Press.

Stevick, E. (1976b). *Memory, meaning and method.* Rowley, MA: Newbury House.

Stevick, E. (1982). *Teaching and learning languages.* New York: Cambridge University Press.

Stockwell, R., Bowen, J., & Martin, J. (1965). *The grammatical structures of English and Spanish.* Chicago: University of Chicago Press.

Strong, M. (Ed.). (1988). *Language learning and deafness.* Cambridge: Cambridge University Press.

Sullivan, E. (Ed.). (1976). *Piaget and the school curriculum: A critical appraisal.* Toronto: Ontario Institute for Studies in Education.

Svanes, B. (1988). Attitudes and cultural distance in second language acquisition. *Applied linguistics, 9*, 357-371.

Swain, M. (2006). Languaging, agency and collaboration in advanced second language learning. In H. Byrnes (Ed.), *Advanced language learning: the contributions of Halliday and Vygotsky.* London: Continuum.

Swinney, D. (1979). Lexical access during sentence comprehension: (Re)consideration of context effects. *Journal of Verbal Learning and Verbal Behavior, 5*, 219-27.

Tarone, E. (1983). On the variability of interlanguage systems. *Applied Linguistics, 4*, 143-63.

Tarone, E. (1985). Variability in interlanguage use: A study of style-shifting in morphology and syntax. *Language Learning, 35*(3), 373-404.

Tarone, E. (1988). *Variation in interlanguage.* London: Edward Arnold.

Tarone, E., & Swain, M. (1995). A sociolinguistic perspective on second language use in immersion classrooms. *Modern Language Journal, 79*, 166-178.

Tavakoli, H. (2012a). *A dictionary of research methodology and statistics in applied linguistics.* Tehran: Rahnama Press.

Teichert, H. (1996). A comparative study using illustrations, brainstorming, and questions as advance organizers in intermediate college German conversation classes. *Modern Language Journal, 80*, 509-517.

Tharp, R., & Gallimore, R. (1988). *Rousing minds to life: Teaching, learning and schooling in a social context.* New York: Cambridge University Press.

Thomas, J. (1983). Cross-cultural pragmatic failure. *Applied Linguistics, 4*, 91-112

Thorne, S. (2004). Cultural historical activity theory and the object of motivation. In O. St. John, K. Van Esch, & E. Schalkwijk (Eds.), *New insights into foreign language learning and teaching.* Frankfurt: Peter Lang Verlag.

Thorpe, W. (1954). The process of song-learning in the chaffinch as studied by means of the sound spectrograph. *Nature, 173*, 465-469.

Tollefson, J. (1991). *Planning language, planning inequality.* London: Longman.

Tomasello, M., & Bates, E. (Eds.). (2001). *Language development: The essential readings.* Oxford: Blackwell.

Tomasello, M., & Brooks, P. (1999). Early Syntactic Development: AConstruction Grammar Approach. In M. Barrett (Ed.), *The development of language* (pp. 161-90). Hove: Psychology Press.

Torrance, E. (1980). *Your style of learning and thinking, Forms B and C.* Athens: University of Georgia Press.

Tosi, S. (1984). *Immigration and bilingual education.* Oxford: Pergamon.

Towell, R., & Hawkins, R. (1994). *Approaches to second language acquisition.* Clevedon: Multilingual Matters.

Towell, R., Hawkins, R., & Bazergui, N. (1996). The development of fluency in advanced learners of French. *Applied Linguistics, 17*, 1, 84-119.

Trask, R. (2005). *Key concepts in language and linguistics.* London: Routledge.

Truscott, J. (1998). Noticing in second language acquisition: A critical review. *Second Language Acquisition Research, 14*, 103-135.

Tseng, W., Dörnyei, Z., & Schmitt, N. (2006). A new approach to assessing strategic learning: The case of self-regulation in vocabulary acquisition. *Applied Linguistics, 27*, 78-102.

Tsui, A., & Fullilove, J. (1998). Bottom-up or top-down processing as a discriminator of L2 listening performance. *Applied Linguistics, 19*, 432-451.

Tsui, A., & Ng, M. (2000). Do secondary L2 writers benefit from peer comments? *Journal of Second Language Writing, 9*, 147-170.

Ungerer, F. & Schmid, H. J. (1996). *An introduction to cognitive linguistics*. London: Longman.

Valdés, G. (2001a). *Learning and not learning English: Latino students in American schools*. New York: Teachers College Press.

Valian, V. (1996). Input and Language Acquisition. In W. Ritchie & T. Bhatia (Eds.), *Handbook of child language acquisition* (pp. 497-530.). San Diego, CA: Academic Press.

Van Lier, L. (1996). *Interaction in the language curriculum: Awareness, autonomy and authenticity*. London: Longman.

VanPatten, B., & Benati, A. (2010). *Key Terms in Second Language Acquisition*. London: Continuum.

Vihman, M. (1982). The acquisition of morphology by a bilingual child: The whole-word approach. *Applied Psycholinguistics, 3*, 141-160.

Vihman, M. (1996). *Phonological development: The origins of language in the child*. Oxford: Blackwell.

Yule, G (2006). *The study of language* (3rd ed.). Cambridge: Cambridge University Press.

Vygotsky, L. (1934). *Thought and Language*. Cambridge, MA: MIT Press.

Vygotsky, L. (1962). *Thought and language*. Cambridge, MA: MIT Press.

Vygotsky, L. (1978). *Mind in society*. Cambridge, MA: Harvard University Press.

Watson. J. (1913). Psychology as the behaviorist views it. *Psychological Review, 20*, 158-177.

Wardhaugh, R. (1970). The contrastive analysis hypothesis. *TESOL Quarterly, 4*, 123-130.

Weinert, R. (1995). The role of formulaic language in second language acquisition: A review. *Applied Linguistics, 16*, 180-205.

Wenden, A. (1999). An introduction. *System, 27*, 435-441.

White, L. (1987). Against comprehensible input: The input hypothesis and the development of L2 competence. *Applied Linguistics, 8*, 95-110.

White, L. (1989). *Universal Grammar and second language acquisition*. Amsterdam: John Benjamins.

White, L. (2003). *Second language acquisition and Universal Grammar*. Cambridge: Cambridge University Press.

White, L. (2007). Linguistic theory, universal grammar, and second language acquisition. In B. VanPatten & J. Williams (Eds.), *Theories in second lan-*

guage acquisition: An introduction (pp. 37-55). Mahwah, NJ: Lawrence Erlbaum Associates.

Whitman, R. (1970). Contrastive analysis: Problems and procedures. *Language Learning, 20*, 191-197.

Whitman, R., & Jackson, K. (1972). The unpredictability of contrastive analysis. Language Learning, *22*, 29-41.

Whitney, P. (1998). *The psychology of language.* Boston, MA: Houghton Mifflin.

Williams, M., & Burden, R. (1997). *Psychology for language teachers: A social constructivist approach.* Cambridge, UK: Cambridge University Press.

Willing, K. (1987). *Learning styles and adult migrant education.* Adelaide: National Curriculum Resource Center.

Wingfield, A., & Titone, D. (1998). Sentence processing. In J. Gleason & N. Ratner (Eds.), *Psycholinguistics* (2nd ed.). (pp. 227-274). Fort Worth, TX: Harcourt Brace.

Wray, A. (2002). *Formulaic language and the lexicon.* Cambridge: Cambridge University Press.